HOUSING

AS IF

PEOPLE

MATTERED

**California Series in
Urban Development**

Edited by
Peter Hall and Peter Marris

Great Planning Disasters
Peter Hall

The City and the Grassroots
A Cross-Cultural Theory of
Urban Social Movements
Manuel Castells

The Suburban Squeeze
Land Conversion and Regulation
in the San Francisco Bay Area
David E. Dowall

Housing as if People Mattered
Site Design Guidelines for
Medium-Density Family Housing
Clare Cooper Marcus and
Wendy Sarkissian

UNIVERSITY OF CALIFORNIA PRESS

BERKELEY   LOS ANGELES   LONDON

CLARE COOPER MARCUS

AND WENDY SARKISSIAN

WITH SHEENA WILSON AND DONALD PERLGUT

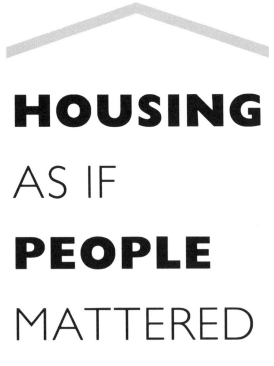

HOUSING AS IF PEOPLE MATTERED

SITE DESIGN GUIDELINES FOR

MEDIUM-DENSITY FAMILY HOUSING

This book is dedicated to Clare's children, Jason and Lucy, who have enriched her life beyond imagining, and to the memory of Alex Ramsay.

University of California Press
Berkeley and Los Angeles, California

University of California Press, Ltd.
London, England

Library of Congress Cataloging in Publication Data

Marcus, Clare Cooper.
  Housing as if people mattered.

  Bibliography: p.
  Includes index.
  1. Homesites—Planning.   2. Architecture—Human
factors.   3. Architecture and society.   I. Sarkissian,
Wendy.   II. Title.
NA7115.M27 1985   307'.336   84-2587
ISBN 0-520-06330-9

Printed in the United States of America

  3   4   5   6   7   8   9

The paper used in this publication meets the minimum
requirements of American National Standard for
Information Sciences—Permanence of Paper for
Printed Library Materials, ANSI Z39.48–1984. ∞

Contents

Preface:
The Authors and Their Environmental Values

However objective one attempts to be, one's own environmental experiences and values will, consciously or unconsciously, color what one writes. Gaston Bachelard first suggested in *The Poetics of Space* that "topoanalysis" might be as important as "psychoanalysis" in understanding our current selves, what we do and say.

After convincing many students and colleagues of the importance of exploring one's own environmental values and biases, we would be less than honest if we told you nothing about ourselves and our values. We do this not to bare our souls, but to give you a little more information than the usual listing of degrees, professional experience, and current position.

Clare Cooper Marcus

I was born into a small middle-class family and spent my first few years in a standard semi-detached house in the North London suburb of Finchley. Mine was a normal upbringing until the onset of the Second World War. My father having left to join the army, my mother, elder brother, and I were evacuated to the Rothschild estate in Buckinghamshire. There, during the most formative years of childhood (five to eleven), I had free run of woods, meadows, overgrown ornamental gardens, and farmland. Although we experienced considerable wartime restrictions and anxieties, our unexpected rural sojourn was, for us children, an idyllic time. We had a wide territorial range, raised rabbits and chickens, and engaged in all the activities of a country childhood—climbing trees, making secret dens, digging tunnels, exploring streams, cooking food over campfires. I am sure that my adult interest in adventure playgrounds stems from a belief, based on childhood experience, that swings, slides, and concrete sewer pipes are not enough to engage most children's creative energies. Although I certainly do not believe that cities are "bad" for children and country life is "better," I do believe that the territorial restrictions placed on urban children by traffic and security inhibit their need for exploration, variety, and a sense of independence. Hence in this book I emphasize children's needs to play creatively, make hiding places, and gradually explore farther and farther away from home. However this emphasis stems not solely (or even primarily) from my own bias, but also from the fact that children's needs have been consistently overlooked in housing design and that virtually every study of residents' reactions to existing housing schemes indicates that success is strongly correlated with fulfilling children's needs. Hence this book attempts to redress an imbalance that for too long has made children's recreational needs in housing areas a low priority.

During two very formative periods of my life I lived in courtyard arrangements. During the war we lived on a courtyard bounded by brick row houses and horse stables, the cobbled court being used for exercising the horses and for children's play. I recall strongly the powerful sense of enclosure and of group territory in that cobbled courtyard. We children knew it was "our space," and when they told us to stay there, our parents knew where we were. Much later, when my son was a toddler and I was pregnant with my second child, I lived with my husband at St. Francis Square, San Francisco, a cooperative apartment scheme arranged around three landscaped courtyards. As a parent I experienced what a godsend a communal courtyard can be, providing play space and playmates within easy reach and calling distance of home. However the undoubted leaning in this book toward bounded spaces and toward the crucial importance of spaces *in between* buildings can be attributed only partially to my own environmental experience. Studies of resident reactions to housing clearly indicate a preference for dwellings bounding human-scale spaces that provide safe and interesting play areas for children and places of casual meeting for adults.

I appreciate living in neighborhoods and housing schemes that have some visual identity, some sense of "placeness." Happily, I have lived in several: in Stockholm; London; San Juan, Puerto Rico; New York; San Francisco; Berkeley; and Sydney. A recent resurgence of interest in neighborhood identity suggests that this need to live in a place that feels like it is "somewhere," not just anywhere, is a strong need for many people. Hence the inclusion in this book of many guidelines dealing with identity, personalization, and communal space.

Strong feelings about gardens and gardening need hardly be justified to a British audience; making and tending gardens might be consid-

ered *the* British art form. Although a U.S. resident for the past twenty-four years, I retain a great love of gardening—both for decoration and for food raising—which I attribute to my British upbringing. This predilection, together with the fact that more than half the research studies cited in this book are British, may have introduced a slight bias toward the importance of garden space. Hence users of this book in other cultures may have to make adjustments regarding local values or norms of behavior in relation to gardens, as well as other culture-bound behaviors (children's games, adult recreation, and so on).

As a feminist I strongly support the needs of women, and particularly the environmental needs of single working parents, of which I am one. It is tragic that for so long women have been underrepresented in the design professions, although they have traditionally been responsible for rearing children and maintaining homes in the housing schemes designed *for* them. It is not surprising that housing design and site planning frequently fail in their support of child rearing when the chief decision makers (housing programmers, designers, managers) are predominantly male and have had little firsthand experience minding small children. It is ironic—and again not surprising—that many of the influential writers on the sociology of housing—how it really *works* for adults and children—have been women (for example, Patricia Bagot, Anne Beer, Connie Byrom, Jane Darke, Elizabeth Gittus, Vere Hole, Pearl Jephcott, Joan Maizels, Alison Ravetz, and Margaret Willis in Britain and

Sandra Howell, Florence Ladd, Susan Saegert, Sue Weidemann, Elizabeth Wood, and Catherine Bauer Wurster in the United States).

Where would *I* prefer to live? I think that is a relevant question for all of us in the environmental professions to consider. My bias is toward medium- to high-density living (although not high *rise*!). I like to feel that other people are living close by, to see people passing by on the street, to walk to neighborhood shops and see people I know. Although not strongly anti-car (it offers us a great deal of freedom), I prefer for myself and my children to live in a neighborhood well served by public transport, where major traffic flows are relegated to neighborhood edges or where traffic is managed so that pedestrians' needs predominate. I admit to being strongly influenced by Swedish new town design during a year's residence in that country. I admire the strong values attached to walking and safe pedestrian movement in residential areas; I see those same values espoused in much British new town planning (although not sufficiently in the latest and largest new town—Milton Keynes), but hardly at all in American suburban design. The development of shopping malls and traffic-segregated cluster housing heralds minor inroads into the dominance of the car in U.S. culture, but it is a top-down approach, rather than one that emanates from a deep cultural value attached to walking.

Are there places where I personally could not live? Yes, indeed, there must be such environments for all of us. For me it is the two extremes of density: low-density suburbia, which I find lacking in street life and public outdoor activity and too dependent on the car, and high-density high rises, which I find unacceptable for my children and too vertically divorced from garden space and urban activity for myself. My ideal would be to live in a community of detached, semidetached, or row housing, each with ample private garden space with each cluster of houses sharing some common space, whether that be a street with limited traffic flow, some community gardens, play space, landscape walking areas, or all of these. My personal experience and my extensive reading of the research literature on housing indicate that numerous variations on this theme are highly suitable environments for family life. Indeed, low rise, high density, as it has come to be known in the United States (cluster housing in Australia, mid-density in Canada), is the form that has been encouraged by housing authorities, the design professions, and some private developers for the past decade. Any bias toward this form of housing in this book is only marginally attributable to my personal preference; increasing evidence suggests that this will be an important housing form of the future because it expresses certain economic, sociological, and ecological values that are increasingly espoused by the public at large.

For the past twenty-five years I have been avidly looking at houses and housing; it is both my profession and my hobby. Even on vacation in foreign parts I gravitate to housing schemes, redeveloped areas, and new towns, as well as to the museums and cathedrals of classical tourism.

Perhaps it is an addiction. Where children play and what they do and how people delimit their gardens, personalize their entries, decorate their homes, and meet each other in neighborhood space are the "stuff" of this book. I hope that some of my enthusiasm for this subject comes through in the pages that follow.

Wendy Sarkissian

While Clare was feeding animals in the English countryside, I was making my start in life in the environment that has become my greatest professional concern: isolated, low-density suburbia—treeless, no services, no public transit. Although I have lived in many countries besides my native Canada, my memories of the limitations of that suburban experience have fired my enthusiasm to campaign for a reform of suburban planning and to seek to develop and explain alternative housing forms.

Accessibility is something I value highly. In my view housing is only as good as the quality of its connections with essential features of the neighborhood: shops, community facilities, schools, recreational areas, and other houses. Travel distances are important to me, probably because my family had access to a car only occasionally (my father traveled away from home on business for several months at a time). Until I was thirty-seven I did not drive a car; so I became a connoisseur of public transit and an experienced urban cyclist. Having grown up in a cold and rainy climate, I am especially sensitive to the interchanges or connections between the elements that make up a neighborhood or a city. I

like safe, well-lit walks from bus stops to front doors, protected places to wait, and easy gradients from bus to home to facilitate carrying a week's groceries, a potted palm, or a stack of books. When you do not have a car, all those access issues assume much greater significance. If there is also a bias in favor of access for disabled persons in the book, I take credit for it. Certainly the years I spent at U.C. Berkeley working on research projects studying barrier-free design dramatically changed my views about access. I now see barriers to access for disabled people everywhere. We have conscientiously attempted to remove them—and the stereotypes they often reflect—in this book.

I seem to have been born with an inability to find my way home, a poor sense of direction; I am easily disoriented spatially. I cannot explain its origin, but I am certain that it accounts for my abiding concern for creating "legible" environments—where you can easily get a mental map, image, or picture and are able to find your way around. I lose myself easily in identical courtyards, am perpetually frustrated by maps with no "you are here" indicator, and complain about poorly lit street signs, unnumbered doors, and ambiguous messages from the environments. I do value complexity, diversity, and a little ambiguity, but in their proper places. I am partly responsible for the focus in this book on orientation, which is designed to help create housing that helps people move about efficiently and easily.

I dislike institutional environments. I have never been a prisoner, but I have been a hospital patient for more time than I care to remember. I lived in public housing as a child and spent almost all my working life in large institutional settings. I have rebelled against institutional sanctity, the philosophy that has given us tiled walls, regulation paint colors, and rules about decorating ("defacing") or in any way modifying those environments. I once painted my office door a brilliant red color called blaze and videotaped the custodian's reaction for my architecture students. I have contributed to this book's emphasis on the need for personalization and individual control.

Writing this book has had a dramatic effect on my environmental values. From the start I have been concerned about errors we might make in cross-cultural comparisons. For example, what might be considered high density in suburban Sydney would be extravagantly low in Hong Kong or Vancouver's West End. I was forced to review both my housing research and my housing experiences in Canada, the United States, England, and Australia and to search for universal themes. We have found, I believe, some essential features that improve the quality of life in medium-density housing, almost irrespective of its context.

While writing the book, we sorted our data a number of times as our views developed. Early in our work we made a conscious decision to remove any sex-role stereotypes that might influence design decisions. We have not assumed, for example, that all households with children (this is a book about housing for house-

holds with children) have two parents who are married to each other. "Family" became "household"; "parent" became "adult"; "mother" is not, we hope, condemned to a lifetime of supervising children while she stands at the sink. My feminist views and experience in the women's movement working for environmental reform for women contributed to those decisions.

Later, with the help of two physically disabled women who have architectural expertise, we examined our guidelines to see whether they fostered the creation of barrier-free housing. They did not, but they do now, to the best of our ability.

Perhaps the most important value that has influenced my work on this book is the view that life is better in environments that are appropriate to people's needs and congruent with their values. Working toward a good fit is a worthwhile cause. Like Margaret Mead, who, at the Habitat Conference in 1976, complained that "none of our teapots pour," I believe in all good things: equity, community, social reform. I also know that people spend a great deal of time in and around their homes. And as we are required to live at higher densities, we might as well use everything we know to make our housing more comfortable, supportive, and life enhancing.

The Experience of Joint Authorship

Although often separated by an ocean while writing this book, we are both totally convinced of the strength of joint authorship. Not only is it

an asset when enthusiasm lags and the task seems impossible, but our experience of working together has amply demonstrated to us that two minds are better than one, that possible biases or misinterpretations of data can be caught and rectified when a manuscript goes back and forth between two authors. Between us we have ninety years of experience of living in the world, have lived for extended periods of time in five different cultures, and have spent countless hours looking at housing in many others. We believe this multifaceted experience, shared with each other, has subtly influenced the form in which this book evolved and has immeasurably added to its quality.

Neither of us would consider writing another book alone. We may not necessarily expect to write other books with each other, but we do expect to find other like minds with whom to engage in the exciting intellectual adventure of joint authorship.

Acknowledgments

When publication time arrives, the authors of any book find themselves indebted to many friends, colleagues, and family members who have assisted, advised, and encouraged along the way. In the case of this book our indebtedness is even greater because the book has had a very long gestation period and has drawn on research and expertise in a range of countries.

Starting in Berkeley in 1977, Cooper Marcus was especially aided by former architecture student Jared Polsky, who made a valuable contribution in reorganizing an early version of the manuscript and pointing out overlaps and omissions. Also at that time many fruitful conversations with research colleague Lindsay Hogue helped formulate ideas about design guidelines. A grant from the National Endowment for the Arts (Art and Architecture Division, spring 1977) enabled work to begin with three Berkeley students—Elizabeth Drake, Nancy Owens, and Peter Bosselmann—on creating the illustrations that form such a valuable part of this book and on a trial mock-up of the book design, created by faculty colleague Mark Treib.

During the academic year 1978–79, following several months of collaborative work, Cooper Marcus resided in London and was able to devote all her time to work on this book while Sarkissian ably took over her courses in Berkeley. We are especially grateful to Barry Poyner and Nigel Hughes, who graciously shared their office space with Cooper Marcus at the Tavistock Institute for Human Relations, London. During this period of intensive work many people made valuable contributions: Jane Darke and Alexi Ferster Marmot were most helpful in reading certain chapters and in accompanying Cooper Marcus on many enjoyable and enlightening expeditions to housing sites in London, Sheffield, Liverpool, and Runcorn New Town. Sheena Wilson (then of the Department of the Environment) was extremely helpful in editing the book at that time and in alerting us to recent relevant research in Britain. The *Architectural Psychology Newsletter* edited by Sue Anne Lee of Kingston Polytechnic School of Architecture put us in touch with many useful British sources.

Our association with the Architectural Press began at this time, and we are grateful to Geoffrey Golzen and Maritz Vandenberg for their editorial advice and generosity in enabling us to browse through the photographic files of *The Architect's Journal* for many useful illustrations that now grace this book.

In 1979–80 the two authors worked closely on the book in Berkeley. A number of students in the College of Environmental Design were very helpful at that time: Patrice Traylor, Colette Meunier, Carolyn Francis, and especially Donald Perlgut, whose work formed the basis of the chapter on security. We undertook many field trips to observe and photograph inner-city and suburban housing, several with Ann Cross (visiting from Australia), who provided valuable insights on the links between design and management.

Since 1980, we have again been separated by an ocean, and work has continued via the mails and annual meetings. While Cooper Marcus was principally engaged in teaching, Sarkissian investigated housing evaluation research in Australia and New Zealand and was especially aided in this endeavor by the support of Marie Mune and Richard Nies of the South Australian Institute of Technology, Adelaide, and by Stephen Cramond, librarian at the South Australia Housing Trust, Adelaide. Two Australian landscape architects read and commented on the manuscript at this time. We are grateful to Kevin Taylor and especially to Ian Barwick for the many creative criticisms of our work. Barwick's comments were particularly enlightening in terms of communicating our findings to the design professions.

Wendy Sarkissian acknowledges the long friendship and professional encouragement of David Yencken of Melbourne, Australia, whose passion for housing reform has sustained her in the conviction that "God is in the details." Both authors thank Mary Ann Hiserman and Cheryl Davis of Berkeley for advice and enlightenment on barrier-free design. Wendy especially thanks Mary Ann for friendship, inspiration, and education.

In another corner of the English-speaking world Jacqueline Vischer Skaburskis of Vancouver, Canada, was very generous in sharing her knowledge of housing evaluation research in Canada and especially her own work on medium-density housing in the False Creek redevelopment area.

Our thanks are also due to Kim Dovey, an Australian Ph.D. student in architecture at Berkeley, for his invaluable work on overlaps and conflicts among the guidelines (summer 1982); to Peter Marris, Ron Bedford, and Franklin Becker, who reviewed the final manuscript for U.C. Press and made useful suggestions that we incorporated in our final editing; and to Carolyn Francis and Anna Kondolf for invaluable assistance in the preparation of the manuscript for composition.

We also appreciate colleagues and government agencies who have granted us permission to use illustrations that previously appeared in published books and reports: John Byrom, Greater London Council, Her Majesty's Stationery Office, Milton Keynes Development Corporation, Oscar Newman, U.K. Department of Environment, and Sue Weidemann.

The University of California Press has been enormously supportive of our work, and we must especially thank Karen Reeds, who carried the book through the first stages of review and acceptance; Sheila Levine, Mary Lamprech, and Sylvia Stein, who ably supervised its editing; and Laurie Anderson, who designed its layout.

We are deeply grateful to the many people who have done invaluable work on editing, word processing, and typing during the many phases of this book's evolution: Kitty Solomon in London; Pauline Cox, Dinah Ayers, and Teresita Valdoria in Australia; Marcie McGaugh and Nancy Laleau in Berkeley; Marilyn Barry in Scotland; and particularly John Taylor of Berkeley, whose expert professional editing transformed an overly long manuscript into the present book. We are grateful to the Farrand Fund of the Department of Landscape Architecture at Berkeley for financial support in this very critical editing phase of our work.

The production of any book is a time-consuming and sometimes stressful and frustrating experience. Inevitably, family members and close friends of the authors have had to put up with much of the fallout. Wendy Sarkissian has been sustained by Leonie Sandercock, who writes books more easily but understands the process very well. She records the most heartfelt gratitude for continued professional and loving encouragement to Donald Perlgut (who was so understanding that she married him during the course of writing this book). Clare Cooper Marcus expresses her deep gratitude to Al Baum and Priscilla Thomas for their friendship and continued emotional support; to Christine, Anthony, and Jane Cooper, her family in London; to family and friends at the Findhorn community in northern Scotland where the final tedious checking of copyediting was done amidst peaceful surroundings; to Stephen Marcus, the father of her children; and especially to her children, Jason and Lucy Marcus, for dealing so patiently with a mother who was sometimes distracted and often tired, but whose passionate concern for her work they somehow understood.

Introduction

Consider these two places: Walking into Green Acres, you immediately sense that you have entered an oasis—traffic noise left behind, negative urban distractions out of sight, children playing and running on the grass, adults puttering on plant-filled balconies. Signs of life and care for the environment abound. Innumerable social and physical clues communicate to visitors and residents alike a sense of home and neighborhood. This is a place that people are proud of, a place that children will remember in later years with nostalgia and affection, a place that just feels "good."

Contrast this with Southside Village. Something does not feel quite right. It is hard to find your way about, to discern which are the fronts and which are the backs of the houses, to determine what is "inside" and what is "outside." Strangers cut across what might be a communal backyard. There are no signs of personalization around doors or on balconies. Few children are around; those who are outside ride their bikes in circles in the parking lot. There are few signs of caring; litter, graffiti, and broken light fixtures indicate the opposite. There is no sense of place; it is somewhere to move away from, not somewhere to remember with pride.

These are not real locations, but we have all seen places like them. The purpose of this book is to assist in the creation of more places like Green Acres and to aid in the rehabilitation of the many Southside Villages that scar our cities.

This book is a collection of guidelines for the site design of low-rise, high-density family housing. It is intended as a reference tool, primarily for housing designers and planners, but also for developers, housing authorities, citizens' groups, and tenants' organizations—anyone involved in planning or rehabilitating housing. It provides guidelines for the layout of buildings, open spaces, community facilities, play areas, walkways, and the myriad components that make up a housing site.

Architects and planners who design housing schemes work under especially severe constraints. The most serious of these, and often the hardest to recognize, is the lack of input from the people who must live with their designs. The immediate clients are usually public or private agencies, not the eventual tenants.

Under such circumstances the ordinary give and take between designer and user that seems a prerequisite to a satisfying design cannot take place. Architects usually are forced to fall back on their own experience and their perceptions of the future tenants' needs. There is, however, an alternative. Architects and planners can also draw on the accumulated experience of people who already live in housing developments. Over the past two decades many designers and social scientists have asked residents to comment on the design of their living spaces. Such postoccupancy evaluations (POEs) provide useful information about what works and what fails from the residents' perspectives.

Architects who have tried to unearth these studies complain with justification that they are hard to come by and to use. This book is the result of a concerted effort to examine and assess as many of these studies as possible from the English-speaking, developed world. The guidelines that make up this book are the outcome of our analysis of nearly one hundred studies of what people like and dislike about their housing environments.

The Emerging Need for Design Guidelines

Long before people built houses, they had already evolved ways of living together that reflected their needs, values, and beliefs. When they began to build shelters and dwellings, these ways were unselfconsciously incorporated into the fabrics they constructed. Materials were what was readily at hand; construction techniques were commensurate with the builders' skills. Form, layout, and decoration reflected what the residents deemed important (Alexander, 1979; Rapoport, 1969). Buildings reflected culture; if it were not so, archaeology and the social history of architecture would have no meaning.

Since the Industrial Revolution and the massive movement of rural folk into cities, however, an increasing proportion of the population has had its homes built by strangers—speculative builders, housing authorities, building contractors, architects, and engineers. There is nothing inherently wrong with this; many activities that we used to do for ourselves, such as growing food and making clothes, are now done for us. Because specialists perform these tasks, we gain free time to follow other pursuits. And, despite

---

1 Primary phase: one actor in the design process

user
client
designer
builder

User-client-designer-builder are one and the same person

2 Craftsman phase: two actors in the design process

a. Wealthy client-user hires and communicates directly with
b. Master mason or builder who draws up plans and executes them

3 Early professional phase: three actors in the design process

a. Wealthy client-user hires and communicates with
b. Professional architect, who interprets needs of client, creates a design, and
c. Contractor who executes making any modifications to original design.

4 Later professional phase: multiple actors in the design process

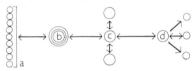

a. Users are separate from fee-paying client; needs are filtered through client;

b. Client is often an institution represented by a committee;
c. Architect interprets clients' needs, communicates with fellow professionals (engineers, landscape consultants, etc.); has to please client not the users;
d. Building contractor executes the design and is dependent on sub-contractors.

5 Contemporary phase

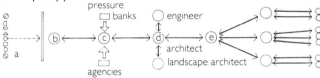

pressure
banks
engineer
architect
landscape architect
agencies

a. Users have increased in number and become more diverse in terms of needs;
b. Barrier in communication with client and designers created by space, time, economics, and politics. Recognition of barrier evokes new professionals of user needs consultant, environment and behavior researcher and design programmer;
c. User needs are filtered to designer via client and take 3rd or 4th place after client's own needs and those of banks, city agencies, federal regulations, etc.
d. Architect becomes process manager, balancing needs of many actors as well as fulfilling own professional needs;
e. Building contractor limited in interpretation of design into reality by manufacturers of building components, union regulations, materials specifications, etc.

Figure 1. Designer-user relations at different periods in history. From *The Form of Housing*, ed. Sam Davis (New York: Van Nostrand Reinhold, 1981).

persuasive arguments to the contrary (Alexander, 1977, 1979), most people probably do not *want* to build their own homes: The majority wants a ready-made dwelling, as long as it fulfills the functional and symbolic needs of "home."

The designer and his or her private client traditionally came from the same social milieu; they "talked the same language" and could at least communicate about the function and symbolism of a proposed new house or other building. Moreover the client and the eventual user of a new building were one. Today, however, the communication process is more complex: Fee-paying clients are often institutions, and they are represented by committees that frequently do not even include eventual (non-fee-paying) users. Time and budget pressures often preclude detailed, analytical consideration of the users and functions of buildings.

Design practitioners seeking a socially responsible approach find little of value in professional criticism. With few exceptions critiques in professional magazines focus either on building science and technology or on aesthetic principles and style. Rarely are buildings evaluated according to dwellers' responses or the way the buildings fulfill daily functions. *The Architect's Journal* in Britain and the *American Institute of Architects' Journal* and *Landscape Architecture* in the United States have encouraged social assessments of buildings and open spaces, but even these exceptions are often not the "studies" they purport to be.

Figure 2. Postoccupancy evaluation studies can inform us of discrepancies between designers' and residents' perceptions. In this London scheme the architects wanted to create a stepped-down effect that would enable the development to "blend into" its surroundings. The residents affectionately named the scheme "Lego Flats" and "The Battleship."

Figure 3. The designer's intent in this scheme was to re-create the essence of a London street of terrace (row) houses. Residents referred to it as "The Prison" and felt overly exposed when walking to and from their houses.

The general public is no longer content to take what is given it or to pay what is demanded of it. The past two decades have seen a phenomenal rise in the degree of public protest and in the number of groups (blacks, Hispanics, Asians, women, gays, the physically disabled) who are ready to fight for their rights. Property tax revolts in California, court cases against highrise housing in Minneapolis, rent strikes in Liverpool and London, and "tent cities" of homeless youth in Australia demonstrate that people are prepared to take action against unreasonable housing costs or forms. In Britain in the late 1970s the image of the architect was perhaps at its lowest ebb since the Second World War. Media coverage of architectural bungling and ethics received wide coverage and generated considerable public debate. There was a BBC TV series in February 1979 entitled "The Way We Live Now" that dealt forthrightly with some of the questionable housing and planning decisions of the previous two decades. In the summer of 1979 a successful play entitled *Can You Hear Me at the Back?* opened in London's West End. Its main character was the disillusioned chief architect of a fictional British new town.

Although designers have made avoidable mistakes (some of horrendous proportions) that people will have to live with for decades to come, the blame also lies with fee-paying clients, design programs, ways in which government standards are applied, social researchers unwilling to stand up and be counted, and bureaucratic departmentalism (passing the buck). Because of this last phenomenon, for example, we frequently find housing officials concerned only with dwelling mix and construction speed, government agencies concerned only with costs per dwelling and compliance with technical standards, and architects concerned only with dwelling design and overall image. Rarely is there a housing coordinator and rarely, except in the relatively unique situation of new town planning, are social services and physical facilities planned in an integrated fashion.

During the past two decades growing concern about the separation between designers and their eventual clients has led to the emergence of a new field of study known variously as environmental psychology, environment and behavior studies, environmental sociology, or architectural psychology. Both the need for a theoretical understanding of the relationship between people and their surroundings and immediate, pragmatic concern over mismatches between people, institutions, communities, and designed environments have provided impetus for this work, and a considerable body of research now exists. Britain led the English-speaking world in pragmatic, case study research in housing with government bodies initiating postoccupancy evaluations of prototype housing forms. Ironically, British schools of landscape and building architecture place little emphasis on the theoretical foundations of environmental psychology or sociology. In the United States virtually every leading school of architecture or landscape architecture requires courses in people-environment studies, but the federal Department of Housing and Urban Development

(HUD) has barely begun to acknowledge the need for postoccupancy evaluations and a more user oriented approach to programming. Australia has tended to follow the American pattern, emphasizing teaching in departments of architecture and environmental design; government sponsorship of basic research has only recently expanded. The Canadian and New Zealand experience falls somewhere between that of the United States and Britain, with a limited role for the teaching of social science in design departments and an expanded and more influential role for a user-oriented approach to housing at local and national government levels.

The Use of POE Research to Generate Design Guidelines

If research on people-housing relations now exists, why are the design professions not using it? A recent U.S. study on the use of social science in architecture revealed that, although 96 percent of the designers surveyed believe that the environment influences behavior and 87 percent are aware of the existence of environment and behavior research, only 20 percent have ever used any in their work (Reizenstein, 1975, 28). Designers did not know where to find research; findings were frequently reported in jargon-ridden language; the design implications were not immediately obvious; and so on.

Designers would be more aware of this research if it had filtered into government housing standards, but little of it has, and most designers currently in positions of governmental authority were trained before it existed. Most

official housing standards, which originated in the nineteenth-century public health laws, emphasize physical health and safety within dwelling units or building complexes and ignore both individual and community *mental* health and crucial aspects of site design. The U.S. Douglas Commission characterizes such codes and standards as "a combination of rule-of-thumb, personal experience, and professional judgment with limited supportive scientific data (National Commission . . . , 1969, 33).

Another kind of government standard has recently appeared in Britain: local authority "design guides" or policy guidelines aimed primarily at regulating the *visual* environment. These control exterior design and road layout in private housing developments. Growing concern for conserving local vernacular architectural styles and a townscape philosophy of urban design influenced the development of design guides, which range from the now-classic Essex *Design Guide* (County Council of Essex, 1973) to numerous less-ambitious pamphlets by local authorities. The design guidelines in this book differ greatly from these. Both address site planning issues, but design guides approach the quality of housing environments from a primarily *aesthetic* perspective, as defined by professional designers and planners; the guidelines in this book address the quality of housing environments from a *social* perspective, as defined by residents.

The most telling fact about the neglect of user-based housing research is that little has found its way into commercially published books,

retrievable in libraries. Many of the studies referred to in this book are reported in government-sponsored research published as monographs, design bulletins, or academic reports. Some are theses or dissertations written by architecture or landscape architecture students. A few have appeared as articles in the design press, a few as papers in social science journals or the proceedings of professional conferences.

Of the approximately one hundred housing case studies used as the research base of this book, forty-seven were published in Britain, thirty-seven in the United States, five in Canada, five in Australia, five in New Zealand, and one in Ireland. Locating, reading, and synthesizing the results of these studies have taken many years. Often we discovered case studies almost inadvertently; in the course of visiting another university a question sometimes led one of us to a thesis or a local report of considerable relevance. In attempting to uncover this research in hiding, we were particularly aided by our own multicultural and interdisciplinary range. The authors of this book are a British geographer and planner, currently residing and teaching in the United States (Cooper Marcus), and a Canadian planner, resident for much of her career in Australia (Sarkissian). Co-workers and advisers on this long-term project include an American planner now resident in Australia (Perlgut), a Canadian architect who did postgraduate work in the United States (Polsky), a Canadian sociologist now residing and working in the United States (Hogue), a British sociologist with research experience in criminology (Wilson), and an Australian architect doing postgraduate work in the United States (Dovey). The illustrators were an American architect/planner (Drake), a German architect now teaching in the United States (Bosselmann), and an American landscape architect (Owens).

We considered only postoccupancy evaluation studies of resident reactions to low-rise, medium- or high-density family housing that used recognized survey techniques of sampling, interviewing, observing, and analyzing. We relied more heavily on those using interviews rather than mailed questionnaires because subtleties and details are lost with the latter technique. The most reliable studies used both attitude surveys *and* behavioral observations; a few studied behavior alone. We rejected "studies" that were, in fact, only designers' journalistic critiques.

Some of the studies utilized sophisticated techniques of multivariate and regression analysis; others relied on simple, noncomputerized cross-tabulations. The former offered interesting data on correlates of satisfaction but often overlooked mundane but significant site-specific data. Less sophisticated analysis techniques may have lacked a grand correlational conclusion but often contained a wealth of human detail. We rejected studies with small sample sizes, atypical population groups, or dubious research methods.

As our research and literature review progressed, overlaps began to appear. Indeed, the occurrence of similar findings in different locations first alerted us to the possibility of formulating guidelines. If ten different studies of

comparable housing in different locations report dissatisfaction with, say, unfenced backyards, that finding is probably true for the majority of people.

Although we relied heavily on evaluative case studies, we also found valuable supporting material in books or articles dealing with child development, residential crime, housing management, social networks, community analysis, and deviant behavior, as well as in collections of guidelines from more technical or aesthetic viewpoints (County . . . , 1973; Department . . . , 1972b, 1972c; Department . . . Transport, 1977). We used two other categories of materials. One was common sense. Some facts about housing design are so obvious and basic that they need no research to prove them; we include them because they are nevertheless sometimes overlooked. The other was the authors' ongoing field observations in housing developments. Sometimes a visit to a housing project led to guidelines that would not have emerged from existing research. For example, a guideline on the need for an orientation map at entrances to large, new developments stemmed from observing people using them on many greater London council estates. Later, during field observations in new medium-density suburban housing in California, this guideline was elaborated and made more specific, primarily because current design and location details sometimes render these maps inoperable.

The observations of existing housing initially focused on public inner-city redevelopment and

private suburban housing in the San Francisco Bay Area. This American bias was balanced by an equally concentrated study of council housing in London, Glasgow, Newcastle, and Liverpool; public and private estates in Milton Keynes, Stevenage, and Runcorn New Towns; and selected observations in Vancouver, Winnipeg, Toronto, Ottawa, Auckland, Wellington, Dunedin, Christchurch, Melbourne, Sydney, Adelaide, Stockholm, Copenhagen, and Amsterdam. Some recent books on design guidelines were especially influential in our thinking: *Changing Children's Hospital Environments* (Lindheim, Glaser, and Coffin, 1972) is a fine example of the translation of observational research into clearly articulated recommendations, with a set of design review questions to use as a checklist at the end. *Low Rise Housing for Older People* (Zeisel, Epp, and Demos, 1977) is an excellent example of succinct guidelines, cogent illustrations, and stimulating (although nondirective) possible design responses. This publication influenced our own inclusion of a similarly titled section for each guideline. Finally, *A Pattern Language* (Alexander et al., 1977) somewhat influenced our organization of the text and particularly influenced our use of a shorthand name for each guideline.

Changing Needs and the Housing Environments

Housing is designed and built and in that sense is a product. But when considered as a sequence from original contract, user participation, alternative designs, final design, and working drawings to construction, occupation, resident evaluation, management, maintenance, and replacements, housing is also a process (Turner, 1976). Too often designers focus on the product and withdraw their professional responsibility when buildings are completed. Contractual arrangements that would retain architects and landscape architects for several years beyond initial occupancy to implement changes and modifications requested by residents (Ministry . . . , 1967a) would require considerable changes in the traditional designer-client relationship. We believe that these changes and new arrangements must be made.

A particular program, and the resulting built environment, may be well conceived to cope with the current daily needs of, say, families with young children, but what happens when the children become teenagers or when half the original nuclear families become single-parent families or groupings of unrelated adults? Design flexibility is often recommended, but an ambiguous space in year 1 is often equally ambiguous (and leads to equally serious problems) in year 15. Perhaps we need the architectural equivalent of the owner's manual supplied with a new car, something that stays with the housing (whatever the management, whoever the residents) and spells out how different spaces or facilities *could* be modified to meet changing needs. It might say, for example, "If the child population becomes predominantly adolescent, the sandbox could be boarded over to become a stage. If the de-

mand arises, the flat next to the preschool play space could be converted into a day-care center. If a higher proportion of residents becomes car owners, the parking area could be decked over to double the number of spaces." If designers make these alternatives explicit from the start and suggest modifications in writing, the long-term usefulness of a project will be enhanced and designers will be forced to think about long-term flexibility.

Postoccupancy evaluation would become an integral part of the design process if specific time and money provisions for it were incorporated in the designer-client contract. We will start to see a systematic upgrading of multifamily housing only when clients and designers can be persuaded that objective user evaluations are essential to the improvement of housing design and the modification of government regulations. It is also essential that the residents themselves have some control over their home environments and can effect changes through tenant participation in management or through cooperative arrangements. This in turn will ensure a continuous reevaluation of design.

We have learned enough now to know that a move to better housing in a "good" environment cannot, by itself, improve the economic circumstances of deprived families, the emotional circumstances of disturbed families, or the general happiness of "normal" families. But we have also learned that the design of environments affects people in a multitude of ways and that, in terms of their well-being, it matters deeply. Because of

this, we offer our design guidelines as a contribution to housing as if people mattered.

Clustered Housing: A Socially and Ecologically Desirable Form

Inevitably, when guidelines are based on existing POE research of a particular housing type (low-rise, high-density or clustered housing), those guidelines will tend to perpetuate that form. We firmly believe that this form of housing, when done well, can serve the needs of many segments of the population better than the other two density extremes—low-density, detached housing or high-density, high-rise housing. Our plea is for a more urban, ecologically aware, and potentially community-oriented residential form.

Low-density suburbia was constructed at a rapid rate after World War II to house newly formed families. The model was set of the commuting male adult returning tired to the serene dream house, whose physical and emotional maintenance was the responsibility of his wife. Home and garden, at least in the United States, were often large enough to represent a full-time maintenance job, not to speak of cooking, shopping, and chauffeuring children to music lessons and school. Built during a time (the 1950s and 1960s) when it was expedient to phase women out of the paid labor force, it was socially and economically convenient to perpetuate a housing form that supported the old adage—"a woman's place is in the home" (Egar and Sarkissian, 1982; Hayden, 1980).

Figure 4. Low-rise, high-density housing became the norm in redeveloped areas of most Western cities after the demise of the high-rise era of the 1960s.

By the 1970s, however, women in every Western country had begun to enter the labor force in unprecedented numbers. By 1975, the two-worker family accounted for 39 percent of all American households (Hayden, 1980, S174). More and more women opted to work, and many—in single-parent families—found themselves the sole breadwinner. Inevitably, working women found themselves doing two jobs: the job for which they are paid plus unpaid home maintenance/child care/cooking. Recent surveys in affluent suburbs of "a large Midwest metropolitan area" (which included both employed and nonemployed wives) indicate that despite liberalizing sex roles and work women still do 80–95 percent of the approximately sixty household tasks investigated (Berk, 1980, 73). The large split-level suburban house in the United States has become a burden to many employed women. Commuting is also a problem in segments of the city where low densities virtually exclude public transport.

In a comparative study of residential satisfaction in a low-density U.S. suburb (Levittown, Pennsylvania) and a higher density Swedish equivalent (Vällingby), sociologist David Popenoe concludes: "With the percent of gainfully employed women in the U.S. sharply rising, the relative disadvantages of a Levittown-type environment for the working woman are increasing. For the woman who can't afford a second car, who has difficulty making child care arrangements, and who has specialized employment needs, Levittown can become a noose around her neck" (1977, 177).

Small wonder that attached or clustered housing, with smaller dwellings and more shared facilities, is gaining in popularity. Some families who can afford it are moving back to the city to be closer to more work opportunities, childcare facilities, public transport, and cultural facilities.

Children, particularly between the ages of six and twelve, need to have access to their peers, need to be able to explore and roam safely on their own, and need to have access to a variety of environments. All of this, and more, is available to children in clustered housing if shared landscaped spaces are designed sensitively. Inevitably, if children are safe and happy in their home neighborhood, their parents' lives are easier.

Research shows that one of the most frustrated population groups in low-density suburbia is adolescents (Gans, 1967; Popenoe, 1977). When young people are entering a stage in which they are seeking more and more independence from their parents, they find themselves in an environment where getting together with friends is made difficult by distance, paucity of public transport, separation of housing from shopping centers, and so on. In his United States–Sweden study, Popenoe found American suburban teenagers more often bored and engaging in vandalism than their counterparts in Sweden living at higher density with easy access to shops, clubs, public transport, and so on (Popenoe, 1977). Teenagers in clustered housing are more likely to find others of the same age living within walking distance and may have access to shared

facilities or hanging-out places where they can spend time together, out of sight of home, yet not far away.

The problems of high-rise, high-density living for families have been too widely discussed to bear repeating here. Low-rise, high-density housing can (potentially) offer residents some of the advantages of the high-rise flat or apartment (privacy, efficient maintenance, shared facilities) without its disadvantages (distance from ground, feelings of anonymity).

Not only does clustered housing offer some distinct *social* advantages; it also addresses some pressing *economic* issues. With rising energy costs, the costs of commuting are affecting all income groups. Clustered housing in the inner city allows people to enjoy a green and quiet environment within easy access to city jobs. Similar housing on the city's fringes will, if repeated often enough, increase overall densities and render public transport more economical. As land costs continue to rise, clustered housing permits more dwellings on a given site. As ecological issues of natural drainage, solar access, and community gardens become more pressing, clustered housing permits the more rational use of any given site—the best soil saved for food growing, existing woodland preserved for play or windbreak, natural drainage patterns preserved.

In short, clustered housing, although not a panacea for all people, offers certain distinct advantages to population segments not previously given much attention in housing design (working parents, children, and adolescents). It also has

distinct ecological merits. Thus we offer guidelines on what we predict will soon be the fastest growing housing type in our cities.

2

Design Guidelines:
What they are and
how to use them

The houses people live in say much about them, about their life-styles and dreams. If we are to design housing to fulfill people's needs—and dreams—we must find out what they want and do not want, and such information must be readily available to designers of future housing and their clients. This book gathers some of this information in the form of design guidelines.

This book has evolved from fifteen years of examining housing, conducting postoccupancy evaluation research, and analyzing comparable studies done by others. It represents what we know at this time about human needs and desires in the housing environment and how they are affected by design. There now exist some obvious truths about how housing does—and does not—work for people. Unfortunately, these truths are not so obvious when housing programs are written or when housing developments are designed on the drawing board. Because budgets are tight, time is short, and immediate functional needs have to be met, more subtle, yet crucial, human needs such as privacy, territory, play space, and security are sometimes overlooked or inadequately fulfilled.

Decrying the usefulness of social science to design has become fashionable among some designers. At best these criticisms have focused on the use or misuse of jargon; at worst they have erroneously lumped together all social research under the rubric of "behaviorism" or rejected all attempts to find links between people's activities and the physical environment as "determinism." Very little of the research on which this book is based was carried out by psychologists, and none of it took a behaviorist viewpoint. Most of the research was carried out by sociologists and designers, often in joint efforts, and consisted of both attitudinal and observational data collection. The guidelines that follow are not intended to force people into a certain pattern of behavior. They are based on sensitive observations of how people apparently *want* to behave, to be, to play and work and socialize in and around their homes and how they *feel* about these activities.

We reject determinism on a macro, societal scale, but we believe that on the microscale of space in and around the home the environment very much influences behavior. Design cannot cause behavior, but it can offer the possibility of certain activities taking place. The physical environment of a housing development, for example, can encourage, discourage, or be neutral to its residents' behaviors.

The environment that influences behavior involves more than merely physical dimensions and design properties. It is laden or encoded with symbolic dimensions and messages, which we read or decode according to our role, expectations, motivation, and other factors (Becker, 1977; Rapoport, 1978). The environment facilitates (or inhibits) behavior simultaneously via several modes of physical, social, and symbolic communication. The placement of a path leading toward a dwelling entry will strongly suggest that you approach the door by this means, but social norms or familiarity with the residents may determine that you cut across the garden or tap on a side window instead. Similarly, the location of a bench in a landscaped area will suggest the possibility of sitting, but by no means dictates it; you might just as easily choose the grass because friends are there already or a retaining wall because it's convenient.

However to say that a design communicates a different message to different people is not the same as saying that people have total free will in relation to design and that their behavior is in no way affected by it. The latter attitude is naive and irresponsible and overlooks the universal human need for predictability, for avoidance of stress and unnecessary ambiguity. In our day-to-day life we seek social-physical settings where we feel comfortable, where there is some predictability as to how we and others will behave. We avoid settings that have no meaning or use for us or where we feel confused, fearful, or under stress. This fact is so obvious that we often overlook it in design considerations and fail to see that the same attraction-avoidance "dance" is operative on a housing site, where people use spaces and settings that have a functional use or aesthetic attraction and avoid those that do not.

Rather than separating design considerations from human behavior, we approach the designed physical environment first and foremost as a setting for human behavior. Thus we consider the design of housing primarily as the design of a place for eating, sleeping, loving, playing, socializing, and raising children. This book is an attempt to guide the residents, clients, and designers of housing toward a better understanding of how design affects these most basic human activities, the activities that take place at home.

Guidelines For What?

The guidelines in this book refer to the site planning of low-rise, medium- and high-density housing in both the private and public sectors. Dwelling interiors are not included. Analysis of a hundred case studies of residents' responses to their housing environments clarified that their chief complaints focus not so much on dwelling interiors as on overall image, milieu, and site planning. Most designers know by now how to design an adequate kitchen and a functioning bathroom, but apparently their skills have not been so highly developed in site planning, landscaping, play design, and creating acceptable images. Hence this book focuses on the arrangement of dwellings on the site, the treatment of facades and entries, and the crucial spaces between buildings.

Because high-rise living for families has been rejected in a number of Western countries (Britain, Australia, Canada) and strongly questioned in others (United States, Netherlands, Denmark, Sweden), this book focuses on what currently appears to be a reasonable alternative—low-rise, high-density housing. With trends in the West toward smaller households, a decreasing proportion of nuclear families, and an increasing proportion of single-parent households and nontraditional family groups, this form of housing becomes an attractive alternative to the expensive, space-consuming, and isolating single-family or detached house.

Figure 5. Design details clearly suggest certain behaviors and discourage others. The designer here wants to discourage use of the waterfront, hence the employment of river-eroded rocks, which are hard to walk on.

Figure 6. Waterfront use, ranging from walking or biking on the boardwalk, to pulling dinghies up on the pebble area (left), to sitting on the lawn (right), is encouraged here.

This book focuses on high-density housing, but because it is such a relative term, its use is avoided whenever possible. (What is considered medium density in Britain is considered high density in California; the highest density acceptable in Sydney's suburbs would be considered relatively low in Manchester or New York.) We have adopted the term *clustered housing* instead, by which we mean any arrangement whereby dwellings are clustered on a site (these could be single-family houses, row houses, or apartments) so that some of the site can be left free to develop communal open space or shared recreational facilities. The guidelines deal only with low-rise housing forms—buildings without elevators (depending on local regulations, three to five stories).

Guidelines For Whom?

This book is primarily about housing for families with children. This group forms the majority of households needing public and private housing. Some members of such households (children, parents at home), because they may be less mobile, are highly vulnerable to environmental oversights; and it is housing for families, especially public housing, that has been most often criticized in evaluation research. By "family" we mean any household that perceives itself as a family (for example, a single-parent family, a couple without children, or a group of unrelated adults who have chosen to live together, as well as the traditional nuclear family). For developments meant exclusively for single people living alone (students, working adults) or elderly households (singles, couples, or groups) other sources of guidelines would probably be more relevant (Zeisel, Epp, and Demos, 1977).

This book emphasizes children's needs not only because they are the chief users of outdoor common space, and the most influenced by their design, but because designers frequently ignore their needs. Virtually every study of medium- or high-density family housing identifies serious problems with children's play. In studies of British "difficult-to-let" projects inadequate provision for children and adolescents has often been *the* crucial factor in the physical and social disintegration of the project (Department . . . , 1981b; Heffernan, 1977).

The emphasis of this book is on housing in the English-speaking world. Virtually all the research cited was carried out in Britain, the United States, Canada, or Australia. Minority groups in such predominantly Anglo-Saxon cultures may have subtly different housing needs and preferences, but evaluation research on specific minority groups is still minimal. For such groups—for example, Asians in Britain, American blacks or Chicanos, Australian Aborigines, New Zealand Maoris—this book can be a starting point for discussion. Useful, culture-specific sets of guidelines could be developed by people who agree or disagree with our recommendations. We acknowledge the difficulties of cross-cultural generalizations; therefore the guidelines should be used with confidence only in those cultures we have cited. How French, Italians, Malays, or Peruvians might respond to comparable housing in their countries is beyond the

Figure 7. Postoccupancy research indicates that the success of clustered housing depends more on how the spaces *between* buildings are handled than on interior design.

scope of this volume, but for them, too, it might be a starting point.

Although we have tried to frame guidelines for general geographic use, the predominant "temperate northern" experience of the authors and their research base undoubtedly shines through. Designers in other climates may need to make local adjustments regarding orientation, microclimate, play norms, gardening behavior, plant materials, and so on.

How to Use This Book

The guidelines in this book are statements regarding human behavior in or attitudes toward the built environment that might be useful to designers and their clients. Most of these guidelines are based on empirical research; that is, a number of case studies suggest that this particular behavior or attitude is so. References within each guideline identify the supporting case studies. A study cited thus may be either entirely a discussion of the guideline topic or some portion of the study may support the findings in the guideline. Where no references are given, the guideline has emerged from intelligent observation of people and their housing environments.

Each new guideline begins a new column; at the top of the column, the guideline is abbreviated to facilitate quick reference. In many guidelines, an illustration depicts graphically a setting in which the need the guideline addresses was either well provided for or obviously overlooked. Thus the guideline statements and illustrations form the basic skeleton of the book; a quick perusal of them will give the reader a good idea

Figure 8. The design of a site for families with children needs unique handling.

of what the book is all about. The "meat" of the book explores the reasoning and research behind the guidelines, cites the references to specific case studies, and suggests possible design responses to the stated need. Thus each guideline comprises four or five distinct components: a key word shorthand title, a brief statement, textual backup, possible design responses, and in most cases an illustration.

At the start of program-writing, during conversations with the designer, or during the sketch design phase, the user of this book might briefly read the guideline statements and glance at the illustrations. At a later stage of design refinement, weighing up alternatives or making compromises among conflicting needs, the user

might read the textual backup of specific guidelines or consider some of the possible design responses suggested. At a final stage the designer, clients, or review board might wish to review the key word guideline titles alongside the plan to see that no essential needs have been overlooked.

Chapters have been ordered roughly as designers might need the material. Chapter 3, the first chapter containing specific guidelines, addresses general issues that need to be considered in the initial program-writing stage. The next chapter addresses image, building form, and orientation because these are issues frequently considered at the beginning of the design—at the sketch on the back of an envelope

Figure 9. A site housing working adults only presents different design demands.

Figure 10. If medium- or high-density housing is to be successful, children's needs must be met. In this high-density London scheme not a single piece of play equipment was provided. There were no yards or safe communal courtyards.

Figure 11. Although the London scheme (shown in Fig. 10 and above) housed over a thousand children, their needs were not addressed.

stage (Darke, 1978). Subsequent chapters deal with increasing detail, moving from the building edge out into site planning issues: personalization, access, private open space, common open space, play areas, facilities for adults, parking, landscaping, security, and services. A breakdown into subsections facilitates use in chapters with many guidelines; for example, in the chapter on purpose-built play areas for children the guidelines are grouped according to the needs of preschool children, children aged six to twelve, and teenagers.

In preparing this book we found that those of us from different parts of the English-speaking world (Britain, Australia, Canada, United States) sometimes used different architectural or planning terms for the same process or item. Because the basic text is in American English, we have compiled a glossary (Appendix A) that "translates" certain terms into British, Canadian, Australian, and New Zealand usage. We hope this book will be useful in all parts of the English-speaking world.

We envisage the users of this book to include professional designers of housing environments (architects, landscape architects), the fee-paying clients who create programs or briefs for design, the non-fee-paying clients (or future residents) who may use this book to help structure an intelligent participatory dialogue with professional designers, design students who wish to base studio decisions on something other than current stylistic fashion, and social researchers who may wish to explore, challenge, or modify its point of view.

Use of Guidelines

A book of this kind might be used in many ways, including the following:

1. A tenant group involved in rehabilitating its housing or a co-op group mobilizing to build its own dwellings might use the information about how comparable populations have responded to their housing in the past as a starting point from which to evolve priorities for discussion with designers. This would facilitate their early participation in the design process and enable them to do more than merely comment on designers' alternative plans.

2. Advocacy groups (for example, married students, children's advocacy groups, disabled people's organizations) involved in housing issues can use this book as a starting point for developing their own specialized guidelines.

3. When an architect is working with a specified resident group, so that its needs must be given priority, the guidelines might form the basis for initial discussions with them or for an interview survey to ascertain their preference and priorities. (To learn more about the techniques of social surveys, we urge designers to consult texts on sociological methods [Babbie, 1973; Lofland, 1971] or social researchers experienced in this field.)

4. Especially where eventual residents cannot be identified and there can be no dialogue with them concerning their needs, the guidelines can be used to identify the needs residents are likely to have and suggest ways of meeting them. Thus the guidelines are useful at the program-writing stage. Most design programs go no further than stating concrete features, such as dimensions, areas, and services. They need to go on to include objectives that relate to the needs and preferences reflected in the guidelines. The guidelines can help designers create programs for socially responsive housing— programs that are sensitive to the quality of spaces, for example, or the social function of adjacencies and boundaries in daily activities such as gardening, minding a child, washing the car, taking out the rubbish, playing, cycling, or meeting neighbors.

5. The guidelines can facilitate a much-needed innovation in the traditional design sequence: the annotated site plan. (We are grateful to John Zeisel for this idea and for conversations discussing its merits.) Annotations to the plan can make explicit how guidelines such as "personalization on and around the dwelling" or "opportunities for exploratory play" have been followed, thus spelling out the connection between social needs and the planned physical environment. Making these connections helps to ensure that the design fulfills the stated program. For this reason the annotated site plan is an effective device for communication between designers and clients. It also can provide materials for entry in a systematic design log (Spivack, 1978), recording

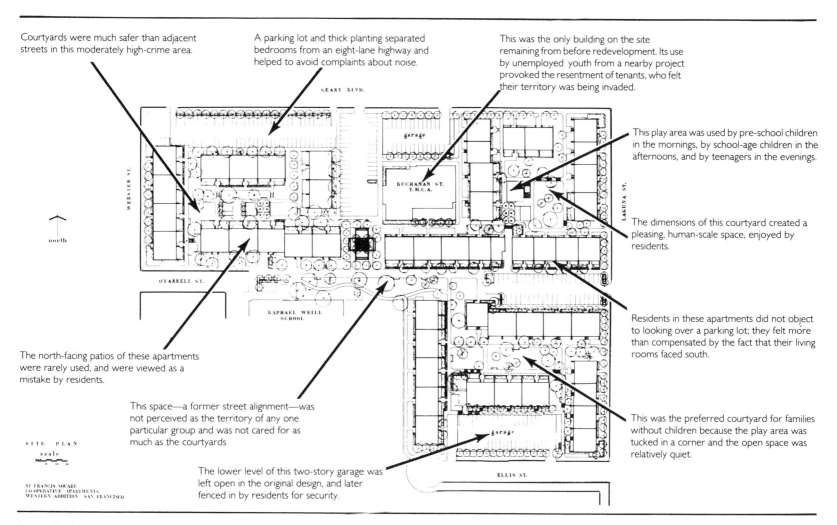

Courtyards were much safer than adjacent streets in this moderately high-crime area.

A parking lot and thick planting separated bedrooms from an eight-lane highway and helped to avoid complaints about noise.

This was the only building on the site remaining from before redevelopment. Its use by unemployed youth from a nearby project provoked the resentment of tenants, who felt their territory was being invaded.

This play area was used by pre-school children in the mornings, by school-age children in the afternoons, and by teenagers in the evenings.

The dimensions of this courtyard created a pleasing, human-scale space, enjoyed by residents.

Residents in these apartments did not object to looking over a parking lot; they felt more than compensated by the fact that their living rooms faced south.

The north-facing patios of these apartments were rarely used, and were viewed as a mistake by residents.

This space—a former street alignment—was not perceived as the territory of any one particular group and was not cared for as much as the courtyards

This was the preferred courtyard for families without children because the play area was tucked in a corner and the open space was relatively quiet.

The lower level of this two-story garage was left open in the original design, and later fenced in by residents for security.

north

GEARY BLVD.

garage

WEBSTER ST.

BUCHANAN ST.
Y.M.C.A.

LAGUNA ST.

O'FARRELL ST.

RAPHAEL WEILL
SCHOOL

garage

ELLIS ST.

SITE PLAN
scale

ST. FRANCIS SQUARE
CO-OPERATIVE APARTMENTS
WESTERN ADDITION SAN FRANCISCO

Figure 12. Annotated site plan of St. Francis Square, San Francisco, indicating how various programming issues were translated into physical design and how residents reacted.

design goals and solutions. Such a record facilitates subsequent postoccupancy evaluation, which is necessary to complete the design cycle.

6. Eventual residents or housing officials might use the design guidelines to appraise alternative designs. They might, for example, work through the list of guidelines, allotting points or weights to each of them according to their perception of its importance, and then use the scores to select the most appropriate plan. (In our eyes any such list of scores would provide better criteria for determining the winners of design awards than the criteria now chiefly operative—professional aesthetic considerations and peer approval.)

7. The guidelines could form the base on which government authorities devise their own, locally based sets of priorities (for example, regional HUD guidelines).

8. Social scientists could use the guidelines as hypotheses to be tested by further research. The guidelines are intended to inspire comment, modification, and even refutation if contrary evidence is forthcoming.

9. There is considerable scope for using guidelines in design studios. Even though many students of architecture, landscape architecture, and city planning now have opportunities to study people-environment research as part of their curricula and are sometimes trained in simple techniques of postoccupancy evaluation, they may have difficulties applying their skills when faced with the pressures of a studio problem. For students, as for practicing professionals, the existence of design guidelines precludes the need constantly to reinvent the wheel. Guidelines can form the base of the design program and/or be used as a checklist after alternative designs are produced. Review judges can use the guidelines in evaluating the social responsiveness of student work.

10. The guidelines are useful in evaluating existing housing developments prior to rehabilitation. They can be used as a checklist to pinpoint missing, poorly located, or badly designed features so that the rehabilitation program is responsive to social needs. With increasing emphasis on rehabilitation rather than demolition and redevelopment this may be one of the most fruitful uses of design guidelines.

What This Book Does Not Do

The guidelines are intended for initial use at the program-writing stage, after a site has been selected and a budget determined, and do not deal with site selection or budget organization. The guidelines do not address city planning issues beyond the site, such as local policies on public transit, community services or facilities, distribution of employment, or density zoning. They do not include space and construction standards prescribed in government building and housing codes. Because we assume that most designers have access to manuals detailing anthropometric and ergonomic information on average human dimensions pertaining to bench design, door widths, counter heights, and such, the guidelines do not cover such matters.

The guidelines avoid quantification as much as possible. Because this book is designed for use throughout the English-speaking world, where local conditions vary so widely, quantified guidelines are often inappropriate. In any case existing quantified standards often lack the support of reliable empirical evidence. Most important, once standards are quantified, they may be applied in a rubber stamp fashion. Where standards relate to psychological and social matters, this encourages a blindness to real human needs.

In the United Kingdom, for example, the Department of Environment (DOE), concerned about housing estates built without adequate play provision, sponsored one of the most detailed studies ever undertaken of children's play in housing areas: *Children at Play* (Department . . . , 1973a). An official circular for local authorities detailing space standards and play equipment that qualified for grants in subsidized housing followed in 1972. When play areas designed to meet these new standards began to appear in housing developments, several studies questioned their literal application (Hill, 1980; Hole, 1966; Holme and Massie, 1970). A Canadian authority on play even went so far as to judge that play opportunities in British council housing had been set back thirty years by the DOE study because it led to the 1972 circular, which demanded a specific number of seesaws, swings, slides, and roundabouts for each project. "What went wrong? The researchers were gathering the wrong data. They counted the times the children used the only equipment available to them, which happened to be traditional playground equipment. They must have had a computer code for seesaw, and none for mud (Hill, 1980, 24).

The list of guidelines is not a universal cookbook or compendium of solutions, and individual guidelines are not recipes. They can be seen, rather, as statements of culinary facts (for example, salt adds zest to vegetables), helping cooks take off on their own creative flights. These facts, essential relationships that the program may not address or the designer may not have time or resources to investigate, are the underpinnings of good design, not substitutes for it.

Thus most guidelines do not demand or prescribe one particular design solution. For example, a guideline that states, "people need to dispose of rubbish somewhere close to the house yet not in a place where the sight of, or odor from, the rubbish can(s) could cause offense" could be fulfilled in countless ways. When guidelines are worded prescriptively, this is because such wording is the clearest way of putting the point across. In fact, however, most guidelines are worded as performance standards (for example, "the entry should be welcoming yet clearly indicate to a stranger that this is the start of a private domain"). In such a case the design of an entry that performs in this way is clearly up to the designer.

Nevertheless, "possible design responses" follow most of the guidelines. In reviewing the manuscript of this book with many architecture students and practicing professionals, we were constantly pressed to say what *we* thought would be possible solutions to the needs stated in the guidelines. For this reason, after considerable debate, we decided to include our suggestions as these possible design responses. These are only suggestions and by no means exhaust the number of possible solutions.

The factors involved in housing satisfaction are many and complex. Lively, viable communities may exist in environments that planners have designated as slums and architects regard as ugly (Back, 1962; Gans, 1962), and the converse of this is true as well. No user of guidelines should suppose that their use will guarantee a happy housing development. The most humane architecture may house an unhappy community unless management, tenant allocation, maintenance policies, and so on are equally enlightened. Although this book only briefly touches these areas, we believe them to be equally important to overall housing satisfaction.

Which Guidelines To Follow

A decision to follow or not to follow any one of the guidelines in this book will be affected by budgetary considerations. Some, such as the guideline pertaining to swimming pools, call for considerable expense; others lead to short-run economies. But in the long run we believe that design according to these guidelines is cost-effective. An enormous amount of public money is currently spent in the United States and Britain on rehabilitating housing developments that have proved ill suited to their residents' needs, and a great majority of the design errors involved could have been avoided had more been known about these needs at the design stage. The use of guidelines will also prove cost-effective in new design work because housing that suits its residents will lead not only to higher levels of satisfaction, but to lower maintenance, replacement, and administrative costs and fewer vacancies and transfers. In the design office itself the use of research-based guidelines will largely eliminate the need for costly original research on user behavior. In fact the cost of user participation—often presented as an argument for limiting or eliminating this crucial phase in the design process—is reduced by the use of guidelines as a starting point for client-designer-user discussions.

These are arguments for the general use of guidelines, but they leave aside the question of which particular guidelines to follow and how to choose among conflicting recommendations. No single design can follow all the guidelines in this book; there are too many for that to be feasible, and in any case some of the guidelines contradict others. Conflicts, and the need to establish priorities in order to resolve them, are an inevitable part of the design process, whether or not the guidelines are taken into consideration.

When conflicts typically arise in the design process, too often they are resolved (1) in favor of the cheapest solution, (2) in favor of the most influential user (the maintenance staff?), (3) in favor of the user with whom the architect identifies most strongly (male, employed, heads of households?), (4) in some totally random fashion, or (5) worst of all, without actually being identified, so that no one's needs are properly met!

In our view there are better means of resolving design conflicts, but we have made no attempt to provide a point system or formula for determining priorities among the potentially conflicting needs different guidelines address. Each designer or resident group will have to make such decisions itself, weighing up local site conditions, community needs, specific group preferences, management policies, maintenance budgets, and so on. Guidelines facilitate this process by highlighting certain needs that might otherwise be overlooked, but they do not render the process unnecessary.

What happens when basic needs have been reasonably accommodated and conflicts still develop? Should a limited budget be stretched to include a preschool play area or visitor parking, a communal laundry room or an extra dwelling? We believe that such conflicts usually can, and should, be resolved in favor of residents who are most at risk environmentally. Thus the needs of a child who may spend most of her waking hours within a housing complex should take precedence over the needs of an occasional visitor. The needs of parents or disabled or elderly people trapped at home most of the day should take precedence over the needs of the employed commuter.

The overall intent of this book is to be a guide to more humanistic design. Individual guidelines may be modified in time; future research may subtly change the import of others. But housing is being planned, built, evaluated, and rehabilitated today and tomorrow. To wait until all the evidence is in would be socially irresponsible.

We believe that the following guidelines will help sensitize and raise the consciousness of clients, residents, designers, students, and researchers to the obvious and not so obvious ways that the design of housing environments affects us.

LIST OF DESIGN GUIDELINES

CHAPTER 3

Basic Considerations of the Design Program

CHAPTER 4

Image, Building Form, and Orientation

CHAPTER 5
Personalization

CHAPTER 8

Common Open Space and the Needs of Children

CHAPTER 9

Purpose-Built Play Areas for Children

*Play Areas for Preschool Children
(Ages Two to Five)*

*Equipped Play Areas for Children
Five to Twelve Years Old*

center is really available to teenage residents.

CHAPTER 10

On-site Facilities for Adults

Casual Social Needs

space should not be less than about 30 feet (9.14 m).

Communal Facilities

CHAPTER 11

Parking

CHAPTER 12

Landscaping, Footpaths, and Site Furniture

Landscaping and Planting

CHAPTER 13

Security and Vandalism

Penetrability

Territoriality

Opportunities for Surveillance

Ambiguity

CHAPTER 14

Management, Maintenance, and Refuse Disposal

serve a specific number of units and be
clearly accessible to them.

3

Basic Considerations of the Design Program

This chapter contains some basic guidelines to consider when preparing the brief or program for a housing site. These particular guidelines are not, of course, presented here as the only ones to consider in the total design of a housing scheme. Rather, they are some of the more basic issues to consider while preparing a written program or contract for design or creating a preliminary sketch design. Any low-rise, high-density scheme should initially give consideration to these guidelines, and only then move on to fulfilling as many of the more detailed recommendations as possible.

I. Density and form

There is no simple relationship between density and satisfaction; other significant variables combining with density affect perceived density and influence satisfaction.

---

a. *Overall size.* Although large projects generally have a negative image, size alone is a relatively weak predictor of overall satisfaction. Keeping a development relatively small facilitates coping with other factors associated with satisfaction, such as noninstitutional ap-

Figure 13. Numerous repetitive units make this scheme seem larger than it really is. It was nicknamed "The Concentration Camp" by people who lived nearby.

pearance and privacy (Francescato, 1979). But in a scheme that is too small providing needed communal facilities such as day-care centers, laundries, or play areas is often deemed unrealistic.

b. *Spacing of units.* Most people's sense of density is fairly straightforward: It pertains to the distance between their lot or building and the one across from them, in front or behind, and building heights. But this distance affects perceived density, depending on the way it is treated. Thus, if the common green space between rows of townhouses or apartments is marginal in width and primarily flat lawn, residents may look straight into the other person's window and feel they are living too close. But if the common space is sensitively landscaped to provide only a filtered view of opposite dwellings, people may be satisfied. Because the locations of doors and windows can affect sight lines, this also affects the sense of density (Department . . . , 1971a, b) and overall satisfaction.

c. *Visual and functional access to open space from the dwelling.* Functional access in itself is not enough; a nearby greenbelt invisible from the dwelling is generally irrelevant to the perception of density, however much it may have figured in the designers' objectives for lowering density. But a feeling of spaciousness within the home—an important component of resident satisfaction in medium-density housing—can be achieved when well-landscaped grounds provide green views from windows.

d. *Protection of privacy.* The higher the density, the more carefully must the design limit visual intrusions into dwellings, patios, yards, and balconies. Privacy can be achieved either by keeping people at a distance (exclusion) or by screening them off (seclusion). Upper-income suburbanites create privacy by purchasing plenty of space around them; those living at higher densities (whatever their income) find it behind fences, hedges, or drapes.

e. *Division into small clusters.* Where the development is one large mass, with hundreds of dwelling units or windows visible from one point, residents are likely to perceive it as massive and unattractive (Department . . . , 1972a; Norcross, 1973). Subdividing the site into small, identifiable clusters renders perceived density lower, and more acceptable, than actual density.

f. *Variety in facade design.* A sense of visual variety can help create a lower perceived density. Similar facades in row or terraced houses tend to create more monotony than those in look-alike detached or semi-detached houses.

g. *Access to buildings.* Almost everyone prefers private entrances at ground level, but where density or site design make this impossible, the smaller the number of households sharing an entry, the more satisfied they will be. Clear distinctions should be made between space and facilities serving a shared entry group and those serving a wider group (that is, a courtyard cluster) (Center . . . , 1973;

Darke and Darke, 1972; Gilmour et al., 1970; Newman, 1972).

h. *Minimum of noise intrusion.* Noisy neighbors and noise from children playing outdoors can increase perceived density (Committee . . . , 1972; Sandvik, Shellenbarger, and Stevenson, 1973).

i. *Well-sited community facilities.* A poorly sited communal laundry may be a worse impingement than the close spacing of buildings; insensitive positioning of play facilities for children in the noisy team sports age group may be a daily reminder of density (Cooper, 1975; Cooper and Marcus, 1971; Department . . . , 1971a, 1973a); and to families with no children the presence of even a few children in a common landscaped space designated for their use may be read as overcrowding.

j. *Parking.* The perception of density is increased if residents are always searching for a parking space. Parking areas that seem large and institutional have a similar effect.

k. *Adequate private open space.* Even the most sensitive spacing, size, or clustering may feel like overcrowding if residents have no access to private open space. Without adequately screened patios or yards people have nowhere to retreat from crowded communal areas or household pressures.

Possible design responses

• Consider grouping dwellings into developments large enough to support play facilities, day-care centers, laundries, and other needed communal facilities.

- Subdivide dwellings in medium to large developments into small, identifiable clusters (thirty to one hundred units).
- Provide sensitively landscaped open space over 30 feet wide (9.14 m) between dwellings to filter views and contribute to privacy.
- Provide variety in facade design through color, roofline variations, and positioning of entrances (which are probably the features most noticed by nondesigners), as well as by staggering and detailing.
- Where entrances must be shared, ensure that no more than five to eight households share each entry.
- Clearly define the boundaries between spaces and facilities belonging to each entry group and to a wider group (say, a courtyard).
- Insulate party walls against sound, especially where access ways run above or next to dwellings.
- Provide double glazing to minimize noise intrusion.
- Locate children's play facilities so that they are within view but do not dominate communal spaces.
- Site buildings and design landscaping and fencing so that groups of older children cannot play close to dwelling units.
- Provide adequate parking in modest-sized lots so that residents do not have to "jockey" for spaces.

Figure 14. This scheme houses three hundred families, but building entries are shared by only six, and dwellings are clustered around three well-planted courtyards. There is a continual waiting list of people wanting to move in. (St. Francis Square, San Francisco)

2. Project size

A multifamily housing development should be small enough to avoid the appearance of a "project," but large enough to provide adequate space for children's activities.

An estate or subdivision can be large in size (in terms of numbers of dwellings and/or spatial extent), yet not seem overwhelming to its inhabitants if, by subdivision into relatively intimate subspaces, it is small in scale (Norcross, 1973; Shankland . . . , 1977a). Because children are the chief users of public open space in housing (Architecture . . . , 1969; Byrom, 1972; Committee . . . , 1972; Cooper, 1975; Cooper and Marcus, 1971; Department . . . , 1972a, 1973a; Parish and Parish, 1972; Shankland . . . , 1969), the expected number of child residents is a more reliable guide to acceptable project density than the number of either adults or dwellings (Shankland . . . , 1967).

Disadvantages of Large Projects: British Experiences

Although council (or public) housing per se does not bear the stigma in Britain that it does in the United States, size and massiveness do. Take, for example, a West London, prewar project that covers forty-six acres and contains more than two thousand dwellings in thirty-seven almost identical buildings. It is now being rejected by tenants, except those in greatest need, even though these buildings (five-story, red brick) are well designed and soundly con-

structed and there has been a program to upgrade dwelling interiors, modify allocation policies, improve security, and extend improvement discussions. A Department of the Environment (1973b, 51–52) appraisal of this scheme concludes that "the estate is simply too large, dense, and uniform for any sense of community ever to have developed there . . . greatest need seems to be to break down the size of the estate in every way possible." It is unlikely that schemes of such size will be repeated in Britain. The density and massiveness of, for example, the Barbican in the City of London or Habitat in Montreal would almost certainly be rejected were they not housing for upper-income families, with fewer children per household, on prime sites.

Stigma and Size: U.S. Experiences

In the United States, where public housing is known to be for lower-income groups or welfare recipients, rejection of massive projects led to a policy of encouraging the private sector to build for local housing authorities and then "turning over the key" on completion (hence the name "turnkey housing"). In one city the neighbors resented the intrusion of welfare recipients, and the buildings they lived in became stigmatized, despite every effort to keep them in a form, scale, and size (eight to twenty families) comparable to their surroundings. The chief complaints, predictably, revolved around children: The households frequently contained many children, and, because small sites precluded provision for play, children's activities

spilled out onto the parking lot, adjacent streets, and vacant lots (Kautz, 1974).

British, North American, and Australian suburban tract housing has been accepted because it provides for a number of basic preferences, including private, enclosed outdoor play space for small children.

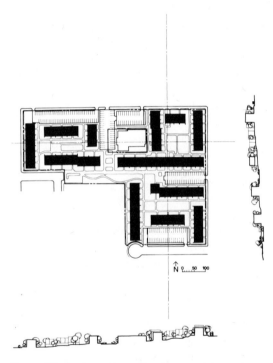

Figure 15. An inner-city redevelopment scheme for three hundred families that serves those with children especially well. There is a play area within each of the three courtyards and plenty of safe pathways for moving around. (St. Francis Square, San Francisco. Source: Francescato, 1980)

Possible design response

- Plan groupings of dwellings large enough (more than thirty units) to support play opportunities for all ages.

See also: Unobtrusive image (16), Superblocks (215), Child density (231), Chapter 8—Common open space and the needs of children, Chapter 9—Purpose-built play areas for children.

3. Children safe from cars

Families with children under ten value highly residential environments where pedestrians are separated from or have precedence over vehicles. (Architecture . . . , 1969; Cooper, 1971; Sandvik, Shellenbarger, and Stevenson, 1973).

Most accidents in residential areas involve children, and half of all road accidents to children occur within approximately 330 feet (100 m) of their homes (Departments of Environment and Transport [UK], 1977). Swedish research indicates that, until the eleventh or twelfth year, various important sensory mechanisms (sight, hearing, and ability to differentiate right from left, fast from slow, or near from far) may not be fully developed. Children are thus especially vulnerable in traffic situations (Sandels, 1975).

A British new town study in Stevenage shows a statistically significant difference in child accidents between two neighborhoods, one traffic segregated and one not (Architecture . . . ,

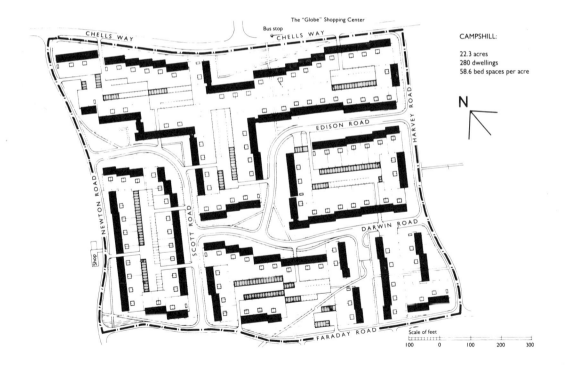

Figure 16. Children in this Stevenage New Town neighborhood played chiefly beside or on the streets. Child accident rates were two to three times higher here than in the nearby neighborhood shown in Figure 17. (Source: Architecture . . . , 1969)

1969). This and other new town corporations continue to build traffic-segregated neighborhoods for families. Recent resident feedback studies, for example, from Milton Keynes New Town, suggest that most families want traffic-segregated neighborhoods (Residential . . . , 1975). In some inner-city redevelopment projects, however, the dogma of traffic segregation has been carried too far: Familiar streets have been bulldozed and replaced by a bewildering maze of culs-de-sac, parking lots, "fire lanes,"

and undefined open space. In such cases the gain in children's safety is more than offset by residents feeling isolated or cut off from the life of the surrounding neighborhoods. Traffic segregation also poses problems for the provision of well-surveyed and accessible parking areas.

The ideal situation would allow each dwelling visual and functional access to a street on one side and to a pedestrian-oriented court or landscape area on the other. The relatively new solution of mixer courts in Britain or woonerfs in

the Netherlands may be a satisfactory compromise between total vehicular-pedestrian segregation and the traditional street. Cars are allowed access right up to the dwelling, but they must pass through a zone where paving, landscaping, and layout clearly indicate that the space is primarily for pedestrians, thus slowing the car to a walking pace and strongly reducing the likelihood of accidents to children, the physically disabled, or the frail elderly.

Possible design responses
- Provide residents with a choice of orientation so that they look out either over a landscaped courtyard or vehicle-free open space, onto a street, or (ideally) both.
- Mix vehicles and pedestrians on a strictly controlled basis (for example, mixer courts or woonerfs).

See also: Pedestrian precinct (67), Traffic management (68), Woonerfs (70), Playing everywhere (79), Unrestricted setting (84), Vehicular segregation (148).

VARDON ROAD
Bus stop
N
Bus stop

VERITY WAY

VERITY WAY

DOUGLAS DRIVE

SISHES END:

25.3 acres
351 dwellings
56.4 bed spaces per acre

Scale of feet
100   0   100   200   300

Bus stop
FAIRLANDS WAY

Figure 17. In neighborhood where most of the play took place on a series of interior pedestrian open spaces, child accident rates were low. Compare Figure 16. (Source: Architecture . . . , 1969)

4. Space Hierarchy

Clearly delineate public space (streets), community space (shared open space, play areas, communal laundries, and so forth), and private space (dwellings and private open spaces). (Newman, 1972).

Figure 18. Where the delineation of private from public space has been less than adequate, residents will attempt to modify their environment.

People are invariably dissatisfied with their residential environment when one or more of the following intrusions occur: (1) outsiders cut through an area that residents regard as communal or semiprivate, (2) outside children use communal play areas or courtyards as public property, (3) passersby peer into inadequately fenced gardens or patios, or (4) children play on common space or footpaths that abut onto dwellings. All these problems could be avoided if, at the sketch-design stage, a hierarchical development from public (at one end of the scale) to private interior (at the other) were envisioned.

A private zone around dwellings (a yard or patio) provides three necessities: visual privacy, a buffer zone for noise between the dwelling and children at play, and a needed outdoor space for such essential activities as toddlers' play, gardening, and drying clothes. In U.S. public housing design of the 1940s and 1950s, however, the absence of yards was semiofficial social policy because the poor did not deserve such "luxury extras." In British housing design of the 1960s and even the 1970s front yards in both private suburban and public inner-city housing were eliminated in the name of "open planning." In both countries, in the public sector, this has proved to be a costly mistake: Rehabilitation schemes for rundown U.S. housing projects frequently put a high priority on the addition of fenced, private open spaces (Cooper Marcus, 1978b; Newman, 1976).

Possible design responses

- Make the distinction between public streets and on-site open space clear enough that residents and nonresidents alike can read it.
- Locate communal on-site facilities (laundries, play areas, seating, and so forth) so that they are clearly for the use of residents and not public amenities.
- Ensure that the lease or sales agreements specify rights, responsibilities, and maintenance arrangements for every category (public, communal, private) of on-site space.
- Provide a visual buffer in the form of a private yard or patio between public pathways, courtyards or streets, and the private area of the dwelling interior.

See also: Community identity (5), Deck connections (46), Group territory (72), Common space boundary (77), Street linkage (78), Site entry barriers (201), Territorial zones (213), Good management (238).

5. Community identity

A sense of community and security is likely to be enhanced when access to the site by outsiders is discouraged.

The more self-contained a housing development is, the more likely are its residents to recognize and look out for each other and to feel a sense of proprietorship and responsibility over the whole site. Strangers are less likely to intrude, and residents will feel more secure about their own and their children's safety (Architecture . . . , 1966; Bagot, 1971; Byrom, 1972; Committee . . . , 1972; Cooper, 1970a, 1972b; Cooper and Corrie, 1970; Department . . . , 1971a,

1972a; Gatt, 1978; Kautz, 1974; Newman, 1976; Norcross, 1973; Parish and Parish, 1972; Sarkissian and Heine, 1978).

Possible design responses

- Where a preexisting street alignment or long-established pedestrian route passes through a new housing site, ensure that it passes through relatively "neutral" portions of the site or is buffered (by planting, level changes, berming, and so forth) from semi-private sectors of the site.
- To avoid passersby perceiving landscaped areas on site as a public park, create relatively narrow and unobtrusive site entries.

- Where a new site provides play spaces badly needed in the neighborhood as a whole, either locate them on the edge of the site so that they are clearly public or locate them on the interior of the site or so that they are clearly not public (but provide comparable facilities in a nearby neighborhood park or public space).
- Subdivide the site into clusters so that residents learn to recognize each other and can spot nonresidents.

See also: Subunit identity (21), Group territory (72), Street linkage (78), Site entry barriers (201), Territorial zones (213).

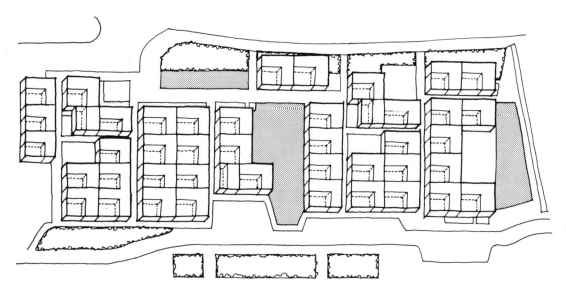

Figure 19. Nonresident children perceived the central common open space of this Scottish scheme as a public park and played soccer there after school. Residents resented this intrusion into their territory. (Inchview, Prestonpans. Source: Architecture . . . , 1966)

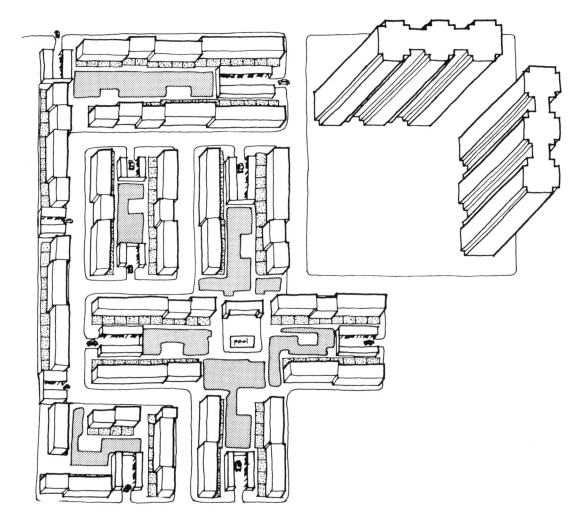

Figure 20. Residents of the two tower blocks made their way to a twenty-four-hour supermarket (bottom, left, off plan) via the common open spaces of a neighboring row house development. Residents of the latter grew so incensed that at one time they seriously considered building a wall around their neighborhood. (Geneva Towers and Terrace, San Francisco)

6. Social homogeneity

A degree of homogeneity is necessary before residents will develop a feeling of community.

Where there is a fairly high degree of neighboring and visiting and a general feeling of well-being about the community, there is usually also a relatively homogeneous population (Gans, 1961a; Ineichen, 1972; Keller, 1968; Lansing et al., 1970; Sarkissian and Heine, 1978). An extensive U.S. study of thirty-seven HUD-assisted projects across the country concludes that "the more other residents in the development were perceived to be similar to oneself, the higher the level of satisfaction with other residents and with living in that development" (Francescato, 1979, ES-4). The most crucial similarities are in life-style, education, income, and child-rearing practices (Keller, 1968). In one San Francisco co-operative, for example, considerable diversity in terms of race, age, and family composition is successfully balanced by relative homogeneity of income, life-style, and educational level (Cooper, 1970b).

A greater degree of heterogeneity of neighbors will (probably) be tolerated where there is a greater separation of dwelling units or adequate buffers, such as fencing (Cooper, 1975; Sandvik, Shellenbarger, and Stevenson, 1973; Sarkissian and Heine, 1978; Zeisel and Griffin, 1975). Of course, a greater degree of homogeneity of values and life-styles is likely to occur

where residents have chosen to live in a particular development. But in housing that is more or less forced upon residents who have been on a housing list it is wise to avoid schemes that compel them to practice neighborly "togetherness."

See also: Group territory (72), Meeting neighbors (130).

7. Life cycle clusters

Create clusters of dwellings for families at the same stage in the life cycle. (Miller and Cook, 1967; Shankland . . . , 1969).

People generally prefer to live close to others of approximately the same age or stage in the life cycle. Students like to live with or near other

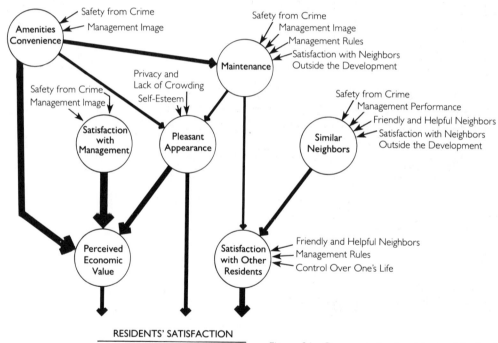

Figure 21. Components of resident satisfaction in thirty-seven HUD-assisted housing schemes across the United States. (Source: Francescato, 1979)

students; families with young children tend to socialize more and exchange more "goods and services" with each other than do families with teenagers or elderly households. Elderly residents complain when their dwellings are placed too close to communal areas used for children's play (Ministry . . . , 1967c, 1969a; Shankland . . . , 1969).

Possible design responses

- Avoid clustering large families together—"child density" may be a problem (Barker, 1976; Shankland . . . , 1969). Cluster according to stage in the life cycle, but mix family sizes.
- Where an age range of households is likely to occur, cluster dwellings for the elderly and screen these households from noisy play areas by landscaping or distance.
- Cluster housing units for families, especially single-parent families, so that facilities to enhance shared child care (connecting doors between dwellings, intercom system, common playrooms, and so forth) can be provided.

See also: Subunit identity (21), Meeting neighbors (130), Friendly encounters (131).

8. Ground-floor households

In multistory schemes preference for ground-floor units should be given to families with small children, elderly households, and physically disabled persons.

More than any other type of household, households with children dislike using stairs. (Department . . . , 1973a). Moreover, children under eleven play outside more if they live in dwellings with ground-floor or first-floor access, and their play is less of a problem for their parents. One study indicates that children seem discontented living off the ground up to about the age of nine, but after that, it makes little difference to them (Stewart, 1970).

Some childless households actually prefer living off the ground (Department . . . , 1971a, b, 1972a). In Britain, where official policy has resulted in many families with children being moved out of tower blocks, those same highrise buildings provide satisfactory dwellings for young single people or students.

Ground-floor units, of course, constitute fewer barriers to physically disabled people.

Figure 22. Minding small children is made much easier when they can move safely out from home into a courtyard or play area shared by a small group of neighbors.

Possible design responses

- House families with small children in ground-level units with enclosed yards or patios, in a slightly elevated position to overlook an enclosed common space for preschool play.
- Where families with small children cannot be housed at ground level, give priority to the largest families.
- Where all elderly and disabled residents cannot be housed at ground level, locate their units in buildings that have elevators.
- In units for physically disabled people, provide ramps for ground-floor units or elevators to ensure easy access to above-ground units.

See also: Accessibility (43), Yard play (87), Door-step play (89).

9. Dwelling mix

Provide a variety of dwelling sizes so that households can move within the same neighborhood or development as their space needs change.

Some families wish to move within the same housing development or neighborhood when their space needs change. Social networks can remain intact; children need not be uprooted from familiar schools; and elderly persons can remain near friends and families.

In public sector housing in England and Australia authorities encourage elderly residents of "empty nests" (highly sought-after larger dwellings with yards) to vacate them for use by larger households. Because they live in deliberately homogeneous neighborhoods, often no small and suitable nearby dwellings are available for them. A policy of providing small, in-fill units in such neighborhoods helps alleviate this problem.

See also: Resident allocation (218).

4

Image, Building Form, and Orientation

This chapter discusses two basic issues in clustered housing design. The first is image and form. The overall exterior impression of a house or group of dwellings significantly affects how residents feel about their homes, sometimes even how they feel about their own worthiness as human beings. A design that violates the local norms of "home" may cause residents of subsidized housing to feel inferior or unworthy of living in the way most families in their culture aspire to live. Rarely is this done from any conscious desire to denigrate a segment of the population; it usually results from constrained budgets, government red tape, or professional aspirations to create novel, eye-catching schemes to impress peers and future clients. Novelty and avant-garde forms may be appropriate for private sector residents who can choose to live in a particular development, but professionals designing in the public sector must be much more aware of currently acceptable images. Accordingly, this chapter emphasizes images and forms preferred by public sector residents, although some of the guidelines could apply equally well to the private sector.

A second issue is that of orientation: how residents and visitors find their way around. This is particularly important in housing schemes not laid out according to a familiar street arrangement.

If certain aesthetic and formal design issues seem to be missing, this is because currently available consumer research in housing has nothing to say on them. In some other areas, such as adult social behavior or children's play, we felt justified in basing some guidelines on informed hunch or field observations, but we did not feel this was appropriate in the case of aesthetics.

Figure 23. Although revered by the architectural critics, this "new brutalist" scheme was much disliked by the residents, who especially resented the overwhelming presence of grey brick and concrete.

10. Pleasing milieu

The total visual milieu of a housing development is an important component of resident satisfaction.

That many case studies of housing developments show attractiveness to be a major factor influencing overall satisfaction underscores the importance of the designers' role (Cooper, 1970b; Department . . . , 1971a, b, 1972a; Ellis, 1977; Francescato, 1979; Gilmour et al., 1970; Lansing et al., 1970; Ministry . . . , 1967c; Shankland . . . , 1969). A pleasing appearance is not associated with any particular housing style, but rather with variety in building height and facades, color, good landscaping, pleasant views from the units, a noninstitutional appearance, and high levels of maintenance.

One extensive study of seven low- and high-rise New York developments reports: "Well-maintained grounds and the absence of litter and junk were a prerequisite to satisfaction with any more specific design features. As maintenance problems decreased, residents became more aware of other aspects of the development's appearance and the 'public face' it presented" (Becker, 1974, 65). Residents in well-designed subsidized schemes that are subsequently well maintained are more likely to take care of them and are less likely to seek transfer to other, more desirable developments. The money invested in good design and upkeep may mean lower management and administrative costs and, in the long run, more money available for investment in housing.

Possible design responses

- Where a rundown or difficult-to-let scheme is being rehabilitated, place a high priority on improving the whole visual milieu, not just the interiors.
- In the preliminary design phase of a new scheme, place as high priorities landscaping, a noninstitutional appearance, variety of spaces and forms, complexity, and pleasant views.
- Ensure that materials used, planting installed, and spaces provided are within the maintenance capabilities (financial and competence level) of the management.

See also: Landscape quality (11), View from the window (12), Unobtrusive image (16), Visual complexity (18), Landscaping importance (163).

11. Landscape quality

Landscaping and site layout contribute highly to resident satisfaction.

It is inappropriate, whatever the budget, to regard landscaping, site layout, play areas, and community facilities as luxury extras. All the evidence suggests that a medium- or high-density family development designed with little concern for these features will be doomed to failure, no matter how much effort and budget were spent on building interiors. One study of private sector housing in London indicates that to most people appearance means landscape and layout first, architecture second (Shankland . . . , 1969). In a highly successful San Francisco co-op residents report that the high-quality landscaping and total visual milieu attracted them to live in the development; few specifically mention the architecture (Cooper, 1970b). Clearly, the highest quality architecture can look stark and unhomelike without the softening effects of planting; conversely, a monotonous or repetitive design can be vastly improved by quality landscaping.

Possible design responses

- Invest considerable design time in site planning; in terms of resident needs this is a more significant area of design than facade treatment.

- Invest a considerable proportion of design time and budget in landscaping and site amenities, limiting the budget on interior finishes if necessary, in order to provide a quality exterior milieu.

See also: Landscape importance (163).

12. View from the window

Most people base their notions of attractiveness on what they can see from their windows.

Designers frequently rely on two-dimensional plans and think in terms of overall design intent, but most residents will judge the attractiveness of their neighborhood simply by what they can see from their windows. Most prefer a visual diversity that includes a distant open view, a closer view of greenery, and some human activity. People dislike views of monotonous facades, buildings that are too close, auto parking, and blank walls (Architecture . . . , 1966;

Figure 24. In this scheme residents have a pleasant green outlook but are not bothered by passersby peering in.

Cooper, 1970b; Department . . . , 1971a, 1972a; Ministry . . . , 1967c, 1970; Shankland . . . , 1967).

It is important that windows designed for good views out are in rooms frequently used during the day. Still, however much green areas are appreciated, they should not be provided at the expense of privacy. Many residents will complain where a pleasant view from the dwelling enables strangers and neighbors to look in (Connell, 1975; Cooper, 1975; Danish . . . , 1969; Department . . . , 1971a).

Possible design responses

- Locate living room and/or kitchen windows to permit "good" views.
- If some windows must look out onto a blank wall, monotonous facade, parking, or other less pleasant outlook, make sure that these are in less frequently used rooms.
- If a view onto a blank wall from some window is inevitable, plant fast-growing vines or creepers on that wall to render it more visually acceptable.
- Where there is a limited horizontal separation of windows from nearby public or communal space, employ fencing, planting, or grade differences to ensure that strangers cannot look directly into the dwelling.
- Design and locate windows so that the view can be seen from a seated position, especially if they will be used by physically disabled or elderly residents.

See also: Home turf (128), Trees (170).

13. House on its own land

The ideal of most families is to live in a house with some land around it; therefore, when a higher density or different form must be used, try to give residents as many of the advantages of house dwelling as possible.

Virtually every housing preference study conducted in the English-speaking world indicates that the ideal dwelling for the great majority of households with children is a simple house with yard. (These studies number many dozens; see, for example, Connell, 1975; Cooper, 1974b, 1975; Darke and Darke, 1969b; Halkett, 1976; Hanson, 1978; Michelson, 1968; Mulvihall and McHugh, 1977; Residential . . . , 1975.) Where family life is concerned, the general public has strongly resisted all attempts by the architectural profession to convince them of the merits of something different (for example, high-rise flats), and it seems unlikely that people will discard this image of home in the foreseeable future.

For this reason, if there were but one guideline for medium- to high-density family housing, it would be this: *The more you incorporate into your design the essential amenities of the detached or semidetached house, the more satisfied the residents will be.*

These essential amenities seem to be (in no particular order): rooms of at least minimum legal size, a private entrance at ground level, a private open space (garden, yard, balcony, patio), parking reasonably close to the dwelling,

Figure 25. Although row houses in this Milton Keynes New Town neighborhood had entries at ground level and small gardens, the use of a thoroughly *un*homelike cladding material (corrugated steel) rendered these houses much disliked.

and an individualized facade or opportunities to personalize.

Rooflines are also important. A New York State study reveals that low- and moderate-income residents prefer apartments with a sloping roofline in the front—the stacking of units violates people's image of a homelike dwelling (Friedberg, 1974). A Canadian study reports similar findings (O'Brien, 1972). Another Canadian study emphasizes that steeply pitched or monopitched roofs look like sheds to tenants and are disliked (Barker, 1976).

In the U.S. suburban housing market, when budgets are tight, people are willing to make do with limited yards or patios as long as a private entrance, convenient parking, and privacy from neighbors are provided. Similarly, in successful British examples of moderate- or high-density housing (for example, Marquess Road, Islington; Setchell Road, Southwark; Byker, Newcastle), where private open space may be minimal and some dwellings may be off the ground and lack the symbolic pitched roof, considerable design attention has still been paid to visual and aural privacy and to providing private entrances that can be (and are) highly personalized.

Possible design responses

- Ensure that as many dwellings as possible have private entrances at ground level and adjacent private open space.
- Give interior visual and aural privacy a higher priority than the provision of large, private open spaces.

- Ensure that each household has an attractive private entry that can be decorated and personalized.
- Use permeable cladding materials, especially around doors and windows, so that residents can easily personalize their dwellings.
- Provide as many dwellings as possible with parking on the lot.
- Provide dwellings with roofs comparable to those in local traditional housing.

See also: Locally acceptable materials (17), Territorial expression (29), Entry personalization (34), Private entry (35), Private front path (37), Front porch (40), "Front" and "back" customs (56), Display garden (62).

14. Popular forms

To minimize the likelihood of jealousy among neighbors, avoid a mixing of housing forms that have differing degrees of popularity.

The common mode of large housing sites in Britain during the 1950s and 1960s was "mixed development." A mix of building forms—two-story row houses, four-story maisonettes, twenty-story tower blocks—aimed at providing for different family types in different building forms. When a mix was used merely to create a pleasingly varied, sculptural effect and similar families were housed in different architectural forms, the potential for envy and dissatisfaction was inadvertently introduced.

In one Liverpool estate, although two-story terraced houses were popular, a mile-long spine of five- and eight-story deck-access maisonette blocks was extremely unpopular and difficult to let. Maisonette residents saw themselves surrounded by much more attractive and socially acceptable houses with yards, and this feeling of relative deprivation must have been further exacerbated by the estate's location in a suburban area of low-rise housing. They had difficulty understanding why *they* had to live in housing that was different (Department . . . , 1981b).

Possible design responses

- Determine the most acceptable dwelling form in the locality and maximize the number of dwellings of that type on the site.

- If it seems appropriate to use two or more dwelling forms for the same type of household, ensure that these cannot be construed as "better" and "worse."
- If a dwelling form that could be construed as being less prestigious than others on the site must be used, ensure that it has some compensatory qualities (lower rent, better views, larger garden, and so forth).
- Where subsidized housing is located close to private sector housing, ensure that the form, materials, and image are comparable.

See also: Social homogeneity (6), Conforming image (15), Unobtrusive image (16), Locally acceptable materials (17).

Figure 26. A much disliked and hard-to-rent scheme in Runcorn New Town (U.K.). Residents could not understand why they had to live in these massive, displeasing structures when similar families nearby had small, "homey" dwellings of traditional materials. (See Figure 24.)

15. Conforming image

Most residents appreciate an image that reflects local prevailing middle-class norms.

Feedback from architects and housing officials suggests that lower-income clients frequently balk at styles, building forms, colors, or materials that are far removed from current local standards of middle-class taste. People want their homes to look individual and different, but only within the confines of these standards. Unusual appearance and novelty are values designers often espouse, but unusual appearance is often considered an undesirable attribute in a home (Architecture . . . , 1966; Department . . . , 1972a; Friedberg, 1974; Griffin, 1973; Ministry . . . , 1969b; Neighborhood . . . , 1973). Particularly disliked in Britain are materials used for institutional buildings (for example, concrete), materials locally branded as lower status for house construction (for example, grey brick, cinder block), or materials associated with vehicles or factory buildings (for example, steel).

The least popular development in one British new town (Milton Keynes) is composed of long rows of flat-roofed attached houses built of steel, with round porthole windows in their front doors (Residential . . . , 1975) (see Figure 25), although they were acclaimed by some members of the architectural establishment as the "contemporary equivalent of the Georgian terrace." One has only to look closely at nearby private sector housing to see what people apparently prefer: pitched tile roofs, red brick fa-

Figure 27. The design of this subsidized scheme in a British new town was appealing to residents, partly because it was comparable in form and materials to local, owner-occupied, private sector dwellings.

cades, rectangular windows, and solid wood doors, often embellished with "antique" hinges, coach lamps, and name plates.

Similarly, in Runcorn New Town some neighborhoods have two-story, red brick, pitched roofed houses and an attractive villagelike atmosphere where relatively few units can be seen from any one point (see Figure 24). In others industrialized building methods have been used; materials such as concrete and steel form the basic cladding; and vast numbers of dwelling entries can be viewed from any one point, as decks or galleries recede into the distance (see Figure 26). Residents clearly prefer the first image to the second (Jowell, Berthoud, and Johnson, 1971).

In designing for those least able to protest (the less well-off, the homeless, the public housing tenant) the architect is most tempted to experiment with novel forms, materials, window shapes, or building components. One Runcorn New Town development designed by an internationally famous architect boasts ribbed steel walls, windows shaped like television sets and ship portholes, and pipes carried overhead between buildings. Units in this development have been the scene of recent arson attacks and are the most difficult units to let in the town.

In a number of studies in which people have been asked to draw or describe their ideal dwelling, they tend to describe dwellings like those of people just above them in social status (Cooper, 1975). It is not the form per se they are relating to, but the social standing in the community that the form symbolizes (Becker, 1974). Clearly, a design for low-income residents that looks institutional or cheap will be very much resented as yet another reminder of the residents' low social status in the community (Cooper, 1975; Newman, 1972; Rainwater, 1966; Sommer, 1974).

Possible design responses

- Avoid avant-garde colors, forms, or materials.
- Avoid novel features such as porthole windows, exposed pipes, innovative rooflines, or unfamiliar entry arrangements.
- Avoid forms or images that are locally associated with nonresidential buildings (factories, office buildings, schools, or warehouses).

See also: Unobtrusive image (16), Conforming signs (27).

16. Unobtrusive image

Low-income residents prefer housing schemes that do not stand out in the neighborhood.

Innovative high-density designs may be fine for middle- and upper-income groups who have chosen to live there, who gain some positive benefits from this choice (for example, closeness to work and urban amenities, status from living in a famous scheme), and who may have access to a country cottage for weekend relaxation. The massive Barbican housing scheme in the City of London, with its waiting list of applicants, is a case in point. But any characteristics that make subsidized housing stand out will tend to be looked on with disfavor, especially if the distinguishing characteristic represents a current design fad. For example, the incorporation of old industrial elements in the site furniture of a San Francisco development built on the site of a famous brewery was praised by architects but hated by residents, who eventually raised the money to have the features removed (Margaret, 1971).

In one Canadian development with a public housing image residents reported that they were aware of "generalized hostility" toward them from people in the surrounding community (O'Brien, 1972). In a California case two sixteen-story towers for subsidized low-income tenants located in an owner-occupied neighborhood of two-story row houses provoked violent opposition from the original inhabitants and more than a decade after construction were still viewed negatively (Cooper and Corrie, 1970). Yet almost identical buildings (same architect and client, but higher-income residents), placed in a downtown, high-density neighborhood, have provoked no negative comment. A building form suitable in one location may be unsuitable in another.

Possible design responses

- In subsidized or low-cost housing avoid design features that could be construed as affected or faddish.

- Use forms, materials, colors, and proportions that allow the development to blend into its surroundings.

See also: Project size (2), Conforming image (15), Small parking lots (152), Superblocks (215).

![Figure 28 photograph]

Figure 28. Residents in subsidized housing resent living in schemes that look to them like factories.

Figure 29. Or that resemble a ship.

Figure 30. Or even a prison.

17. Locally acceptable materials

In rental housing select building materials of comparable quality and image to those used in local owner-occupied housing to minimize the likelihood of stigma.

In some cultures (such as the United States) renters are accorded lower status than owners. It is particularly important in these circumstances not to stigmatize renters further by using unacceptable building materials. Unacceptability, of course, is relative. The risks involved in cross-cultural generalizations cannot be overstated, and every area, even different regions of the same country, has its own preferred materials. Most people have strong feelings about the kinds of materials from which their homes are built, and in every locality some materials are viewed as more or less homelike. On the East Coast of the United States, for example, where brick and stained wood are often used in single-family homes, rental housing developments in those materials are looked on favorably by their inhabitants (Becker, 1974). Some of the best of the Urban Development Corporation's low-to moderate-income developments in New York State are indistinguishable, in terms of form and materials, from nearby upper-income, private developments.

The same is true in the suburbs of certain British cities (for example, Sheffield), where successful public rental and private owner-occupied housing are very similar in form, style, and materials. Also in Britain many of the subsidized

rental schemes of the late 1970s that have been well received by residents and the architectural profession (for example, Marquess Road, Islington; Setchell Road, Southwark; Palace Fields, Runcorn) are built primarily of traditional materials (red brick and tile). This is in marked contrast to many disliked developments of the

1960s, which employed nontraditional concrete or grey brick, and innovative new town schemes using steel or cinder block as exterior cladding. In fact where client or designer perceives the future residents as not caring about their environment and selects an "indestructible material" (such as concrete), the decision may

Figure 31. Subsidized housing schemes using traditional local forms, rooflines, and materials are generally more popular than those employing experimental materials or the latest architectural styles. (Setchell Road, Southwark, London)

backfire (Sommer, 1974). "The belief that it is a waste of money to provide quality materials because they will only be destroyed often results, ironically, in the construction of very expensive prisonlike buildings, which by their attempted indestructibleness, invite challenges to destroy" (Becker, 1977, 89). In the long run it may actually be more economical to use high-quality, homelike materials (Sommer, 1974).

Not surprisingly, cladding material that is seen as not wearing well is viewed negatively by residents. In a consumer study of reactions to the design of a British new town (Milton Keynes), those neighborhoods using traditional, hard-wearing brick were generally ranked as well liked while residents generally disliked the external cladding where the materials were not wearing well (cedar boarding, painted panels) (Residential . . . , 1975).

Possible design responses

- Avoid materials that could be construed as institutional or not homelike.
- Select hard-wearing but not indestructible materials.
- Include materials used in popular, local middle-class housing and/or those indigenous to the locality.

See also: Conforming image (15), Unobtrusive image (16), Personal additions (32), Attractive materials (234), Good management (238).

18. Visual complexity

Regardless of architectural style, most residents prefer some degree of aesthetic complexity and variety in their neighborhood.

In a nationwide U.S. study of HUD-assisted projects those developments that residents rank high on appearance have in common a degree of architectural complexity. In one case row houses were differentiated by the use of materials, textures, roof shape, trim, and size; in a second case complexity was achieved by breaking down the total volume of buildings into

Figure 32. Endless rows of identical dwellings can increase perceived density and create a monotonous environment for passing pedestrians. (Milton Keynes New Town, U.K.)

smaller units and varying the shape, size, and placement of windows and balconies; in a third, where facade materials, roofline, and building form remained consistent, buildings were combined in a number of different ways (Francescato, 1979).

Conversely, the least liked developments range from traditional to contemporary styles but have in common monotonous facades, messages of institutionality (unscreened clotheslines, pipe railings), little or no landscaping, or very poor maintenance.

Possible design responses

- Employ variety in height, color, setback, roof shape, trim, and size to create a degree of visual complexity within a recognizable whole.
- Break down the volume of buildings into smaller units or clusters.
- Vary the shape, size, and placement of windows and balconies.
- Use imaginative landscaping to add complexity to relatively simple building facades.

See also: Chapter 5—Personalization, Display garden (62), Varying spaces (75), Landscaping importance (163), Personalized landscape (180).

19. Exterior design control

Residents will not perceive facade variety if too much design control is enforced.

Although designers, recognizing people's need to feel that their houses are individual, sometimes provide a varied facade, color control tends to remain in the hands of the designer and management. Similarly, the effect of a pleasing articulated facade may be negated by a semi-public, open plan layout that precludes the planting of front yards or the erection of fences. The message of the vertical plane is individuality, but the horizontal plane says hands off. In the same vein the glassed-in porch, which became a common added-on feature of British suburban houses from the late 1960s on, has now been co-opted by housing clients and architects, thus short-circuiting the original do-it-yourself idea (Ruddick, 1969).

Possible design responses

- Ensure that sales or lease agreements do not preclude reasonable alterations to the facade or front landscaping.
- In design detailing create possibilities for residents to add their own touches to the dwelling exterior.

See also: Visual complexity (18), Chapter 5—Personalization, Display garden (62), Landscape installation and modification (179), Good management (238).

20. Color

External color schemes should be carefully considered to reflect residents' tastes.

Although the general public is probably as attuned to color as to any other aspect of architectural design (Cooper, 1975), it is naive (and presumptuous) to assume that it will be attracted to bright or bold housing colors, especially if the local middle-class norm dictates more subtle ones. Most people's tastes with respect to their dwellings are fairly traditional and conservative, and this is even more true among lower-income residents, who have enough evidence of their degraded status in society without the further humiliation of housing that looks "funny." For example, residents of a San Francisco redevelopment project in which facades were painted in striking shades of orange, brown, and ochre strongly disliked the color scheme (Margaret, 1971). In the rehabilitation of a rundown, north of England project in the mid 1970s, it was reported, "the houses were given

a dramatic facelift, being painted in bold colours—pillar box red, yellow and ochre—giving the estate the rather apt designation of 'toy town'" (Department . . . , 1981b, 27).

Tastes in colors vary according to culture and region; the currently fashionable earth tones of much western U.S. housing, for example, might seem bleak and drab in Britain.

Possible design responses

- Select colors, including roof colors, that reflect prevailing local norms.
- Avoid bright or dramatic colors for low-income housing, especially where local tastes in middle- or upper-income housing differ widely from those colors.
- Permit residents to choose colors wherever possible, or at least to paint one feature of the exterior (front door, porch, garage door) themselves.

See also: Exterior design control (19).

Figure 33. In this California condominium development the residents are allowed to make very few external changes.

21. Subunit identity

Each subunit of a scheme should have some elements of uniqueness to create a sense of place and identity.

Where considerable numbers of units are being designed en masse, a particular form or cluster arrangement may be repeated. In a housing scheme in south London (Pollards Hill, Merton) six virtually identical courtyards are surrounded by flat-roofed, two-story, terraced houses clad in white vitreous enamel. No attempt has been made to plant trees to screen opposite houses, and in each court the dimensions, planting, grading, and positioning of paths, lights, and benches are virtually identical. Visitors and residents report feelings of disorientation; two-fifths of the residents consider the outlook from their home unpleasant (Victoria . . . , 1975). It is bad enough that people have to live in identical units clad in an unfamiliar and impermeable material that cannot be personalized without adding to this the message that not even *groups* of dwellings are to be allowed a sense of identity. This absurd example of "architectural integrity" is by no means an isolated case.

Possible design responses

- Where a basically identical group of dwellings is repeated, ensure some uniqueness for each subgroup.

- Design the common open space of each cluster so that the size, dimensions, grading, planting, site furniture, and play equipment of each are different.
- Provide spaces where the residents themselves can jointly create unique milieus.

See also: Community identity (5), Life cycle clusters (7), Street names (25), Varying spaces (75), Landscape installation and modification (179), Personalized landscape (180), Territorial zones (213).

Figure 34 (a, b, c). No wonder residents and visitors in this Milton Keynes New Town (U.K.) neighborhood feel disoriented: At least three courtyards are almost identical.

22. Edge treatment

Residents are particularly sensitive to conflicts that occur at the edge of a development.

Methods of dealing with the outer edge will vary considerably. With inner-city redevelopment sites the outer edge should conform as closely as possible to local norms of orientation, setback, materials, height, and form. It is important that residents not find themselves precluded from joining in the life of the neighborhood or street by the inward orientation of doors or useless buffer landscaping.

However, a suburban greenfield site or a redeveloped industrial area may be near no existing street life and provide the designer with no compelling reason for orientation toward the street. In suburban California, where cars rather than people dominate the surrounding streets, many successful medium-density schemes place parking (and communal trash collection points) in landscaped peripheral locations so that the site is approached by foot. The effect is that of entering a quiet green oasis, with peaceful outlook, high-quality landscaping, birdsong, and neighbors talking over fences—a complete contrast to the car-dominated periphery.

Possible design responses

- When designing a site in a neighborhood where there is some degree of street life, avoid an entirely introverted site plan.
- Locate and design buffer landscaping so that it does not inhibit residents' functional and visual access to the street.
- Ensure that the design of buildings and landscaping on the outer edges of new developments is consistent with local norms.
- Where there is little likelihood of street crime, minimal street life, or car-dominated peripheral streets, consider creating an interior "oasis."

See also Conforming image (15), Unobtrusive image (16) Chapter 11—Parking.

23. Site map

When the design of a development does not follow the normal street pattern, orientation maps should be placed at major entry points.

Clustered, medium-density dwellings are often not oriented in an easily comprehended street arrangement. Virtually every user study of Radburn-style medium-density housing reports that visitors, delivery people, police, and ambulance people have problems finding a particular apartment; new letter carriers have trouble understanding the address system; and new residents become disoriented on the site.

Figure 35. Although well located at the entry to a California suburban scheme, this site map is positioned too high for many adults (and most children) to read.

Orientation maps should be located at entry points. These maps should be designed by the site planner as an integral part of his or her job to ensure that the original intent of the layout is made clear (Architecture . . . , 1969; Center . . . , 1969; Cooper, 1970b, 1972b; Department . . . , 1981b; Gilmour et al., 1970).

Possible design responses

- Locate maps at every entry point.
- Make each map clear, bold, and readable by those not familiar with architectural plans.
- Clearly indicate the dwelling numbering system, location of visitor parking, major community facilities, major landmarks, and management office.
- Indicate clearly "You Are Here" on all maps.
- Place all maps under glass so that they do not become weathered, or make them of non-weathering material. Update them whenever necessary.
- Position maps low and close enough to walkways so that children, persons with poor eyesight, or persons in wheelchairs can read them.
- Locate at least one map so that persons approaching by car can use it without leaving their vehicles.
- Light all maps for nighttime use.
- Locate maps so that planting will at no time obscure them from view.

See also: Name sign (24), Accessibility (43), Visitor parking (158).

24. Name sign

If a development is generally known by its name, this should be prominently displayed at frequently used entry points.

Clustered developments often become known by their names rather than by street locations; yet rarely is this name publicly displayed. With new, private developments, promoters often exploit the image evoked by a particular name (Woodlake Meadows, Village Square, Lakeview Homes) and erect prominent signs displaying it. But when the development is well established, such signs are generally removed, and the development may be difficult to locate and identify.

Possible design responses

- Locate well-lit name plates, large enough to be read from approaching vehicles, at main entry points.
- Design high-quality name plates of vandal- and weather-resistant material. If the housing is subsidized, do not draw attention to this fact.
- Locate the name plate so that planting will at no time obscure it from view.
- Where the entire development has one street address instead of, or as well as, a name, display this prominently.

See also: Site map (23), Street linkage (78), Site entry barriers (201).

Figure 36. Even when the "Now renting" sign is removed, this housing development will be distinguishable.

25. Street names

To assist in finding addresses, name all internal streets, courtyards, and other identifiable common areas.

Where allowed by city bylaws, internal streets should be given their own names. If they are extensions of local streets, they should be named accordingly (Beck, Rowan, and Teasdale, 1975b). Where courtyards form identifiable and used locations within the development, these should also be named and labeled. These names may be used in community discussions or in identifying a residence, and these actions may tend subtly to reinforce the residents'

identity with a particular subspace within the development.

Possible design responses

- In a clustered scheme name all internal streets and walkways, and ensure that these names are prominently displayed and well lit at night.
- Name identifiable common areas, such as courtyards, and include these names on site plans given to new residents and orientation maps at site entries.

See also: Subunit identity (21), Group territory (72), Territorial zones (213).

Figure 37. Finding your way around the upper-level "streets" of this London low-rise, high-density scheme is facilitated by adequate signs and a clear numbering system.

26. Dwelling addresses

The street number and address of every dwelling should be clearly identified.

Public housing projects are notorious for the almost universal lack of legible and logical systems of dwelling addresses. Institutional numbers (or letters) are often assigned to buildings, and dwellings often have two numbers—one referring to the housing authority's designations and the other referring to the postal department's. If, as one Canadian study asserts, "a family's identity and individuality are related to having a clear and distinct address," it is incumbent upon designers and management to create a simple, logical system (Beck, Rowan, and Teasdale, 1975b). A confusing or even nonexistent address is just one more message that the individual does not matter.

Possible design responses

- Develop a simple, logical numbering system and adhere to it throughout the development.
- In row or attached housing provide each entry (front and back) with a small plaque indicating its full number and street address.
- In buildings with shared entries attach a similar plaque, listing the numbers of all apartments off that entry.

- Design a street and numbering system that corresponds to
  —The system used by postal authorities
  —The identification of units on the orientation maps
  —The identification used by management, police, fire, and ambulance personnel
  —The system of labeling designated parking spaces

See also: Visible dwelling numbers (28).

27. Conforming signs

Site signs and numbering should conform as much as possible to the surrounding neighborhood.

A signage and numbering system that is unique to the site and not related to the system used in adjacent neighborhoods may reinforce the separateness suggested by a unique form of architecture and site plan (Beck, Rowan, and Teasdale, 1975b). Most residents of public housing would prefer not to be identified as such. In private developments, however, "setting apart" often accommodates residents' desires for some kind of separateness and uniqueness.

Possible design responses

- When considering signage, street names, and numbering, you must strike a delicate balance between giving the development some identity and totally separating it from its neighborhood.
- Especially in subsidized schemes graphics and signs should be of high quality and should not convey to outsiders that this housing is "different."

See also: Conforming image (15), Locally acceptable materials (17).

Figure 38. Many housing projects have a confusing array of street addresses plus housing authority numbering systems.

28. Visible dwelling numbers

Visitors approaching by car should be able to read the numbers on street-oriented dwellings at night.

First-time, after-dark visitors are confused when dwelling numbers are too small to be read from an approaching car or are not well lit. Daytime visitors, too, will have difficulty when the numbers are too small or positioned so that they can be obscured by shared entry doors propped open for children's access.

Possible design responses

- Use medium- to large-sized numbers.
- Locate numbers so they are well lit at night by porch or street lights.
- Locate numbers at shared entry locations on the wall beside the door, opposite the hinges, rather than on the door itself.

See also: Visible entry (36), Back and front entries (41).

5

Personalization

Figure 39. When houses look basically the same, residents often like to make personal modifications that say "This is *my* house."

A house can only be considered a "home" to the extent that the occupiers can give it their own meaning. . . . It may even be said that "homes" develop "in spite of" rather than "because of" the house design (Ruddick, 1969, 115).

Since the Industrial Revolution, local authorities and speculative builders have increasingly provided housing for people in middle and lower socioeconomic groups. As a result, individuals have become more and more divorced from the design of their own homes. The phenomenal rise of do-it-yourself activities around the home and the increasing popularity of gardening among urban house dwellers and apartment dwellers alike are both reactions to this divorce. Another is the wholesale rejection and frequent vandalism of anonymous mass housing.

Most people need, if not to design their dwellings, at least to give them some touch of uniqueness that says: "This is mine; it is a reflection of me/my family; and I/we are worthy and unique beings." But architectural opinion, at least as reflected in the architectural press, continues to favor strict limitations on opportunities for personalization. There is little discussion of the exterior clues that stimulate personal expression on house facades, of ways the initial design can support later desires for increased privacy or territorial definition, or of arrangements of dwellings, access, and public space that facilitate gardening (Rapoport, 1968). One could almost say that, after completing the formal contract, design professionals are loathe to conceive of the design process as *continuing*.

Such discussion of direct involvement as exists has focused on movable partitions, kits of parts, and innovative flexibility, although there is little clear evidence that the general public wants the kind of involvement characterized by, for example, the early technical solutions of Habraken's "Supports" (Habraken et al., 1976, 1972). Architects like this kind of playing around with spaces, and they assume the public would

Figure 40. There are few touches of external personalization to enliven the environment in this scheme because the material (stove enamel) is virtually impossible to alter or add to, because front doors (a favorite location of personal touches) are out of sight, and because balconies have solid front walls so passersby cannot see plants in pots. Was this deliberate? (Pollands Hill, Merton, London)

like to do the same, given the chance. Although some do, what little evidence there is suggests that, once the walls are in place, very little rearranging of spaces takes place, by either the first or subsequent owners (Rabeneck, Sheppard, and Town, 1973, 1974a, b). As Amos Rapoport (1968, 303) states in his argument for open-ended design: "The general symbolic and emotional ties with the house, the need to territorialize and personalize, the need for expression, may be more important than physical flexibility, although they are related."

A. Rabeneck et al. propose rooms highly flexible as to function and use by virtue of their size, shape, and wiring (Rabeneck, Sheppard, and Town, 1973, 1974a, b). But this too fails to address the exterior of the dwelling. Architectural literature does not confer approval on "chaotic" front yards and unmatched exterior finishes, even though such elements of personalization encourage pride of ownership and involvement outside the house.

Personalization is used here to mean any modification of or addition to the dwelling exteriors, garages, or front or back yards effected by residents. The guidelines in this chapter are concerned with ways design can gently encourage the completion or continuing modification of dwellings by residents. They are in line with Rapoport's significant observation that the environment is important to people to the extent that they give it their own meaning (Rapoport, 1978).

This chapter emphasizes personalization in mass housing (in both the public and private

sectors) rather than in individual, freestanding houses. It seems clear that, with increasing wealth and the ability to choose one's dwelling, personalization as we understand it becomes less and less relevant, or rather, the symbols of personalization become different. For example, in a typical California blue-collar community of almost identical mobile homes (caravans), personalization by means of plaster gnomes, nymphs, burros, lions, and frogs is much in evidence in the minute front yards before each unit. In British middle-class suburbs "historic" doors, windows, and hardware are added to otherwise standardized dwellings. But in the stockbroker belt south of London the house itself (and its location) becomes the symbol of personal status: individual, added-on symbols have disappeared, except for the odd Rover or Jaguar parked prominently in the front drive. And for the very wealthy even the car and house are screened from view; the very size of the property, and its often impenetrable boundaries, become personal symbol enough.

Most renters are permitted to personalize only the interiors of their dwellings. However, many housing authorities are now encouraging residents to take over responsibility for improving and repairing their dwelling exteriors because of rising maintenance costs; so an increasing need for designers to facilitate these changes arises. If personalization and modification are discouraged (through lease arrangement, lack of ownership, or an inhibiting design), a significant, incremental, long-term opportunity to upgrade the housing stock is forgone. In Britain much do-it-yourself improvement in old and new housing areas is being encouraged by government grants (of up to half the cost) and low-interest loans from building societies (the British equivalent of saving and loan institutions). The building component market has responded with inexpensive building additions (porches, sun rooms, garages, bathrooms) that can be ordered from catalogues and erected with little or no professional assistance. Similarly, soaring U.S. house prices of the late 1970s and early 1980s have forced many to modify and add to existing homes rather than move.

The responsibility of new-home designers—given this social and economic climate—is to establish a framework in which each individual can work. Site planning of streets, access, parking, and common open space is crucial because it is the common frame within which individuals can express—internally and externally—their own symbols of home. A framework is needed in which each dwelling can be more or less assertive without knocking the overall aesthetic off balance.

Personal modification of the environment not only allows people to give their homes meaning, but also facilitates changes that enable occupants to stay, rather than move, as family size and needs change; it also encourages neighbor cooperation in the swapping of ideas, tools, and skills in do-it-yourself home improvements. The cumulative result may be a naturally occurring complexity and variety in the exterior visual environment, which most people regard as a necessary component of aesthetic attractiveness.

Figure 41. Personal touches to the dwelling exterior are hardly necessary in the London stockbroker belt because the house and its address are enough of a "status" statement.

Figure 42. A British new town scheme with little room for the kind of personalization that might have humanized this monotonous street scape. Plants on balconies cannot be seen, front doors are deeply recessed at the back of the garage, and there is no room to "extend" the dwelling into the public domain. (Fishermead, Milton Keynes New Town, U.K.)

29. Territorial expression

Provide opportunities for residents to experience or express a sense of territory around their dwellings.

Most people feel a deep need to know where their domain ends and another begins. Researchers in the United States (Worthen, 1975), Ireland (Mulvihall and McHugh, 1977), and England (Ruddick, 1969) note that one of the first acts of a new house buyer is to define clearly the property lines—by planting vegetation or erecting a fence or low wall. Observations in British council housing estates where dwellings are now for sale indicate an intense concern about boundaries and the symbols of ownership with a change of status from renter to owner (Poyner and Hughes, 1979).

In U.S. public housing of the 1940s and 1950s the clear although unspoken policy was that the poor did not deserve a yard and that territorial boundaries might give them the erroneous notion that they owned their dwelling. Front yard definition has also been discouraged by designers of new private sector housing to maintain a coordinated environment or controlled aesthetic; the expression of territory and personalization might interfere with overall visual coherence. But studies of older housing projects where fenced yards *were* provided and recent research linking private and group territorial definition to the sense of security (Newman, 1972) are beginning to convince housing authorities that the inclusion or addition of private

Figure 43. A few judiciously placed tubs and planter boxes can soon establish a sense of territory.

open space has distinct payoffs in increased resident satisfaction and lower maintenance costs.

Possible design responses

- Provide front and back yards.
- Allow residents to define their domain by means of fencing, hedges, planting, and so forth.
- Establish rental or sales agreements that permit residents to alter the means by which they define their private open space.
- Even where open plan landscaping is provided at the front of new row or semi-detached housing, permit residents to modify this to reflect their personal tastes.
- Design environments that offer hints to residents that territorial definition is possible.
- Ensure that there are convenient and comfortable places to sit in semiprivate areas.

See also: House on its own land (13), Visual complexity (18), Exterior design control (19), Transitional filters (39), Privacy screening (57), Display garden (62), Personalized landscape (180), Resident responsibilities (245).

30. Added privacy

Give residents the option of increasing the sense of privacy around their homes.

One of the basic motivations behind the demarcation of territory is the need to create a greater sense of privacy. A low fence or hedge around a front yard can successfully exclude roaming dogs and children. Higher planting or fencing prevents passersby from looking directly into the house or yard, cuts down on the noise and "busyness" of an adjacent street, or enhances the sense of security. In the United States typical suburban houses for sale have become increasingly "private" over the past few decades—with floor plans changing from living rooms and large picture windows at the front in the 1940s and 1950s to living or family rooms at the back of the house facing onto a private patio or garden and smaller bedroom windows facing the street in the 1970s. In Britain, by contrast, new suburban houses of the late 1970s often have extensive glazing facing the street, causing residents considerable expense on net curtains and on double glazing (to reduce energy loss).

In older suburban areas such as Berkeley, California, many older homes have been subdivided into apartments. To create two areas of private open space, front fences are being erected, and front yards are becoming private spaces for sitting out, vegetable growing, or children's play. Privacy is a more basic and universal need than community or neighborliness. The architectural concern with neighboring and community is commendable, but privacy must be established before people will reach out into the community.

Possible design responses

- Specify solid rather than glass front doors.
- Where the front door must be a light source, specify glass that cannot be seen through from the outside.
- Carefully consider the size of front windows, and avoid windows that extend to the floor.
- Include a semiprivate front porch.
- Stagger units so that wall extensions at right angles to the main facade create a sense of enclosure at the entry.
- Make territorial definitions clear (if only symbolically) so that stronger demarcations can be added.
- Specify building materials that allow do-it-yourself additions that create privacy—a porch, canopy, or trellis—to be fixed to the facade.
- Position the entries to semidetached or row housing so that porches can be added without intruding on car access to garage or carport.
- Include a planting area or window boxes beneath the front window and around the entry or wide exterior sills for flowerpots.
- Provide a windowsill just inside the main front window so that houseplants can increase the sense of privacy within.

See also: Exterior design control (19), Private front path (37), Entry path location (38), Transitional filters (39), Front porch (40), Neighborly surveillance (42), Privacy planting (176), Peeping out (205), Informal surveillance (219).

Figure 44. In these British new town row houses a wood-framed "window" in the backyard wall permits residents to add trellis and climbing plants for privacy or to leave it open.

31. Articulated facade

The more articulated the facade, the more likely are residents to add their own touches to the design.

A plain box or flat-fronted row house requires a strongly assertive statement to distinguish it from its neighbors. An articulated facade, with elements breaking out from the basic box or terrace, allows residents to intrude into semi-public space without leaving the domain of the house.

In the case illustrated in Figure 46, the resident has made personal modifications without "stepping out of line," either with neighbors or with the scheme's overall appearance. The addition is more protected than if it were "plugged on" to a flat-fronted house. Similarly, a wall at right angles to the main facade is more likely to be decorated or planted because it appears to have a more private position than one facing the street.

The British semidetached house, long sneered at by architects, remains one of the most adaptable of house types. The party wall reduces construction and servicing costs; yet the open side wall allows for a variety of extensions without interrupting the line of the buildings. The small-scale articulation of the front porch and bay windows allows an enclosed porch to be added without any noticeable change to the street scape (Ruddick, 1969). Even small articulations, such as the slight projection of one room

at right angles to the main facade or the provision of a "skeleton" porch, can provide a cue for adding trellis work, climbing plants, or a built-in porch.

A design student elaborated on these opportunities and on prevailing "architectural" attitudes: "The more 'elements' there are to a design, the more they are likely to be adapted because as the number increases, so the average size of each element decreases. . . . This idea, of course, runs contrary to the architectural concept that tries to limit the number of colours,

Figure 45. There are many personal touches in this scheme because adding porches, lamps, and trellises to brick walls is relatively simple, because the front door is visible, and because subtle articulations in the facade allow residents to appropriate walls and corners at right angles to their unit. (Marquess Road, Islington, London)

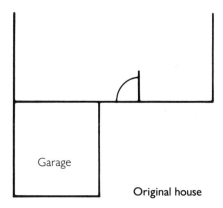

Garage

Original house

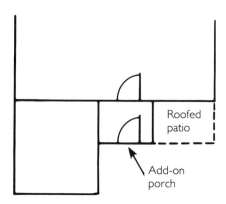

Roofed
patio

Add-on
porch

With adaptations

Figure 46. Additions are easier where there is a projection in the house facade.

materials, etc., to create an integrated whole" (Ruddick, 1969, 123).

Possible design responses

- Provide articulations in the facades of row or semidetached houses or ground-level flats.
- Specify permeable cladding material so that additions can easily be attached to the facade.
- Ensure that the arrangement of elements in the facade does not inadvertently create barriers to the disabled (for example, changes in floor level, tight corners, or enclosed spaces that are difficult for a person in a wheelchair to turn around in).

See also: Visual complexity (18), Exterior design control (19), Front porch (40), Upper windows (208), Resident responsibilities (245).

32. Personal additions

Use permeable cladding to facilitate the addition of personal touches to house exteriors.

Probably the two most versatile and adaptable building materials are brick and timber. These materials are easily fixed to, torn down, poked through, and added to. Hence they continue to be more popular than "modern" materials such as concrete panels, tiled walls, PVC panels, or stove-enameled steel.

Designers go to great lengths to create uniqueness in a new housing scheme yet often ignore the needs of the individuals within it to feel similarly unique. When this happens, their consistent use of materials precludes additions, and their bold architectural forms defy individual embellishment. This points up a basic—and perhaps insoluble—dichotomy between the designers' and the residents' ways of looking at the environment. Despite protestations of social concern, designers focus on the whole scheme, on consistency, on integrity, not on the needs of individuals within the whole. Residents focus on their own part of the whole and, looking around, perceive that same consistency and integrity as unrelieved monotony, if not imposed standardization.

The trick is to design a form with elegance and beauty that does not inhibit residents from making their mark. Le Corbusier's Pessac, which shows that the trick can be done, allows the addition of domestic accretions (shutters, cornices, windows) while still retaining the integrity of its form (Boudon, 1972).

Possible design responses

- Use brick, timber, or other locally acceptable building materials that can easily be added to.
- Specify permeable finishes and trim so that residents can add shutters, awnings, trellises, and so forth.

See also: Locally acceptable materials (17), Exterior design control (19), Articulated facade (31), Resident responsibilities (245).

Figure 47. The addition of personally selected cladding material allows the owners of this house to distinguish their dwelling from. . .

Figure 48. . . . the one next door.

33. Component replacement

Use standard-sized doors, windows, and balconies so that residents may replace or modify these if they wish.

As people upgrade their economic position in Latin American self-built shantytowns, one of their first acts is to buy or make an impressive front door. In North American suburbia the type and design of the door ("double-paneled doors" for higher priced houses) is always a feature of advertising literature. In British suburbia of the early 1980s removing the standard glass-paneled front door and replacing it with a solid, wood-paneled door is one of the first acts of personalization by new home buyers. Heavy paneled doors are very popular, as are "historic" accoutrements such as large door knockers, brass knobs, "antique" carriage lamps, and "old" hinges. Many of these symbols have status overtones; indeed, three of the four best selling "historic" doors marketed by one of the largest manufacturers in Britain are named after royal residences: the Balmoral, the Sandringham, and the Osborne.

Windows also function symbolically. In Britain standard steel windows have lower status than wood-framed windows or, better still, mullioned leaded or bow-front windows. The latter clearly have historic associations.

Because doors and windows—the links between inside and outside—are apparently such significant symbols, it might be possible in some new schemes to leave them off and supply the first group of occupants with a catalogue of available parts and let them choose their own. An experiment of this sort was attempted in the London estate of Thamesmead, where residents were given money to buy their own garage doors. Because the garages were a prominent element in the overall design, the resultant personalizations created an interestingly varied effect in what was, at base, an industrialized housing scheme.

In many British mass housing schemes, where window design is unchangeable, residents add a personal touch with elaborate net curtains or by positioning ornaments on the windowsill or painting frames in different colors. Residents often try valiantly to overcome the monotony of high-rise projects by using multicolored curtains, which can create an exciting, colorful mosaic from a distance. In most U.S. projects even this form of identity is precluded; the designer/client provides identical neutral drapes for every unit.

Where balconies form part of the design, it would be desirable to use dimensions such that standard-sized glass panels or sheetrock can be used to enclose the balcony, if the household would prefer additional interior rather than outdoor space. In one San Francisco development more than 10 percent of the residents have enclosed their balconies to make sun porches or extended living rooms; with foggy and windy weather through much of the year, sitting out in the sun was not as appealing as the designer expected (Cooper, 1970b).

Possible design responses

- Specify standard-sized fixtures to enable easy purchase and fitting of replacements.
- Experiment with allowing the first occupants to select doors, windows, or garage doors from a catalogue of available parts.
- Allow residents to choose and hang their own curtains and drapes.
- Design balconies so that standard-sized panels of building materials could be used to enclose them.

See also: Locally acceptable materials (17), Exterior design control (19), Privacy screening (57), Good management (238).

34. Entry personalization

Allow for personalization of the front entry.

Because of its symbolic meaning, the front entrance is more likely than any other part of the house to be personalized. Here especially one is likely to observe flowerpots, window boxes, ornaments, door mats, wind chimes, and so on. People like to see these personal touches as they come and go; they like visitors to see them also. In some high-density schemes even a subtle embayment, or nook in the access way, is often sufficient for residents to "lay claim" and decorate their entry. Even in high-density transient housing—for students, young working adults, and so forth—doors are often made unique and personal with posters, cartoons, name plates, and such.

Possible design responses

- Provide environmental cues at the dwelling entry that help residents lay claim to this territory and personalize it.
- Provide ground-level entries with skeleton porches or roofed overhangs for window boxes, hanging planters, or other personal additions or modifications.
- Provide space for a door mat outside the entry.
- Avoid placing a hard-surfaced path up against the front facade of ground-level dwellings or along any wall at right angles to that facade. Allow for "foundation" planting.

Figure 49. When acquiring a new house, many British families like to give it a name.

Figure 50. Americans are more likely to display the residents' names.

Figure 51. Along this institutional corridor—ironically named "Meadow Row"—there were no signs of entry personalization.

Figure 52. At ground level in the same building, however, where doors seemed more personal, there were many individual additions.

- Avoid a combination of car and pedestrian access to the house or any arrangement that leaves no room to personalize around the front entry.

See also: Added privacy (30), Articulated facade (31), Private front path (37), Transitional filters (39).

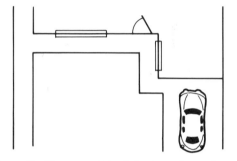

Figure 53. There would be little chance here of personalizing the front facade or entry through foundation planting.

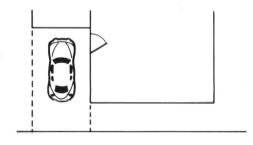

Figure 54. An entryway shared by people and cars allows little room for personalization around the door.

Access to Dwellings

Access refers to the spaces—outdoor and indoor—traversed between the entrance to a development, project, or estate and the front door of the individual dwelling. This threshold is the point at which public and private spaces and interests converge and may conflict; it should therefore receive serious design attention.

The traditional street provides for many functions in one setting: direct access to the dwelling, link to adjacent dwellings, location of many service activities (refuse collection, postal delivery), place for casual social activities (neighboring and play), and framework and linkage to other parts of the city (Victoria . . . , 1975).

With increasing rates of car ownership the juxtaposition of many of these functions in one place began to be challenged in new housing. Pedestrianized developments have proliferated in response to demands for car parking and pedestrian safety. Precinct planning and traffic management schemes have led to the separation of local and through traffic; land use planning and zoning have encouraged the separation of residential and commercial areas. Many activities that used to take place naturally on or near the street are now dispersed to playgrounds, shopping centers, parks, and community centers. Despite these further steps in the compartmentalization and dilution of urban functions, urban dwellers cling to what is known: the traditional sequence of street, pavement, front yard, porch, front door, and hallway. In housing that breaks away from this pattern designers and residents may be equally at sea as to the appropriate behaviors in each location.

In grouped or clustered housing developments access generally falls into one of the following categories:

1. Individual ground-level access to dwellings (that is, detached, semidetached, or row dwellings) from either a street or an interior courtyard
2. Walk-up access to apartments or maisonettes via a shared exterior or interior stair
3. Vertical access via stairs or elevators leading to horizontal access via half-open galleries, wide decks, upper-level "streets," or interior corridors
4. Access shared by a limited number of dwellings via one elevator leading to a relatively compact circulation system and approached via one point of entry at ground level (that is, the tower block)

The predominant form of access in higher density British subsidized housing has shown a distinct pattern of change since World War II. The elevator-access tower blocks and medium-rise, gallery-access blocks of the immediate postwar years began to be superseded in the late 1960s by lower-rise, deck-access schemes. In the mid 1970s these began to be superseded in turn by high-density, low-rise schemes with an accent on ground-level, private access and yards. Britain has therefore been in a unique position to monitor the social effects of different forms of access; we thus draw primarily upon British research in this chapter.

These studies demonstrate the overwhelming popularity of the private entry at ground level

(Cooper, 1972b; Department . . . , 1972a, 1981b, c; Victoria . . . , 1975). This is what people expect a house or home to be like. In the United States dangerous criminal activities in shared access areas have been highlighted in Oscar Newman's "Defensible Space" and other studies. In a more recent British study focusing on resident reactions to different forms of access, semiprivate stairs, elevators, and decks in

subsidized housing were frequently reported as the locale for vandalism, littering, and fouling by animals or humans (Victoria . . . , 1975).

Access is a consideration of particular importance for users who are physically or sensorily disabled or impaired. Arrangements must not constitute barriers to people using wheelchairs or other devices for assistance.

Figure 55. Shared access ways are often problematic environments. Would it be considered appropriate for residents to put doormats and plant pots outside their front doors here? Or for children to play or roller-skate? Or is it just for walking back and forth to home?

Figure 56. There is an overwhelming preference for ground-level, private entries among upper-income home owners.

35. Private entry

Provide as many dwellings as possible with a private entrance at ground level.

Private entrances and a footpath from the sidewalk to the door are closely associated with images of home (Architecture . . . , 1969; Becker, 1974; Connell, 1975; Cooper, 1975; Front . . . , 1967; Kuper, 1953). You can come and go without unwanted interactions with neighbors; your friends can find your home; and you can personalize your entry. If you have children, they can engage in doorstep play without creating noise or confusion in shared corridors or stairways and can have easy and ready access from the home into the yard or adjacent play areas.

Figure 57. Lower-income renters have the same strong preference as upper-income owners.

This guideline particularly applies to families with children. Reducing the separation between child and parent is one of the most important design issues in family housing; it is most complex, of course, where access (stairs, decks, corridors, elevators) has to be shared and where immediate access to the ground is not possible. It is most satisfactorily solved where private entries are at ground level.

See also: Ground-floor households (8), House on its own land (13), Entry personalization (34).

36. Visible entry

Ensure that the main entry to the dwelling is clearly visible from the nearest public circulation path.

The image of front doors or porches lined up along a street is strong in most people's minds. They expect that they and their visitors will be able to see their front door—its unique color, design, or decoration—as they approach it. They do not want the main entry at the end of a narrow, shadowed passage or at the back end of a garage. Privacy at the front door is important, but a tunnellike entry may render the house number invisible and create a security problem.

Possible design responses

- Ensure that each front door—its number, personalization, mailbox, and so forth—is clearly visible from the nearest circulation route and from a number of other dwellings. Where this is impossible, locate the pathway to the front door clearly.
- Avoid access via a tunnellike space or via a utilitarian space such as a garage or carport.

See also: Visible dwelling numbers (28), Entry personalization (34), Transitional filters (39), Neighborly surveillance (42), Informal surveillance (219).

37. Private front path

Avoid sharing private, ground-level front paths.

The front path leading from a public street or footpath to an individual dwelling entry provides a strongly symbolic image: a space within view of the public domain, yet clearly the territory (and responsibility) of the individual household. Opening a garden gate or passing through an entry gap in a fence or hedge further emphasizes the public-to-private transition. A household sharing its entry approach with other households is in a potentially uncomfortable situation. Whose job is it to sweep up the leaves? Whose visitor is it coming down the path? Why do they not tell their children to keep their bikes off the path?

Possible design responses

- Provide each ground-level dwelling with a separate, private front path.
- Design paths that extend at least five or six paces from main circulation routes to signify a threshold. (In tight situations grade changes can substitute for length if they do not constitute barriers—most steps are barriers—or create tight corners difficult for a disabled person to maneuver.)

See also: House on its own land (13), Visible entry (36), Footpath privacy (188), Running the gauntlet (229).

Figure 58. Although this looks quite pleasing, an entry area or path shared by two households may lead to problems of responsibility and territoriality.

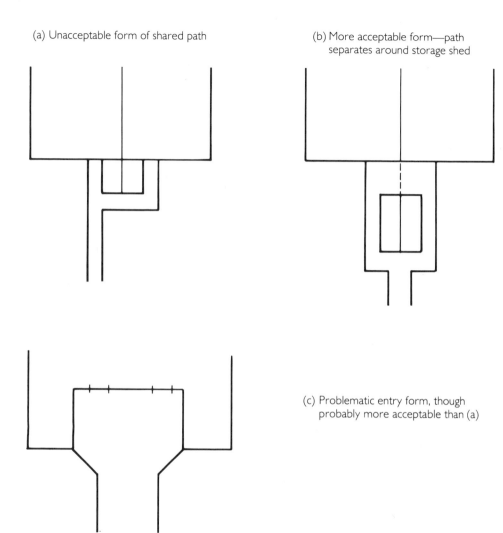

(a) Unacceptable form of shared path

(b) More acceptable form—path separates around storage shed

(c) Problematic entry form, though probably more acceptable than (a)

Figure 59. If a shared entry path is unavoidable, some arrangements are better than others.

38. Entry path location

Ensure that the positioning of the front path does not violate interior privacy.

The path leading from public circulation to the dwelling must be visible from the house—to note the approach of visitors—and yet not pass too close to the windows of private interior living space, especially living rooms and bedrooms. Drawn curtains are a heavy price to pay for privacy.

See also: Added privacy (30), Private front path (37), Doorstep play (89), Footpath privacy (188).

39. Transitional filters

Provide a series of transitional filters for pedestrians passing from public spaces to the private domain of the dwelling.

Most people find it preferable that visitors or strangers pass through a series of zones or filters that make them more and more aware that they are entering a private domain as they approach the dwelling (Gehl, 1977). Residents passing through the same transitional points relax as they are surrounded more and more by their own symbols and handiwork. The transition filters extend, of course, into the home: A

Figure 60. The progression from front gate to front path to front porch or patio allows for increasing degrees of privacy.

visitor, but probably not a vendor, may be invited into the hall or, if the visit is to be extended, into the living room or parlor; a visitor who is actually "one of the family" may be ushered into the kitchen.

The desire for these filters seems to have been maintained, if not increased, over the years; and in Britain, for example, the richer you are, the greater the number of transition points you provide yourself. For example, a working-class row house (dating from the nineteenth century) may have a step leading from the street straight into a formal front room or parlor. Beyond this are private rooms into which few except family are invited. The lack of additional filters such as a front gate, front path, porch, and hall is often made up for by an almost ritualistic attention to the front door (polishing brass door knobs and whitening the step daily) (Young and Willmott, 1957) and by display behavior in the front parlor (which frequently contains the best furniture, family heirlooms, photos, and ornaments). A contemporary house in the stockbroker belt, in contrast, may have a hedged yard, a front gate and drive, a porch, a formal entry hall, a formal living room, and a less formal family kitchen. In Melbourne, Australia, a study of seventeen residential streets supported the need for "soft interfaces"—gradual transitions from private to public providing opportunities to stay on the public side of the house and to interact passively or actively with people in the street or in other front yards (Gehl, 1977).

All these transition points are means of handling visitors and maintaining control over the privacy of the home.

Possible design responses

- Provide essential transition points, however limited in size or subtlety these may be. At ground level they might include a front gate (or opportunity to add one), a private front path, a porch (or opportunity to add one), and a foyer or entrance hall. With entries at higher levels, employ features such as planters on either side of the front door, a small, porchlike overhang at the entrance, or a recess off the access deck or corridor.
- If spatial dimensions are limited, use grade changes to create a sense of transition. However, a simple step up or down can constitute a significant barrier to a disabled person: small ramps are better. Particularly avoid using only a few steps, which are dangerous, especially for a stranger at night.
- Ensure that these filters do not block visual access to the main entry of the dwelling.

See also: Added privacy (30), Private front path (37), Front porch (40).

40. Front porch

Provide a porch or porchlike space at every front entry.

Chats over backyard fences or exchanges while puttering about in adjacent front yards often lead to initial contact with neighbors in multi-family housing. The porch, which provides a more private transition space between the home and the more public footpath or access way, provides a comparable locale for casual socializing (Architecture . . . , 1966; Cooper, 1970b; 1975; Shankland . . . , 1967). Even the addition of a canopy over a front door or a recessed space off a long access corridor is often sufficient to suggest semiprivacy. Such a space has important functions as a psychological breathing space between the public and private domain: as a place to stack groceries and find one's key, as a shelter from darkness, cold, and damp, and as a place for added welcoming touches to the home (doormat, plants, ornaments, and so forth). An enclosed porch can serve as a draft excluder, a house enlarger, a storage unit, a conservatory, and a secure point from which to view strangers.

Possible design responses

- The ideal porch space is
  —Large enough for two people to stand under cover, even when the outer door (or screen door) is open

Figure 61. This tiny front porch in a London scheme for the elderly allows for the addition of personal touches and enables resident or visitor to stand out of the rain.

—Large enough to hold a small table or shelf where bags or packages can be rested

—Well lit at night with a light-sensitive or exterior switch or preset timer, both to deter intruders and as a convenience late at night

—Large enough in very wet regions for an umbrella to be propped up open to dry

—Large enough to sit in

—Insulated, ventilated, and glazed where geographically appropriate to insulate the building

—Designed and located to enable surveillance from windows

—A level space of nonslip finish large enough for a person in a wheelchair to turn around (5 feet [1.52 m] minimum diameter), with no barriers between the porch, door, and street

—Built of wood so that residents can easily secure personalized additions such as a window box, hanging basket, ornaments, or house numbers

• Especially where initial building entry is via a shared transition space (corridor or stairs), provide a further transition space at the dwelling entry by recessing doors, changing floor covering material, or providing shelves or places for plants.

See also: Entry personalization (34), Private entry (35), Transitional filters (39), Doorstep play (89), Home turf (128), Casual meetings (129).

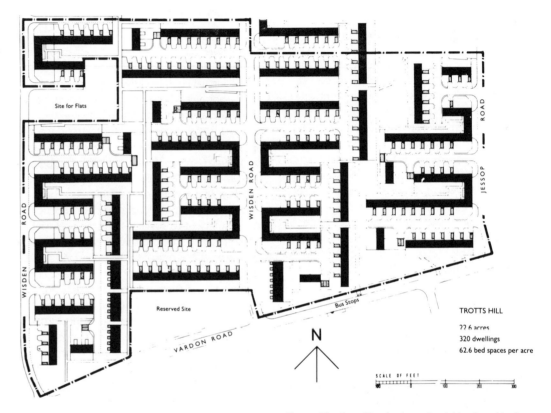

Figure 62. A traffic-segregated neighborhood in Stevenage New Town (U.K.) in which residents complained that visitors and delivery men always came to the back door (approached via vehicular culs-de-sac) and infringed on the privacy and security of the fenced backyard. "Front" doors faced onto interior landscaped spaces and visitors could not find them. (Trotts Hill. Source: Architecture . . . , 1979)

41. Back and front entries

Back and front entrances to the dwelling should be clearly identified and distinguished from each other.

The front of the dwelling is its more formal facade, on show to the neighborhood, approached first by visitors. The back is the informal aspect, where utilitarian functions take place, private household functions occur, and children come and go with ease. Each society, or indeed region within a country, may have different customs about which door to approach. In many Australian suburbs, for example, the accepted convention is to go to the front door if one has been invited but to the back door if one is just calling casually.

In Western societies, houses traditionally front onto streets, and public norms determine appropriate front behavior. But with the emergence of clustered or Radburn-type layouts some confusions have arisen. In one New York condominium development of semidetached homes, where front entries were on the *sides* of street-facing dwellings, a minor uproar occurred and the condominium bylaws were eventually amended when a resident planted tomatoes in front of her unit. Such confusion about front and back entries is recorded in a number of studies (Architecture . . . , 1969; Byrom, 1972; Front . . . , 1967; Gatt, 1978). For example, in Stevenage New Town, road access in three neighborhoods studied was at the backs of houses, and, when delivery persons approached dwellings via backyards, residents complained that this impinged on the privacy of their yards and the security of small children and pets left there

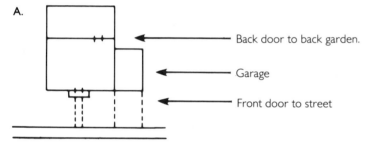

A.

Back door to back garden.

Garage

Front door to street

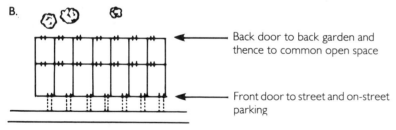

B.

Back door to back garden and thence to common open space

Front door to street and on-street parking

Figure 63. Some possible back and front arrangements: In situations (a), (b), and (c) back and front entries are clearly distinguishable from each other; situation (d) may create some confusion.

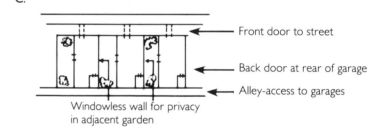

C.

Front door to street

Back door at rear of garage

Alley-access to garages

Windowless wall for privacy in adjacent garden

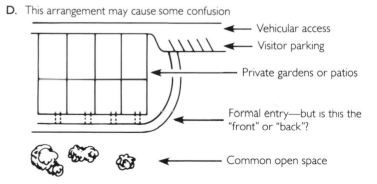

D. This arrangement may cause some confusion

Vehicular access

Visitor parking

Private gardens or patios

Formal entry—but is this the "front" or "back"?

Common open space

(Architecture . . . , 1969). The study recommends a return to the "true Radburn system," with the front door located on the road side of the house, where it can better cater to formal occasions and special visitors (Architecture . . . , 1969).

Similarly, in two middle-income, medium-density projects in Vancouver residents had difficulty distinguishing between front and back doors (Gatt, 1978), mainly because "front" was located near the kitchen.

Possible design responses

- Provide each housing unit on the ground with both a formal and an informal entry.
- Where dwellings have two doors, clearly indicate which is formal and which is informal by the location of guest parking, layout of sidewalks, address designation, or design of dwelling approaches.
- Avoid ambiguity by obscuring back entries or designing them so that they cannot be reached by strangers.
- Locate back doors near kitchens or laundries.
- Put house numbers and mailboxes near front entrances.
- Locate front doors facing streets or clearly visible from the street to facilitate strangers finding the right address.

See also: Visible dwelling numbers (28), Visible entry (36), "Front" and "back" customs (56), Common space at the back (76).

42. Neighborly surveillance

A delicate balance must be struck between designing for ease of surveillance and designing for privacy.

"Watching out for each other" can mean noticing the mail carrier trying to deliver a parcel to neighbors on vacation, a child perilously close to a busy street, a visitor having trouble finding an address, or a stranger acting suspiciously. Such casual responsibility sharing can be enhanced by site layout, window placement, and building access.

Care must be taken, however, that privacy needs are not violated. Complaints about lack of privacy come most frequently from residents of dwellings with inadequate buffers between dwellings and public pathways or open space and from residents of gallery-access blocks where low windows look out onto the access area. Fewer complaints regarding privacy come from residents of houses with adequate solid fencing around their yards, flats with clerestory windows or no windows looking out into access areas, tower blocks, and internal corridor blocks (Cooper, 1970b, 1975; Cooper and Corrie, 1970; Department . . . , 1971a, b,

Figure 64. Most people are glad when neighbors can casually view their dwellings but do not want to be continually under scrutiny.

82

1972a; Ministry . . . , 1970). Because crimes most commonly occur in interior shared access areas, approaches to the main building entrances should be designed to permit surveillance from neighboring windows.

Nevertheless, these measures may fail to prevent crime where some or all of the following conditions exist:

1. Residents fear recriminations for identifying or reporting potential lawbreakers. (This situation commonly occurs in large-scale U.S. low-income public housing projects, where most heads of households are women.)
2. Residents are tenants without opportunities to control or exercise responsibility toward the spaces around their dwellings.
3. Management-tenant relations are strained.
4. Poor maintenance of common or public spaces leads to alienation from the exterior physical and social environment.

Possible design responses

- Locate windows so that surveillance of semi-public open spaces and footpaths is possible from frequently used rooms, without permitting close views in from these areas.
- Provide solid fencing or a mixture of fencing types to permit views out but limit visual access to dwellings and private open spaces.
- Avoid low windows in gallery-access blocks.
- Provide lighting that illuminates entries and approaches without shining directly into windows.

- Design short, articulated decks that provide good supervision of dwelling entries (Vancouver . . . , 1978).

See also: Added privacy (30), Tot lot location (90), "Opportunities for Surveillance" in Chapter 13—Security and Vandalism, Resident responsibilities (245).

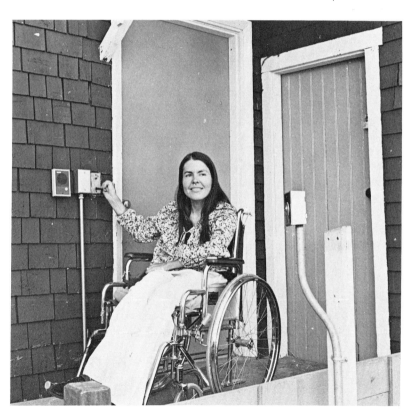

43. Accessibility

Dwellings should be accessible to physically disabled people.

Most countries now require that buildings meet certain standards for accessibility to persons having a wide variety of impairments, especially those dependent for mobility upon wheelchairs,

Figure 65. Dwellings designed for ease of access by physically disabled persons allow them the freedom and dignity of living independently.

walkers, canes, and crutches. In Britain these regulations take the form of the British Standard Code of Practice, CP96, Part I: 1969: Access for the Disabled to Buildings. In the United States they are the American National Standards Institute's Specifications for Making Buildings Accessible to, and Usable by, the Physically Handicapped (A117.1-1-1961, R-1980), which is incorporated by reference into state and federal laws and regulations.

Minimal accessibility often yields poor results, as in the case of a ramp whose location is inconvenient and difficult to discern. Moreover, confining accessibility to a few facilities that, according to prejudice, disabled people use perpetuates social isolation, dependency, and fragmentation stresses upon the family. Finding housing suited to their needs may be difficult or impossible for single disabled persons and families with disabled members, especially those of low or moderate income. For the designer to ameliorate this situation is always desirable, often required, and usually possible.

In new construction the cost of providing full accessibility to buildings has been shown to be less than 0.1 percent. For site design, the subject of this book, costs should be far less.

Guidelines now widely available to facilitate barrier-free site planning (American . . . , 1980; American . . . , 1975; Goldsmith, 1967) are not universally supported by compliance mechanisms, but they should be used to ensure that the requirements spelled out in the following design responses section are met.

Possible design responses

- Site entrances accessible to disabled persons should be easily identified and clearly marked with signs and maps.
- If an accessible path is not easily discernible, provide a sign at the site entrance with the international symbol of access.
- Provide level (2 percent grade maximum), well-lit, and clearly designated parking spaces for disabled persons (at least one in every development, or 2 percent of all spaces). They should be at least 12 feet (3.64 m) wide (preferably more) to permit transfer from a wheelchair to car or van, to accommodate vans with side-mounted lifts, and to enable disabled people to maneuver easily around their vehicles. Parallel parking spaces for disabled persons should be at least 28 feet (8.53 m) long or situated at the rear of a row to allow for vans with lifts at the rear. They should be related directly to the units they serve. Stalls for disabled users should be closest to building entries (100 feet [30.48 m] maximum preferred).
- Provide unobstructed curb ramps that can easily be reached from parked vehicles. Curbs should be no higher than the maximum height of one step (6½ inches [16.5 cm]). Do not provide double or stepped curbs, which are difficult to negotiate.
- Provide parking spaces in garages with a minimum width of 13½ feet (4.1 m). Travel distance to the dwelling should be minimized and the route protected against inclement weather. Switches for lights or automatic garage doors should be easily accessible. At least part of the garage should be high enough for vans (minimum 7 foot [2.13 m] ceiling height for an unconverted van).
- In addition to residents' parking spaces, provide clearly identifiable drop-off zones, with curb ramps if necessary, as close as possible to entries of units designed for physically disabled people.
- Design clear and direct access routes, following regularly traveled footpaths, unless they create cross-slope difficulties. They should be at least 3½ feet (1.07 m) wide (preferably wider) and paved with firm, even-textured, nonslip, hard-surfaced materials. Avoid loose gravel, pebbles, raised cobblestones, brick, and quarry tiles. Joints between paving stones or tiles should be even and no more than ½ inch (12.7 mm) wide. Paths should be well lit and contain no steps (unless accompanied by a ramp). Handrails, where needed, should extend 1 foot (0.3 m) beyond the top and bottom of a run of stairs or ramp, turning under, so as not to catch at sleeves. Overhanging trees near pathways should be trimmed to 7 feet (2.16 m) to safeguard visually impaired people.
- Integrate ramps into the design of routes used by ablebodied and disabled people alike; housing need not look different in order to be accessible. The area extending from the top and bottom of a ramp should be clear and level for a distance of 5 feet

(1.52 m), and similar level areas should be provided at least every 30 feet (9.14 m). The gradient of ramps should not exceed 1:12 (8.33 percent).

- Provide adequate draining of walkways and parking areas; depressed surfaces constitute a particular hazard. Drainage should be flush with the surface; openings between grates and bars should not exceed ¾ inch (19.05 mm). To avoid hazardous water buildup, do not locate drainage structures between a curb ramp and the corner of a street or immediately downgrade from a curb ramp.
- Where outdoor stairs are necessary, design them to accommodate the needs of people with walking difficulties and impaired vision. Stairs should not be used where there are only a few steps in a series. They should have a minimum clear width of 3 feet (0.91 m); the maximum rise between landings should be 4 feet (1.22 m) in unprotected stairs and 6 feet (1.83 m) in protected stairs. Individual steps should be of a minimum tread width of 11 inches (279.4 mm) from nosing to nosing. Open risers should not be used (for fire stairs they must not be used). Nosings should be absent or chamfered; avoid abrupt, square nosings, which provide less resistance and can cause tripping. Light should be cast down toward the risers so that treads are not in shadow.
- Where access ways meet dwelling entrances, provide protected, level platforms of non-slip material (minimum size 5 feet by 5 feet

[1.52 m by 1.52 m]) to permit persons using devices for assistance to maneuver with ease. The platform should include a clear area at least 1½ feet (0.45 m) beside the door on the side opposite the hinges, for similar reasons. The platform may be sloped ⅛ inch (3.17 mm) per foot to provide drainage.

- The threshold at the front door should preferably be flush with floor surfaces or have a maximum height of ½ inch (12.7 mm) and be beveled on either side.
- Equip gates and doors with easy-to-operate levers, bars, handles, or locks mounted at convenient heights (30 to 32 inches [762 to 813 mm] above the floor, 36 inches [914 mm] maximum). Round door knobs are particularly difficult for arthritic hands to grasp; gate latches that can be manipulated with the side of the hand are relatively easy.
- Mount doorbells and mailboxes at a convenient height (3 feet to 3 feet, 9 inches [0.91 to 1.14 m]).
- Provide rest areas along pathways. Walls 18 to 22 inches (457.2 to 558.8 mm) high and at least 1 foot (0.30 m) wide can double as seats and package rests. Higher walls are useful to lean against.

See also: Ground-floor households (8), Site map (23), Visible entry (36), Transitional filters (39), Ramps and elevators (50). [For further information about barrier-free site design, see American . . . 1975; American . . . 1980; Goldsmith, 1967; Lifchez and Winslow, 1979.

44. Shared entry

When one building entry serves a group of dwellings, the number sharing should be between three and eight households.

The fewer the doors opening off one corridor, stairway, or balcony, the more people's privacy and security needs will be met, the more responsible they will feel toward shared facilities,

Figure 66. Access shared by four households. (Private sector cluster housing, California suburbs)

and the more likely they are to make positive social contact with neighbors (Gilmour et al., 1970; Habraken, 1972; Newman, 1972; Shankland . . . , 1977a; Victoria . . . , 1975). Although such space tends to be viewed as shared private space in inverse ratio to the number of people using it, the number of units should be great enough to indicate that the space is shared in common. A lower limit of three or four may be preferable to just two (Cooper, 1971; Front and Back . . . , 1967; Shankland . . . , 1967; Vancouver . . . , 1978; Zeisel and Griffin, 1975), which may imply private possession and thus lead to conflict. In a U.S. project where six families share each entry and stairway, a high degree of neighboring and assistance (borrowing, taking in parcels, baby-sitting) was reported among this group. Within the same neighborhood residents of neither a luxury high rise nor a low-income high rise, where several hundred shared each entry, displayed a comparable degree of cooperation and neighboring (Cooper, 1971, 1972b). Problems increase when large numbers of residents are forced to share facilities such as foyers, access stairs, and refuse hoppers (Beck, Rowan, and Teasdale, 1975b). When this sharing is compounded by poor quality materials, a high child density, a confusion over maintenance responsibilities, or inadequate maintenance, it is small wonder that resident complaints frequently focus on access ways and what must be encountered—aesthetically and socially—when using them.

There is no magical maximum number of households that can share an entryway successfully, but research suggests that an upper limit of eight to ten is advisable and that five or six is preferable (Brill . . . , 1979b; Cooper, 1970b; Front . . . , 1967; Ineichen, 1972; Mayhew et al., 1979; Newman, 1972; Shankland . . . , 1967; Zeisel and Griffin, 1975). Perhaps this number is most conducive to neighboring, whatever the building form. In one U.S. study, where residents of a suburban, medium-density scheme were asked to define the area where they had fairly frequent interaction with neighbors, all indicated an area embracing six to eight adjacent dwellings. This was true for apartment dwellers sharing a stairway, townhouse dwellers facing a street, and single-family home owners on culs-de-sac.

See also: Life cycle clusters (7), Subunit identity (21), Doorstep play (89), Casual meetings (129), Meeting neighbors (130), Visible lobbies (202), Entrance group (214).

Figure 67. Access shared by six households. (Public sector housing, inner London)

45. Outdoor Gallery Access

Be cautious in providing access via long, shared-access galleries.

Exterior shared access has more potential for problems than any other form of access in subsidized housing (Department . . . , 1981b; Heffernan, 1977; Shankland . . . , 1977a). In Britain especially, noisy play, vandalism, lack of upkeep, and an institutional feeling have rendered deck-access spaces unacceptable, and some estates containing them have been officially designated "difficult to let." One British study concludes, "It is unlikely that this type of housing, slab blocks with deck access, will ever be popular with families" (Department . . . , 1981b, 41).

We should be wary, however, of totally condemning this form of access. Gallery access (single-loaded corridors) is commonly and successfully used in the United States for small, low- or middle-income apartment buildings. If elevators are provided, gallery access offers disabled persons accessibility to many apartments in a cost-effective manner. Where such access ways are small and do not serve as shortcuts to outsiders, they are not perceived as semipublic places. If childless households and households with children are housed on different floors, neighbors' children may not be a problem.

Gallery access in Ralph Erskine's Byker Wall Newcastle is successful. Galleries are curved, avoiding an institutional image of rows of front doors; each dwelling has a raised step, place for a doormat, planter for flowers, and a bench

seat. In a modified deck-access scheme in Stapleton Houses, Staten Island, New York, windows from the kitchen-dining room look out over a glass-enclosed deck, and entrances are set back from the deck 4 feet (1.22 m). The glass enclosure helps define the space and creates a weatherproof area for doorstep play. What had been officially designated as public space was perceived as semiprivate by the tenants (Newman, 1972).

As with other seeming architectural "mistakes," we should analyze not only the problematic features of deck access, but also the cases in which such features are successful.

Possible design responses

- Provide appropriate, safe, attractive, and interesting play areas for children on site so they are not tempted to play on the decks.
- Set back entrances to define entries as areas for doorstep play for very small children.
- Provide high-quality finishes and lighting.
- Ensure that the deck is naturally lit (during daytime hours) and ventilated, has a pleasant view, and is constructed so as to minimize noise transference to dwellings below or adjacent.
- Ensure that gallery widths reflect the number of dwellings served and other critical environmental criteria (for example, sun lighting, weather protection, entrance privacy). Decks should not be less than 6 feet (1.83 m) wide and preferably wider, especially when they serve dwellings with children.

- Provide for good visual supervision of decks by neighbors without allowing passersby to look directly into windows.

See also: Front porch (40), Neighborly surveillance (42), Deck connections (46), Territorial zones (213), Entrance group (214).

Figure 68. An impersonal access way such as this is just another reminder to residents that they live in a huge institutional housing project.

46. Deck connections

Be cautious about providing above-ground deck connections to adjacent neighborhoods.

Some deck-access developments have deliberately attempted to connect on-site circulation to the general neighborhood pattern. Then the same space doubles as access to dwellings along it and a through route for people walking, say, from a shopping center to a more distant housing cluster. This is laudable on some accounts, but decks' accessibility to outsiders has encouraged the use of access ways by nonresidents for passing through, playing, hanging out, or exploring by youth. Residents thus have trouble feeling that these spaces are theirs.

Possible design responses

- Ensure that above-ground deck connections to local shopping centers, schools, and so forth do not provide shortcut routes for nonresidents.
- Ensure that the means used to prevent cutting through by nonresidents do not preclude accessibility to disabled persons.

See also: Space hierarchy (4), Group territory (72).

Figure 69. This massive institutional housing block is rendered even more impersonal by the fact that access corridors double as pedestrian routes from a shopping center to more distant housing.

47. Quality detailing

In linear-access schemes provide high-quality design details, finishes, and lighting and stipulate maintenance responsibilities.

In a development in Manchester where decks link a number of low- and high-rise buildings in a complex, linear scheme, only 18 percent of residents surveyed complained about the distance they had to walk from dwelling to building entry (maximum 131 feet [40 m]), but two-thirds complained about the *quality* of the environment they had to pass through—poor finishes, rough appearance, monotony, low-grade materials (Victoria . . . , 1975).

A comparison of two other British housing schemes suggests similar attitudes. In a scheme of linked blocks of deck-access maisonettes and flats (Queen's Park Maisonettes, Blackburn), the incidence of socially disapproved activities on the decks (fighting, breaking in, vandalism, littering, fouling by animals and humans) is high. This can be contrasted with a higher-density London scheme (Marquess Road, Islington), where three- to five-story blocks of maisonettes and flats are linked by ramps, elevators, and upper-level streets. Residents approve of most of the behaviors in these access ways (sitting out, engaging in hobbies, hanging laundry) and their location.

There may be a host of interlocking factors affecting these differences, but it is interesting that the access ways in the first scheme are conventional inset decks with dwellings above and below, with one side open to the elements, and with very poor construction and detailing (easily broken glass panels, flimsy paneling).

The London scheme, by contrast, has access largely via upper-level streets—completely open (as a street would be), with dwelling entries recessed on either side, with attractive and hard-wearing brick and blue asbestos cement slates as wall cladding on either side, and with brick or traditional paving slabs as the walking surface. These access ways are extremely well maintained and highly approved of by most of the residents, many of whom have placed tubs of flowers outside their doors to add color to the "street" scene. Could it be that the nonroofed design, the paving slabs, and all the messages that declared this a "street" discourage some of the disapproved behaviors that have become associated with the no-man's-lands of decks?

People are likely to accept the basic design form because it is hard to imagine anything different; they are nevertheless acutely aware of the ancillary aspects of design—the details they encounter in day-to-day life.

Possible design responses

- Avoid materials and fixtures in shared access ways that are easily damaged or vandalized or difficult to clean.
- Ensure that high-quality lighting and furnishings are provided in shared access ways, if necessary limiting the budget for interiors to do this.

Figure 70. A London housing scheme where upper-level "streets" of good-quality materials have been highly personalized by residents. (Marquess Road, Islington, London)

- In an open or semiopen access deck create an image of "street" so that people will understand what is appropriate behavior.
- Ensure that maintenance responsibilities for shared access ways are clear; preferably, it is management's (not residents') job to keep such places clean.

See also: Outdoor gallery access (45), Vulnerable materials (233), Attractive materials (234), Maintenance responsibilities (240).

48. Street activities off the ground

Design off-ground linear access ways to accommodate as many activities as possible that would normally occur on the street, sidewalk, or front porch or path.

The street provides for many more functions than just coming and going, and so must any access way that replaces it. In an extensive study of play in fifteen British housing schemes of varying forms and densities, play behavior was more frequently observed in access ways within buildings than in any other location (Department . . . , 1973a). (See Figure 71.) Yet when play, socializing, courting, and dog walking—all "street activities"—take place in the access ways of linear-access developments, residents frequently disapprove (Victoria . . . , 1975). In a deck-access development in Manchester, for example, two thirds of the residents felt that the decks were an unsuitable location for play, and 28 percent felt that they were unsuitable for courting. Ironically, more than half the residents questioned reported that they themselves used the deck for casual socializing, although none considered this unsuitable.

This study, and a number of comparable ones, indicates a kind of time lag: What was perfectly acceptable on the street is not yet accepted on the upper-level deck. Yet whatever adult residents think, five-year-olds will continue to play house and fifteen-year-olds will still flirt in the access ways of housing schemes. Adolescents traditionally socialized in the front parlors

or on the front porch or stoop, and children played on the doorstep or the front path. The same activities merely spill out into whatever is the contemporary equivalent—the deck, the corridor, the access stairs. Where possible, households with children should be housed on ground floors (see guideline 8). Where that is not possible, the following design responses should be considered.

Possible design responses

- Design off-ground pedestrian ways to reflect the activities likely to occur there (that is, activities that would traditionally occur on the pavement, on the porch, or over the garden gate).
- Provide high-quality soundproofing between the deck and dwellings underneath it.

Figure 71. Twelve-foot (3.6 m) wide "streets in the sky" in a Sheffield (U.K.) housing scheme successfully accommodate doorstep play, tricycling, roller skating, milk delivery, and casual neighborly encounters.

- Provide improved soundproofing (including double glazing) between deck and adjacent dwellings.
- Locate socializing and play areas with seats in "neutral" territories at the ends of decks or heads of access stairs.
- Design recessed entries to dwellings, perhaps with a planter box or seat (as nicely incorporated in Newcastle's Byker Wall).
- Design wide access ways (6 to 12 feet [1.83 to 3.66 m]) with adjacent semienclosed "eddy spaces" to accommodate the needs of play and adolescent socializing.
- Include design features that will render the whole access area safe for unsupervised children.

See also: Street names (25), Front porch (40), Neighborly surveillance (42), Group territory (72), Children on the move (80), Doorstep play (89), Casual meetings (129), Friendly encounters (131), Running the gauntlet (229), Maintenance responsibilities (240).

49. Corridor access

Avoid corridor-access buildings for households with children.

Problems frequently arise where small children are housed in interior, double-loaded corridor schemes; their play activities spill out into the corridor, and the space, being enclosed, very effectively carries noise. Children play outside the dwelling less in corridor schemes than in those with any other form of access (Department . . . , 1972a, 1973a; Stewart, 1970), and when they do, problems frequently arise.

On one Newcastle estate the six-story corridor blocks of three-bedroom dwellings intended for families were extremely unpopular. The corridors were long and noisy—"the slightest sound reverberates through them" (Department . . . , 1981b, 64). The estate had a high child density; large numbers of children used the corridors as transit routes. When the local authority started letting the flats only to single people or couples without children, it had no trouble finding tenants (Department . . . , 1981b). Technological shortcomings, in other words, were less of a factor than the presence of children.

Possible design responses

- Avoid housing families with children in interior corridor schemes.

- Where children must be housed in buildings with corridor access, provide supervised interior and exterior play areas.
- Where corridor access is unavoidable, define entries by setbacks and such for use as doorstep play areas.

See also: Life cycle clusters (7), Ground-floor households (8), Quality detailing (47), Doorstep play (89), Visible lobbies (202).

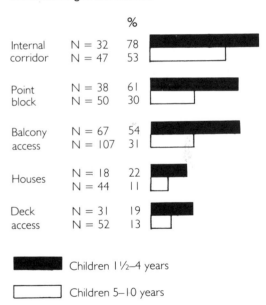

Housewives who said their children played mainly in the dwelling in fine weather

		%
Internal corridor	N = 32	78
	N = 47	53
Point block	N = 38	61
	N = 50	30
Balcony access	N = 67	54
	N = 107	31
Houses	N = 18	22
	N = 44	11
Deck access	N = 31	19
	N = 52	13

■ Children 1½–4 years

□ Children 5–10 years

Figure 72. Location of children's play reported by residents in British housing schemes with different access designs. (Source: Department . . . , 1972a)

50. Ramps and elevators

Provide ramps or elevators for people unable to use stairs.

Where linear access is approached by stairs, ramp, or elevator, alternative access should be included at certain points so that persons with strollers, wheelchairs, or shopping baskets are not inconvenienced. Even if disabled people do not live in the development, they may want to visit friends who do.

Possible design responses

- Design ramps or elevators to be unobtrusive but simple to locate.
- Locate ramps or elevators in relation to stairs so that disabled and ablebodied people circulate by similar means or proximate routes.
- Provide accessibility to units intended specifically for disabled people that does not make them look different from other units.
- Construct ramps of fire-retardant materials with nonslip finishes, and ensure that they are well lit and protected from rain or snow.
- Provide ramps and stairs with uninterrupted handrails that extend at least 1 foot (0.30 m) beyond their ends.

See also: Unobtrusive image (16), Accessibility (43).

51. Entry storage

Provide storage space for strollers, bicycles, shopping carts, and so forth close to the main entries of dwellings or groups of dwellings.

Dwellers in medium- to high-density housing frequently complain that there is nowhere safely to store children's outdoor toys, strollers, bicycles, and so forth. They must be stored on balconies, chained to stairways, or left lying around in communal areas, which creates an unpleasant image (Wirthensohn, 1976). Having to carry bicycles, baby carriages, or shopping carts up and down stairs frequently places an unnecessary burden on women; theft of equipment left in semipublic spaces places additional hardships on families of limited means.

Possible design responses

- Provide a lockable storage area within the yard or patio for ground-level units or close to the main entry for above-ground units.
- Locate storage spaces in communal areas as close as possible to the dwelling (ideally adjacent).
- Provide weatherproof storage.
- Choose observable locations where there is natural through traffic.
- Ensure that storage areas have secure doors and locks.

- Provide lockable bicycle racks outside building entrances for daytime use.
- Provide lockable indoor bicycle storage adjacent to building entrances for nighttime use.
- We do not recommend a return to the traditional British pram sheds and outdoor stores: Sheds are normally damp, are located too far from the dwellings themselves, are in vulnerable positions (that is, not overlooked and therefore broken into and vandalized), utilize valuable ground space, and are a source of visual blight (Heffernan, 1977, 31).

See also: Shared entry (44).

52. Furniture moving

Access ways should be designed to facilitate moving furniture.

Moving into medium- and high-density housing can be a trying experience. The van often cannot come right up to the front door, and heavy furniture must be carried along footpaths. Or, if the building incorporates shared access, the stair, corridors, or foyers may not accommodate large items of furniture.

Possible design responses

- Locate housing so that furniture vans can load and unload within 50 feet (15.24 m) of each unit.
- Align stairways with main entries to facilitate large-item removal.
- Locate railings with care. For example, avoid central railings, which make it difficult to move large items.
- Provide landings with at least 8 feet (2.44 m) of clearance between the elevator or stair doors and the nearest opposite wall or other obstruction (Edmonton . . . , 1978).

7

Private Open Space

Private open space provides a number of benefits. Functionally, it can offer a visual buffer around or between homes, as well as space for growing flowers or vegetables, drying washing, doing minor repair jobs, airing clothes, keeping pets, or enclosing a toddler at play. Symbolically, such space is a piece of the environment, partially or totally in view of neighbors and passersby, that we can personalize and make our own. Psychologically, these functional and symbolic activities can be a welcome relief from stressful work activities or tense in-house relations.

Reviewing the U.S. experience, Franklin Becker notes that residents of low-income housing tend to personalize the exterior of their homes in order to disassociate themselves from the negative overall image their housing conveys. "Fewer instances of personalization occur in high-income apartments where the building itself conveys high status, respectability, and worth" (Becker, 1977, 52). Becker also finds more evidence of personalization (fences, outdoor lighting, patio furniture, and gardens) in low-income projects with well-defined private entrances or yards than in projects with no prior cues to delimitation of territory (Becker, 1974). Other studies and observations in many housing projects confirm this finding.

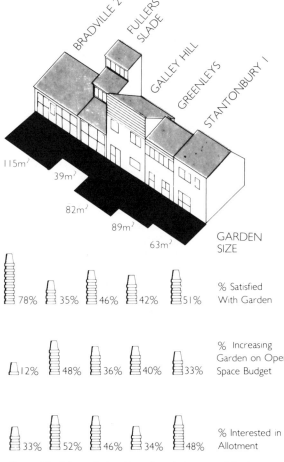

GARDEN SIZE AND ALLOTMENTS

Figure 73. The relationship of yard size to satisfaction and the desire for an allotment (victory garden) in a British New Town neighborhood (Source: Residential . . . , 1975)

53. Yard amenities

Provide a private garden, yard, patio, or balcony for every unit, appropriately furnished with amenities to facilitate its use.

Studies made throughout the English-speaking world indicate that most households consider it important to have some private open space attached to the house (Architecture . . . , 1966, 1969; Byrom, 1972; Committee . . . , 1972; Cooper, 1970b; Cooper and Corrie, 1970; Department . . . , 1971a, 1974b, 1972a; Gilmour et al., 1970; Griffin, 1973; Halkett, 1976; Ministry . . . , 1967c, 1979b; Norcross and Hysom, 1968; Parish and Parish, 1972; Shankland . . . , 1969; United States Department . . . , 1975). The most frequent uses by low- to moderate-income families are for drying clothes, sitting out, gardening, having toddlers play, and storing things (Architecture . . . , 1966; Auckland . . . , 1974b; Department . . . , 1971a; Ministry . . . , 1967c, 1969a, 1969b; Parish and Parish, 1972). Well-tended yards may have beneficial side effects. A Greater London Council report concludes that private yards, as well as being a source of pleasure to individual residents, cumulatively create an impression of security, of value to the estate as a whole (Shankland, 1977a).

Possible design responses

The appropriate amenities to facilitate use of ground-level space include:

- A level hard-surfaced area (deck or patio) for chairs and table adjacent to the house
- An extensive area of bare soil for plants, lawn, trees, and so forth
- A back porch roof, especially in snowy or rainy regions
- A lockable storage shed for garden equipment, bikes, and so forth
- A clothesline—in small patios or gardens a rotary line or one that folds against the wall of the house
- An outside tap with adequate provision for drainage (The design of taps should be carefully considered if use by children, physically disabled, or elderly arthritic people is expected.)
- A protected electrical outlet for use with radios, lighting, power tools, and so forth
- In hot climates pergolas, trellises, or lattice-work over porches to support deciduous vines, which can provide shade in summer but shed leaves to admit winter sun

---

See also: House on its own land (13), Territorial expression (29), Common space boundary (77), Yard play (87), Yard surveillance (220).

Figure 74. A yard that accommodates family needs yet is convenient to maintain is an essential component of successful housing design.

54. Access to private open space

The private open space of all units should be visually and functionally accessible from inside the dwelling.

Residents of above-ground dwellings tend to neglect private ground-level outdoor space assigned to them to which they have no direct access (Department . . . , 1981b). Where physical access is straightforward and direct, adults and children are more likely to use private open space for casual leisure pursuits, brief walks to look at the plants, or short periods of play between school and dinner. If there is clear visual access, interior space will be perceived as enlarged (the Japanese notion of borrowed scenery); planting and flowers can be appreciated from inside the unit.

Use of private open space for children's play depends less on its size than on its intimacy and security, its location close to the kitchen, and its ease of access to main pedestrian routes (Department . . . , 1973a; Ministry . . . , 1967a). Small children need to be watched; so it is generally preferable to locate gardens adjacent to the kitchen and/or living room.

Possible design responses

- Locate kitchen, family room, or living room windows so that one may look directly into private open spaces.

- Provide sliding glass doors leading via direct level access into private open spaces from the dwelling.
- Avoid sliding glass doors in high-crime areas or in cold climates, where they tend to freeze shut.

See also: House on its own land (13), Yard play (87), Sliding doors (206).

55. Yard linked to common space

The needs of children—and their parents—will be best served if there is direct access from a fenced yard to a safe communal play area.

Private open spaces should be located so that small children's play flows uninterruptedly from the dwelling to the yard and from the yard into

Figure 75. An enclosed yard visible from kitchen or living room permits easy supervision of small children. Direct access from the yard to communal play space allows older children greater freedom to explore.

safe communal recreation spaces (Architecture . . . , 1969; Eikos Group, 1980; Ministry . . . , 1967c; Shankland . . . , 1969). Even where yards are adjacent to communal spaces, if no gates allow direct access to them, these spaces are rarely used, and children tend to cluster around entrances on the opposite (often the street) side of dwellings. In one Canadian study of one hundred ten family co-op units, children report negative perceptions of play areas where fences isolate playgrounds from backyards (Eikos Group, 1980).

Possible design responses

- Provide gates between yards and communal areas.
- Provide childproof latches on gates (to prevent toddlers from escaping).
- Provide barrier-free access between private and communal open space so that elderly and disabled people can also use the spaces.

See also: Group territory (72), Interesting landscaped spaces (73), Common space at the back (76), Common space boundary (77), Yard surveillance (220).

56. "Front" and "back" customs

Design and delimit front and back yards according to locally accepted norms of "front" and "back" behavior.

Culture, class, and region considerably affect the use of the front and back of the dwelling. In British middle-class housing the front is frequently developed as a display garden, and the back is largely devoted to flowers, lawn, and a patio (for summer tea and drinks). Vegetables are likely to be screened from view in a kitchen garden. In British working-class neighborhoods, though, there may be no front gardens and the back is likely to be used for flowers, vegetables, storage, and a small shelter to house some hobby or money-earning sideline such as raising pigeons or doing electrical repairs.

In the United States and Canada the use of the front and back varies by region, life-style, and class. In California suburbs front yards are primarily lawns and maintenance-free shrubs.

Figure 76. Among British families it is customary to put sleeping infants outside in the fresh air during part of the day.

The Pacific Northwest has a tradition of flower gardens, in part because of the wet climate. Middle-income dwellers generally tend to develop the front for display but rarely use it. The more private backs, in contrast, often comprise an extensive patio, with access from the kitchen and/or family room for barbecuing, sun bathing, having drinks, and so forth.

In U.S. working-class and lower-income neighborhoods the stoop and the front steps, porch, or yard space are used for play, for socializing, and for watching the world go by. When people from such neighborhoods move into multifamily projects, they may bring out folding chairs (and sometimes tables for cards or drinks) to the entry that most resembles "the front," even if it faces the parking lot. Not only are norms variable, but the situation is not static. Even in Britain, where the flower garden is virtually *the* national art form, the younger generation is not as keen on this pursuit as its elders. Open-plan schemes, where lease or sale agreements preclude territorial definition and individual landscaping at the front, are apparently popular in some upper-middle-income developments.

Young singles (age twenty-five to thirty-five) in rental accommodations are rarely interested in gardening, but the ablebodied elderly frequently are. In San Francisco, a multiethnic city, a housing scheme for elderly Jewish people found few interested in garden plots, but schemes with residents of predominantly Chinese origin could not provide enough.

With so many regional, cultural, and life-style variations and with changing norms, a definitive guideline is inappropriate. Designers and clients must deduce local idiosyncratic needs, offer a choice of solutions, and provide flexibility in lease or sales agreements.

See also: Back and front entries (41).

57. Privacy screening

Provide screening for yards where private activities are likely to occur and to delimit private from communal open space.

Despite variations in what yards are used for, the need for clear boundaries between one's private open space and adjacent uses is wide-

Figure 77. An adequate barrier between private and communal open space is essential in housing for families with children.

spread. Numerous studies document the emergence of neighbor tensions where definitions between private and public spaces and between adjacent private spaces are unclear (Barker, 1976; Becker, 1974; Byrom, 1972; Committee . . . , 1972; Connell, 1975; Cooper, 1972b, 1975; Department . . . , 1971b; Gilmour et al., 1970; MacLeod, 1977; Ministry . . . , 1967c; O'Brien, 1972; Parish and Parish, 1972; Sandvik,

Shellenbarger, and Stevenson, 1973; Shankland . . . , 1969; Worthen, 1975). Delimitation is especially necessary where private open spaces abut onto a communal landscaped area. In a Massachusetts housing development, where the builder eliminated patio fences to cut costs, the omission had serious consequences: Where patios faced onto interior communal green space, few residents attempted to plant or personalize

their space. Only a quarter of the ground-floor residents sat outside on their patios, compared to three-quarters of those who lived above ground, with semiprivate balconies. The sliding glass doors providing access from living rooms to the unfenced patios, which otherwise might have enhanced the setting, only served to create a "fishbowl" feeling. The authors conclude that the effects of fencing for privacy are "a lesson in priorities: architects and developers must both begin to realize the importance of 'foolish little' things that are fundamental to a livable environment" (Zeisel and Griffin, 1975, 63). Privacy in a dwelling's adjacent open space is an important contributor to overall housing satisfaction (Architecture . . . , 1966; Becker, 1974; Byrom, 1972; Connell, 1975; Cooper, 1971, 1975; Lansing et al., 1970; Parish and Parish, 1972; Shankland . . . , 1967; Wirthensohn, 1976), and visual privacy, which requires some sort of screening, is more important than auditory privacy. However, most people dislike feeling totally cut off from activity outside their yard or patio (Eikos Group, 1980), and the smaller the area, the less suitable is a solid wooden fence or brick wall because it can cut out all views, create shadows, and result in unpleasant, pitlike space. For this reason slatted fences, which permit fleeting glimpses, are often preferable to solid ones. Residents generally prefer to see outside without letting outsiders see into their whole space (Byrom, 1970; Cooper, 1970b; Ministry . . . , 1967c, 1969a), especially if they are at home most of the day (for example, the elderly and parents of preschool children).

Figure 78. A barrier may not be so necessary where the dwellings are for adults only or the elderly.

Possible design responses

- Provide fences 5 feet (1.5 m) minimum height for complete privacy.
- Provide a hinged or louvered section of the fence that can be left open when necessary.
- Provide a fence or wall with a cutout or window that can be filled in, planted with climbing plants, or left open, as desired.
- Provide a fence one section of which is high (for privacy) and one low (for supervision).
- Provide a wide gate that can be left open for child surveillance.
- Provide semiprivate fencing, slatted so that fleeting views in and out are possible (6 inch [150 mm] slats and 2.0 inch [50 mm] gaps).
- Provide open trellis fencing that residents can plant creepers or vines to grow over.
- Provide brick or stone walls, as long as the resultant yard or patio space does not become too shaded or, if it is small, pitlike.
- Provide hedging if residents have the time and energy necessary for its maintenance.

See also: Territorial expression (29), Added privacy (30), Privacy planting (176), Yard surveillance (220).

58. Overlooking

Arrange dwellings so that windows of neighboring units do not overlook private open spaces likely to be used for private activities.

Figure 79. In moderate- to high-density housing some overlooking may be unavoidable, although overlooking front or display gardens is preferable because these are rarely used for private activities.

Designs that carefully provide adequate fencing around patios or yards may still violate residents' needs for privacy if windows of neighboring units look directly into those spaces. This is especially true if units have been staggered and neighbors' bedroom windows look directly down onto patios.

Possible design responses

- In above-ground units provide high-level windows that admit medium to distant views but inhibit overlooking into adjacent yards.
- Locate walls, fences, trellises, and boundary line trees to interrupt views from upstairs windows.
- Stagger units and locate windows so that overlooking is not possible.

See also: Added privacy (30), Neighborly surveillance (42), Casual meetings (129), Privacy planting (176).

59. Orientation to Sun

People will use only private outdoor spaces that are oriented for a comfortable daytime temperature.

This may seem obvious, but we include this guideline because some multifamily housing is still designed without adequate consideration for this factor. In relatively cool San Francisco, residents in one study complained that their north-facing patios were wasted space because no one ever used them (Cooper, 1970). In Australia buildings are often oriented east-west, with careful attention to rooflines and shading, so that the winter sun will warm northern windows but severe summer sun will be excluded. In such hot climates of the Southern Hemisphere the yard ideally faces south, the cool side of the house in summer.

Possible design responses

- In mild or temperate regions ensure that private open space receives summer sun.
- In hot climates orient private open space so that it is shaded in summer.
- Locate outdoor living areas according to local climate conditions to provide the most comfortable outdoor conditions in both summer and winter.
- Use building elements to modify climatic conditions. For example, fences may stop cold winds but still allow winter sun onto a patio; pergolas with deciduous vines may block summer sun but allow winter sun to penetrate.
- Plant trees to modify climatic conditions (for example, deciduous trees that block summer sun in hot climates but whose branch density is open enough to permit adequate sun penetration in winter).

See also: Outdoor drying (138), Microclimate (173), Privacy planting (176).

60. Square backyards

To facilitate use, make private open space approximately square.

The bottom end of a long, narrow yard tends to be neglected or used for storage. Privacy is also a problem; for example, in one British neighborhood where all units had gardens of nearly identical length, almost three quarters of the residents felt overlooked where the garden was very narrow (22.5 feet [6.9 m]), but less than a

Figure 80. Yards that are roughly square or broadly rectangular are generally more desirable than those that are long and narrow.

third did where gardens were 28.5 feet (8.7 m) wide (Residential . . . , 1975). In another neighborhood satisfaction regarding size varied considerably from less than 40 percent satisfied in narrow-frontaged houses, 14 feet 9 inches (4.5 m), to 100 percent where the frontage was 29 feet 6 inches (9.0 m).

Possible design responses

- Avoid narrow house lots.
- Where narrow, long yards are unavoidable, take extra care to provide private boundaries between adjacent units.

See also: Front of modest size (63).

61. Yard size

Where minimally sized yards are inevitable, compensate residents with access to communal space.

Residents tend to complain when yards are less than 200–300 square feet (18.6 to 27.9 sq m) (Architecture . . . , 1966; Department . . . , 1971a, 1972c; Ministry . . . , 1969b; Parish and Parish, 1972; Residential . . . , 1975). In Britain, however, the desirable yard size seems to be declining, or at least expectations are becoming lower (Architecture . . . , 1969; Residential . . . , 1975). In the United States, as suburban housing and land and construction costs rise, yards are becoming smaller. One British new town study concludes that a smaller garden is acceptable provided that activities generally concentrated in the garden can still be conducted elsewhere (for example, in communal landscaped space or allotment [victory] gardens) (Residential . . . , 1975). In many Western countries allotments or community gardens satisfy the increasing interest in "growing our own."

Possible design responses

- Provide yards with minimum size of 323 square feet (30 sq m) for families or large

Figure 81. Common landscaped space that is attractively designed and well maintained is, for many residents in U.S. clustered housing, more than adequate compensation for small, private yards. Unfortunately, in this scheme the design does not allow direct access from patios into the shared space.

households and 215 square feet (20 sq m) for other households.
- If yards must be below this minimum size, ensure that shared landscaped space is enclosed, attractive, identifiable, immediately accessible from the dwelling, and furnished with needed communal facilities (for example, play space, seating, and attractive footpaths).
- If yards must be below the minimum size, provide space near home for allotments or victory gardens.

See also: Woonerfs (70), Adjacent public facilities (71), Interesting landscaped spaces (73), Common space at the back (76), Community garden (141).

62. Display garden

Provide residents with the opportunity of maintaining a semipublic (or display) garden around the front entry.

In a British new town, where the development corporation maintained open frontages, almost a third of those surveyed in six typical neighborhoods wanted to work on them themselves (Residential . . . , 1975). In a detailed study of a U.S. rental housing project in which residents were required to take care of their open-land frontages, the majority of residents wanted to do it themselves, despite their low incomes (Cooper, 1975). A recent study of a high-crime housing project in Los Angeles confirms these

Figure 82. In these British row houses residents have created attractive flower gardens around their front doors.

findings (Berkeley . . . , 1980), as does a study in the eastern United States that found a high correlation between gardening and crime-related outcomes and that "signs of appropriation are proven powerful security features if they reflect the continuing presence of the resident." Although planting was found to be a "powerful territorial sign," display of ornaments was not. Planting implies continuing and current investment (Dockett, Brower, and Taylor, 1983). By taking care of the front yard a resident can manifestly be a good housekeeper and legitimately be outside, casually contacting neighbors or passersby. This in turn may lead to a greater level of casual surveillance and community responsibility.

Beyond these interpersonal considerations, there is an aesthetic one. Although avid rose or dahlia growers might not phrase it in such terms, the front yards where they grow their flowers are clearly displays, and display gardens can make a substantial contribution to the attractiveness of the street scene. Project management's reason for insisting on landscaping the front yards before occupancy or on doing the maintenance themselves is often either a belief that residents lack good taste or a compulsive desire for aesthetic conformity. In either case management is interfering with individual freedom of choice, and designers might well question such a policy.

Possible design responses

- Provide yard space around the front entry to every ground-level unit.

- Where space is very limited, provide planters or space to place flowerpots or window boxes.
- Locate at least one window so that the front yard can be seen and enjoyed from inside the dwelling.
- When initial landscaping is installed, provide lease or sales agreements that give residents the right to modify it.
- Ensure barrier-free design and provide low-maintenance vegetation and materials or raised planter boxes to enable frail elderly and physically disabled residents to take care of their own spaces.
- Provide opportunities (possibly in the lease or rental agreement) for the sharing of responsibilities among residents who wish to help frail or disabled neighbors with more strenuous work.
- Avoid locating structures, such as carports or garages, so that they completely block front yards from public view.
- Do not fence front (street-oriented) yards; residents can add symbolic boundary fencing or planting as they desire.
- Allow front yards to be sloped or terraced toward the street to enhance their display function.

See also: View from the window (12), Exterior design control (19), Chapter 5—Personalization, Transitional filters (39), Yard play (87), Meeting neighbors (130), Personalized landscape (180).

63. Front of modest size

Front-entry yards should be deep enough for privacy but not so large as to inhibit personalization.

Where front yards face onto a street or traffic way in the traditional pattern, setbacks must be designed with care; the relationship of depth and privacy is not simple. Factors influencing privacy include the width of the dwelling (that is, how much of the dwelling is exposed to the street), the amount of passing vehicular and pedestrian traffic, legal and financial restrictions on residents' opportunities to fence yards and plant gardens, and privacy requirements in the street-facing room.

"More open space is better" is a planning cliché that is truer in theory than in practice. In a British study of two-story row house neighbor-

hoods in Milton Keynes (Residential . . . , 1975), the only substantial group of residents who considered their open frontage a waste of space had very deep and relatively narrow front yards. Few of these yards were personalized, although in the same neighborhood residents with smaller front yards were likely to lay claim to them and plant them attractively.

Possible design responses

- Avoid large front yards, which require a great deal of effort to maintain and seem overwhelming so that some residents do not even make a start.
- Avoid long and narrow front yards.

See also: Chapter 5—Personalization, Neighborly surveillance (42).

Figure 83. In this neighborhood the larger front yards (background) were not personalized, and one-third of the residents considered them a "waste of space." Narrower frontages at the corner of each courtyard were more frequently fenced and planted with flowers. (Galley Hill, Milton Keynes New Town)

64. Above-ground balconies

Units above ground level should have access to private balconies of usable dimensions.

Most apartment dwellers in all climates prefer having a balcony to having additional interior space with no balcony (Cooper, 1970b; Department . . . , 1972a; Ministry . . . , 1970). In the Northern Hemisphere, however, interior space is probably preferable to a north balcony. Balconies should be generous in size; smaller balconies tend to degenerate into storage space.

Possible design responses

- Design balconies no smaller than 10 feet (3m) by 6 feet (1.8 m).
- Provide balconies only if they can have an east, west, or south orientation (in the Northern Hemisphere).
- Ensure that balconies are reasonably private by providing space, side wings, or vegetation buffers.

See also: Overlooking (58), Orientation to sun (59), Balcony play (88).

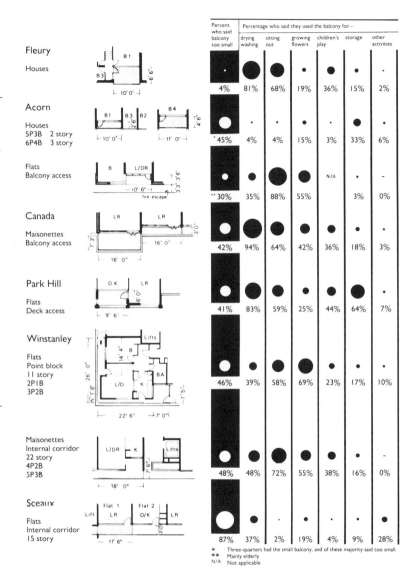

Figure 84. Satisfaction with, and use of, balconies of different dimensions in several British housing schemes. (Source: Department . . . , 1972a)

	Percent. who said balcony too small	Percentage who said they used the balcony for:—					
		drying washing	sitting out	growing flowers	children's play	storage	other activities
Fleury — Houses	4%	81%	68%	19%	36%	15%	2%
Acorn — Houses 5P3B 2 story, 6P4B 3 story	*45%	4%	4%	15%	3%	33%	6%
Flats — Balcony access	**30%	35%	88%	55%	N/A	3%	0%
Canada — Maisonettes Balcony access	42%	94%	64%	42%	36%	18%	3%
Park Hill — Flats Deck access	41%	83%	59%	25%	44%	64%	7%
Winstanley — Flats Point block 11 story 2P1B 3P2B	46%	39%	58%	69%	23%	17%	10%
Maisonettes Internal corridor 22 story 4P2B 5P3B	48%	48%	72%	55%	38%	16%	0%
Sceaux — Flats Internal corridor 15 story	87%	37%	2%	19%	4%	9%	28%

*   Three-quarters had the small balcony, and of these majority said too small.
**   Mainly elderly
N/A   Not applicable

65. Balcony off living room

Where possible, locate the balcony adjacent to the living room.

Balconies tend to be used more, especially by adults, when they have glass doors and lead off a living room (Gatt, 1978). The notion of the "master" or "mistress" of the house relaxing on the bedroom balcony is a myth of the media. Glass doors allow the balcony to become an extension of the living room and make it seem larger; they also permit plants, flowers, and so forth on the balcony to be appreciated from inside the dwelling.

Possible design responses

- Use sliding glass doors, except in high-crime areas or in very cold climates (where they tend to freeze shut).
- Provide recessed, rather than cantilevered, balconies for greater privacy and protection.
- Provide solid or semisolid walls between balconies to enhance privacy.

See also: Access to private open space (54), Balcony play (88), Sliding doors (206).

66. Balcony drainage

Ensure that balconies are adequately drained.

Drainage is important not only for rain and snow, but also to permit watering of plants.

Possible design responses

- Ensure that storm water from one balcony is not directed onto the balcony floor below it before reaching an exterior pipe.
- Locate drainage pipes so that they do not gush directly into landscaped areas or across public footpaths.
- Make sure the balcony is designed so that it will drain away from the dwelling.

8

Common Open Space and the Needs of Children

One of the potential aesthetic and social benefits of medium- or high-density housing is that clustering units onto part of a site allows other parts to be left in their natural state or to be landscaped into attractive communal areas. This is fundamentally different from streets of detached or attached houses, where every parcel of buildable land is divided up into individually owned lots.

The first successful contemporary model of housing combined with communal open space was designed by Clarence Stein and Henry Wright in Radburn, New Jersey, in the 1920s. Although repeated in a few other locations in the next decade (for example, Baldwin Hills, Los Angeles, and the New Deal Greenbelt towns), this form of site layout was virtually forgotten in North America until the development of suburban cluster housing in the 1960s and 1970s.

Instead, the idea of traffic-segregated layouts with communal landscaped space was taken up with enthusiasm in Western Europe and England. The new postwar suburbs of Vällingby and Farsta, outside Stockholm, were almost entirely planned from this viewpoint; so were the later phases of the first set of British new towns (Stevenage, Harlow, and Basildon). Studies evaluating the success of these first British Radburn-type layouts showed that a majority of residents liked them; but one objective was usually not achieved as planned: While landscaped areas meant for play remained virtually unused, many children played on roads and culs-de-sac, and an appreciable proportion of parents understandably worried about their safety (Miller, Courtis,

and Cook, 1965; Miller and Cook, 1967; Ministry . . . , 1968b).

Despite these failings, the values of Radburn-type layouts were accepted without argument, and planners and designers persisted in modifying and improving the components of pedestrianized layouts. In 1958 Stevenage New Town Corporation adopted a policy of traffic and pedestrian segregation in residential areas. In an evaluative survey of the first implementation of this policy (Architecture . . . , 1969), the Pin Green neighborhood of thirty-six hundred dwellings (mostly terraced houses), researchers from Edinburgh University studied layouts that improved on earlier Radburn-type schemes in the following ways: Private and communal spaces were clearly demarcated; landscaped spaces were easily entered from dwellings and comprised interesting sequences of large and small open spaces with paths suitable for playing on, equipped play areas, and safe linkages to neighborhood shops and schools (see Figure 17). The study revealed that 85 percent of the children used these communal open spaces for play; only 15 percent played on roads and parking areas. Parents and teachers appreciated the positive advantages of the layouts, and the child accident rate was half that of a nearby street-oriented (nonsegregated) layout (see Figure 16).

Other studies in Britain and the United States document similar rates of children's use of communal areas and correspondingly positive reactions from parents. The earlier "failures" in child safety are clearly attributable to communal spaces not being made attractive enough for

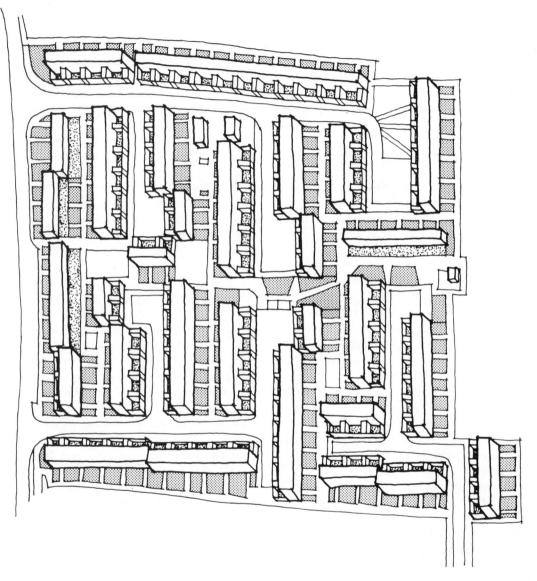

Figure 85. An influential postwar British clustered housing scheme where the designer expected children would play on the pedestrian open space. (Source: Ministry . . . , 1968b)

Figure 86. In fact residents perceived these spaces as their front lawns and discouraged the play of children.

Figure 87. Children found the hard-surfaced open spaces of the garage courts more to their liking. (Woodway Lane, Coventry)

children and do not invalidate the Radburn principles. Merely laying out some grass between two sets of houses and expecting children to flock to it reflects a naiveté about what children actually do when they play.

Children are more deeply affected by the environment than any other age group. They may be physiologically and psychologically harmed by constant restrictions on their play and movement within it (Jephcott with Robinson, 1971; Perez and Hart, 1980). Children learn from the environment what society values, for the environment itself is a potent communication medium (Becker, 1977). If a housing environment implies that kids are low-priority users, they will decode the message as "we do not count." Vandalism could be looked on as a form of nonverbal protest against environments that are hostile to the young (Ward, 1973).

Three principal factors render an environment suitable for child rearing: (1) direct access to private open space for easily supervised outdoor play by small children, (2) direct, safe access to an area for communal outdoor play for school-age and older children, and (3) reasonable auditory and visual privacy so that children's daytime noise and prying eyes or infants' nighttime cries do not disturb the neighbors.

One study indicates that children in aboveground (walk-up) apartments went outside less than those in nearby row houses and therefore suffered higher rates of diseases caused by lack of vitamin D (sunlight). Their mothers suffered higher rates of psychoneurotic complaints (Fanning, 1967). Another study, by a doctor with a

Figure 88. Buildings were not placed so as to enclose and define communal green space, which formed 60 percent of this neighborhood. In an evaluative study 90 percent of the residents said they would have preferred a reduction in the size of the communal outdoor spaces and reallocation of the land saved for larger gardens, play areas, and allotments (victory gardens). (Fullers Slade, Milton Keynes New Town)

practice in a Liverpool estate, reveals that mothers isolated in five- to eight-story deck-access blocks exhibit relatively high rates of psychiatric disturbance and that their children tend to suffer from respiratory ailments caused in part by lack of fresh air and sun. These mothers fear to let their children out to play on vandalized decks, stairways, and elevators (Goodman, 1974). Several studies show that lack of auditory privacy causes parents to restrict children's indoor play severely. This may limit outlets for aggression and creativity, lead to tension between children and irritable adults, and encourage sedentary, passive activities such as TV viewing (Cappon, 1971).

Basic Needs of Children

We discuss the play needs of children in residential settings at some length here to correct an imbalance: In the past they were largely ignored.

1. Children need safe, uninhibited outdoor play for their physiological and mental health.
2. Parents need to be able to allow their children outside without constant, close supervision.
3. The environment around children's homes needs to be safe from traffic, pollution, and unnecessary physical and social hazards.
4. Children should be able to experience the pleasures of finding bugs, picking leaves, smelling flowers, collecting things, and so on without their parents or the management harassing them. Through such contact with nature they may develop, among other

things, an understanding of basic ecological principles.

5. Children need to create private spaces for themselves (for example, tree houses, forts, or clubhouses) on wild or unmaintained ground away from public view.
6. Children need easy, casual access to other children without a formal invitation to play.
7. Children need places in the communal environment that are undeniably their territories where they can expect to find other children.
8. Children need to be able to move around their home neighborhoods safely and to take little trips farther and farther from home to gain a sense of independence.

Many of these needs were met naturally in rural settings. Only in the city are normal childhood activities such as exploring, climbing trees, building dens, digging holes, damming streams, and lighting camp fires labeled delinquent or antisocial. But if no standard urban (or suburban) setting is ideal for meeting these needs of children, clustered housing with direct access from the home to safe and attractive communal areas is clearly the best alternative. Hence guidelines in this chapter deal jointly with the provision of common open space and the general outdoor needs of children. Later chapters deal more specifically with the landscaping and furnishing of common open space, the particular needs of different age groups of children, the design of play equipment areas, and the outdoor needs of adults.

Common open space cannot always be landscaped. In new or rehabilitated clustered housing in inner areas common open space may be available only through the rehabilitation of surrounding streets and pavements. Since the pioneering work of Jane Jacobs, who refocused attention on the much-maligned street as a place for children, other researchers have looked at how the street is used (Appleyard and Lintell, 1972; Zerner, 1977) and made recommendations for its redesign (Jacobs and Jacobs, 1980; Weininger, 1980). The most heartening changes hail from the Netherlands, where "woonerfs" have restored the balance between pedestrians and vehicles on the street (Woonerf, 1977, 1978; Verwer, 1980).

The first part of this chapter deals with the street as communal open space; the latter part concerns landscaped common areas.

Figure 89. The residents in this neighborhood were highly satisfied with their courtyards because they were human in scale, accessible only to residents through their backyards, provided for preschool play, and gave the scheme a "desirable open feeling." (Stantonbury IV, Milton Keynes New Town)

67. Pedestrian precinct

Within reasonable bounds provide as extensive a traffic-free area as possible.

Children aged two or three may want to range 30 or 40 feet (9 or 12 m) from their dwelling on tricycles; at five or six pulling a wagon around the block alone is a great adventure. Children learn self-reliance by ranging farther and farther away from home. We can translate this into environmental terms by providing an area of private open space attached to the house for initial exploration and a farther area, still within the aura of home, for broader patterns of play.

The relative danger from vehicular traffic is a primary consideration in both areas. Research suggests that a limited street-access pattern has distinct safety advantages. In a study in which accident rates in a U.S. grid pattern neighborhood and in a limited-access neighborhood ("curving streets, culs-de-sac, and through traffic routed around") matched for area and population were compared, the rates were found to be 77.7 per year and 10.2 per year, respectively (Marks, 1957, p. 314).

Safety considerations notwithstanding, children should be presented with an environment that is varied and tempting to explore, that they can comprehend, and that has an inherent feeling of enclosure and security. Open space in itself is not enough. In one neighborhood of Milton Keynes New Town (Fullers Slade), where

60 percent of the estate is landscaped in sweeping greenswards (which, significantly, are not enclosed or identified with any particular group of dwellings), smaller children tend to play in clusters on the culs-de-sac, where row houses create some feeling of enclosure and of being close to home, and to ignore the common landscaped spaces. In another neighborhood, where small groups of houses enclose child-scale green courtyards that contain play equipment, children play in these safe and attractive areas and very few are attracted to the streets (Residential . . . , 1975). (See figs. 88 and 89.)

Possible design responses

- Provide vehicle access via short culs-de-sac and non—through streets.
- Ensure that the natural focus of dwellings is equally onto the street and onto the common landscaped areas.
- Provide a reasonable balance between landscaped common open space and private open space so that one is not provided at the expense of the other.
- Provide play spaces and footpaths in communal landscaped areas.

See also: Children safe from cars (3), Woonerfs (70), Interesting landscaped spaces (73), Comfortable space dimensions (74), Vehicular segregation (148), Superblocks (215), Incorporating the street (216).

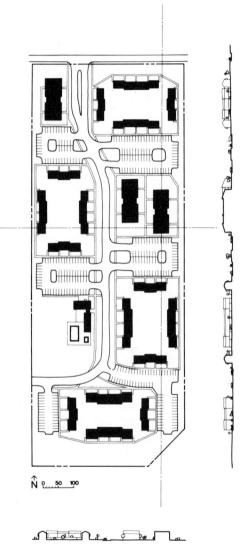

N 0   50   100

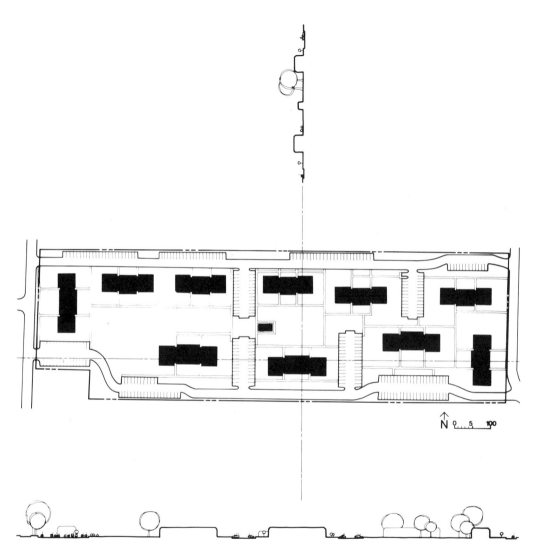

Figures 90 and 91. In these two schemes (U.S. subsidized housing) residents were highly satisfied with site design: Parking is provided close to the dwelling; yet dwellings look out on, and enclose, attractive, human-scale, landscaped spaces. (Source: Francescato, 1980)

N 0   5   100

68. Traffic management

Reduce the speed and volume of traffic on residential streets.

Children will always at times be attracted to streets, whether or not they have access to landscaped courtyards and play areas. On a small inner-city site peripheral parking is a high priority; whatever common space remains can then be designed for safe use by children. But on a more spacious and lower density site complete segregation of vehicular traffic may not even be desirable. In either case traffic management (slowing speed and reducing volume) is crucial for children's safety.

In neighborhoods that limit traffic access, children may start to be careless and need to be shielded from the heavier traffic flows of peripheral distributor roads. Even where segregated sidewalks and culs-de-sac are provided, sidewalks should be provided along all traffic ways as well.

Possible design responses

- Employ appropriate means to slow traffic, such as
  - Narrowing roadways
  - Limiting the length of straight stretches
  - Creating culs-de-sac
  - Closing off streets
  - Placing speed bumps at intervals in the roadway
  - Erecting barriers to eliminate through traffic
  - Routing through traffic around the periphery of the neighborhood
- Place adequate sidewalks along all streets (see next guideline).

See also: Children safe from cars (3), Woonerfs (70), Vehicle speeds (149), Incorporating the street (216).

Figure 92. One of many traffic barriers in Berkeley, California, which have successfully transformed residential through streets into quiet and safe culs-de-sac.

69. Sidewalk activities

Design sidewalks as part of community space

Since the widespread use of the car, the street has increasingly been seen as the domain of vehicles, with children's needs relegated, at least officially, to houses, yards, parks, and schools. Recently, however, planners and designers have started to redress the imbalance between vehicles and people. The street—and more particularly the sidewalk—has begun to reassert itself as a legitimate community space (Jacobs and Jacobs, 1980; Jacobs and Charney, 1975; Weiser, 1980).

In fact city children never really stopped using the sidewalks. According to one study (Ward, 1978), nine- and eleven-year-olds in three streets in Haifa, Israel, are aware of the continuity of the "objective" or planner's street, but more meaningful to them is the subunit they refer to as "my street." This area ranges from 165 to 490 feet (50 to 150 m) from the home (in particular traffic-segregated areas, 1,300 feet [300 m]) and serves as an extension of their private domain. Its physical/functional structure is defined, like that of the house, by walls, surfaces, and objects located in it, with particular attention paid to features an adult might pass by and barely notice—the fence, street sign, edge of the sidewalk, garbage can, steps, paving stones, and fire hydrant. On "my street" children do what adults normally do in (or from) the home: watch people go by, talk to friends, play quiet games.

The street truly can be a dwelling place for children, but for this to happen on all streets we may have to start perceiving them as places to be and not just places to pass through.

The extent of street play depends on sidewalk width as well as on the relative availability

Figure 93. The sidewalk outside the house is an obvious and natural place for children to play.

of alternative play areas. The sidewalks of Brooklyn and other congested parts of New York City, for example, prove to be excellent locations for play, despite heavy traffic on adjacent roads, because their width easily accommodates passing adult pedestrians as well as group play. Jane Jacobs (1961, 86–87) describes such play:

> An immense amount of both loitering and play goes on in shallow sidewalk niches out of the line of moving pedestrian feet. . . . If the sidewalks are skimped, rope jumping is the first play casualty. Roller skating, tricycle and bicycle riding are the next casualties. The narrower the sidewalks, the more sedentary incidental play becomes. The more frequent too become sporadic forays by children into the vehicular roadways.

Jacobs recommends that inner-city sidewalks be 35 feet (10.6 m) wide but concedes that even pavements 20 feet (6 m) wide can accommodate a range of play and adult traffic. In an inner-city area where children may be attracted to inner courtyards with play equipment as well as peripheral sidewalks where the "action" is, sidewalks should be about 20 feet (6 m) wide, or a hard-surfaced area should be located near on-street dwelling entries, paralleling the public sidewalk. The total width of the two might then be 20 feet (6 m). In a suburb or new town such sidewalk width is inappropriate because the density of use does not warrant it.

It is important to determine local adult attitudes toward the street. Perez and Hart (1980) found that Hispanic children frequently use the sidewalks close to their Manhattan homes, but children of Irish, Jewish, and Italian descent in the same neighborhood, who are allowed to go to certain parks and playgrounds, have limited access to streets and sidewalks. Black children are mostly confined to the housing projects where they live.

Similarly, a local planning exercise in inner-city, working-class Baltimore failed to attract children off the streets into a new play area at the back of the houses because planners had overlooked the intense, traditional use of the street for playing and adult socializing. In subsequent schemes they recommended reclaiming the street as pedestrian space by reducing traffic speed and volume, widening sidewalks, and designing street furniture to accommodate and withstand play (Brower, 1974; Neighborhood . . . , 1973).

In middle- and upper-class areas there is often a fear of the street and strict instructions to children *not* to play on sidewalks. In such areas a play area at back is more likely to be used. In a Berkeley, California, neighborhood where the middle-class residents of one urban block voluntarily removed their backyard fences to create a single, large communal area, the space was much used and appreciated for children's play, as well as for adult socializing. Play on peripheral sidewalks was minimal (Cavanna, 1974). However, this should not be interpreted as a directive to provide for working-class play at the front and middle-class play at the back. Rarely has anyone thought of play as a legitimate sidewalk activity. If we start to create sidewalks in such a way that playing and socializing are not only legitimized but subtly encouraged, all kinds and ages of people may start to reinterpret this ubiquitous but underrated city environment.

Possible design responses

- Where a sidewalk forms a component of the site plan (and there is no room for traffic-free, landscaped play space), ensure that the sidewalk is wide enough for play and socializing—ideally 20 to 30 feet (6 to 9 m) at the widest points.
- Remember that children relate to small-scale articulations of the environment at their level. Create sidewalk elements that children can touch, smell, climb on, sit on, jump from, sit against, roll model cars down, hide behind, crawl under, and so forth.
- Design entrances to dwellings and the adjacent street to enhance children's perceptions of these as complementary parts of one continuous experience.
- Create articulations in the building facade so that nooks and crannies can be temporarily claimed by groups of children. These spaces can be thought of almost as lay-bys (or pull offs) from a road.
- Create spaces—benches under a tree, a wall at sitting height, or a space for a wheelchair—where adults meeting casually on the street can stop and chat.

- Ensure that the main route of the sidewalk is smooth and unobstructed with good sight lines at intersections for children on bicycles, roller skates, skateboards, and so on.

See also: Playing everywhere (79), Children on the move (80), Hard-surface play (82), Doorstep play (89), Casual meetings (129), Incorporating the street (216).

70. Woonerfs

Consider the controlled mixing of pedestrians and vehicles by means of woonerfs or mixer courts.

Since the early 1970s, the woonerf has been developed in the Netherlands and modified in Britain as the "mixer court." By the elimination of curbs (designating separate zones for vehicles and pedestrians) and by the sensitive combina-

Figure 94. A woonerf in a Dutch city: a street where vehicles and pedestrians use the same space but pedestrians have the right of way.

tion of paving, street furniture, and planting, the woonerf enables slow-moving local traffic and children at play to use the same space without hazard to either.

As often happens with the introduction (or demise) of an environmental innovation, a tragedy triggered serious consideration of woonerfs. A Dutch journalist whose child had been killed in a street accident joined with similarly bereaved parents and formed an action group called Stop de Kindermoord (stop the child murders). They lobbied for traffic restrictions on residential streets, particularly the narrow streets of older Dutch cities where children were especially vulnerable, and published a persuasive and influential brochure in 1975 (Stop . . . , 1975).

By 1980 woonerfs had been developed in many Dutch cities and had spread to many parts of West Germany, Denmark, and Sweden. In Britain the impetus for the development of mixer courts was planners' desire to find a better way of accommodating cars in new, medium-density housing. At least one major developer (Wimpey) now reports that its houses (semidetached) on mixer courts often sell better than do houses with a traditional street or cul-de-sac frontage.

Possible design responses (drawn largely from Dutch experience) [Woonerf . . . , 1978]).

- Create a woonerf only where the normal traffic flow can be accommodated. Dutch experience suggests a limit in the order of one hundred to three hundred vehicles per hour during the peak period.
- Permit only vehicles with an origin or destination within the woonerf.
- Limit their speed to a walking pace of 8 to 12 miles per hour (12 to 20 k.p.h.) by humps (sleeping policemen), sharp bends, or narrow sections of roadway no more than 164 feet (50 m) apart and located to be related to vertical elements in the overall design. Avoid long sight lines, which might encourage higher speeds.
- Avoid causing a vehicle to pass too close to dwellings facing onto the street. (According to Dutch regulations, the minimum distance is 2 feet [0.6 m].)
- Avoid cues—different paving, long curbs, separate roadways—that seem to separate moving vehicles and pedestrians. The whole of the street is the pedestrian's domain. If any feature—a plant or paving—suggests a footpath, create breaks in this feature clearly visible to motorists at 80-foot (25 m) intervals.
- Create a pleasant milieu for pedestrians with paving, planting, street furniture, play equipment, and so on.
- Identify and separate play equipment areas from traffic by bollards, fences, or chains. However, do not create the impression that such areas are the only place for children; the whole street is their domain.
- Constrict the vehicular portion of the street in sections where children are allowed to play over the full width of the street.
- Do not restrict visibility with vertical elements. (Planters used to indicate humps or twists in the roadway should not exceed 2 feet 6 inches [0.75 m]—the height of the hood of a car.)
- Limit parking to locations where it causes no inconvenience to other street users, and inhibit it elsewhere by means of obstructions (planters, bollards, bike racks). Because the designation of woonerfs normally leads to reduced parking capacity, they should not be developed if there are not adequate special parking facilities nearby.
- Designate parking spaces with distinctive paving.
- Design lighting so that speed-reducing features are clearly visible at night. (In Dutch cities lighting poles are 10 feet 2 inches [3.5 m] high, spaced about 82 feet [25 m] apart.)
- Clearly designate entrances and exits of a woonerf by a change in paving or a sign; most people are unfamiliar with the concept.

See also: Children safe from cars (3), Traffic management (68), Vehicle speeds (149), Incorporating the street (216).

71. Adjacent public facilities

In designing or rehabilitating a site of limited dimensions, make maximum use of existing adjacent public space or unused public facilities.

One way of converting public spaces to communal use is to close off streets—permanently or for part of the day. In a successful street closure conversion in San Francisco, for example, five blocks of a street passing through a number of housing projects with high child densities were redesigned as an attractive linear park (Buchanan Street Mall). All the social implications of street closure, however, must be considered. Noise from increased concentration of play may annoy adults; the space may become a gathering place for "undesirable elements"; criminal access to adjacent houses after dark may be facilitated; and residents may resent the lengthening of local car journeys. It may prove more desirable to limit (but not ban) traffic, widen sidewalks, install shade trees and benches, and create more of a community space (Neighborhood . . . , 1973). (See previous guideline.) A San Francisco study of street quality found that the lighter the traffic flow, the greater the likelihood of cross-street neighboring (Appleyard and Lintell, 1972).

Little or underused public facilities are another potential resource for community use, although conversions may require considerable capital investment. In a number of difficult-to-let

Figure 95. A new low-rise, high-density scheme in London made good use of an adjacent redeveloped waterside park.

housing schemes in Britain, redesign proposals include converting unused car-parking areas to space for children's play, ball games, workshops, and storage (Heffernan, 1977). In a San Francisco housing development where an underground garage is unused because of security problems, tenants have requested its conversion to a much-needed gymnasium (Margaret, 1971). The opening of a school yard after hours or on weekends can radically enlarge the open space potential of a congested neighborhood. The problem in cities is less the *lack* of space than the insensitive allocation of space or the inadequate scheduling of the times for its use.

Possible design responses

- Close streets permanently or for part of the day.
- Convert underused adjacent facilities, such as car parking, for children's play.
- Investigate arrangements to enable shared use of school yards after school hours or the communal use of other neighborhood facilities.

See also: Sidewalk activities (69), Woonerfs (70), Children's rights (85), Play on site (101), Off-site facilities (127), Child density (231).

72. Group territory

Recognition of a common open space as the indisputable territory of a group of dwellings provides, for many residents and their children, a needed sense of place and belonging.

Child rearing benefits from the provision of common landscaped space of modest dimensions, every part of which is visible from the dwelling, where children can recognize familiar landmarks and understand that this is "our territory." As they acquire the ability to engage in cooperative play (at three to five years), their need increases for such an environmental setting beyond dwelling and garden, where social encounters and group play can occur naturally. In schemes where such space has been successful all dwellings have had ready access to it (Architecture . . . , 1969; Barker, 1976; Byrom, 1972; Cooper and Corrie, 1970; Cooper and Marcus, 1971; Gilmour et al., 1970; Residential . . . , 1975).

Supervision by adults is facilitated if the space is roughly square or rectangular. Irregular shapes, fragmented open space, large spaces, or multiple exits make supervision difficult. The

Figure 96. When neighbors frequently pass through a space where they see each other and can stop for a chat, the seeds of community are sown.

communal landscaped spaces of two traffic-segregated estates in Stevenage New Town were arranged in tight, fragmented patterns, fulfilling neither of the basic objectives of such areas: visual amenity and a place for children's play. The narrow "alleys" of open space between opposite rows of terraced houses caused too much infringement on privacy and easily allowed children to "disappear" (Architecture . . . , 1969).

A greater territorial sense can develop if residents frequently walk through communal spaces on their way to parking, laundries, recreation facilities, and so forth (Cooper, 1970b; Cooper and Marcus, 1971; Newman, 1972). They begin to feel comfortable in the space, to greet others, and to perceive it almost as an extension of their dwelling. Thus it is essential that the *shortest* distance to parking, shopping, laundries, and play areas be through or around the common open space.

If residents feel comfortable in and responsible for a portion of communal open space, they develop a protective attitude toward landscaping and facilities, thereby providing a significant payoff in lower maintenance costs.

Possible design responses

- Provide communal open spaces that are semienclosed or totally enclosed by the dwellings they serve and can be seen from all those dwellings.
- Ensure that each communal area is clearly the territory of a specific group of dwellings.

- Provide access to communal open space, either directly from the dwelling or via ground-level private open space.
- Design common open spaces that are roughly square or rectangular to enable supervision of children at play.
- Locate pedestrian ways so that adults will walk through communal landscaped areas en route to parking, laundries, and other facilities.
- Restrict the number of households using any one common open space to no more than a hundred.
- Provide direct visual access, preferably from kitchen, living room, or dining room, to common open space.

See also: Space hierarchy (4), Community identity (5), Neighborly surveillance (42), Pedestrian precinct (67), Courtyard width (133), Landscape installation and modification (179), Territorial zones (213), User group territories (227).

73. Interesting landscaped places

Children will be attracted to safe, interior landscaped areas only if they find them more interesting play spaces than surrounding roads or parking areas.

Mere provision of open space is *not* sufficient to fulfill the needs of children (and their parents). Landscaped spaces without the attraction of play equipment, games areas, wide paths for cycling, or other features attractive to children are like hotel lobbies or airport lounges devoid of furniture. Design must pay attention to the spatial organization of the environment, but no less to the landscape elements that furnish it and give it character. Otherwise children will tend to play more frequently on roads and in parking areas, and the common open space will remain unused for play or adult social activity (Architecture . . . , 1969; Barker, 1976; Byrom, 1972; Cooper, 1970b; Cooper and Marcus, 1971; Miller and Cook, 1967; Ministry . . . , 1967c; Sandvik, Shellenbarger, and Stevenson, 1973; Zeisel and Griffin, 1975).

Possible design responses

- Ensure that communal landscaped spaces are
  - Easily accessible from dwellings and attached private open space
  - Within sight of kitchens or other focal places of indoor adult activity
  - Provided with a variety of play equipment
  - Provided with wide, hard-surfaced paths

—Located on the direct route to schools and other off-site facilities
- Ensure that these spaces are large enough to minimize conflicts between groups of children or between children and adults.

See also: Children safe from cars (3), Group territory (72), Comfortable space dimensions (74), Common space at the back (76), Playing everywhere (79), Leftover spaces (83), Children in the landscape (165), User group territories (227).

Figure 97. Children will play in pedestrian spaces only if they are attractively furnished for play and if the design makes clear that their use of such spaces is legitimate.

74. Comfortable space dimensions

The design of comfortable landscaped spaces requires attention to locally accepted notions of size, dimension, and height/width ratios.

"Uncomfortable" common open spaces generally fall into two categories: Either they are too cramped, so that children's play intrudes on dwelling privacy, or they are too large, and children tend to congregate in other, more intimate places (doorways, garages, driveways, and so forth).

The results of a user study in Milton Keynes New Town indicate the following rates of satisfaction with shared landscaped courtyards (Residential . . . , 1975):

Size of Courtyard	Percent Satisfied
1,673–3,337 square yards (1,400–2,790 sq. m)	80
3,061 square yards (2,560 sq. m)	80
1,555 square yards (1,300 sq. m)	55

In a Milton Keynes neighborhood of excessively large courtyards, the great majority of children and adults shunned these spaces and congregated on the opposite (street) side of these dwellings, despite the architect's sketch of how the courtyards were meant to be used (see Figures 98 and 99).

In a highly successful, three-story inner-city redevelopment project in San Francisco the courtyard that best accommodated children's and adults' needs—which felt enclosed without feeling claustrophobic—was a modest 150 by 150 feet (46 by 46 m). A recent evaluation of this and other U.S. medium-density projects (from the viewpoint of site design and children's needs) recommended that courtyard spaces be squarish and 150 to 200 feet (46 to 61 m) on a side (Cohen et al., 1979).

The most comfortable ratio of building height to open space width is 1:3 to 1:5 (Introduction . . . , 1978), considerably wider than a narrow street. A traditional London mews, with a height/width ratio of 1:1, or a typical nineteenth-century London minor street of row houses (ratio 1:2) is generally acceptable partly because the roadway and passing traffic create a kind of "moat" between opposite neighbors (Cooper, 1975). Judicious earth moving and planting in landscaped common space, however, can provide an offsetting factor. In California even ratios as tight as 1:2 are acceptable in private sector apartment complexes when fast-growing trees screen one building from another. Tighter ratios may prove acceptable to single persons, childless couples, or students, but not to families with children: The difference is that children actually *use* the common open space.

Possible design responses

- Design square or nearly square common open space.
- Avoid large courtyards (more than 200 feet [60 m] per side) with no "intimate" subspaces.

Figure 98. The reality of how an environment looks and is used is often different from how the designer envisioned it (see Figure 99).

Figure 99. Note that three-fourths of the people in this sketch are shown as adults and only one-fourth as children. Research on common open space use shows an exact reversal of these proportions.

- Design open spaces so that the ratio of building height to open space width is in the range of 1:3 to 1:5, or as tight as 1:2 with careful landscaping.
- Provide open spaces with dimensions that range from 100 to 200 feet (30 to 60 m) on each side.
- Use landscaping to increase the feeling of privacy.

See also: Courtyard width (133).

75. Varying spaces

A series of connected, medium-sized spaces of varying shape and appearance is more suitable than one large or several identical spaces. (Architecture . . . , 1969; Barker, 1976; Becker, 1974; Byrom, 1972; Cooper and Marcus, 1971; Cooper, 1971; Eikos Group, 1980)

Where several connected open spaces are virtually identical in size, shape, and landscaping, disorientation and lack of identity, especially for children, may result. In one such scheme in suburban Copenhagen (Albertslund) large graphic signs of different animals had to be attached to each court so that children could find their way home. Clarity and integrity of design cannot be allowed to eclipse the identity of each subspace in any repeated scheme.

Possible design response

- In large developments devise ways to give character to individual courtyards or dwelling clusters by varying the shape of open space, as well as earthforms, planting, play equipment, and site furniture.

See also: Visual complexity (18), Subunit identity (21), Street names (25).

Figure 100 (a, b, c). In this housing scheme identical dwelling units look out onto shared courtyards that are almost identical in terms of dimensions, circulation, and lack of planting or play equipment. The majority of residents disliked what they could see from their windows, and first-time visitors soon became disoriented. (Pollards Hill, Merton, London)

76. Common space at the back

Care should be taken in connecting dwelling entries with common open space.

Take the case of a house with its front or "display" garden, front door, and living room all looking out onto a communal landscaped space; car access is via the back. The advantages of this arrangement—that living spaces look onto a pleasant green space and children do not have to cross a road to reach the communal area—can be more than offset by disadvantages. Visitors or delivery personnel approaching by car are likely to enter via the "back" entrance; neither "front" doors nor "front" yards face the street, so the personal touches added to these spaces do not contribute to the overall street aesthetic. The street, with its boundaries formed by back fences and/or garages, may take on the appearance of a service alley; and children going back and forth to the communal areas may track dirt in through the "front" door or living room (see example 1, Figure 101).

The advantages of example 2 in Figure 101 seem to outweigh the disadvantages. The house seems to be oriented the "right way," and it is a simple matter for a visitor to locate a street address and approach the house via the "front." If the garage does not block views into the front yard, individual gardening efforts can add personal touches to the street.

Both examples 3 and 4 in Figure 101 incorporate the hazard of children crossing a road to reach the landscaped area, although this can be

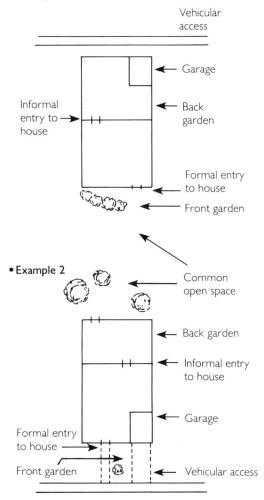

• Example 1

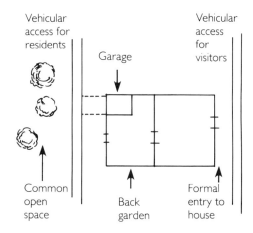

• Example 3

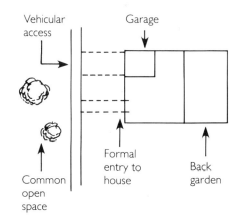

• Example 4

Figure 101. Different arrangements of dwellings vis-à-vis common open space.

minimized by judicious use of "Go Slow" signs and speed bumps at the cul-de-sac entry. Example 4 has perhaps a slight aesthetic edge in that home owners enjoy the double advantage of a street-oriented house *and* a pleasant green outlook (on the Georgian square model).

Possible design responses

- Ensure that the dwelling orientation is unambiguous, that a visitor approaching for the first time would be able to distinguish between front and back door.
- Where possible, orient the front (formal) entrance toward—or within view of—the street.
- Orient the back (informal) entry toward the yard or patio, and provide direct access from it to communal open space.
- Avoid situations where children have to cross a street to reach the common open space.
- Avoid situations where children have to pass through the formal living room in order to gain access to the common open space.

See also: Visible entry (36), Back and front entries (41), Yard linked to common space (55), "Front" and "back" customs (56), Informal surveillance (219), Buffer zone (228).

Figure 102. Groups of six apartments, each sharing an exterior stair and a small play court for toddlers, are linked by a low gate into a safe interior street used only occasionally for fire truck and garbage truck access and used frequently by older children for cycling, roller-skating, and playing games needing a hard surface. The whole scheme houses 234 households. (Cedars Road, Lambeth, London)

77. Common space boundary

Ensure that the boundaries between private and communal outdoor space are clearly defined.

Private open space contributes to the symbolic image of "home" and supports outdoor activities requiring privacy. Because different and potentially conflicting activities occur in such space and in communal outdoor space, a clear separation between the two types of space is necessary. Semipermeable boundaries also enhance community surveillance of common areas. A frequently occurring oversight in the site planning of clustered housing is the lack of boundaries of this kind (Appleyard and Lintell, 1972; Byrom, 1972; Connell, 1975; Cooper, 1970b, 1975; Cooper and Corrie, 1970; Cooper and Marcus, 1971; Department . . . , 1971b; Gilmour et al., 1970; Griffin, 1973; Milne, 1976; Newman, 1972; Norcross, 1973; Sandvik, Shellenbarger, and Stevenson, 1973; Zeisel and Griffin, 1975). This lack is especially significant where children use the communal open space for play (Eikos Group, 1980; Milne, 1976; Newman, 1972; Norcross, 1973; Ziesel and Griffin, 1975). Unless adequate separation is provided, increased use of shared space around the home by chil dren decreases the general use of private open space. Even if children do not use it, adults may avoid common space for fear of intruding on neighbors unless it is defined by fencing or

planting (Tulin, 1978). Where backyard fences are seen as "barriers" by children, however, backyards are less frequently used as play spaces (Eikos Group, 1980).

Most people will also avoid private, ground-level open spaces lacking a barrier and abutting directly onto public spaces. Indeed, some may go further and keep their blinds closed all day—a clear behavioral response to the lack of privacy and protection afforded by a fence. (For more details see Chapter 7—Private Open Space.)

See also: Yard linked to common space (55), Privacy screening (57), Yard surveillance (220), Buffer zone (228).

78. Street linkage

Design the linkage between common open space and adjacent public streets with care.

Residents, especially North Americans, sometimes become territorial about "their" space and resent the intrusion of outsiders. North

Figure 103. The entry from a San Francisco street into a semiprivate courtyard shared by numbers of row houses is marked by a street light and an unobtrusive opening between buildings.

Americans tend to use land ownership (whether real or assumed) as a means of defining status, whereas in Europe, particularly Britain, the lingering class system is more frequently used to define "who you are." Nevertheless there are indications that, as status hierarchy loses its power in a society, territoriality tends to take its place as a social balancing mechanism (Sommer, 1969).

Closing off a common landscaped area entirely is generally impractical, but subtle "filters" can be provided to create narrow, half hidden entry points obvious to residents but less so to passersby. When entering via a narrowed-down access point, outsiders are unlikely to mistake the interior space for a neighborhood park or public playground and likely to perceive it as semi-private territory. The narrower the entry point, the more easily residents can subsequently add a gate.

Possible design responses

- Use planting, building arrangement, level changes, and fencing to create semiprivate entry points to communal open space.
- Ensure that entry points do not become a security hazard or a barrier to disabled people.

See also: Community identity (5), Edge treatment (22), Site entry barriers (201).

79. Playing everywhere

Children tend to play anywhere and everywhere, not just in designated play spaces.

Children are by far the greatest users of shared outdoor spaces in multifamily housing (Architecture . . . , 1969; Blackman, 1966; Byrom, 1972; Committee . . . , 1972; Cooper and Marcus, 1971; Cooper, 1974; Department . . . , 1973a; Miller and Cook, 1967; Ministry . . . , 1969b; White, 1970) and most housing evaluation studies indicate that problems with children's play are one of the most frequent subjects of complaint (Architecture . . . , 1966, 1969; Committee . . . , 1972; Cooper, 1972b, 1975; Department . . . , 1972a, 1973a; Kautz, 1974; Lansing et al., 1970; Ministry . . . , 1969a, 1970; Norcross, 1973; Parish and Parish, 1972; Sandvik, Shellenbarger, and Stevenson, 1973). Although the total outdoor environment in a housing area should be regarded as primarily for children, adults need to be able to predict with some accuracy what will happen in it and where. Some place structuring of activities is therefore required, with noisy activities occurring in certain places, digging in others, and sitting quietly elsewhere. In certain places—tot lot, playground, basketball area—but not others, children can have full autonomy. In one successful Vancouver family co-op, where most children were aged six to twelve, high levels of children's satisfaction were reflected by one child who remarked that he could play "anywhere in the cosmos" (Eikos, 1980).

Possible design response

- Avoid hazards (steep slopes, high retaining walls, pools, poisonous or thorny plants); assume that children will be everywhere.

See also: Children safe from cars (3), Children in the landscape (165), Grassed areas (169), "Keep off" planting (174), Shrubs for play (175).

80. Children on the move

Moving around the neighborhood is children's most frequent outdoor activity.

From the age of two or three years children learn to deal with separation by making small, exploratory trips away from home. This activity is strongly affected by neighborhood layout and traffic patterns.

Between six and twelve, children perfect their motor coordination by riding bicycles, running, climbing, skating, and so forth. Because they need to practice these skills, and their perceptual development permits them to find their way home from a variety of neighborhood locations, children during this "middle age" of childhood seem to be constantly on the move. Such children may still be careless about traffic and other pedestrians, so pathway systems should be free from traffic and wide enough for children on bicycles as well as walking adults. Because it is safer if children use pedestrian routes, and they tend to ignore notices prohibiting bicycle use in any case, design pathways for multiple use from the start. In one Canadian study bicycle riding in culs-de-sac was regarded by children as a highly valued play activity (Eikos Group, 1980).

Children often seek out slopes where they can engage in bicycle "jumping," and small landscaped mounds are very tempting because they increase the excitement of going fast (Eikos Group, 1980).

Possible design responses

- Provide on-site, multipurpose paths at least 8 feet (2.4 m) wide that
  - Following interesting and varied circuits
  - Are rounded at the corners to prevent cutting across and wider at intersections to reduce collisions
  - Do not invite cutting through play areas or across lawns
  - Are lighted for evening cycling
- Provide opportunities for bicycle jumping through mounds for that specific purpose or safe alternative places (for example, wide concrete areas) where "jumps" can be created out of planks and boxes. Eliminate mounds not specially set aside for jumping.
- Provide paths with moderate changes in level, banks, and pull-off areas for use by children on bicycles.
- Ensure that elderly or physically disabled people and very small children are not threatened by designs to accommodate bicycle riders.

See also: Children safe from cars (3), Footpath design (183), Pedestrians passing by (187), Footpath play (189), Running the gauntlet (229).

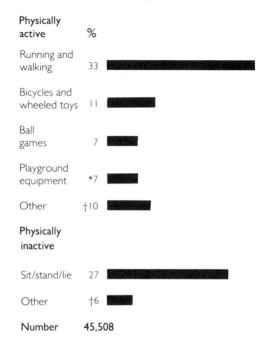

What the children were doing

Physically active	%	
Running and walking	33	
Bicycles and wheeled toys	11	
Ball games	7	
Playground equipment	*7	
Other	†10	

Physically inactive		
Sit/stand/lie	27	
Other	†6	

Number   45,508

* This percentage was adjusted to exclude the numbers of children observed on the estates which did not have play equipment.

† These percentages were adjusted to exclude the numbers of children observed on the estates where the activity categories were not divided into physically active and inactive.

Therefore totals exceed 100%.

Figure 104. Children's activities in communal open spaces near home in six British high-density schemes. Note the relatively low use of playground equipment and the high proportions moving around or engaged in physically inactive "observing" behavior. (Source: Department . . . , 1973a)

81. Children's spaces

Children need to play and move around in settings that are varied and full of surprises.
(Becker, 1976; Bengtsson, 1970; Brill . . . , 1976b; Cooney, 1974; Cooper, 1974a; Cooper and Marcus, 1971; Department . . . , 1973a; Hart, 1978; Hole, 1966)

Children are rarely engaged for long in any one activity. They like secluded places to hide in, and they like to explore the natural world—plants, earth, rocks, water, insects—at close range. But they are equally likely a short time later to be running races across a wide open space, climbing up high to have a view over things, or rolling toys down a slope.

Possible design responses

- Provide a variety of spaces, surfaces, levels, and plant materials. (Variety and irregularity in the design of communal space, however, should not create barriers for physically disabled people.)
- Provide mounding or "berming" to permit views and rolling down slopes.
- Provide secluded or private subareas by means of planting, retaining walls, and site furniture.

See also: Varying spaces (75), Leftover spaces (83), Unrestricted setting (84), Play nests (116), Children in the landscape (165), Ground shaping (166), Shrubs for play (175).

82. Hard-surface play

Children tend to play more frequently on hard surfaces than on grass, given the choice between the two.

Many studies observing children's play in medium- or high-density housing confirm that most play occurs on pathways or other hard surfaces (Architecture . . . , 1969; Becker, 1976; Byrom, 1972; Committee . . . , 1972; Cooper and Marcus, 1971; Cooper Marcus, 1974; Department . . . , 1971, 1973a; Hole, 1966; Ministry . . . , 1967c, 1969b), even when adequate grassed areas are present. This is both because moving around is one of children's favorite activities and because many children's activities

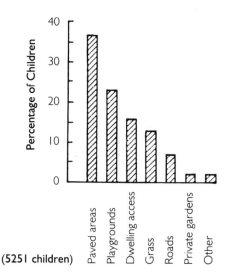

(5251 children)

(cycling, roller skating, bouncing a ball) require hard surfaces.

Possible design responses

- Provide a variety of hard-surfaced areas in the form of wide pathways (at least 5 feet [1.5 m] and up to 12 feet [3.6 m]) and small areas off the circulation system for hopscotch, small ball games, jump rope, jacks, playing with model cars and tricycles, and cycling. However, for reasons of aesthetics and noise control, do not create a predominantly hard-surfaced site.
- Provide some hard surfaces on which chalk marks for hopscotch will show up clearly.

See also: Traffic management (68), Woonerfs (70), Footpath design (183), Footpath play (189).

Figure 105. The types of surfaces on which children play, recorded in nine London housing developments. Note the predominant use of hard surfaces, an observation confirmed by many other studies of urban play in Europe and North America. (Source: Hole, 1966)

83. Leftover spaces

Because children play creatively in wild or leftover spaces, leave part of the site undeveloped.

When designing a housing development on a suburban or rural site, leave a portion of the site in its "wild" state, not even providing maintenance or cleanup from site personnel. The castoffs of the adult world (hubcaps, milk crates, pieces of lumber) can be rich treasures for children bent on building a fort or a clubhouse. Children will spend more time playing in such a setting than they would on even the best designed play sculpture (Eikos Group, 1980). In fact, where natural landscapes no longer exist, Dutch landscape planners even plant "wild" areas or urban forests well ahead of construction so that they are ready for use when families move in (Laurie, 1979). Recent housing developments in Denmark include "play woods" adjoining traditional equipped play spaces, and they have been well used (Chase and Ishmael, 1980).

However, an observation study of children's play in a U.S. suburb where numbers of houses backed onto wooded or tall grass lots found that some parents, unfamiliar with such areas, discourage their children from using them. It may be necessary to educate parents as to the creative and educational benefits of wild areas and to legitimize them as places by fencing, a gate, or a name.

Possible design responses

- Retain the most attractive and stimulating natural portion of the site as an unmaintained, creative play area.

- Where no natural vegetation exists, plant fast-growing, "wild" forests before the site is developed but well away from builders' work areas or parking places.

Figure 106. A portion of the original rural landscape left untouched between newly built neighborhoods in a British new town. It is used by six- to twelve-year-old children for exploratory play, building dens, tree climbing, and so on.

- Leave the creative play area unmaintained. If possible, permit the collection of "junk" (perhaps leftover building materials) on that portion of the site.
- Screen or fence the area to give children using it a sense of enclosure and privacy and to screen it from adults who may not find the appearance acceptable.
- Plant fast-growing, hardy shrubs and trees that are resistant to harsh treatment (such as willow and dogwood).
- Plant shrubs and trees that are particularly attractive to wildlife (birds, butterflies, insects).
- Where appropriate, fence and name the wild area to designate it as a legitimate child's place.
- Include an account of the potential use and worth of a wild area in the tenant's or home owner's manual.
- Where possible, locate natural areas in central locations, within calling distances of dwellings.

See also: Children safe from cars (3), Playing everywhere (79), Unrestricted setting (84), Children's rights (85), Complementary play (103), Children in the landscape (165), Taking risks (232), Resident's manual (241).

84. Unrestricted setting

Create an environment that channels children's play without the need for rules and regulations.

In street-oriented houses parents set the rules in and around the home regarding permitted activities by their children, but in medium- or high-density housing certain rules for kids are set by the management ("No ball games after 9:30," "No children over nine allowed in play area."). Because parents may resent such restrictions on their children's behavior, an environment designed holistically from the start—on the understanding that children will attempt to play anywhere and everywhere—may prevent conflict. Where rules are too strict, children will shift their play to locations outside the housing development.

In one Vancouver low-rent development with most children under five, children expressed a low level of satisfaction with the exterior environment in terms of play potential because of strictly enforced rules prohibiting play on roadways, paths, yards, and grass (Eikos Group, 1980).

Possible design responses

- Ensure that as much of the site as possible is potentially available for children's play.
- Use design cues to channel activities.

- Avoid creating spaces whose exclusive use by one age group may need management enforcement.
- Avoid "Keep off" landscaping.
- Avoid areas that are fenced off for no apparent purpose.

See also: Children safe from cars (3), Interesting landscaped spaces (73), Playing everywhere (79), Children's rights (85), "Keep off" planting (174), User group territories (227).

85. Children's rights

A resident's manual or lease-sales agreement should make clear that communal open spaces are intended primarily for children's play.

In cases where it has not been made explicit that communal space is for children, residents without children, who see it as an aesthetic amenity, have complained of "misuse," and management has attempted to forbid play (Byrom, 1972; Department . . . , 1971b, 1973a; Gilmour et al., 1970).

Possible design responses

- Make it clear, by means of child-oriented facilities in communal landscaped areas, that these spaces are intended for children's use.
- State in the sales or lease agreement that communal landscaped spaces are intended for play as well as being aesthetic amenities.
- Communicate information about children's use of communal open space during an orientation session for new residents.

See also: Open space maintenance (86), Resident's manual (241).

86. Open space maintenance

Maintenance of communal open space is strongly linked to overall resident satisfaction. (Barker, 1976; Byrom, 1972; Cooper, 1970b; Lansing et al., 1970)

Unless the responsibility for maintenance of communal open space is clearly identified at the design and construction stage, and budgeted for, the space will tend to become a source of contention among neighbors, between residents and management, or between residents and the local maintenance authority (Byrom, 1972; Griffin, 1973; Ministry . . . , 1969b, Norcross, 1973; Parish and Parish, 1972; Shankland . . . , 1969).

Maintenance arrangements generally follow one of the following schemes in the United States (Whyte, 1964):

1. Landlord maintenance in private or public rental housing
2. Municipal ownership and maintenance where open spaces are very large and are accessible to the public at large
3. Special service districts where the boundaries coincide with those of the housing development. (The district maintains the space and has power to levy assessments on the residents. This procedure has been used successfully in Connecticut, Colorado, and California.)
4. Home owner associations where dwellings are owner occupied, the extent of common

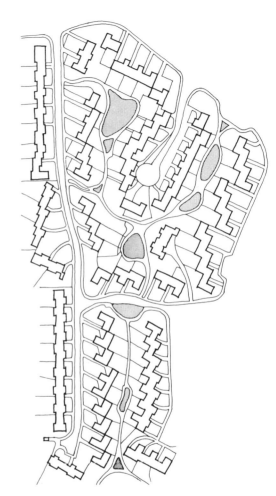

Figure 107. In this private sector Scottish scheme the small scattered pieces of common open space were barely usable and proved to be a source of contention because no prior maintenance arrangements had been made. (Source: Byrom, 1972)

open space is not large, and the general public is for the most part excluded from use of that space

In a study of 349 U.S. home owner associations (quoted in Whyte, 1964) six characteristics were found to be common to successful associations, all relevant to situations where home ownership combined with communal open space is contemplated:

1. The home owner's association must be set up before the dwellings are sold.
2. Membership must be mandatory for each buyer and each successive buyer.
3. The open space restrictions must be permanent, not just applicable to a set time.
4. The association must be responsible for liability insurance, local taxes, and maintenance of recreational and other facilities.
5. Residents must pay their pro rata share of the cost; the assessment levied by the association can become a lien on the property.
6. The association must be able to adjust the assessment to meet changing needs.

Possible design responses

- Before embarking on the design of housing that will incorporate common landscaped spaces, ensure that the client or management has clear and reasonable plans for its maintenance.
- Ensure that the open space design does not include any particular maintenance or replacement problems. (See Chapter 12—Landscaping, Footpaths, and Site Furniture.)

See also: Pleasing milieu (10), Safe play (105), Tree maintenance (172), Landscape maintenance (181), Footpath design (183), Maintenance policies (239), Maintenance responsibilities (240).

Figure 108. In this private sector Scottish scheme a former field boundary with mature trees was saved as common open space. Because it was open-ended, outsiders perceived it as a park, and neither the local authority nor the residents were willing to pay for its upkeep. In adult eyes it became something of a problem area, although it was a great resource for children. (Source: Byrom, 1972)

Purpose-Built Play Areas for Children

PROVISIONS FOR PLAY

The child shall have full opportunity for play and recreation, which should be directed to the same purposes as education; society and the public authorities shall endeavor to promote the enjoyment of this right (Declaration of the Rights of the Child, adopted by U.N. General Assembly, November 1959).

Society often places a low priority on the need for children's play. This is both because it is erroneously seen as frivolous and because we assume that families—in particular, women—will cope on their own with growing children. But times are changing. More and more women have to work to support their families or prefer to do so. More people are living—or will have to live—in medium- and high-density urban neighborhoods or "densified" suburban communities, and many play activities that were considered natural in rural settings—climbing trees, digging tunnels, lighting camp fires, making dens, damming streams, sneaking fallen apples—are labeled delinquent in urban areas, if they can occur at all.

In Western Europe great strides have been made in understanding the developmental significance of play and in devising new forms of play for urban children (adventure playgrounds, play parks, and city farms), but no legislation specifically dealing with the overall need of play yet exists in Britain or the United States to compare with legislation for public health, housing, and education. The provision of play space for local authority housing seeking central govern-ment subsidies is now mandatory in Britain (but not in the United States). However, more than space is at issue. For example, although the out-cry against high-rise family housing has precipi-tated a swing to low-rise, high-density housing, the play needs of two- or four-year-olds are a problem even at ground level if there is no en-closed yard, traffic-free communal space, or ap-pealing play equipment within sight of home.

The lack of national legislation relating to play results in scattered and uncoordinated responsi-bilities at local levels, with the responsibility to lobby for funds for children's play provision de-volving onto local pressure groups. A study of inner-city play in Liverpool shows how this leads to ad hoc provision, with articulate local groups obtaining improved facilities for their areas and areas that could not muster a group (but whose needs were as great or greater) being left with inadequate facilities. This study argues that local authorities have been able to relinquish their responsibilities for play by allowing the growth of the voluntary sector (Wilson and Womersley, 1977).

Several recent British studies find close cor-relations between rates of vandalism and num-bers of children. The Lambeth Inner-Area Study, for example, concludes that, where child density exceeds thirty per acre, problems of noise, van-dalism, and neighbor disputes are likely to be-come more marked (Shankland . . . , 1977b). A study of vandalism on fifty-two inner-London estates predicts that vandalism is likely to occur in all building forms once ratios of children (aged five to sixteen years) exceed five children per ten dwellings or twenty per apartment building (Wilson, 1977). But because some, perhaps most, vandalism results from the *normal* use of scarce resources of equipment and open space, it is likely to continue, whatever the child density, as long as children's needs are a low-priority budget item. A 1971 study of fifty British council housing schemes built during 1968–69 reveals that, of the thirty-nine estates intended for families, only eight had made any provision for children (and of these only four had any equipment) (Department . . . , 1974). After a detailed study of two problem-ridden London estates, the Architectural Research Unit (Edinburgh) concluded that vandalism increases as the provision for children's needs decreases (Heffernan, 1977). The evidence from many postoccupancy studies suggests that "adequate provision" does

not mean adding a couple of play areas to an already cramped site plan, but seeing the whole site from the start as potential play space and acknowledging the needs of children (often constituting 40 percent of the population) as not only valid but crucial.

Low-income children are not alone in being deprived of play opportunities. An increasing proportion of middle-income U.S. families with children are purchasing condominiums (generally row house or apartment clusters) because they can no longer afford the preferred detached house. These condominiums have often been designed *without* children in mind; ironically, many originally designed as "swinging singles" complexes have tennis courts, saunas, and jogging trails—but no play areas for children.

But providing play areas *alone* will not fulfill children's needs. As Chapter 8—Common Open Space and the Needs of Children—makes clear, children need to have access to the whole site or neighborhood, to explore and discover their own play spaces, to watch and cooperate with adults engaging in their daily activities. We cannot buy off our children by merely providing playgrounds.

Because children's needs in housing areas are so varied and complex, we cannot confine them to one chapter. Chapters 7 and 12 also contain guidelines relating to children's play. This chapter deals specifically with purpose-built play equipment spaces. Although children are likely to use these for less than 20 percent of their time outdoors, such areas are used, in proportion to their size, far more than any other on-site

Percentage of mothers finding play a problem, by building types

Building types	Number of estates	%		No.
Low-density houses	11	56	▰▰▰▰▰	161
High-density houses	11	61	▰▰▰▰▰	576
Deck access	2	61	▰▰▰▰▰	125
Balcony access with elevators	4	72	▰▰▰▰▰▰	161
Walk-up blocks	6	72	▰▰▰▰▰	81
Corridor blocks	3	73	▰▰▰▰▰	92
Point blocks	7	81	▰▰▰▰▰▰	137

Figure 109. Percentage of mothers in a British study finding play a problem, by building type. (Source: Department . . . , 1973a)

Reasons why play was thought to be a problem

Reasons given	Families with young children	Adult households	Elderly households
Not enough play facilities in area/nowhere to play	75%	56%	56%
Children not safe from traffic	16%	10%	5%
Play areas not safe	9%	2%	3%
Children play too close to dwelling/are a nuisance	8%	33%	41%
No supervision	5%	1%	1%
Older people complain	5%	2%	2%
Differences in age groups/nowhere for particular age group to play	5%	4%	2%
Difficult to keep child in sight	3%	1%	1%
Other	2%	14%	13%
Number	329	536	318

Figure 110. Reasons for which play was thought to be a problem by various resident groups in a British study of children's play. (Source: Department . . . , 1973a)

NB—Percentages do not add up to 100% as mothers could give several reasons for play problem.

spaces. The criteria for children's play that follow are designed to provide a research-based, balanced view between the extremes of quantified "rules" and vague generalities. The guidelines in this chapter are arranged under three major headings: preschool children (age two to five), six- to twelve-year-olds, and teenagers. This differentiation, of course, does not imply that these three age groups should be segregated or that they are incompatible. Because of disparate levels of social and physical maturity, however, their environmental needs are different and are thus considered separately.

Play Areas for Preschool Children (Ages Two to Five)

From the age of about two, children are increasingly drawn to explore the outside world, and the residential environment must accommodate this exploration in the crucial preschool years.

Following Hart (1973) and Pollowy (1977) the major developmental attainments of this period can be summarized:

1. Children begin to form mental representations of the environment as a fixed spatial system centered on the home. Their desire to get "into," "out of," "on top of," and "under" things (furniture, play equipment, old boxes) expresses a need to expand and solidify this growing sense of spatial relations.
2. Children become more confident and daring in their motor skills and want to practice them using simple play equipment (swings, slides, balancing beams, climbing frames)

Figure 111. The environment close to home is highly used by two- to five-year-olds and should provide for their needs.

and self-propelled vehicles (scooters and tricycles).
3. Children enjoy learning through experimentation (for example, by combining elements in the environment in new ways—sand and water made into "food").
4. At four or five, children like to explore a limited area away from home on their own, but they can cope only with easily conceptualized site plans—pulling a wagon, say, "around the block."
5. By the end of their fifth year most children can cross safe, local streets and go on simple errands to a shop or visit a neighbor.
6. By four or five (and considerably earlier for some very independent children) children

are able to accept the temporary absence of a parental figure as long as they can reestablish contact by running home or calling out. (The impossibility of doing this in high-rise housing was one of its major pitfalls for families with young children.)
7. By four or five, most children are drawn to small groups of playmates and are capable of simple cooperative play (dressing up, playing house or shop).
8. This is a period of experimentation with independence and going it alone, when a child is likely to run ahead and hide from adults while on a walk or play hide-and-seek with a group of peers (hence the importance of small nooks and crannies and places to hide).

87. Yard play

Yards should meet the needs of children under five.

The use of the yard for play will vary, depending on what other opportunities are available. For example, in a U.S. suburban area where there were few other attractive play locations, more than 70 percent of observed play occurred in yards (back and front) (Aiello, 1974); yet in a study of play in high-density London estates a very small proportion of children were observed in yards (Department . . . , 1973a).

More than any other age groups, children under five use yards for play (Cooper, 1975; Newson and Newson, 1968; Residential . . . , 1975). The yard is a continuation of the home environment, an accessible outdoor room where, given reasonable weather, they can play throughout the year. They can "escape" from adults and yet be within easy calling distance, and they can feel a greater freedom to move and express themselves than in the confines of a kitchen or playroom.

Possible design responses

- *Visual access:* The yard should be visually linked to the room in which supervising adults will predictably spend time.
- *Entry to house:* Access should be via an informal transition space (back porch, family room, kitchen) so that dirt or mud is not tracked into the "best room." The back door

should be designed so that it is easily managed by a two-year-old.

- *Access to communal areas:* Where a back gate opens onto shared open space, a latch high enough for four- or five-year-olds but too high for a toddler should be provided.
- *Site:* Yards should be 120 square yards (100 sq. m) or more in size (Cook, 1969). One study asks us to "remember that the under-fives are most affected by the lack of play spaces because they are least likely to have satisfactory alternatives as they cannot wander far from home" (Lamanna, 1964, 57).
- *Surfaces:* Three kinds are essential: grass (to roll or run on), dirt and sand for manipulative play, and smooth, hard surfaces for tricycles or model cars.
- *Sense of enclosure:* Young children should be able to glimpse the larger world beyond the yard. Slatted fences high enough to prevent climbing over but with vertical slats wide enough to allow peeking out are ideal; horizontal slats encourage climbing.

See also: Ground-floor households (8), Access to private open space (54), Yard linked to common space (55), "Front" and "back" customs (56), Yard size (61).

88. Balcony play

Where families must be housed off the ground, provide a safe and usable balcony for children's play.

Families most penalized by living off the ground are those with children from one through five, who need a considerable amount of supervision, are likely to get themselves into dangerous situations, and are unable to negotiate elevators on their own. A recent British study of flats, families, and under-fives reveals an alarming number of serious and fatal falls from poorly designed windows, balconies, and access decks (Gittus, 1976).

If children of this age must be housed above ground, a safe balcony must be provided for the kind of casual outdoor play normally associated with the backyard; moreover, it should *appear* to be safe. A survey of London flat dwellers found evidence of a general fear of balconies, although two-thirds still appreciated having one and 40 percent of the under-fives regularly played there (Willis, 1957, 372–76). A Melbourne study finds a similar mixture of appreciation and apprehension (Stevenson et al., 1967).

Children like to see what is going on outside, and they will be tempted to climb up and look over solid balcony walls. For this reason balconies should ideally have slatted screening. Because very small children enjoy pushing toys off balconies or under railings, balcony fronts should be designed to enable the easy addition of a protective screen. In Sweden a building regulation requires an insert (usually glass or a slatted panel) in every balcony to allow a crawling toddler to see out and yet be safe. The clear spacing between slats or bars is not to exceed 3½ inches (89 mm).

Parker Morris standards in Britain require that balconies be no less than 40 square feet (3.7 sq. m). The width of the balcony is more crucial than its length; for example, a 10-foot long (3 m) balcony may contribute aesthetically to the building facade, but it is useless unless it is deep enough to accommodate a baby carriage, a play pen, or a deck chair.

Possible design responses

- Provide screening that permits views out but maintains some degree of privacy for balcony walls. Slatted screening is recommended.
- Ensure that solid-walled balconies have transparent insets.
- Avoid horizontal bars or projections, which might encourage climbing.
- Ensure that the space between the balcony floor and the wall is either too small to shove things through or climb through (less than 3½ inches [89 mm]) or capable of being fitted with a protective screen.
- Ensure that balconies are at least 6 feet (1.8 m) deep and 10 feet (3 m) long.

See also: Access to private open space (54), Orientation to sun (59), Above-ground balconies (64), Balcony off living room (65).

89. Doorstep play

Design dwelling entries to accommodate doorstep play.

Design should acknowledge an important characteristic of small children's play: they tend to play close to the most frequently used entrance to a dwelling (Ackermans, 1970; Architecture . . . , 1969; Barker, 1976; Cooper and Marcus, 1971; Cooper Marcus, 1974; Danish . . . , 1969; Department . . . , 1971a, 1973a; Gilmour et al., 1970; Gittus, 1976; Norcross, 1973; Sandvik, Shellenbarger, and Stevenson, 1973; White,

1970). An extensive British study finds that three-quarters of all children, but especially children under five, irrespective of density or building form, play within 33 feet (10 m) of the door to their home. A study of an Illinois housing project reported that 36 percent of all observed toddlers' play took place outside the kitchen door, while only 13 percent took place in the toddlers' play area (Saile, 1971).

The old front stoops of New York brownstones and the wide covered porches of older houses in the midwestern or southern United States were ideal in this regard. The porch provided an intimate space; railings met at a right

Figure 112. In all cultures children aged two to five play most frequently round the doorway, staying close to home yet not *in* it.

angle where sticks and old drapes could quickly create a "house" or "shop"; the roof provided shade and shelter. Porch steps or stoops were ideal places to sit and talk or play jacks or cards. Under the steps were hiding places for secret meetings or for spying on adults. The angle between the steps and the facade of the building provided an "eddy space" out of the sidewalk traffic where elaborate ball games were invented.

But the porch and the stoop have largely disappeared from modern housing design, and the entry has atrophied to a minimal recess or token front step. Children living in streets of row houses dating from the last century often enjoy the most comfortable play spaces. In the narrow streets and alleys of San Francisco's Chinese and Latin American districts, for example, there is a great range of highly creative play on and around the front steps of older houses (Zerner, 1977). Play is usually more varied and creative than in the lower-density suburbs to which many parents move "for the sake of the children."

Where groups of terraced or row houses face onto a common pathway, designers need to bear in mind that doorstep play will inevitably spill over onto it. Pathways should be hard surfaced, wide, and able to accommodate sheltered "niches" with low walls, balancing rails, steps, and a child-scaled bench and table. In developments where shift workers are likely to be present, it would be appropriate to locate bedrooms away from areas of doorstep play. Dwellings that share staircase access can easily accommodate a variant of doorstep play. A successful London example places a semiprivate, outdoor fenced court—a kind of oversized playpen—at the bottom of each set of three-story access stairs, serving six to nine dwellings (Gilmour et al., 1970). It is visible from all the dwellings it serves, adequately fenced and gated to keep small children from straying, and discouraging to older children because of its small size and level changes (see Figure 102).

Even deck (or gallery) access can be designed to accommodate doorstep play if the deck is wide enough to fulfill access *and* play needs. The 10-foot-wide (3.4 m) decks of Parkhill, Sheffield, have proved particularly successful for children's play, even accommodating roller skating, cycling, and skateboarding five or ten floors above ground (see Figure 71). At Thamesmead, London, the wide access decks are covered with the same concrete paving slabs visible on every sidewalk in London, thus emphasizing the message that this is intended for use like a sidewalk.

Possible design responses

- Wherever possible, provide a dwelling entry with the following features:
  - A semienclosed, roofed space around the entry
  - Steps for sitting, talking, or viewing activities in streets or courtyards
  - A smooth-surfaced path for running model vehicles or tricycles
  - A flat-topped step or porch area for laying out a board game or playing cards
  - Easy access to the house via a hall or foyer (that is, not directly into the "best" room)
  - Visibility from inside the dwelling
  - Easy access to a downstairs toilet
- Design the area immediately outside a cluster of entries or a shared entry with the following characteristics:
  - Surface of smooth concrete or asphalt
  - Wide enough to allow two or three children to play
  - Separated from lower-floor windows to prevent intrusion on neighbors
  - Visible from inside the dwelling for adult supervision
  - Sheltered "niches" with low walls
  - Located away from bedrooms
  - Child-scaled bench or bench and table
- Consider providing a semiprivate fenced outdoor court at the bottom of access stairs in multiple-unit access designs.
- Especially in deck-access developments provide adequate sound insulation, rubber floor cladding, and double glazing near potential play areas.
- Ensure that deck-facing windows permit views out while protecting residents' privacy.

See also: Visible entry (36), Front porch (40), Shared entry (44), Street activities off the ground (48), Hard-surface play (82).

90. Tot lot location

Provide purpose-built play areas for children under five within sight and calling distance of home.

When they leave the domain of the dwelling, most children under five like to play within sight (or calling distance) of their parents or other adults known to them (Barker, 1976; Becker, 1974; Cooper and Marcus, 1971; Cooper Marcus, 1974; Department . . . , 1971a, 1973a; Gatt, 1978; Hole, 1966; Larsson, 1980; Ministry . . . , 1967c; Norcross, 1973). Where tot lots are out of view of the majority of houses, they are virtually never used (Department . . . , 1971b; Gilmour et al., 1970; Ministry . . . , 1967c). Even if the tot lot is within view but requires a circuitous route to get to it, parents may not want to leave their children there (Sandvik, Shellenbarger, and Stevenson, 1973). An extensive British study of play in housing estates notes that no more than a third of the under-fives playing outside in public areas were with an adult (Department . . . , 1973a). Designers need to make the working assumption that parents have busy lives. As Elizabeth Gittus (1976, 203) concludes: "the adequacy of play arrangements, especially for young children in multi-storey homes, . . . turns not so much on the amount of play space per child as on the guarantee of supervision, however informal and unobtrusive." A detailed policy statement from the City of Sheffield recommends that a play area for small children be included whenever the number of dwellings on a site exceeds eleven (Scottish . . . , 1978).

See also: Life cycle clusters (7), Neighborly surveillance (42), Yard linked to common space (55), Common space at the back (76), Friendly encounters (131), Daycare center (136), Pedestrians passing by (187), User group territories (227).

Figure 113. A play space for small children should always be sited within view of the dwelling to allow casual surveillance from home.

91. Tot lot catchment

A tot lot, or play space for preschool children, should be located in every court or subspace of a family housing development.

When parents supervise children, they are more likely to meet neighbors; meeting people "through the children" is often cited in multi-family housing as one of the principal means of making adult contacts in the neighborhood. For this reason, as well as because children may become somewhat territorial about "their" play area, it is doubly important to provide one tot lot for each distinct cluster or subarea of the site (MacLeod, 1977). In one Canadian development where this was not done the cluster of chatting parents and children around the one tot lot inhibited parents from other courts from coming to use it; they felt they were intruding (MacLeod, 1977).

Several studies indicate that groupings of anywhere from around twelve to a hundred dwellings can be designed so that each unit is within sight and calling distance of a play area, depending on form and density. Naturally, the higher the proportion of households including children, the lower the number of dwellings that can reasonably share a preschool play space before it becomes overcrowded. In one San Francisco development households ranging from those with small children to those with school-age children to those with no children were grouped in clusters of a hundred walk-up apartments, and the courtyard play area serving each group of a hundred was never overcrowded (Cooper, 1971). One hundred seems to be an upper limit. Alexander et al. (1977) argue for an ideal cluster size of sixty-four households, showing statistically that this size is the "critical mass" necessary for each child—children representing one-quarter of the population—to have a 95 percent chance of reaching five potential playmates of his or her own age. Much successful Swedish housing of the 1950s and 1960s is made up of clusters of this order; a common form is three-story walk-up apartments around a courtyard with twelve entrances, each serving six households (that is, a total of seventy-two dwellings share a play area).

A study of current and recommended play standards in family housing areas of U.S. military bases reports a preference for one tot lot for every fifty families.

Where the density is relatively low, to ensure that all dwellings have visual access to a play area, the number sharing may be considerably less. To ensure some certainty that a child will find playmates, however, a lower limit of twenty is advisable.

Possible design responses

- Provide one tot lot for every twenty to one hundred units.
- Ensure that all family units have visual access to tot lots.
- Where a development is subdivided into a number of clusters, ensure that each cluster has its own preschool play area.

See also: Subunit identity (21), Group territory (72), Varying spaces (75), Dwelling cluster (132).

92. Hazard-free play

Play areas for young children should be physically separated from potential hazards.

Potential hazards for small children include roads, parking areas, steep slopes, high retaining walls, ditches, pools, and—less dramatically— older children's bicycles, large dogs, and cold and windy locations.

For these reasons, and for psychological security, a small child's play area must be enclosed in some way, either by mounding, planting, or a fence. Multifunctional boundaries are ideal—for example, a solid wood or brick wall high enough to keep toddlers in (and some hazards out), but low enough to function as seating for adults.

Sunken play areas whose round forms are nurturing and womblike have been successful in Denmark. They are appealing to small children as long as they do not become pitlike, cutting off views of the play area from homes, or become a drainage problem.

Possible design responses

- Ensure that children are adequately screened from potential hazards en route from dwelling to preschool play area.
- Enclose play areas with multifunctional boundaries (fences or low walls that double as seating).

Figure 114. Boundary to a play area that is both unsuitable and dangerous: Children can be injured by the palings and scratched by the thorns on the rose bushes.

- Avoid enclosing elements that might be hazards (for example, thorny shrubs or pointed fences).
- Provide fences with locking gates.

See also: Children safe from cars (3), Pedestrian precinct (67), Conflicting uses (230).

93. Tot lot design

Design tot lots with careful consideration for children's needs.

Sensorimotor play tends to dominate the period from infancy through the second year, as the growing child learns to master physical skills and to explore the environment through his or her senses. This period of development requires op-

portunities for large muscle development (climbing, running) as well as small muscle coordination (playing with sand or small toys, manipulating loose parts).

Suitable play equipment includes slides, swings, climbing blocks, and sand pits, ideally with a water tap or drinking fountain. Sand pits should be edged to prevent sand spilling out and located a short walk from home so that sand falls off feet or shoes before the child reaches the building entrance. Sand pits should have flat

Figure 115. A more suitable boundary, which can double as a play feature or a place to sit.

surfaces surrounding or within the sand area for sand castles, small wheeled toys, and so forth. Hard-surfaced paths for tricycling around the sand and equipment areas and, beyond these, grass for rolling on are a bonus. Finally, comfortable, shaded benches are needed for adults; some should be close to the sand area for parents of very small children and some farther away for supervision of older preschoolers.

Because infants and toddlers develop rapidly, it is important that a play area offer a variety of graded challenges. Exploring, experiencing, and repeating a variety of sensory activities provides the growing child with a sense of increasing mastery over the environment, and an imaginatively designed preschool play area should offer opportunities for the child to develop crawling, sitting, standing, walking, and climbing skills. Slight barriers can be created between subspaces (by smooth rocks, beams, or platforms) so that infants have access to more of the play area as

they learn to overcome them. A crawling area floored with turf might be separated from a walking area floored with sand, with a series of progressively more difficult logs, ramps, steps, and slides. Another subarea might have bucket-seat slides and other simple equipment requiring adult assistance. Children at this age are learning about the spatial properties of the environment, and the play area can assist this process by providing varied spaces to experience—on, beside, behind, over, in, along, under, before, between, through, against, around, across, by, from, toward, above, below, and so on.

Possible design responses

- In temperate climates locate play areas so that they are both sheltered and sunny at midday.
- In hot climates locate play areas in a partially shaded position.

- In hot climates provide (potentially barefooted) children with the option of walking across grass to and from tot lots—concrete burns!
- Locate play areas far enough from home so that sand falls off feet before the child gets there.
- Provide a variety of graded challenges (blocks, ramps, steps, platforms) and scaled-down slides and swings. (Remember that a toddler's eye level is 20 inches [508 mm].)
- Provide for a variety of spatial-motor experiences (up/down, in/out, above/below).
- Provide a sand area with a water tap or drinking fountain, good drainage, and edging of sufficient height to prevent sand spilling out. (For more detail on sand play, see guideline 95.)
- Provide surfaces surrounding or within the sand area for sandcastles, small wheeled toys, and so forth.

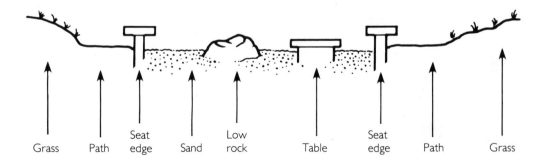

Grass   Path   Seat edge   Sand   Low rock   Table   Seat edge   Path   Grass

Figure 116. An ideal sequence of surfaces in and around a tot lot.

- Provide hard-surfaced paths around equipment areas for tricycling.
- Locate a flat grassy area bounded by smooth rocks or beams to enclose crawling infants, whose eye level is about 8–10 inches (20–25 cm).
- Provide a sloped grassy area, beyond equipment and tricycling paths, for rolling on.
- Provide shaded comfortable benches with a view for supervising adults: some close to the equipment for those supervising very small children and some farther away for those supervising older preschoolers.
- Create an area between about 1,000 and 4,000 square feet (93 to 372 sq. m). Even the lower size could result in a sandbox and equipment area of about 32 feet (10 m) square—large enough to accommodate the needs of a number of toddlers and infants.

See also: Sand play (95), Water play (96), Microclimate (173).

94. Supervising adults

Provide seating areas for adults supervising children's play.

Figure 117. This play area creates an unpleasant pitlike environment for children. It is out of sight of most of the dwellings, and even if a parent decided to bring a child here, there is nowhere to sit.

Adults need comfortable and attractive places to sit, with shading—through planting, arbors, or canopies—where local climate renders this appropriate. Because they may or may not want to socialize, some seating arrangements should permit conversation (sociofugal), some allow for sitting comfortably alone (sociopetal). A table and benches accommodate the needs of adults who want to read, write a letter, or study while their children are playing.

Possible design responses

- Locate benches in sheltered spots.
- Provide benches with backs.
- Provide some table and bench combinations.
- Provide at least one sociofugal and one sociopetal seating arrangement.

See also: Outdoor seating (192), Sunny/shaded seating (193), Seating variety (194), Seating environment (195).

95. Sand play

Provide sand beneath all play equipment.

A British government policy report on housing (Ministry . . . , 1961, 79) recommends that "local authorities should persevere with this provision, in spite of complaints from parents that the sand

Figure 118. Sand is one of the safest surfaces for children to fall onto (accidentally) or jump into (deliberately).

gets in the house, or from caretakers that it has to be swept up, because of the enjoyment which it gives to children."

Although accidents related to playground equipment represent only a small proportion of all children's accidents (Wilkinson and Lockart, 1980), it is important to avoid them. For this reason locate all equipment over impact-absorbing surfaces. One study at University College Hospital, London, shows that three-quarters of children injured in playgrounds severely enough to be admitted to hospital were injured by falling onto a hard surface (Department . . . , 1976).

The impact force that can cause concussion in a child is fifty times the force of gravity (50G). This is how existing surfaces compare (Danger . . . , 1978):

Materials	Height of fall needed to achieve 50G impact
Concrete	Less than 1 foot (0.3 m)
Asphalt, tarmacadam	Less than 1 foot (0.3 m)
Packed earth	About 2 feet (0.6 m)
Standard rubber tile	About 4 feet (1.2 m)
Double rubber tile	About 8 feet (2.4 m)
Wood chips (6-inch [152 mm] depth)	About 10 feet (3 m)
Pea gravel (4-inch [101 mm] depth)	About 12 feet (3.6 m)
Sand (12-inch [305 mm] depth)	About 12 feet (3.6 m)

Concrete, asphalt, and coated macadam have intolerable impact levels. Tarmacadam is also highly water retentive and can corrode metal supports in under two years in wet conditions. Grass under equipment looks attractive at first, but it has a low resistance to wear and can become muddy and slippery in wet weather; the hard-packed earth it is likely to turn into is almost as dangerous as concrete. Although rubber tiling is considerably safer, no evidence is yet available about its long-term durability and vandal resistance. Wood chips are good energy absorbers, but they get wet and rot and are easily thrown about. In some regions of the United States they are said to harbor fleas.

For purposes of providing a double function—impact absorption and play material—we highly recommend sand. It is cleaner than wood chips and less wearing on clothes than gravel. Although, like sand, wood chips and pea gravel can break falls and are hard to ride bicycles through—a decided safety advantage—neither is a molding and building agent. Manipulating sand is a favorite activity among children, who will find their own places to dig and build castles in the dirt or in planting beds if sand is not provided.

The sand area needs to be well enclosed with concrete or wooden walls high enough to prevent the sand from being kicked or blown onto surrounding paving or grass and yet low enough so that small children can climb over it and adults and children can sit on it.

The sand area beneath play equipment should extend far enough so that kids can come down slides, jump off swings, or romp around and still land on it. There should be sand areas well beyond the equipment for general sand play.

Possible design responses

- Use sand in preference to other impact-absorbing materials beneath play equipment.

Figure 119. The design of a sandbox edge is critical. In this case sand that spills out over adjacent pathways causes maintenance problems.

- Never use materials with low impact levels, such as concrete, asphalt, tarmacadam, packed earth, or rubber tile.
- Avoid using grass because it becomes muddy and slippery in wet weather.
- Enclose sand areas with concrete or wooden walls at least 10 inches (254 mm) above sand surface. (Railroad ties work well and provide wide, flat surfaces for children to use as seats and tables.)
- Ensure that the sand extends well beyond the equipment to leave areas free for general sand play.
- Ensure that sand is deep enough: 15 to 18 inches (381 to 457 mm).
- Ensure that sand is raked at least once a week and replaced at regular intervals.
- Provide adequate drainage, via percolation, drainage to a storm sewer, or a tile and drain leach field.
- Select sand with a balanced mixture of particle sizes (0.06 inches [1.5 mm] to very fine). Avoid crushed sand with hard edges.
- Wash sand before using in sandboxes.
- Use seaside, estuary, or clean, natural sand. Avoid building sands, which may stain hands and clothing.
- Never cover sand with solid material because this shuts out air and sun. If sand must be covered, use a wire mesh screen.
- Ensure that sand areas are well defined and at a different level from the surrounding area, with a step up and a step down before entering the sand pit. This discourages animals

from entering the sand area and also provides a rough surface for children to scrape some of the sand off their shoes as they leave.
- Locate part (but not all) of a sandbox in shade to keep some of the sand damp and malleable.
- Part of the area should be open and exposed to the morning sun to permit the sand to dry out and sanitize itself.
- Direct sun at midday in hot summer will render the sand too hot to use. Sand should be shaded by trees, trellises, or the play equipment itself.
- Sand areas should be protected from prevailing winds, both to protect children from blowing sand and to minimize maintenance problems.

See also: Water play (96).

96. Water play

Provide opportunities for children to play in or with water.

Throughout childhood there is a magnetic attraction to water, whether it is available in official wading pools or unofficial puddles, gutters, hydrants, or leaks from faulty irrigation pipes.

Possible design responses

- Provide a simple tap that children within a sand play area can manipulate.
- Position a drinking fountain on the edge of the same area so that the overflow keeps an area of sand damp and so that water can be collected in containers to create a river system in the sandbox.
- Ensure that there is adequate drainage around areas where water is available.
- Provide smooth concrete surfaces close to a water source so that children can "paint" them with water or do "water writing" with spray bottles.
- In regions with hot summers consider a spray or paddling pool. The pool area boundaries should be secure against animal entry; the pool coating must be lead-free and nontoxic; and the pool area must be checked frequently for broken glass. Water should be no deeper than 8 inches (203 mm).

See also: Sand play (95), Drinking fountains (198)

Figure 120. Water has a fascination at all ages, but especially so in childhood.

97. Established play areas

Basic play equipment areas should be on site and ready to use when the first residents move in.

As much as resident participation in the active running, management, and eventual modification of a housing environment is to be encouraged, it is not generally desirable to design a project without any play facilities in hopes that residents will get together and do it themselves. The people who get together will usually be women because taking care of children is still seen as their primary responsibility. But with increasing proportions of women acting as heads of households or working outside the home, fewer are going to have time to pressure for funds for facilities or programs that should have been there in the first place. For this reason the operating and replacement budget should have contingency funds for the modification of play areas after occupancy.

See also: Landscape installation and modification (179), Maintenance policies (239), Resident's manual (241).

Equipped Play Areas for Children Five to Twelve Years Old

Some of the developmental features of this period of middle childhood include the following (Hart, 1973; Pollowy, 1977):

1. Children are able to create a fairly accurate mental map of their neighborhood, comprehend distances, and move around on foot or by bicycle without getting lost. They wish to explore areas at increasing distances from home and to use bicycles and public transport alone.
2. Children attain adult capacities of distance perception (very efficient to 100 yards [86 m], quite efficient to 1 mile [1.6 km]); by age ten they have auditory accuracy comparable to adults (very efficient to 20 feet [6.1 m], one-way communication possible to 100 feet [30.5 m]). They can engage in games that require considerable perceptual skills (for example, baseball and cricket).
3. Motor coordination continues to improve, and many activities evolve around new skills (for example, hopscotch, skipping, jumping, climbing, bicycling, skating, and swimming).
4. With the mental capacity to understand and obey rules and with the necessary motor skills at their command, children of eight or nine start to be interested in and skilled at team sports.
5. There is an intense desire to explore the world through creative play—digging tunnels, building tree houses, collecting bugs.
6. From the age of about six years on there is a desire for periods of privacy and quiet, which children seek out in their own room or in secret places in the outdoor environment.
7. Children increasingly spend time away from home, with their own peer group. In the earlier years of this period (six to eight) groups are haphazard and informal. From seven or eight on groups tend to be made up of same-sex peers and to engage in true cooperative play, with group decisions and rules adhered to. From about ten on groups may become highly structured, gathering around specific interests, with a stable membership and special observances such as rules and passwords. This is a period when adult-sponsored programs (sports, hobbies, crafts) are generally well received.
8. This is essentially the period of *social play*, which may include cooperating on projects, talking, and watching and playing traditional games (tag, hide and seek, hopscotch). It is also the period in which *cognitive-intellectual play* (emerging in the late preschool years) is further developed. This mode of play includes fantasy, role playing, problem solving, and simple experiments (damming streams, building forts).

98. Middle-childhood users

The whole site must be designed with high priority to the needs of five- to twelve-year-olds, who will be the predominant user group.

Children aged approximately five to twelve are generally the most frequent users of outdoor areas for play. A major study of play on fifteen modern estates in Britain reports that 30 percent of five- to ten-year-olds, but only 17 percent of under-fives and 13 percent of over-tens, were seen outside at any one time.

This age group tends to use the whole site area for play activities (Architecture . . . , 1969; Committee . . . , 1972; Cooper and Marcus, 1971; Cooper Marcus, 1974; Department . . . , 1973a, 1974; Gehl, 1971; Hole, 1966; Ministry . . . , 1967c; White, 1970). Thus in specifying planting, site furniture, pathways, entries, and communal spaces remember that these children will inevitably try to climb trees, leapfrog over bollards, cycle down pathways, hang about at entrances, and kick a ball around in any flat, grassy space. It is legitimate that they should do so, and it is up to the designer to create circumstances where this can happen with minimal problems for other children, adults, and management.

Possible design response

- Design every portion of the site as if it were going to be used by children—it probably will be!

See also: Playing everywhere (79), Children in the landscape (165), User group territories (227).

99. Children as planners

Children need to be included in the process of designing areas they will use.

If grown-up users of the physical environment have been excluded from the planning process, children have been doubly excluded. Many adults regard them virtually as "nonpeople," not as thinking human beings with opinions and preferences and the ability to express them. Hart and Moore have been pioneers in working with children as research collaborators. Hart's study of where and how children play in the landscapes in and around a small Vermont town is full of rich detail about the children's own perceptions of these activities and places (Hart, 1978). If he had not used children as informants, his conclusions would have been very different. The same is true of Moore's studies of children's play in inner-city, suburban, and rural settings in Britain and California (Moore, 1985). Yet such studies are few in number, largely because carrying out this work takes time, patience, and a particular empathy with children.

Most designers and planners, like other adults, seem to have virtual amnesia about their own favorite childhood play spaces. When people are asked to draw or recall their own favorite places of childhood, the majority tend to remember semienclosed or "secret" places—leftover spaces (Cooper Marcus, 1978a). Yet the planning and design process leaves little to chance and eliminates potential hiding places (although sometimes reasonably, because of security). Perez and Hart (1980) point out the need to have children describe and map the environment in their own terms, and this would be especially relevant in rehabilitating an existing housing site; a leftover corner, which may seem ripe for "tidying up" in adult eyes, may turn out to be a perfect clubhouse in the eyes of children.

Pollowy, in *The Urban Nest* (1977, pp. 108–9), summarizes three kinds of play planning processes:

1. A process *for* children—involving a professional "expert" designer, noninvolvement of the clients (that is, children), and a strong orientation to a final "aesthetic" product
2. A process *with* children—where "experts" work with children, where process becomes as important as product, but where there is a final physical, fixed outcome
3. A process *by* children—where the "expert" ceases to exist and is replaced by a facilitating manager or play leader, where children create, destroy, and re-create their play environment, where orientation is toward pro-

Figure 121 (a, b, c). There is a place for the "expert"-designed play area, but not if it results in facilities like these. What self-respecting, creative child would want to play in any of them for more than a few minutes?

cess and involvement, and where there is no finite product

An example of the first process (*for* children) is the standard equipped playground, designed and constructed on a housing site before residents move in. Examples of the second (*with* children) are more difficult to find but probably include British play parks where leaders and children develop and modify the playground together. Examples of the third (*by* children) are adventure playgrounds, now thoroughly accepted in Western Europe (Bengtsson, 1970) and making tentative inroads into American recreational programs (Cooper, 1970a). All three approaches (and "products"), with certain provisos, have their merits and should be included in any new (or redeveloped) housing area.

Possible design responses

- In rehabilitating an existing housing site:
  - Ask children to map, name, and rate their current outdoor environment. Preserve spaces and places that are significant to them.
  - Involve children and adults in selecting areas of the site that are currently un- or underused and that might be redeveloped as adventure playgrounds or play parks.
  - Involve children in determining which existing play areas should remain and which should be modified or removed.
  - Ask children to take you on their major walking routes through the site. Locate new play areas close to these routes.

- Take children, where feasible, to existing play areas of different types in the town and ask them to rate them and their component parts. Select equipment that children prefer.
- Ensure that the operating budget can provide funds for a play facilitator who can help children create their play preferences.
- Where a site is too small to provide all three types of play provisions cited, provide at a minimum a designed play equipment area on site, and ensure that local voluntary or municipal agencies have plans to create, with local children, a safely accessible adventure playground or play park in the neighborhood.

See also: Adventure playground (113), User-oriented landscaping (164), Landscape installation and modification (179), Taking risks (232), Tenant involvement (244).

100. Equal play opportunities

The outdoor environment close to home must provide equally for boys and girls.

In Britain and North America girls do not play outside as much as boys, and once there they are much more restricted by their parents in the distance they can range from home (Bussard, 1974; Carrasco, 1977; Hart, 1978). This may be partially because girls have been acculturated to prefer more indoor pursuits and have more domestic duties than boys, but mainly it is because girls are seen as more vulnerable to sexual molestation. Restrictions may also be placed on boys, but these are seen as much more "flexible." If boys violate their restrictions, parents tend to shrug it off as "boys will be boys." Unlike the positive reinforcement girls receive for staying close to home, the negative effects of punishment do not serve to dissuade boys from their adventures.

In a study of a Manhattan neighborhood, Perez and Hart (1980) found that eight- to nine-year-olds of both sexes are able to travel to the end of their block or on an errand on their own but that by ten or eleven boys' free ranges are considerably larger than girls'; girls are frequently restricted to the same range they were allowed at eight or nine. If girls are to be permitted as much environmental freedom as boys—and for psychological and developmental reasons this is extremely desirable—residential settings must be designed so that parents perceive them as safe. This means a setting sub-

What the children were doing, by age and sex

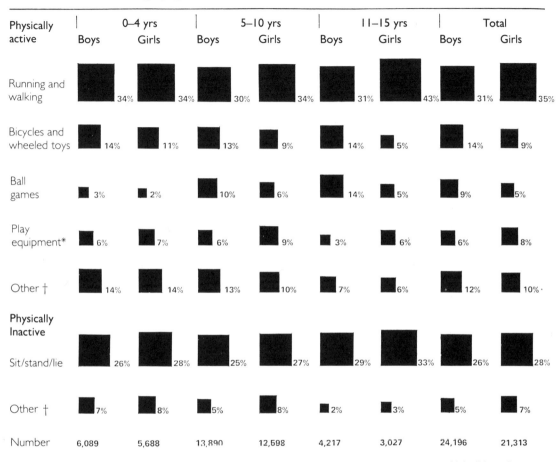

Figure 122. Children's outdoor activities by age and sex, as recorded in a British study of moderate- and high-density housing. (Source: Department . . . , 1973a)

Physically active	0–4 yrs		5–10 yrs		11–15 yrs		Total	
	Boys	Girls	Boys	Girls	Boys	Girls	Boys	Girls
Running and walking	34%	34%	30%	34%	31%	43%	31%	35%
Bicycles and wheeled toys	14%	11%	13%	9%	14%	5%	14%	9%
Ball games	3%	2%	10%	6%	14%	5%	9%	5%
Play equipment*	6%	7%	6%	9%	3%	6%	6%	8%
Other †	14%	14%	13%	10%	7%	6%	12%	10% ·
Physically Inactive								
Sit/stand/lie	26%	28%	25%	27%	29%	33%	26%	28%
Other †	7%	8%	5%	8%	2%	3%	5%	7%
Number	6,089	5,688	13,890	12,698	4,217	3,027	24,196	21,313

* Percentages were adjusted to exclude the numbers of children observed on those estates which did not have play equipment.

† Percentages were adjusted to exclude the numbers of children observed on those estates where the activity category was not divided into physically active and inactive.

Therefore totals exceed 100%.

divided into reasonably sized and enclosed "clusters" so that adults have a sense of responsibility toward "their" portion of the neighborhood and strangers (particularly antisocial ones) are cautious about entering such "defensible space."

Both sexes in the under eleven age group enjoy play with wheeled vehicles and toys. Above that age it tends to be more of a male pursuit. Small children rarely play ball games; after age eleven such games are predominantly engaged in by boys. Girls of all ages tend to wander around the site more than boys, especially during adolescence (Department . . . . , 1973a).

Whether by "nature or nurture," boys above nine or ten tend to be attracted to open spaces, such as playing fields, where they can engage in competitive field sports. There is a tendency in housing design—perhaps because most designers, who are men, recall their own boyhoods—to go overboard on such flat, featureless spaces. Thus the response of (male) planners in a typical Australian suburb to the fact that children were bored and unstimulated in their home environments was to propose more playing fields (Lynch, 1977)—despite the fact that existing playfields were ample and largely unused. This does little for girls, who are more attracted than boys to play equipment, to wandering about in the neighborhood, or to gathering at the edges of "wide open spaces" in small groups.

Possible design responses

- Without removing excitement, interest, or challenge from the environment, subdivide residential settings into enclosed "clusters" to create a sense of safety and enclosure.
- Use "defensible space" (Newman, 1976) and "manageable space" (Perlgut, 1982) criteria to allocate spaces and provide opportunities for resident surveillance and control.
- Provide challenging play equipment.
- Provide safe (but interesting) pedestrian networks.
- Provide "prairie" or large, featureless open space on the edges of developments or between neighborhoods rather than as the core of a housing scheme.
- Provide a *variety* of play spaces and environments so that boys and girls can use areas other than those they have traditionally been expected to use—or rewarded for using.

See also: "Opportunities for Surveillance" in Chapter 13—Security and Vandalism, Group territory (72), Interesting landscaped spaces (73), Comfortable space dimensions (74), Varying spaces (75).

101. Play on site

Neighborhood play provision should never be regarded as a substitute for play space within the housing development for this age group.

Play space within the neighborhood but beyond the bounds of a specific housing development is not a realistic substitute for areas close to home that children can use casually, without relying on adults or older siblings to take them there (Cooper, 1970a; Department . . . , 1973a; Hole, 1966; Holme and Massie, 1970; Parish and Parish, 1972).

A study of city children reveals that only 14 percent (mostly teenagers) use parks for play; the remainder used space in and around the home (yard, sidewalk, street, alley). Parks are seen as too vast and unchallenging compared to the excitement and more human scale of sidewalk and street, and the more formal team games in parks do not allow for the "pickup" spontaneity of play on the street (Jacobs and Jacobs, 1980). Most children play in brief spurts and close to home. However a park can substitute for teenagers' on-site play space because this age group is more mobile, more likely to want to play out of sight of home, and more likely to be able to relate to the large open spaces that have little meaning for small children.

Possible design responses

- In housing developments of more than twenty dwellings provide on-site play equipment areas for school-age children.
- If the housing site is divided into two or more sections by busy streets, provide a play area for this age group in each section.

See also: Children safe from cars (3), Sidewalk activities (69), Woonerfs (70), Adjacent public facilities (71).

102. Walk to play

Provide on-site, well-equipped, and challenging play areas for school-age children within five minutes' walk from home.

Every school-age child should have access to an equipped play area no more than five minutes' walking distance from home. Reaching it should entail crossing only minor streets (and preferably none at all). The area should foster spontaneous play rather than be the focus of formal outings with parents. This area should not be located too close to dwellings or be placed between the end walls of buildings, where noise transmission can be exacerbated. When residents complain about the noise of children's outdoor play, it is frequently *this* age group (five to twelve) that is the problem.

However, in siting play areas for school-age children give their safety needs precedence over adult needs for peace and quiet. On no account should a site be placed "across the road" or tucked in a corner of the parking lot. Give careful consideration to the flow of children to and

Figure 123. If a local park is situated across a busy road from the housing area it is supposed to serve, it might as well be miles away in terms of accessibility to children.

from the playground. They will inevitably move to and from it to the corner store, stopping places for the ice cream van, bus stops, and nearby but different play spaces (school yard, ball games area, cycling path, and so on). All these facilities should therefore be seen as an integrated system, and their siting and connections should be carefully considered.

Possible design responses

- Provide a play area with the following qualities:
  - If adjacent to dwellings, sunken or screened by mounding (berms) and/or heavy planting to reduce annoyance
  - Located in a central position along frequently used children's routes through the site (not in a corner)
  - Safely linked to attractive off-site facilities by pedestrian crossings, traffic lights, subway, or bridge so that only minor streets must be crossed
- Locate equipped playgrounds no farther than 440 yards (400 m) from dwellings and unequipped play areas no farther than 220 yards (200 m) away.

See also: Pedestrian precinct (67), Interesting landscaped spaces (73), Pedestrians passing by (187), Footpath play (189), User group territories (227), Conflicting uses (230).

Figure 124. A poorly equipped and badly located play area in a high-density housing scheme: There are busy roads on three sides, and a landscaped space on the left has no access from it to the play area. (For its location see bottom right corner of plan depicted in Figure 224.)

103. Complementary play

Locate play equipment for school-age children near other play opportunities.

At about age ten or twelve children start to find equipment such as slides and swings boring or "sissy" and need other kinds of stimulation. In many London parks a particularly happy arrangement seems to be the juxtaposition of a traditionally equipped area and a supervised play park. In new Swedish suburbs play parks provide a series of "outdoor rooms," each of which caters to a different kind of play—playing cards at a table, climbing on equipment, building with oversized wooden blocks, and so on. In a highly successful redeveloped Berkeley school yard a natural area of grass, bushes, ponds, and wildlife is adjacent to a large asphalt area for running and ball games; children move back and forth between these two very different environments to engage in an astonishing variety of activities (Moore, 1980; Moore and Young, 1978).

In a behavioral mapping study of a low-income housing project in North Carolina, Coates and Sanoff (1973) found that, of three potential wooded play areas, the one closest to a play equipment area (merry-go-round, paving, and benches) is the one most heavily used. Both the woods and the equipment are predominantly used by six- to nine-year-olds, and the authors speculate that the proximity and visual contact between children in these two areas is what makes both of them so popular.

Where the spatial scale and budget of a housing development precludes generous provision of different kinds of play spaces, the environment must be even more sensitively designed to maximize opportunities for different activities. For example, why not make fences in such a way that they double as a seating or balancing surface or create artificial mounds for potential play, socializing, or viewing surfaces?

Possible design response

- Locate play areas with traditional equipment within sight of those with different play opportunities (for example, a supervised play park or adventure playground, wild area, ball game area, and so forth).

See also: Children's spaces (81), Hard-surface play (82), Leftover spaces (83), Adventure playground (113), Ball games (123), Grassed areas (169).

104. Sibling play

Play areas for different age groups should be separated for safety reasons, but not necessarily segregated.

In a Vancouver study of subsidized family housing a number of children interviewed mentioned that they were not allowed to go to other sections of the site because "older children beat up

Figure 125. A play area for five- to ten-year-olds felicitously located next to a basketball area used primarily by older brothers.

kids there . . . and get mad if we make noise" (Eikos Group, 1980). Where many children are involved—as in a large housing development or an actively used neighborhood park—preschoolers should be segregated from children five to ten for safety reasons. But in small to medium-sized developments (about twenty to three hundred dwellings) segregation may not be necessary or desirable. Unofficial "time zoning" creates a natural segregation: Smaller kids tend to use play areas in the morning; older kids use them after school; and teenagers use them in the evening (Cooper Marcus, 1974).

In a study of a low-income housing project in North Carolina, Coates and Sanoff (1973) observe that play areas close to a teen basketball court were more heavily used, and by children in a greater age range, than other play areas on site. This was partly the result of teenage residents supervising younger siblings, partly the result of children preferring to cluster "where the action is."

Possible design responses

- In developments with large numbers of children (over three hundred dwellings) provide separate facilities for preschool children and those aged five to ten.
- In developments with under three hundred dwellings amalgamate play areas for these two groups or locate them within sight of each other.
- In developments with separate but connected court areas locate one play area to serve all age groups in each court.

- Locate basketball courts for teenagers within sight and calling distance of a play area that can accommodate a wide age range of younger children.
- Consult with parents and children about their preference for age-segregated play facilities.

See also: Friendly encounters (131), Pedestrians passing by (187), User group territories (227), Conflicting uses (230).

105. Safe play

The whole environment should be designed with the safety needs of children in mind.

Figure 126. A paved slope outside the pub in a London housing estate. Although not intended for play, it is nevertheless used for sliding. One child has reportedly died here from a skull fracture. (Thamesmead, London)

Once children start to crawl it is virtually impossible for an adult to watch them every moment of the day. In one urban region of Britain alone (Tyneside) nineteen children under fourteen were killed in 1966 in falls from windows or balconies. Although some local authorities (Birmingham, Greater London Council) have imposed their own compulsory requirements for window catches, for example, no national building regulation makes them compulsory everywhere (Gittus, 1976).

Once a child is old enough to play outside the home, the risks are clearly greater. The British Design Council estimates that a total of twenty thousand playground accidents a year need hospital treatment. Another estimate puts the number requiring medical attention (from doctor or hospital) at one hundred fifty thousand.

A recent British report on dangers in the playground points out that, in Britain at least, a civil lawsuit following a playground accident is costly and prolonged. Many parents settle out of court, but because the law of negligence depends greatly on legal precedents, any settlement out of court (approximately 95 percent of the total) does not take its place in official records and does not constitute a legal precedent.

Thus the law fails to accept that the child is a special kind of victim, needing far more protection against accident than an adult. . . . It is ludicrous that unsafe playgrounds can be excused legally on the grounds that children "ought to know" the dangers, and act accordingly. Those who design and manufacture playground equipment, those who install and maintain it, those who supervise playgrounds must be made to face their responsibilities squarely. They are being paid to provide an environment that is as safe as possible for unsupervised children. If the children use the equipment in ways that have not been forseen, the charge of thoughtlessness and neglect should be levelled against the adults, not against the children. (Danger . . . , 1978, 18, 21).

A U.S. study on playground safety reported by Wilkinson and Lockhart (1980, 91) finds that in public playgrounds climbing apparatus accounts for most accidents (43 percent), then slides (38 percent), swings (10 percent), and seesaws (10 percent). A British study finds that the types of equipment most often involved in accidents are swings (the most used apparatus), merry-go-rounds, slides (although accident levels are low compared with usage), and climbing frames (low usage and low accident rate). Whatever the equipment involved, the most common cause of the actual injury is falling onto hard surfaces. In half the accidents reported in this study the child fell onto concrete, gravel, or asphalt. (See guideline 95 for details on playground surfaces.) The next most common accident is being hit by a swing—usually walking or running into its path. The most serious accidents (fractures, concussion, and so forth) seem to involve slides and climbing frames. (Department . . . , 1976).

Another serious hazard in play areas is lack of maintenance. A study of playgrounds in four British communities finds numerous cases of playground surfaces littered with broken glass or old bricks, splintered wood on swings and seesaws, wobbly climbing frames, steps missing on ladders up to slides, merry-go-rounds' handrails missing or loose, broken or uneven surfaces around or under equipment, and numerous cases of loose, rusted screws and nails extending from the equipment (Department . . . , 1976).

Figure 127. A parent-sponsored study of dangers on the playground found this to be among the most lethal pieces of equipment—a rocking horse under which small legs can slip and be permanently crippled. Such is the lack of collaboration on play provision— typical of many countries—that an official British government paper actually recommended this same equipment.

None of the really serious faults was found in *supervised* play areas: "Broken equipment, whether from lack of maintenance or vandalism, is clearly a potential source of accidents. However, supervision—which is appreciated by mothers and children—does seem to be one way of reducing the risk, if only because serious hazards don't go unnoticed" (Department . . . , 1976, 4).

The same study finds children using equipment in all kinds of unconventional ways (crawling up chutes of slides, using swing frames for climbing, sliding down the central pole of a spiral slide). The authors note that supervision could reduce accidents but conclude that misuse of equipment is not a major source of accidents: "It seems natural that children should experiment with equipment as we saw them doing. It is unrealistic to expect them to use equipment only as the designer intended" (Department . . . , 1976, 4).

It is indeed ironic, as a Canadian authority on play points out, that providing (traditional) playground equipment, some of which is actually dangerous, is seen by the authorities as "doing something for the children. . . . it serves the housing authorities as a way out, a scapegoat. Plunk down a few pieces of equipment and your conscience is clear. The fact that . . . the choice of equipment is inappropriate to the children it is supposed to serve is not admitted. Somehow that does not count, because the user—the child—is not the client. I know of no other product on the market that continues sales

when it is defunct, little-used and often dangerous" (Hill, 1980, 30).

We reiterate that the *whole* environment will be used for play, whether or not specific play areas are present, and that every feature should be designed or specified with the exploratory, accident-prone characteristics of children in mind.

Possible design responses. (Department . . . , 1976; "Getting down . . .", 1975).

- Use impact-absorbing surfaces (preferably sand) under equipment from which falls are possible, particularly climbing frames and slides.
- Design freestanding slides so that their height does not exceed 8 feet 2 inches (2.5 m). The ladder should have deep, child-spaced steps made of nonslip material and be paneled in at the side. There should be a cabin structure at the top of the slide. The slide itself must have curved protective sides made as one continuous section because panels can buckle and leave knife-edged projections.
- Locate slides so that there is plenty of room at the landing place.
- Build slides to follow the contours of existing or specially made mounds or embankments; position steps at the side of the slide or children will beat their own path back to the top. In the Northern Hemisphere all slides should, where possible, face north: Sun-heated metal can cause severe burns.

- Slides built into embankments are particularly suitable for some disabled children, who will benefit from not having to climb conventional steps.
- Provide impact-absorbing swing seats such as those made out of old car tires or heavy-duty webbing. A moving swing attains a speed of 25 miles (40 rm) per hour. A child hit at that speed by the hard edge of a wooden or plastic seat is struck with the impact of a five-ton truck.
- Locate swings (or fence them off) so that children are not forced to go too close to them on their way to and from other activities, or erect a barrier at the front and back of a row of swings, one that is clearly a barrier, not seen (and used) as another piece of climbing apparatus.
- Ensure that moving equipment is designed so that fingers, arms, and legs cannot be trapped between moving and stationary parts or moving parts and the ground.
- Provide for daily inspections of play equipment. Provide more detailed inspection, including consideration of effects of corrosion and other gradual deterioration, every one to three months. Provide certified inspection by a professional engineer every six to twelve months (Getting . . . , 1979). (See guideline 239 for details of maintenance checks needed.)
- Provide a notice display at each site indicating the address and phone number of the responsible person to whom people should re-

port defects, the telephone number and address of the nearest hospital with an emergency department, and the location of the nearest public telephone.
- Repair vandalism and other damage promptly.
- Ensure that playground managers keep a record of all playground accidents and make it available for public inspection.

See also: Above-ground balconies (64), Playing everywhere (79), Open space maintenance (86), Hazard-free play (92), Sand play (95), Child density (231), Play equipment upkeep (247).

106. Equipment variety

Provide play equipment for a variety of experiences.

Because children generally spend very little time in any one activity, the degree of use of an equipped playground depends largely on the variety of the equipment provided (Byrom, 1972; Committee . . . , 1972; Cooper and Marcus, 1971; Cooper Marcus, 1974; Department . . . , 1971a, 1972a, 1973a; Eikos Group, 1980; Hole, 1966; Larsson, 1980; Sandvik, Shellenbarger, and

Stevenson, 1973). One British study concludes that "the amount of equipment provides a clearer basis of differentiation [between frequently and infrequently used playgrounds] than does the area. The well-used playground offered a minimum of three items but had on average six items, whereas those which were not much used had an average of 1.7 items" (Hole, 1966, 8). But because standards are most easily quantified in terms of space—"20–25 square feet (1.8–2.3 sq. m) per person on the estate, not counting people in 1 and 2 person dwellings" (Ministry . . . , 1961, 42)—equipment does not receive its proper share of scrutiny.

Figure 128. Although this equipment is sculpturally appealing, there is little variety of things to do on it.

Equipment should stimulate a variety of activities; a playground with three different swings promotes only one kind of activity, but a sensitively designed wooden play tower may incorporate opportunities to climb, hide, swing, slide, turn somersaults, and fantasize.

Children need to be able to see older children doing things they cannot yet quite achieve. For this reason the whole play equipment area should encourage movement through progressively more difficult developmental tasks, with both graded challenges and places where children can retreat and watch when the challenge is too difficult. Children's drawings in a Vancouver study of children's perceptions in three housing developments showed that they value creative, stimulating, and challenging environments and a diversity of activities (Eikos Group, 1980).

Possible design responses

- Provide a tall, eye-catching feature that clearly announces "This is a playground."
- Provide in any one play area:
  - Facilities for climbing, swinging, jumping, and sliding (gross motor activity)
  - Opportunities for digging in and manipulating the environment, especially by the combination of sand and water (small muscle coordination)
  - Places to hide or play "secretly" in small groups—under hardy shrubs or part of a climbing tower (cognitive and social play)
  - Peripheral places for quiet contemplation, rest, or fantasy (cognitive and social play),

such as a grassy slope beside the active area, benches or retaining walls, shady nooks beneath trees, or nooks and crannies in the play area boundary. (Both children and adults naturally feel more secure at the edges of spaces because a peripheral position allows them to observe from a safe viewing point. But these places should not provide hiding spots for adults after dark.)

See also: Flow of play (110).

Figure 129. Here a child can choose to slide, swing, climb, hide, balance, dig—or just watch from the sidelines.

107. Children's preferences

Play equipment should be selected with children's preferences in mind.

Children prefer equipment that moves (swings, merry-go-round), equipment on which they can move (slides), equipment on which they can climb (jungle gyms, climbing towers), and places nearby where they can sit and watch the activity, talk, and play quiet games (benches and low tables) (Cooper and Marcus, 1971; Cooper Marcus, 1974; Department . . . , 1973a; Hole, 1966).

In a study of the play preferences of a sample of British seven- to twelve-year-olds the Research Institute for Consumer Affairs (U.K.) found the following order of preference: spiral slide (in a class of its own in terms of popularity), high slide, swings, ocean wave, plank swing, tile swings, plane swings, tank climbing frame, small slide, merry-go-round, jungle gym, and seesaw (see Fig. 130). For all these the majority questioned liked the item. More children disliked the following than liked them: rocking horse, whirling platform, logs, tent-shaped climbing frame, and joy wheel (Department . . . , 1976). The study concludes that "attempts to provide safer playgrounds which ignore children's preferences may drive them away to other more dangerous situations" (Department . . . , 1976, 2).

Children's imaginations are stimulated and their interest maintained by ambiguous subjects/structures/spaces with which they can choose to play at rocket ships, school, hospital,

Play equipment preferences of a sample of
7–12 year olds in Manchester and London, U.K.

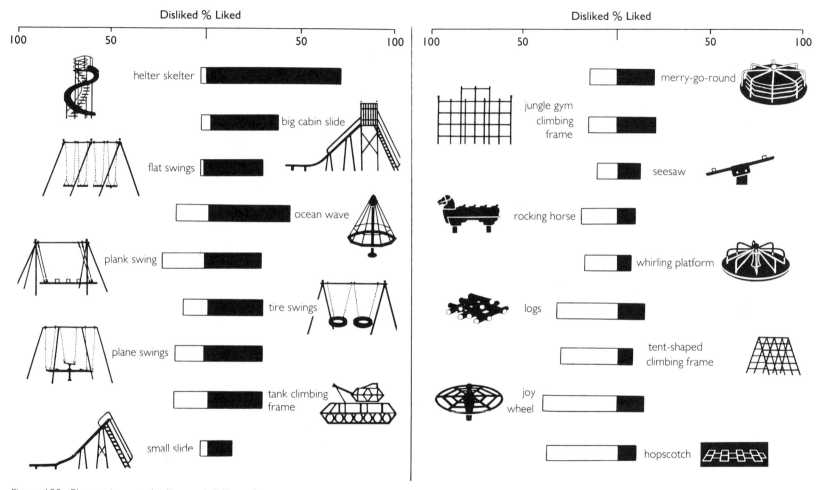

Figure 130. Play equipment: the likes and dislikes of
children seven to twelve years old. (Source: Department . . . , 1976)

or whatever. They are not interested in concrete turtles and tubular steel dinosaurs. When given the choice of both, children tend to play much more frequently on conventional playground equipment (such as swings and slides)

Cost and use of play areas, by estate

Estate	Cost per sq ft*		Percentage of use	No.
	£	%		
Winstanley	1.74	11		3,562
Curnock	1.58	15		2,846
Acorn	1.32	13		3,732
Canada	0.95	13		3,780
The Bonamy	0.95	8		3,163
Warwick	0.92	3		4,773
Edith	0.87	3		4,861
Sceaux	0.75	4		1,732
Park Hill	0.74	18		4,424
Woodway	0.50	5		3,215
St Mary's	0.47	18		5,169

* The costs per sq ft quoted in the table are not actual scheme costs, but are a comparable valuation based on prices ruling for average local authority schemes in early 1972. They therefore eliminate the many variables between individual schemes. They include the cost of: construction; play equipment; seats, litter bins and lighting; enclosing walls, fencing and ballustrading; planting; paving, grassing and turfing; drainage and general excavation.

Figure 131. More money spent on play areas does not necessarily result in higher use. Comparative costs and degree of use of play areas on eleven British housing estates. (Source: Department . . . , 1973a)

than on architect-designed play structures (Department . . . , 1971a, 1973a; Hole, 1966; Holme and Massie, 1970). Specially designed play structures *have* proved popular, however, if they provide for a variety of children's preferred activities—for example, those that involve a number of different ways of climbing up and coming down again (slides, slippery poles, pulley swings), a variety of levels and sizes of spaces, small and partially hidden spaces accessible only to smaller children, and larger, high-up spaces where older children can congregate, survey the scene, and feel a sense of mastery over the environment.

Figure 132. This playground of conventional and well-liked equipment had the lowest cost per square foot and was among the most frequently used. (St. Mary's, Oldham, U.K.)

Commercial play equipment manufacturers in the United States and Canada now produce attractive "kits" of logs, bolts, rungs, rings, and slides that can be assembled on site in many different ways. Unless components include plenty of moving parts or other features that children enjoy, however, they will become abandoned wooden sculptures, useless to children, however aesthetically pleasing they are.

Possible design responses

- Use "catalogue" play structures only if they provide challenging play opportunities, such as:
  - Equipment that moves
  - Climbing up and coming down in a variety of ways
  - Variety of levels
  - Variety of sizes of spaces
  - Hidden spaces
  - Higher spaces to survey the scene
- With a tight budget or space specify "old favorites" rather than expensive, commercially produced creations.
- Include several pieces of equipment that allow children to enjoy pleasurable and unusual kinesthetic experiences—for example, swings, slide, and merry-go-round.
- Avoid equipment that is totally static and has no moving parts.
- Avoid catalogue play structures that resemble real objects—a metal dinosaur, spaceship, airplane. Select structures that provide challenging play opportunities, including the opportunity—provided by *ambiguity*—to exercise the imagination.

See also: Children as planners (99), Equipment variety (106).

Figure 133. This play area cost almost twice as much as that at St. Mary's and was used by only 3 percent of the children living in the housing project. (Warwick Estate, Paddington, London)

108. Tarzan swings

Children enjoy testing their skills and courage in daring experiences.

Children growing up in the country frequently sling a rope over a suitable tree to create a Tarzan swing, preferably over water or a long drop. In new housing lacking mature trees it may be necessary to design settings for such swings.

Possible design responses

• Where a suitable mature tree exists on site, create a Tarzan swing from the strongest branch and ensure that no paths or play areas are in its path and that a soft ground cover is provided underneath (Eikos Group, 1980).
• Design a play tower that permits swinging or sliding from one level to another or swinging back and forth in a large arc and returning to the starting place.
• Where no mature trees exist on site, plant fast-growing, tall trees that will eventually have branches suitable for hanging Tarzan swings.

See also: Taking risks (232).

109. Children's lookouts

Children like to climb up high and gain a sense of mastery by looking out over the environment.

We spend the first dozen or so years of life looking up—literally—to superiors. Thus in reaction children often climb up a tree, on a chair, or up ladders to get a "superior" view. They particularly like semisecret spaces up high—a "nest" in a tree, a "room" in a play tower, a window in a house—from which they can secretly watch adults and passersby. Of a group of young adults asked to recall their favorite childhood environments, more than half spontaneously recalled just such places (Cooper Marcus, 1978a).

The climb up and down may also test gross motor skills, not to mention courage. The element of risk is inevitably part of the experience.

Possible design responses

• Plant sturdy, fast-growing, low-branching, climbable trees with thick outer foliage (and do not enact rules against tree climbing!). If such trees already exist on site, save them.
• Create wooden climbing towers with platforms, "rooms," or "nests" at various levels and climbing steps that become increasingly more difficult.

See also: Children's rights (85), Children as planners (99), Native species (171), Taking risks (232).

Figure 134. A successful play area with sand, perimeter seating, swings, slides, ladders, and places to climb up to and look out of. (Valencia Gardens, San Francisco)

110. Flow of play

Link activities in the play equipment area so that there is an obvious flow of play options.

Children have relatively short attention spans and move quickly from one activity to another. A linked play structure in which connections between activity features themselves become play elements or different activities spiral off a looped circuit accommodates this natural movement (Cohen et al., 1979). Although space must be left around certain equipment (such as swings) for safety purposes, the more integrated the activities, the more attractive the play areas will be to children. If connecting features—catwalks, stepping stones, and so forth—are varied in color, texture, and size, children may use these for self-generated games and contests.

Possible design responses

- While creating a variety of play possibilities via equipment provision, create the links between these (for example, catwalks, balancing poles, platform, and stepping stones) as potential play features also.
- Create a central, eye-catching play tower with different activities extending from it, like spokes of a wheel.

- Create a looped path system with different activities spiraling off it.
- Offer a choice of linkages between activities (horizontal, vertical, slanting) so that children are faced with easier and more difficult choices.

See also: Equipment variety (106).

111. Attractive play materials

Although play facilities should be built of sturdy materials, they should also fulfill children's and adults' aesthetic needs.

To reduce maintenance costs, play equipment in early public housing was made of tubular steel and set into concrete. The wooden and "log" play structures of more recent years are more appealing and speak to children's needs to move around on different levels and find semihidden platforms and enclosures. Although children may carve their initials or use spray paint on them, they are as durable as steel equipment and undoubtedly more attractive. Also, unlike steel, wood (and fiberglass) does not get uncomfortably hot in hot climates.

Concrete sewer pipes and the "new brutalist" concrete blocks still seen on some housing schemes are an insult to children and their needs and should be avoided at all costs.

See also: Attractive materials (234).

112. Supervised play

As more and more parents work, access to supervised after-school and summer play becomes essential.

In a study of a British new town more than half of all families interviewed in five middle-income, rental neighborhoods expressed a need for a supervised play area (Residential . . . , 1975). This is not a child-care center (although many used and wanted those too), but a play area where parents could feel their children were safe to go alone because a paid play leader was present at specified times (after school, Saturday mornings, and so forth). Significantly, in those estates that did *not* meet the criterion of an equipped play area within a safe, enclosed courtyard, visible from the dwelling, the proportion of resident families requesting a *supervised* play area rose to more than 80 percent for those with under-fives and 60 percent for families with five- to ten-year-olds. If the site design cannot provide for safe preschool play beyond the yard, the designer and client should seriously consider the need for a paid playground supervisor.

Probably the best developed model of supervised play areas comes from Sweden. In a typical new town or new, medium- to high-density suburb each neighborhood will have a supervised play area, approachable safely on foot from all the housing areas it serves ("lek-parker"). In Stockholm and other cities the parks department also runs a summer series of "child paddocks" in central area parks so that parents can leave their children with trained play leaders while they shop or attend to appointments. In low- and medium-rise apartment blocks in the newer suburbs a ground-level flat (often a problem space in terms of privacy) is generally given over as an after-school play center, with adjacent communal landscaped spaces available for outdoor play.

In Britain and the United States provision of supervised play areas still has a long way to go. Two successful supervised schemes in Britain are the "1 o'clock clubs" and "play parks" initiated by the Greater London Council Parks Department. The former, located in small, fenced areas in existing parks and open from one to five in the spring and summer, are staffed by play leaders who help the children and provide them

Figure 135. A supervised summer play scheme (day camp) for disabled and able-bodied children in a Berkeley, California, school yard. (Project PLAE)

with materials; the parent or child minder is expected to stay also. For many isolated parents and children in high-rise London estates these facilities have been a means of introducing children to others and for parents to meet other adults.

In "play parks" unconventional play structures are built and maintained by the full-time play leaders with the assistance of the children; these parks are generally located in corners of existing, mature parks. The presence of one or more play leaders with whom to play games or chat is undoubtedly a crucial element in the great success and drawing power of these play areas. A good play leader can expand the children's range of activities by encouraging play, by producing games, equipment, and materials (which could never be provided on an unsupervised playground), by organizing more intensive use of a given space, and by training the children in maintaining it themselves. On a supervised playground a small child from a minimal high-rise flat can engage in sand and water play, paint at a large easel, tricycle, climb, or meet friends— none of which may be possible within the confines of home. A play leader can help a socially deprived or immigrant child adjust to local play norms or a teenager acquire self-confidence through constructing a "house" or assisting with younger children.

Another possibility is the establishment of a "children's house" in each neighborhood. The first children's house was developed by Olive Kendon and the children of a working-class neighborhood in wartime Stockport (England) in 1941 (Kendon, 1979). An empty, rundown house was cleaned and decorated by and for the children and opened every day after school for activities the children chose and organized themselves (sewing, carpentry, cooking, games, singing). Although adult "guardians" were always present for advice and encouragement, the children themselves were in charge. They helped decorate the house, decided on preferred activities, elected their own committees, made their own rules, and determined when and how other neighborhood groups (old people's groups, preschool play groups) could use the building. Guardians treated the children as partners and gave them any help they needed without bossing (Scottish . . . , 1978). After the success of the Stockport children's house others were developed in other cities, using derelict houses, an abandoned pub, or purpose-built wooden structures. The children's house is an ideal model for areas where children would otherwise be at home alone or on the streets with keys around their necks.

A popular U.S. model for supervised summer child care is the "day camp," where programs of supervised sports, arts and crafts, games, and nature study are organized in local parks during the summer vacation.

Where there is a high proportion of working parents, the siting and design of a whole neighborhood or housing development should enable children to walk home alone safely or to walk from school to a supervised play center to home without adult assistance. Care should be taken, however, that the routes children use are inviting and interesting; otherwise they will stray to other—possibly more dangerous— routes. Supreme examples of good planning for the child pedestrian are the new suburbs around Stockholm—Vällingby, Fårsta, and others. The whole environment is safe and interesting enough so that children from about seven years on (school starting age in Sweden) can amuse themselves or drop into supervised playgrounds or play centers until their parents return from work.

An environment designed as a whole, with the safety of children in mind, will help liberate parents from continued home-based and isolating child care. The same criteria that make for "defensible space," to use Oscar Newman's term, also ensure an environment that is physically and socially protective of children, especially when they are temporarily alone (Newman, 1972).

Possible design responses

- Design the whole site so that children will be safe as they play alone between the end of school and their parents' return from work.
- Provide child-safe routes from home to schools, parks, and supervised play areas.
- Provide a ground-level dwelling with adjacent landscaped space for use as an after-school center.
- Convert an empty house (or designate a new dwelling) as a children's house.
- Consider providing play parks, with unconventional play structures and full-time play leaders.

- Consider the possibility of local parks or on-site open space being used as a summer holiday day camp. (For a very specific form of supervised play—the adventure playground—see next guideline.)
- Provide supervised fenced areas ("1 o'clock clubs") with toys, equipment, and materials for use by children accompanied by adults.
- Consider providing child paddocks, with trained play leaders, for casual, short-term child care.
- Investigate ways for parents and other adults to share supervisory responsibilities or the costs of trained play leaders.

See also: Adjacent public facilities (71), Supervising adults (94), Loose parts (114), Small meeting room (134), Day-care center (136), Footpath systems (182), Child density (231).

113. Adventure playground

Provide an adventure playground on site or nearby.

Adventure playgrounds are generally created on undeveloped lots, where loose spare materials (wood, sand, rope, bricks) are deposited. One successful playground in inner London (Notting Hill Gate) covers the site of three bombed houses. An equally successful playground in Huntington Beach, California, which occupies a much larger site, contains an abandoned quarry where children float rafts in shallow water. What makes such sites adventure playgrounds is the presence of a play leader to encourage and supervise children as they build, dig, climb trees, and so forth. The success of an adventure playground depends on the skill and personality of the play leader and on a steady supply of loose materials.

The advantages of adventure playgrounds include the possibility of establishing them on temporarily available sites, their low capital cost (although running costs are high), the reassuring presence of a play leader (male play leaders often become father figures for children from female-headed households), and the length of time children spend on such playgrounds. A comparative study of three New York City playgrounds found that the "traditional" playground (swings, slides, and so on) attracted children for only short periods of time (median twenty minutes); the "contemporary" playground (architect designed, with novel forms of fixed equipment),

for slightly longer (median thirty-two minutes); and an adventure playground, for the longest lengths of play (median seventy-five minutes) (Rothenberg, Hayward, and Beasley, 1974, 127–28). Most children came almost every day to the adventure playground and named it as their favorite. Although the largest age group attracted to this playground was school-age children (45 percent of total), 32 percent of those who attended were teenagers. (Of the users of the traditional and contemporary playgrounds only 10 percent and 7 percent, respectively, were teenagers.)

The activities in an adventure playground will vary, depending on the site, the play leader, and the children's interests. Abiding interests appear to be making houses, building structures, digging, taking care of animals, lighting fires, and cooking. Although a fire is not essential to an adventure playground (some security-conscious U.S. communities have balked at this element), the experience is especially important for today's city child, living in a centrally heated home with little chance to play and experiment with fire under safe conditions.

Although such playgrounds have been accepted rather slowly in North America, there were by 1980 a number of successful ones in Canada and around twenty in the United States. There is now abundant literature on their siting, design, and management (Balmforth and Nelson, 1978; Bengtsson, 1972; Cooper, 1970a; Ineichen, 1972). Despite initial fears of accidents and being sued, playground facilitators have had little trouble obtaining insurance, and accident rates have proved to be no different from those on conventional playgrounds (Wilkinson, Lockhart, and Luhtanen, 1980). Informed observation by the police, play leaders, and community workers and one documented study (Department . . . , 1981b) indicate that there is a likely reduction in neighborhood vandalism rates after the opening of an adventure playground.

A recent variation on the adventure playground is the German and British "youth farm" or "city farm." Vacant lots—on inner-city sites in Britain and mostly suburban sites in Germany—are turned into minifarms where children can help raise chickens, rabbits, sheep, goats, and horses. Many learn to ride the horses. Naturally, such an endeavor would be more appropriate at the neighborhood than at the housing site level.

Figure 136. A British adventure playground where part of the site is for risk-taking play, and part is given over to children for building houses and dens.

Possible design responses

The following are the basic requirements of an adventure playground:

- A *site* suitably scaled to its location. (A Swedish authority recommends a site no smaller than 1,794 square yards [1,500 sq. m] and no larger than 12,000 square yards [10,000 sq. m] [Bengtsson, 1972].)
- *Fencing*, both to create a sense of enclosure and privacy and to shield the sometimes chaotic appearance from passing adults
- Two *entries*, one for children and one for a vehicle delivering loose materials
- A *play hut* with electricity, water, toilets, and a phone for alternative forms of play, for play in inclement weather, and for play leaders' office and storage
- A *play leader*, whose qualities and experience are crucial to playground success
- A *management committee* of local parents to work with the leader to ensure funding and community interest (The typical story begins with a volunteer group raising its own funds to pay the play leader. Once the group has established the playground, it may then be taken over by a local parks or housing authority.)
- *Sequencing* of the several components of an adventure playground (A detailed study of problems at three adventure playgrounds in inner Liverpool stated that the ideal chronological sequence is, first, an effective and responsible management committee, second, two full-time play leaders, third, a site, fourth, a fence, and, fifth, a building. The example of one site they studied in which the sequence was fence, play leader, building, management committee was an object lesson in how not to do it [Wilson and Womersley, 1977].)

See also: Leftover spaces (83), Children as planners (99), Supervised play (112), Taking risks (232).

114. Loose parts

Provide children with the opportunity of playing with manipulable or "loose" parts.

If the site is not large enough for an adventure playground or parents object to smaller children using tools and rough lumber, the manipulative qualities of an adventure playground can be provided on a smaller scale and with "neater" results. The requirements are merely a storage locker, a responsible person to unlock it, and loose parts. Sturdy but light play blocks are manufactured in Sweden (together with a purpose-built, lockable storage chest). Alternatively, large-scale, modular parts could be constructed of light, durable wood or molded fiberglass (or a sympathetic milk wholesaler could be persuaded to part with a collection of indestructible plastic crates). The storage locker might be kept in an on-site day-care center and the loose parts made available alternatively to children in the center and to older children on site who do not attend the center.

Although a qualified play leader would be necessary where this facility was provided for many children, in a small housing site supervision might be entrusted to maintenance staff responsible only for locking and unlocking the storage area daily at appointed hours.

Possible design responses

- Create a space where children can play with large building blocks or loose parts.
- Provide durable modular units—cubes, solid rectangles, planks, rounds—that even small children can move around. They might be made of light wood or molded plastic and should be finished with nontoxic materials and be virtually indestructible.
- Provide suitable locked storage space where they can be kept after hours.
- Make arrangements for an adult to unlock and lock storage area at specified times.

Figure 137. Children frequently find driveways and parking areas fascinating places to play—especially when they are being constructed.

See also: Entry storage (51), Adventure playground (113), Secure storage (211), Resident caretaker (243).

115. Children's gardens

Children need to relate to the natural world and to have opportunities to care for growing things.

Especially in urban settings children should have firsthand opportunities to understand the growth and care of plants, the maintenance of soil fertility, the water cycle, and so on. If children are introduced to basic ecological principles when young, it seems reasonable to assume that they will be more attuned to appreciating and protecting the environment as adults.

Possible design responses

- Provide small garden plots (around 24 square feet [2.25 sq. m]), no more than 2 feet (0.6 m) wide (Coates and Sanoff, 1973) for use by children near adult allotments.
- Divide plots by frequent narrow pathways.
- Provide a water source and a lockable storage shed for tools nearby.

See also: Yard size (61), Display garden (62), Community garden (141), Personalized landscape (180).

116. Play nests

Children need to withdraw, to play alone or in small groups in sheltered, enclosed spaces.

We are too concerned that every corner should be in full view. . . . Must we really know everything and control everything in a child's life? Nobody imposes anything like the same interference on the country child. They have haystacks, barns, woodlands, and so on, and no one sees anything dangerous to society in that (Bengtsson, 1970, 154).

Children have varying moods and requirements through a typical day. A period of rough play may need to be balanced by a period of quiet reading, fiddling with grass and stones, or intimate conversation. A face-saving retreat may be the best solution to a painful encounter or an activity that has proved to be difficult.

Outdoor space needs to accommodate such behaviors, especially when the space-saving elements of modern, medium-density interior design leave so few nooks or crannies. Few props are needed to trigger a game of "house" or "racing car drivers" or "play school"—an old cardboard box or a milk crate is sufficient. But because adults tend to perceive old boxes and crates as trash and remove them, the design itself must provide comparable spaces and places. Semienclosed levels in a play tower can become rooms in a house; a bench can become a stage or a shop counter; bushes to crawl

under can become secret tunnels. The mere suggestion of enclosure is often sufficient; fantasy does the rest.

Cohen et al. (1979) report research that indicates that most spontaneous play groups in outdoor spaces are made up of from three to five

Figure 138. These boys at a California summer day camp have made their own teepee out of sticks and palm leaves.

children or among preschoolers two to four children. Play nests should be scaled to groups of these sizes.

Possible design responses

- Provide child-scaled enclosures (3 to 6 feet [0.9 to 1.8 m] wide and long, 3 feet [0.9 m] high) with single access, which catch the sun and are dry.
- Plant "nests" of shrubs or medium-high ground cover close to quiet, manipulative activities (sand play, children's gardens).
- Build wooden spaces (or create them out of old packing cases) on the edge of play areas.
- Create the potential for children to make their own "nests" by the arrangement of planting, berms, walls, site furniture, and so on.
- Leave part of the site in a wild state so that children can find natural nesting places or provide them with materials to build their own.

See also: Playing everywhere (79), Children's spaces (81), Leftover spaces (83), Shrubs for play (175).

117. Children's seating

Provide places for school-age children to sit.

Children spend much free outdoor time quietly socializing, daydreaming, or watching other children. A study of British children's outdoor play found that 27 percent of their time outdoors was spent in passive pursuits: sitting, standing, lying down, and/or watching others (Department . . . , 1973a). A comparable study of play in two West Coast American housing projects by Cooper Marcus (1974) shows that the number of children observing others playing frequently exceeds those actually engaged in active play. This often overlooked component of play must be accommodated.

Children find and use many places other than benches (steps, retaining walls, and bench-type edges of planters or play areas) to sit informally or to rest and play quietly after a period of strenuous activity. Edges are especially important; if a group of older children "invades" the play area, smaller children may want to retire to the edge to observe.

Possible design responses

- Provide benches, steps, retaining walls, and bench-type edges for planters or play areas.
- Ensure that space is provided for children (and supervising adults) in wheelchairs.

- Design benches with wide backs so that children can choose to sit on the backs or on the seats.

See also: "Site Furniture" in Chapter 12—Landscaping, Footpaths, and Site Furniture.

118. Children's toilets

Provide accessible toilets near major play areas.

Although the need for a toilet is obvious when a play area is separated from home, the authors of an extensive British study of play facilities conclude: "Hygiene has, on the whole, a low priority in playground provision. W.C.'s are in short supply, often filthy, and where they exist, only the minority are accompanied by wash basins" (Holme and Massie, 1970, 66).

Possible design responses

- Provide toilets under the informal scrutiny of an adult employee (for example, in the entry hall of a high-rise building near the manager's office, in a community building near the playground where a supervisor or janitor is always present, or adjacent to a communal laundry) (Holme and Massie, 1970).
- Locate clearly marked toilets at ground level, no farther than 50 yards (46 m) from play area.
- Ensure that at least one toilet is accessible to people in wheelchairs and clearly identified as such.

See also: Walk to play (102), Management office (223), Safe meeting places (224), Resident caretaker (243).

119. Undercover play

Provide a facility for sheltered play in wet weather.

An extensive British study of urban play concludes that children have few opportunities for play outside the home in winter and in bad weather (Holme and Massie, 1970, 66). Similar findings come from the United States (Becker, 1974) and Canada (Barker, 1976). Yet where indoor group play in inclement weather is not accommodated and children congregate in warm indoor corridors, stairwells, or laundries with their toys, balls, and vehicles, it is frustrating to them and annoying to adult residents.

Possible design responses

- Provide a roofed, semienclosed structure (gazebo, "bus shelter") adjacent to the play equipment area with benches and a table.
- Provide play equipment that itself forms sheltered spaces—for example, a climbing tower with platforms that forms shelters or a wide A-frame slide.
- Where appropriate, raise parts of buildings on pillars so that a sheltered indoor/outdoor play space with seating is created. (This would be especially appropriate in regions with heavy snowfall.)
- Provide a porch awning or overhang extending out from a play hut, storage structure, laundry room, or other nonresidential building and seating under it.

Figure 139. A sheltered corner space in a garage court that was intended for play in wet weather. It is rarely used, due in part to the lack of "props"—benches, a table, shelves—that might have stimulated children's use of the space. (Eaglestone, Milton Keynes New Town)

Figure 140. Play equipment that in itself forms a shelter is a good solution to the problem of wet-weather play.

- Plant clusters of trees with good rain protection qualities and with circular seats around their bases.
- Make a ground-level indoor recreation room available for children's play. (Above-ground indoor space is unsuccessful unless adequate physical comforts and supervision are provided.) In wet and cold climates provide a "mud room" for clothes, boots, and umbrellas.
- Consider providing a shared indoor play room, accessible and visible from a group of apartments that share in its use.
- Where cold or wet weather lasts for a number of months, consider providing a mobile indoor play area (a converted bus or large van that would be removed in the summer or drier months, for example).

See also: Supervised play (112), Children's toilets (118), Small meeting room (134), Safe meeting places (224).

120. Ice-skating

In areas with cold winters provide a location that can easily be converted to an ice rink.

In Canada and many northern states of the United States skating and hockey are the most popular winter sports for children and teenagers. Open spaces or tennis or basketball courts can be flooded in winter to form hockey rinks. If appropriate space for flooding is not thought about in advance, children will end up playing hockey in an inappropriate space, such as a parking lot—hazardous for themselves and for parked cars (Beck, Rowan, and Teasdale, 1975b).

Possible design responses

- Locate an ice-skating area to minimize noise problems for residents.
- Provide flat or shallow bowl-shaped areas that can easily be flooded.
- Provide a warming house (which might double as an adventure playground storage or play hut in the summer) (Cohen et al., 1979).
- Where possible, provide two rinks, one for casual skaters and one for hockey players.

See also: Hard-surface play (82).

121. Snow play

Where snow clearance routinely occurs in roadways and parking lots, take account of where children will slide on deposited snow piles.

When designing the parking lot and adjacent buildings, take care that snow piles can be deposited after snow clearance in such a way that children slide *away* from vehicular traffic. In one Canadian development the relationship of buildings to parking lots (20-foot [6 m] separation) virtually forced children to slide into the parking lots (MacLeod, 1977).

See also: Cold weather parking (160).

122. Winter playgrounds

In cold winter regions play areas should be designed for winter as well as summer use.

An Ontario study found that more than half the municipalities surveyed put major items of play equipment in storage between fall and spring. Reasons include safety (although there is no evidence that playgrounds are more dangerous in winter), maintenance, and "traditional practice." In fact playgrounds will continue to be used in winter if equipment is available. In the Ontario playgrounds left open, equipment was used and

a number of innovative field sports developed, including snowshoe softball, snowball, snowshoe soccer and football, and snolf (winter golf).

Possible design responses (Wilkinson, Lockhart, and Luhtanen, 1980)

- When designing a playground for potential winter use, employ berms, planting, and fencing so as to maximize sun exposure and wind protection. Place coniferous trees, shrubs, and mounds on the northwest, north, and east (in the Northern Hemisphere) to shelter the playground from cold winds and to trap the sun.
- Locate barriers so as to reduce snow buildup around the equipment and seating and en-

courage drifting in areas where it is desirable—for play or for further protection.
- When placing equipment, consider how its use will be affected when snowpack raises the playground floor by a foot or more and flow patterns may be different from in summer.
- Place the playground far enough from potential ice-skating areas to discourage children from using play equipment while wearing their skates.

See also: Ice-skating (120), Snow play (121), Snowmelt (177).

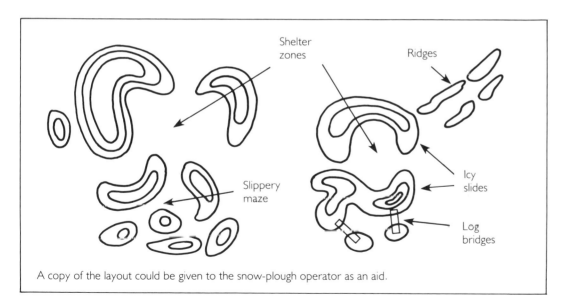

A copy of the layout could be given to the snow-plough operator as an aid.

Figure 141. Snowfall on a play area that has no equipment could be plowed into interesting shapes and slopes to stimulate winter play. (Adapted from Charles H. Thomsen and A. Borowiecka, *Winter and play*. Ottawa: Canada Mortgage and Housing Corporation)

RECREATION OPPORTUNITIES FOR TEENAGERS

At the onset of adolescence young people sometimes turn their backs on play as it has so far been discussed in this chapter; they start to notice the opposite sex, to take pains with their appearance, to spend as much time as possible with their peers, and to learn about world and self through social relationships. They "hang out" ("hang about" in Britain), a pastime adults tend to condemn as "wasting time" but that is a necessary component of growing up.

Teenagers have many of the same needs as adults—for places to get together, to have fun, to compete in sports—yet unlike many adults, they are dependent on public transport. Hence if these places are not within easy access of home, teenagers are likely to become bored and frustrated; some may even begin to engage in vandalism to relieve boredom.

The guidelines that follow cover only the broadest and most obvious of teenage needs close to home. The needs of smaller children are met mainly at and near home, but many teenage needs will be met at school, in the community, and in local parks, not within the housing site.

123. Ball games

On larger developments space should be provided for informal ball games.

Studies of children and teenagers in all kinds of housing areas report considerably less play on grass than on hard surfaces. This is primarily because so many small children play on or close to the doorstep and because so many popular games (skipping, bouncing a ball, roller skating, bicycling, hopscotch) require a hard surface. Nevertheless, uninterrupted level areas of grass are extremely popular for team ball games, essentially for boys aged eleven to fifteen.

Children are remarkably adaptable and do not necessarily need a regulation sports field to play softball, cricket, football, or soccer. Especially if they are boys between eleven and fifteen, they will inevitably use any reasonably level, well-drained, relatively obstruction-free space for ball games. In a New York study of public housing, Becker observed that up to 60 percent of teenagers playing outdoors played on parking lots (1974). It is unrealistic to expect children to take any notice of signs prohibiting ball games. Where prohibition of play on lawns is absolutely necessary, a combination of grading and planting can render a grassy area difficult to use (although not impossible—children are very

Figure 142. Boys play ball more often than girls. They will use any reasonably uncluttered space, whether intended for games or not.

ingenious!). In such cases make provision elsewhere on the site or adjacent to it for casual ball games.

In the United States and Canada, where basketball takes the place of cricket and soccer, half courts for basketball will always be well used.

Possible design responses

- Where possible, provide a good-sized space for soccer and other ball games on site: 110 by 60 feet (33.5 by 18.3 m) is recommended in Parker Morris standards (1978). Where site space is more limited, 100 by 50 feet (30.5 by 15.2 m) or 80 by 40 feet (24.4 by 12.2 m) are smaller but useful spaces (Ministry . . . , 1961).
- Where a ball game area is to be at ground level and screened only with a wire fence, locate it 65 to 100 feet (20 to 30 m) from the nearest dwelling (Shankland . . . , 1977). Where it is to be sunken or walled and noise is likely to be more contained, locate it 30 to 50 feet (10 to 15 m) away.
- Give close attention to the location of rooms and windows and the design of yard fences in dwellings closest to the ball game area.
- Where appropriate, provide for basketball. If space is limited, provide a half court and, if possible, a second area with a lower hoop where smaller children can play.
- Provide lighting for nighttime use.

See also: Paved areas (167), Grassed areas (169).

124. Teenage hangouts

Teenagers need informal gathering places.

Teenagers need "hangout" places where they can socialize and which they can claim as their own. They like to socialize, flirt, show off, and see and be seen by their peers (Bowlby, 1969; Cooper, 1971, 1975; Cooper and Marcus, 1971; Cooper Marcus, 1974; Newman, 1972). Adults are sometimes threatened or embarrassed by such activity or perceive it as "wasting time." Therefore, although places for teenagers to gather should be relatively close to home, they should not impinge unduly on adult residents. If thoughtful provision for these areas is not made, teenagers may take over areas intended for others, such as bus-stop seating or school play areas (Bagot, 1971; Cooper, 1972b). Teenagers will want to hang out whatever the weather conditions and may take over warm laundries or hallways if no provision is made for them.

Possible design responses

- Locate benches at popular street corners, overlooking a sports area, on the edge of a parking lot, or at major pathway intersections.
- Group benches in a right-angled or U-shaped arrangement to facilitate group conversation.
- Locate benches against a retaining or freestanding wall so that teens can choose to sit on the wall as well as on the benches.
- Locate a litter receptacle and (in hot climates) a drinking fountain nearby.
- Ensure that planting will not be damaged in any seating area that teenagers may take over; allow plenty of standing, sitting, and sprawling space around benches and trash containers.
- Install unbreakable lighting fixtures near places that teenagers may use.

See also: Sibling play (104), Outdoor seating (192), Seating variety (194), User group territories (229), Running the gauntlet (231), Conflicting uses (230).

125. Teen center

Where the housing development is large enough, indoor social space should be provided for teenagers.

In one study of seven public housing projects in New York State, almost every teenager and nearly 90 percent of adult residents surveyed wanted a separate room or center for teenagers' use only (Becker, 1974). Such a youth center would allow teenagers to socialize on their own turf and have a say in setting rules. It would also allow them to gather and apparently "do nothing" without aggravating adults or police.

Possible design responses

- Provide (or locate) an indoor space with a small kitchen and toilets that teenage residents might take over and decorate.
- Locate (or "buffer") it to minimize noise intrusion on nearby dwellings, but ensure that it is located near activity areas.
- Ideally, provide several rooms—for quiet games (chess, checkers), for more active games (Ping-Pong), for listening to records and talking, for quiet reading or studying, and for do-it-yourself activities (a small workshop).
- Ensure that there is sufficient operating budget to hire—as a line item—a sympathetic,

nonauthoritarian facilitator who would work out programs, physical equipment needs, and so forth with the teenagers but who would clearly be identified as the person willing to take responsibility.

See also: Adjacent public facilities (71), Small meeting room (134), Supervised facilities (140), Safe meeting places (224).

Figure 143. Poor locations for basketball hoops include parking lots.

126. Teen entertainment

Provide challenging and interesting activities for teenagers to minimize the likelihood of boredom.

In addition to hanging out, teenagers need active pursuits in which they can challenge themselves and each other, overcome fear, and be one of

Figure 144. Spaces where there is little room for play around the net are also poor.

the gang. Vandalism, one such active pursuit, engaged in (primarily) by boys aged twelve to seventeen, may sometimes be motivated by the lack of opportunity to engage in socially acceptable alternative pursuits—that is, by boredom with the local environment (both social and physical) and anger at its limitations and restrictions (Clarke, 1978). Indeed, it may be an effective means of communicating grievances in unresponsive settings (Becker, 1974; Pollowy, 1977).

In two recent studies of difficult-to-let public housing in Britain, projects with high rates of vandalism were often found to be those where a high density of adolescents was combined with a notable lack of recreational facilities. One such project, a large, high-density London slum-clearance project, was bordered by a desolate milieu of semiderelict neighborhoods and boarded-up shops and cinemas. The study concludes that one of the most urgent priorities is for sports facilities, discos, and youth clubs (Heffernan, 1977).

One cross-cultural study of the United States and Sweden found that, regardless of residents' socioeconomic status, there appear to be more problems with vandalism (and drugs) in remote suburban locations, where there are few commercial facilities or bus routes, than in inner-city locations or planned, medium-density new towns, where there is a variety of activities, commercial facilities, and public transportation (Popenoe, 1977).

Possible design response

Ensure that teenagers have easy access—on foot or by public transportation—to the following:

- Sports facilities (swimming pool, gymnasium, sports field, bowling alley, soccer field, basketball court)
- Spaces for fast pick-up games in a central, visible area, with benches for onlookers and lighting for evening use
- Areas for "dangerous" activities (skateboarding, dirt bike riding, and so forth)
- Inexpensive commercial recreation (cafes, soda fountains, discos, hamburger stands)
- A space on site for tinkering with a car

See also: Adjacent public facilities (71), Off-site facilities (127), Supervised facilities (140), User group territories (227), Child density (231), Taking risks (232), Prompt repairs (235), Good management (238).

127. Off-site facilities

Where sports facilities on site are seen as unnecessary because of the proximity to sports or leisure centers, ensure that the centers are really available to teenage residents.

The most obvious limitation to the exploitation of commercial sports facilities by teenagers is the cost of travel and use, but there are other, less obvious ones: not being able to afford the right gear, intimidating staff, facilities for sports that do not appeal to teenagers, and predominant use of the center by a different class or racial group. An inquiry into the use of an inner-London sports center intended to cater to the whole community reports:

Most people who use the centre are in the white collar professions. 90% come from a catchment area of 2 miles, and 80% come by car. . . . It's worked out to be squash, badminton and tennis which are traditionally higher income sports. This was not the original idea, but it was a response to demand. . . . The management committee had no clear objectives when they opened the place. The main thing was to get it running smoothly and get the place used. . . . The more articulate came. The marketing of it encourages those who work in offices, who can use the phone and book 6 days in advance (Department . . . , 1977, 8).

In some instances middle-class skills in using facilities (aided by management) result in what are in effect "takeovers" of sports facilities in lower-income areas. A project leader in East London reports marked resentment from local people and a reluctance to use the local sports facility: "People like us don't go." A community worker in another area remarked: "There's a marked reluctance of the whole community, mostly immigrants, to use the sports hall. It's not related to them, by the way it's run, the attitudes and manner of the staff and the reception. The building is intimidating. The users come from all over the city and park their cars in the side streets . . . we get a lot of complaints from residents who feel resentful" (Department . . . , 1977, 8).

Provision for adolescent leisure should be part of any housing program. If existing facilities are to be used, the designer and client must see to it that these are truly available.

Possible design responses

When off-site facilities for teenagers are being substituted for on-site facilities, ensure that:

- Facilities can cope with additional projected use.
- Facilities appeal to local youth.
- Facilities appeal to girls as well as boys.
- If in a low-income area, be sure sports gear is not expensive or is available on loan.
- The staff is sympathetic.
- Opening hours are suitable for local residents.
- Facilities are available on a drop-in, casual basis.

10

On-Site Facilities for Adults

Although this book deals principally with site planning and outdoor space design, this chapter considers both indoor and outdoor communal facilities, specifically those catering to adults. In creating medium-density housing for the future, clients and designers need to be aware of the increasing need—both social and economic—for on-site communal services to residents. With increasing proportions of married women and mothers in the labor force in every Western country, incorporating within the site of new housing schemes or new neighborhoods facilities that will ease the burdens of house care and child care is essential. Despite some liberalizing of sex roles and work, such burdens still devolve largely onto women. Because informal social contact is also important in the day-to-day lives of residents—both men and women—we suggest certain guidelines pertaining to neighboring and social interaction.

CASUAL SOCIAL NEEDS

People differ in their needs for casual social contact in the neighborhood and in how they make that contact. A person with an active work life may wish to be quiet, even reclusive, during evenings and weekends; a person whose life is rather sparse in face-to-face contacts may seek opportunities to chat with neighbors or socialize on the way to shops. Site designs need to provide choices so that the second group of residents can meet neighbors casually and the first group is not forced into contact with them. Because social relations within housing developments are highly complex and vary with culture, personality, season, and location, the guidelines that follow tend to be general enough to allow for a range of opportunities.

Figure 145. Being able to sit in their own front room and look out at passersby gives older people a welcome window on the world.

128. Home turf

Provide opportunities for residents to watch the world go by from their own "turf."

People have varying needs and opportunities to venture out into the community to meet others. For example, elderly or disabled people or stay-at-home parents may have to remain in their dwellings more than they wish. Such people, or those who are naturally reclusive, may wish to sit observing but unobserved in their living rooms or fenced yards or to sit out on the slightly more public porch or access way and watch passersby. Whether such vicarious socializing is all that is needed, or possible, in the form of contact with others, the design of the dwelling and its access ways should allow for it to happen naturally. Jan Gehl (n.d.) calls the space that permits this interaction a "soft interface."

Possible design responses

- Design windows facing public or communal outdoor spaces so that a person can see out from a seated position.
- Design porch or balcony edges so that a seated person can have a filtered view of passersby.
- Design some fences low enough to see over yet high and strong enough to lean on (Gehl, n.d.).

- Ensure that the distance from the footpath to the front of the house is small enough to allow easy communication between a person sitting near the house or standing at the front door or window and a person on the footpath, yet large enough to provide an effective barrier against "uncomfortable intimacy" between them (Gehl, n.d.).

See also: View from the window (12), Transitional filters (39), Front porch (40), Neighborly surveillance (42), Shared entry (44).

129. Casual meetings

Many adults appreciate opportunities for casual outdoor encounters around the home.

Although people vary in their desire to be on visiting terms with neighbors, most feel more comfortable if they can recognize those who live

Figure 146. A rich community life may grow from numerous, seemingly unimportant, casual meetings with neighbors.

close by and perhaps observe some simple aspects of their daily routine: "She has a spaniel and takes it for a walk before breakfast." "The children opposite got new bikes for Christmas." "The man next door is polishing his MG again."

Many people find it easiest to make initial contact with neighbors while standing on home territory—for example, when gardening, sweeping the path, or fixing a car in the driveway. Thus a small display garden or parking space in front of the dwelling may provide the opportunity to say hello to a neighbor or passerby. Once the ice is broken, common stairways, laundries, play areas, or footpaths available to a group of dwellings may form the locale of further contacts.

Possible design responses

- Design dwelling entries so that a resident casually tending plants, sweeping the path, or fixing the car is within visual and speaking distance of adjacent public circulation space.
- Locate windows so that people can look out on neighbors engaged in day-to-day chores around the front of their dwellings.

See also: Visible entry (36), Front porch (40), Neighborly surveillance (42), Street activities off the ground (48), "Front" and "back" customs (56), Display garden (62), Convenient parking (151).

130. Meeting neighbors

Dwellings should be arranged so that it is possible for neighbors to meet one another, but not so that neighbor contact is forced.

A tendency persists among designers, particularly in the United States, to be overly concerned with manipulating the site plan to "encourage neighboring." Most people, whatever their needs for neighboring, prefer some choice in the matter. For example, it will be satisfactory for two attached houses to share a common path and porch only if two very compatible households live in them. Similarly, front doors too close together on corridors, or exactly opposite each other in a narrow, unscreened courtyard, may make people feel that everyone is on top of one another and cause withdrawal rather than neighborly contact (Kuper, 1953; Ministry, 1969a; O'Brien, 1972; Shankland . . . , 1967). By the same token the location of some dwellings in isolated positions may make neighbor contact seem impossible or, worse still, suggest to their inhabitants that they are not part of the neighborhood at all (Festinger, Schacter, and Back, 1950; Kuper, 1953).

Medium-density developments where residents are satisfied tend to be those where a relatively small number share a common access way and where opportunities for neighboring are present without being forced. Proximity alone is not sufficient for friendship formation. U.S. research demonstrates that nodding ac-

quaintanceships between neighbors will lead to friendships and home visits only if a level of homogeneity of values, interests, and background is also present (Festinger, Schacter, and Back, 1950).

Possible design responses

- Design entrances so that doors do not face each other unless screening is provided (by fencing, planting, mounding, and so forth).
- Avoid pathways or stairs shared by only two households.
- Avoid locating some dwellings in isolated positions.
- Cluster dwellings around some common outdoor access way or landscaped space.

See also: Social homogeneity (6), Life cycle clusters (7), Private front path (37), Shared entry (44), Street activities off the ground (48), Group territory (72), Common space boundary (77), Courtyard width (133).

131. Friendly encounters

Sharing a common pedestrian open space enhances the potential for neighborly social contact.

Casual neighboring close to home tends to take place most easily when neighbors frequently

Figure 147. Seeing neighbors out of the window or meeting each other at the tot lot or en route to the bus stop—all these brief encounters are enhanced when a limited number share a common open space.

walk through a common open space on the way to shared facilities such as parking, a laundry room, a tot lot, local shops, or school (Cooper, 1970b, 1975; Cooper and Corrie, 1970; Gatt, 1978; Lansing et al., 1970; Parish and Parish, 1972; Shankland . . . , 1969). Such casual encounters are especially important for those who spend all day caring for small children. Several studies show that mothers at home with children under 5 (Department . . . , 1972a; Stewart, 1970; Taylor and Chave, 1964) and elderly women (Department . . . , 1972a) are more likely than other women to experience loneliness in residential environments and that women in general are more likely than men to experience loneliness in residential environments (Grady, 1967).

Casual encounters in a shared entryway (door, hallway, or stairs) are more likely to evolve into neighborly exchanges if the number sharing the entry is relatively small—say, fewer than eight. Seeing, recognizing, and greeting neighbors on a common pathway is more likely to occur when the pathway is shared by a specific cluster of dwellings than when it is a more heavily used and anonymous public sidewalk.

Possible design responses

- Ensure that major on-site pedestrian routes pass through communal open space that is attractive to pass through or to spend time in.
- Ensure that the shortest and most convenient route from dwellings to shared laundries, parking, local shops, and so forth is through this communal open space.
- Ensure that on-site pathways are used principally by residents so that the chances of seeing someone you recognize or know are increased.
- Avoid creating pathways cutting through a site or courtyard that will be used principally by outsiders.
- Provide adequate and attractive seating along major routes to further casual encounters.
- Ensure that maintenance responsibilities for shared spaces—preferably by management—are clear: Lack of maintenance can become a source of neighbor friction.

See also: Shared entry (44), Street activities off the ground (48), Group territory (72), Tot lot location (90), Footpath systems (182), Pedestrians passing by (187), Outdoor seating (192), Site entry barriers (201).

132. Dwelling cluster

The number of dwellings grouped around a common landscaped space should be somewhere between twenty and one hundred.

Where housing is clustered around communal landscaped space, the potential for casual meetings is enhanced—as long as walking through that space represents the shortest and most pleasant route to nearby facilities (parking, bus stop, shops). But the number sharing the space must be neither too many nor too few. A small number may unduly restrict the choice of friends; with a large number any potential group cohesion may be lost. A Scottish study reports that schemes were successful where the number of households grouped around a communal landscaped space varied from fifteen to forty-five (Byrom, 1972). A successful California example reports a hundred households sharing each landscaped communal court (the density of the development is thirty-eight units per acre) (Cooper, 1970b). Four successful cluster developments on the East Coast of the United States had between sixteen and twenty-four households sharing a common court (the average density of the developments was sixteen units per acre) (Parish and Parish, 1972). In other words there probably is no "ideal number"; but with present knowledge we can reasonably assume an acceptable range of somewhere between twenty and one hundred.

See also: Density and form (1), Project size (2), Tot lot catchment (91).

Figure 148. This courtyard is shared by a hundred households whose apartments look onto it. It is well used, especially by children, but rarely feels crowded or overused. (St. Francis Square, San Francisco) (For site plan see Figure 12.)

133. Courtyard width

The distance between units facing each other across a communal landscaped space should not be less than about 30 feet (9 m).

Clustered housing increases the possibility of neighbors meeting and of a sense of community developing, but community can emerge only when privacy is first protected. Where windows face each other across a space considered too narrow, residents may respond to invasions of privacy by keeping blinds or curtains permanently drawn (Cooper, 1975; O'Brien, 1972).

Site restrictions, local regulations, and privacy considerations will clearly influence actual distances. A New York study recommends, for example, that staggered units facing each other should be no closer than 35 feet (Becker, 1974), but in suburban situations much larger distances may be appropriate. Similarly, residents whose houses face each other across a flat, grassy open space only 30 or 40 feet (9 or 12 m) wide are likely to be more concerned about privacy than residents whose dwellings face each other across a street of similar width. Streets with passing traffic offset feelings of being too close to opposite neighbors. With common landscaped space between opposite dwellings one has to ensure that planting, grading, and positioning of windows contribute to feelings of privacy.

Possible design responses

- Locate dwellings facing each other across common landscaped space no closer to each other than 30 feet (9 m).
- Be conscious of what rooms face onto the open space: For example, it may be possible to site opposite rows of dwellings slightly closer when, say, bedrooms face living rooms (used at different times of the day).
- Stagger windows and buildings to foster privacy.
- Provide appropriate planting and earth mounding to enhance privacy.

See also: Density and form (1), Overlooking (58), Group territory (72), Comfortable space dimensions (74), Varying spaces (75), Common space boundary (77).

Figure 149. Too much space can be as much a problem as too little. Neighbors on opposite sides of this area will probably never get to recognize or meet each other. Most pedestrian movement takes place along adjacent streets.

COMMUNAL FACILITIES

134. Small meeting room

However small the development, a simple meeting or multipurpose room is desirable.

Where a development has been designed as a conscious entity—with, perhaps, a name, a home owners' (or tenants') association, and so on—it needs a meeting room or neutral space for meetings. Such a space can also be used as a teen club or play center.

In Milton Keynes New Town a successful arrangement in new developments is the designation of one regular dwelling as Neighborhood House, open at certain hours, often containing a washer and dryer for communal use, a place to make coffee, and a room where local parents can organize a play center. In the United States and Australia, when subsidized schemes have not made funds available for purpose-built meeting rooms, regular houses or flats have been converted (or two or three adjacent row houses amalgamated) to form successful meeting spaces (Egar and Sarkissian, 1982).

Possible design responses

- Locate the meeting space in a central, visible location adjacent to high-traffic areas, such as ground-floor lobbies or major routes to the shops—*not* in a basement!
- Provide a toilet and at least minimal kitchen facilities.
- Provide it with storage space for chairs, toys, and so forth.

See also: Sharing work (135), Multiservice centers (144), Safe meeting places (224).

135. Sharing work

Provide for the possibility of neighbors collaborating on tasks that have traditionally been undertaken in private dwellings.

People are likely to meet and socialize casually when using facilities that meet a common need—when folding clothes in a communal laundry, fixing the car in a shared parking lot, or supervising children at a play area (Cooper, 1971; Cooper Marcus, 1978a; Department . . . , 1972a; Festinger, Schacter, and Back, 1950; Zeisel and Griffin, 1975). It is now generally accepted that providing communal laundry facilities in medium- and high-density housing is both economically and socially more acceptable than providing costly equipment in each individual dwelling. But there are still other tasks—such as cooking, child care, and repairs—that some might prefer to do collectively, given the opportunity. Creating such opportunities takes some forethought on the part of the designer or client and some rethinking of the spatial needs of traditional tasks.

For example, a kitchen in a community meeting room might be used by a group of families that wish to cook collectively on a regular basis. Two or three adjacent units might be linked by internal connecting doors so that a single parent could baby-sit for one or two neighbors without leaving home. Some unused garages might be connected to form a community workshop, play group center, or toy-lending library. Modeled on existing Swedish and German examples, a collective dining room/kitchen might be included in a new development so that meals can be prepared and served collectively, thus replacing formerly private "women's work" performed in the household (Hayden, 1980).

In a recent paper on what a nonsexist city would be like Dolores Hayden speculates on how spaces in a typical suburban block could be connected so that "women's work," traditionally performed in isolation in each household, might be shared both by men and women in the same family and between families. She proposes pooling backyards to create a central communal space for play, vegetable growing, and community social events; front and side yards would be fenced to create private open spaces. Some larger houses would be converted to multiple units; some private garages, tool sheds, and utility rooms would be converted to community facilities such as a day-care center, a collective food-purchasing depot, a laundry, a dial-a-ride garage, and a kitchen providing lunches for the day-care center, take-out evening meals, and meals-on-wheels for the elderly.

The use of these collective services would be voluntary; everyone would also have space in the home for their children to play, to cook meals, and to do the laundry. Traditional design and planning practice is based on the assumption that "a woman's place is in the home"; yet women have been entering the labor force in larger and larger numbers. "Dwellings, neighborhoods, and cities designed for homebound women constrain women physically, socially, and economically. Acute frustration occurs when women defy these constraints to spend all or part of the work day in the paid labor force. I contend that the only remedy for this situation is to develop a new paradigm of the home, the neighborhood, and the city, to begin to describe the physical, social, and economic design of a human settlement that would support rather than restrict the activities of employed women and their families" (Hayden, 1980, s171). In many ways the suburban, middle-class woman entering the labor force is even more constrained than her counterparts in middle- or low-income multifamily housing. At least in the latter some communal facilities (laundry, play area, day care, meeting room) are now taken for granted, even if their design is not totally satisfactory. The zoning of a suburb is likely to place commercial laundry, eating, day-care, or shopping facilities at some distance from dwellings; public transport is often unsatisfactory; and the employed male in the household (if there is one) has most likely taken the car to work. One U.S. study found that 70 percent of the people without access to a car are women (Hayden, 1980, 170–87).

Possible design responses

- Provide a community center kitchen so that families might cook together or perform seasonal kitchen tasks (jam making, pickling) as a group.
- Provide a collective dining room and kitchen so that restaurant style or take-out meals can be provided on a semicommercial basis.
- Provide connecting double doors or an intercom system between some units to facilitate shared baby-sitting.
- In converting a low-density neighborhood to a more collective life-style, consider pooling backyards and converting unused garages to play group facilities, shared storage space, or community workshops.

See also: Small meeting room (134), Day-care center (136), Laundry facilities (137), Outdoor drying (138), Workshops (139), Community garden (141), Multiservice centers (144).

136. Day-care center

Provide accessibility to day care.

In most Western countries an increasing proportion of families in both subsidized and private sector housing are single-parent households or families where both parents work. Accordingly, access to nearby full-time day nurseries or child-care centers is an essential planning consideration.

"Access" to day care means not only a center located on site or nearby, but also administrative and financial accessibility. In one subsidized San Francisco scheme, for example, a day-care center laudably provided on site was subsequently leased out to a private entrepreneur who set prices so high that only wealthier, off-site families could use it. In another case a day-care center was already filled with the children of middle-income families when a low-income development was opened next door (Cooper Marcus, 1978b). The development designers proudly pointed to "adjacent day care," unaware that it was inaccessible to their clients.

Although day care at the workplace may be preferable for the care of infants (so that the working mother can continue nursing, for example), there are distinct advantages to home neighborhood day care for children aged one to five. First, the children and their parents have a better opportunity to get to know their neighbors. Second, the journey to work with a child, which is likely to be wearing for both parents

and children, is eliminated. Third, the center may offer part-time employment for local working parents or teenagers. Fourth, payment in kind (working part-time) or voluntary assistance (furniture painting, play area construction) arrangements are more likely to be feasible if the center is in the home neighborhood.

In developments of more than two hundred households, on-site day-care centers for the exclusive use of residents are preferable. In smaller schemes, where access to a local center is essential, local day-care agencies should be lobbied to provide facilities if they are unavailable.

It is not possible (legally or functionally) for an on-site play area to double as a day-care outdoor space, although, of course, children from a day-care center may be brought *to* such a play area for a visit. Each day-care center must have its own fenced play area. Day-care center design is a large topic in its own right. (See also Kritchevsky and Prescott, 1969; Leoffler, 1967; Osmon, 1971; Tonigan et al., 1970; Evans et al., 1971.)

Possible design responses

- Investigate local day-care opportunities.
- If space is locally available, notify center(s) of projected new residents.
- Where space is not locally available, convince clients of the need for on-site facilities, especially if the development is for more than two hundred households.

- Where the site is too small for an on-site center, lobby local agencies to provide more day-care spaces.
- Where the potential demand for day care is impossible to gauge, designate one ground-level flat or house on site, with adjacent space for a play yard, for eventual conversion to a day-care center.

See also: Tot lot location (90), Supervised play (112), Multiservice centers (144).

137. Laundry facilities

Provide easily accessible communal laundry facilities.

Several studies of low- to moderate-income developments show that, regardless of family size or stage in the life cycle, communal laundry facilities are among the most desired and appreciated shared facilities (Becker, 1974; Cooper, 1971, 1975; Margaret, 1971; Sandvik, Shellenbarger, and Stevenson, 1973).

A comprehensive Swedish study (Pederson, 1980) recommends small communal laundries, for a maximum of ten households. When ten or fewer households share the laundry, the user group can easily organize scheduling and responsibility for keeping the space clean. When large laundries are provided for numerous households, people irritated with the distance from home and with having to wait for machines purchase expensive private laundry equipment, which cramps space in the home.

Possible design responses

- Allocate space and utility connections for washers and dryers in dwellings with three or more bedrooms, when residents are likely to own machines.
- With smaller dwellings provide communal laundries for groups of around ten households.
- Locate communal laundries in highly visible, well-trafficked areas to reduce vandalism, preferably within the same building as those using it. Limit access to residents with keys.
- For a laundry serving ten households provide a minimum of two front-feed or four regular washing machines, two trolleys, one tumble drier, one sink unit 2 feet by 3 feet 3 inches (60 by 100 cm), and one chair and work table 2 feet by 5 feet 7 inches (60 by 180 cm) (Pederson, 1980).
- To enable people in wheelchairs to do their laundry, observe the following spatial requirements: a free floor area of at least 4 feet 3 inches by 4 feet 3 inches (130 by 130 cm) so that a wheelchair can be turned 180

Scale 1:50

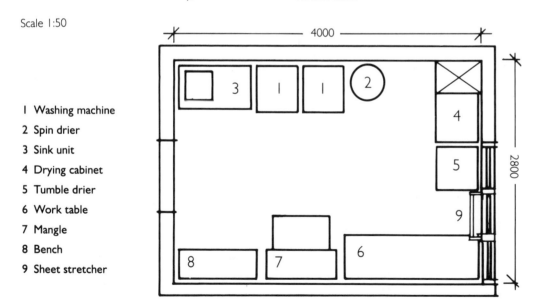

1 Washing machine

2 Spin drier

3 Sink unit

4 Drying cabinet

5 Tumble drier

6 Work table

7 Mangle

8 Bench

9 Sheet stretcher

Figure 150. A sample layout of a Swedish communal laundry of 12 sq. yds. (10 sq. m) for a maximum of ten households. (Source: Britt Pedersen, *Small communal laundries in blocks of flats*. Stockholm: Swedish Council for Building Research)

degrees, a work area in front of the sink unit of 3 feet 3 inches square (100 by 100 cm), and work areas in front of the washing machine and drier, each of 4 feet square (120 by 120 cm). The sink unit, washer, and drier should be designed so that the wheelchair footrest can enter beneath it; machine controls should be located 3 to 4 feet (90 to 120 cm) above floor level; and the detergent filling compartment should be no more than 3 feet 3 inches (100 cm) above floor level.

- Clearly display operating instructions, in several languages where appropriate.
- Outline residents' rights and responsibilities clearly in a handbook and on a notice board in the laundry.
- Allocate laundry room operation hours in accordance with family life-style. (For example, working adults may want to use the laundry in the late evening or on weekends.)
- Provide seats and a communal notice board within and a pleasant sitting area outside to foster casual encounters among neighbors.
- Locate laundries so that heat and noise do not annoy residents of adjacent dwellings.
- Consider connecting a heat exchanger to the drying equipment so that waste heat can be used to heat the laundry room or an adjoining room or greenhouse.

See also: Friendly encounters (131), Outdoor drying (138), Multiservice centers (144), Safe laundry rooms (225).

138. Outdoor drying

Provide opportunities for outdoor drying.

Outdoor laundry drying has greatly declined in most North American cities, but not in all comparably prosperous areas. In Australia, for example, clothes driers are not common: One study in South Australia shows that 99 percent of residents in all types of housing use their private open space to dry laundry (Halkett, 1976). In view of rising fuel costs and energy conservation needs designers in all areas need to provide the opportunity for outside drying.

In climates wetter than much of Australia (Britain, northwestern United States) alternative solutions have to be considered. Possible alternatives are individual driers, communal driers, individual outdoor drying areas, and communal outdoor drying areas. In low- to moderate-income housing the two best alternatives might be drying lines in private yards, patios, or balconies and shared drying rooms or mechanical driers in locked communal laundry rooms. Coin machines should not be the only provision because there may be families who are temporarily or permanently too poor to afford to use them. A Swedish study recommends a drying cabinet as a supplement to the tumble drier for drying woolen articles. A cabinet of 2 by 2 feet (60 by 60 cm) is suitable for a communal laundry shared by a maximum of ten households (Pederson, 1980).

Many studies in Britain and the United States show that, because of limited size, theft, vandalism, and inconvenience, communal drying yards are generally *not* a viable solution (Cooper, 1970b; Gilmour et al., 1970; Hefferman, 1977; Ministry . . . , 1969a).

Possible design responses

- Provide alternatives to private individual driers.
- Provide at least one tumble drier in each small communal laundry (serving a maximum of ten households).
- Locate private outdoor drying areas where they receive sun, particularly during cold and rainy seasons.
- Protect drying areas from incinerator, barbecue, and chimney smoke.

See also: Orientation to sun (59).

139. Workshops

Provide community workshop space and tool loan services.

Communal workrooms on British housing estates and in some U.S. public housing have generally not been used because they are unattractive, prone to vandalism, provided with inadequate storage, unstaffed or inadequately provided with equipment, or simply because people prefer working at home. However a more complete workshop space would probably encourage use in some cases.

The successful communal workshops established in the British new town of Milton Keynes are generally located in small neighborhood shopping centers and draw their clientele, who pay a small user fee for each visit, from a much larger area than the immediate neighborhood. At least one paid supervisor is always present to assist people in several dozen arts and crafts.

Possible design responses

- Provide lockable workshop space in an attractive, central location.
- Ensure that facilities are supervised, maintained, and accessible (keys should be provided and hours should meet users' needs).
- Ensure that the workshop is run by staff in tune with the potential users' needs.

- Where workshops are not practicable, provide tool loan services for gardening, house repair, and carpentry.

See also: Sharing work (135), Supervised facilities (140), Multiservice centers (144), Car maintenance (159).

140. Supervised facilities

Indoor recreation facilities should be provided only if supervision by salaried personnel is possible. (Redevelopment . . . , 1972)

The viability of indoor recreation facilities depends on the availability of a reliable supervisor or play leader on a regularly scheduled basis during times when residents (especially children) are most likely to use facilities. A supervisor's presence and personality have more effect on the use of a facility than does its design (Larsson, 1980).

If a private developer cannot employ a director (at least initially) to establish a community center or if a government funding agency is unable to provide it with staffing, it is perhaps wiser not to build one at all: An unsupervised center raises expectations that can only be disappointed. Where the size of the proposed development does not permit hiring staff, consider increasing the size of the development so that it is economically feasible to hire paid staff (Larsson, 1980).

See also: Project size (2), Teen center (125), Multiservice centers (144), Safe meeting places (224).

141. Community garden

Provide residents with opportunities to have a plot in a communal vegetable garden.

Increasing numbers of Westerners are allocating part of their yards for growing fruits and vegetables and for recycling organic kitchen wastes. With rising food costs and concern about the freshness of produce, the demand for allotments or community gardens is likely to continue. This is especially so in higher density housing where internal and outdoor space may be at a premium.

In five middle-income rental neighborhoods in Milton Keynes (Residential . . . , 1975) 29 percent of the families expressed a serious need for an allotment within fifteen minutes' walk of home. Some with a house garden of 1,075 square feet (100 sq. m) or more still required larger, separate areas for growing vegetables. The Milton Keynes study found more enthusiasm for allotment gardening in smaller families than in larger families and in the professional classes than in other socioeconomic groups. In a housing scheme in Davis, California (Village Homes), "edible landscaping" is provided throughout the site to allow residents to harvest from fruit and nut trees and to raise money for the home owners' association through the sale of produce.

Possible design responses

- Allocate a sunny area within the communal landscaped space for residents to use for a community garden or individual allotments.
- Ensure that there is a water source nearby and access to dry, ventilated, lockable storage.
- Provide comfortable seating nearby.
- Provide some kind of attractive hedging or fencing, or create raised planter beds so that vegetables are not damaged by dogs or children.

See also: Yard size (61), Children's gardens (115), Sharing work (135).

Figure 151. A community garden developed by low-income Spanish-speaking families in an Oakland, California, neighborhood.

142. Access to facilities

Easy access to adequate commercial and community facilities is especially needed by less-mobile population groups.

Less-mobile population groups include those who cannot drive, such as children and the elderly; those who cannot afford a car, such as teenagers and the poor; those who have no access to a car because the one car in the family is used by the breadwinner; and those who are tied to home because of disabilities or child-care responsibilities. The larger the housing scheme, and the farther it is from existing commercial or social facilities, the more essential it is to such residents that these facilities be planned from the start as an intrinsic part of the design.

A number of studies show a correlation between resident dissatisfaction and the lack of convenient facilities and amenities (Pickett and Boulton, 1974; Weinberger, 1973; Young, 1934). For example, on the outskirts of Liverpool there is a sprawling, subsidized development of five thousand dwellings housing over twenty thousand people, but full shopping facilities are an expensive—and for parents with small children, exasperating—bus ride away. Shopping is not only a functional necessity, but a form of recreation and a healthy change of environment. Isolated mothers in the development, deprived of easy shopping opportunities, describe their

situation as "being like puppets in a machine when trapped at home all day looking out at endless rows of windows on the massive uniform facades opposite them" (Department . . . , 1978, 39).

The need for amenities in housing areas has been officially promulgated in Britain since the 1918 Tudor Walters report on the provision of dwellings for the working classes. The report argues that it is not enough to cover the ground with streets and houses. Any housing site should be considered as the future location of a community.

The 1944 Dudley Report on the Design of Dwellings cites the lack of community and amenity buildings as one of the most serious omissions on interwar estates. Twenty-three years later the Ministry of Housing and Local Government again officially emphasized the need for community facilities early in the occupancy of a new housing area (Ministry . . . , 1967b). Clearly, there is a need for close control of new development on the lines of the Norfolk Structure Plan (1976), which stipulates that no new housing scheme be approved unless essential facilities are provided within eighteen months. In New South Wales, Australia, recent state legislation requires a cash "developer levy" to provide social and physical infrastructure (including neighborhood centers and playgrounds) in new housing areas.

At first glance these problems may not seem nearly as acute in the United States: Car ownership is more widespread; subsidized housing is

much less common; and middle-income families moving into new suburban housing are quickly followed by shopping center developers seeking new markets. But in a car-dominated society those without vehicles are even more severely penalized because public transit is generally inadequate and, in typical low-density suburbs, nonexistent. Thus the adult in a two-adult, one-car family who stays at home (usually the woman) is virtually isolated. A recent California study indicates that 70 percent of those without access to a car are women (quoted in Hayden, 1980). Common zoning practice places shops and other needed commercial facilities well out of residential neighborhoods in all new suburban areas. The practice of locating stores for local daily use within walking distance in all neighborhoods—as evidenced in European and Australian new towns—is virtually unheard-of in new housing areas in the United States.

Possible design responses

- Ensure that a new medium- or large-scale housing development has easy—preferably walking—access to adequate community and commercial facilities.
- Ensure that pedestrian access to local stores is pleasant, quiet, and safe so that children can easily be sent on errands or do their own shopping.
- Examine legal and financial mechanisms to ensure early provision of community facilities.

- Investigate opportunities for providing a single neighborhood store or corner deli, including possible subsidies, where necessary.
- Where facilities cannot be provided within walking distance, ensure that careful location of public transit stops and frequent, convenient scheduling links the development with adequate facilities.
- Where public transit access is not available and there is no guarantee of its provision in the near future, seriously question the social feasibility of the development if it is intended for low-income residents.

See also: Local services (143), Footpath system (182).

143. Local services

The more traumatic the breaks with old neighborhoods experienced by residents of a new site, the more crucial is the local provision of adequate social and community services for them.

The move from one residential environment to another—particularly the move from inner-city, extended family neighborhoods to new suburban or new town developments—can be traumatic. A series of studies of Boston's West End, formerly a stable working-class community (Gans, 1962), documents this phenomenon. Planners labeled the community "substandard" and a "slum." Residents were dispersed to other parts of the city, and the neighborhood was demolished. But psychiatrists who followed up former residents found that even two years after the disruption a large proportion was suffering severe sadness and depression, akin to grief (Fried, 1969).

Painfully similar stories come from Stockholm, Paris, Melbourne, Lagos, Rio de Janeiro, London, and Liverpool (Department . . . , 1981b; Weinberger, 1973). Management renting and transfer policies can alleviate some of this suffering by keeping existing social support networks intact. If child rearing is assisted by grandparents, aunts, and uncles in the old neighborhood, for example, extended families should be kept together. If this is impossible, programs and physical facilities should be provided instead.

In an evaluation of a South London estate, where an established community failed to form even after thirty years, the author comments:

If large groups of people who are strangers to each other are moved into high density flats with no individual outdoor space, and this in an area where they have no roots, then the delicate mechanism of community—a network of friendships, trust, expression of oneself through doing things with others—has to be relearnt and to an extent become contrived. There must be informal public places where people can meet (pubs, meeting halls, school buildings, advice shops, play centres) and initially there must be specialized personnel to generate social and community activities for both adults and children; the aim would be to get tenants to take over these activities themselves eventually (Department . . . , 1981c, 36).

Not only the poor need such services. Senior citizen housing developments of the U.S. Sun Belt and the successful "swinging singles" complexes of California also cater to people who are strangers to each other and to the locale and whose prime need (beyond a comfortable dwelling) is for ways to alleviate loneliness. For this reason, although these environments contain fairly modest apartments or houses, lavish attention is paid to club rooms, social centers, swimming pools, sports facilities, crafts workshops, saunas, and community newspapers.

Figure 152. The provision of local shops and services proved especially important in Runcorn New Town (U.K.), where many residents came from working-class, inner-city Liverpool neighborhoods where the corner store and extended family support systems had been a way of life.

Those best able—economically and psychologically—to overcome loneliness can purchase such "packaged environments" with everything delivered. The disadvantaged in all societies, by contrast, have little control over the supply of needed community and recreational services. Therefore it is incumbent upon suppliers of subsidized housing to regard these services and facilities as an integral part of community design. Adequate social and community services for *all* age groups are needed from the inception of a new estate. Before writing a program for new housing at the very least a detailed inventory should be made of the social and community services in the neighborhood and plans should be made with appropriate local agencies for filling projected needs. "Housing" is clearly more than a roof over one's head. It must incorporate provision of those services and facilities that enhance and ameliorate all aspects of daily life in the neighborhood.

Economically expanding and developing countries could benefit from the hindsight of the developed countries, where we have learned that a housing authority cannot merely state a program in terms of dwelling mix, and an architect cannot responsibly accept such a job. Agencies responsible for the physical fabric, for community development, for services provision, and for housing management must collaborate at the planning stage or they will find themselves with even more "problem" areas in the 1990s than exist already.

Possible design responses

- Inventory local service provision and negotiate with appropriate city or voluntary agencies to provide needed services to a new development.
- When moving people from an existing community, document informal social support systems (neighbors trading child care, grandparents baby-sitting, and so forth) and make every effort to ensure that arrangements can easily continue or be supplemented in the new setting.
- Provide facilities and personnel to help new residents meet each other and form their own special-interest and support groups.
- Advertise local services and community functions on prominent notice boards and in local newspapers.

See also: Access to facilities (142), Multiservice centers (144), Resident's manual (241).

144. Multiservice centers

In large subsidized developments provide facilities for a multiservice or advice center.

In large developments where, in effect, new communities are being created, it is important to provide employment referral, health information, library study, and welfare and counseling services. Time and again, when an information or counseling service has been established on site, the level of awareness and use of services has increased markedly.

A report assessing the impact of an advice and information center installed in an empty ground-floor flat on a large "problem" estate in the London borough of Lewisham concludes:

> Advice and information staff are needed in many cases to give the sort of personal attention which increasingly impersonal bureaucracies cannot give, not only with regard to welfare benefits, but on housing queries, fuel bills and legal rights; they are needed too to fill a cultural gap, to pass on the sort of information which neighbours and parents could give if they were in close touch (Department . . . , 1981c, 36).

The center received up to six hundred callers a month from a population of five thousand residents. The staff—two part-time housing assistants, a full-time social worker, two community workers, and two clerical information officers—were meeting needs that had gone unrecognized in the previous thirty years of the estate's existence.

Possible design responses

- Provide a centrally located space to be used as a small advice and referral center; in a small housing development a converted flat might suffice.
- In larger developments provide a purpose-built center as a base for community and welfare workers, citizens' advice, child care, and neighborhood associations and groups.

See also: Supervised play (112), Teen center (125), Small meeting room (134), Day-care center (136), Workshops (139), Local services (143), On-site office (242).

145. Adult sports

Provide facilities for adult outdoor leisure and sports.

In this era of sedentary jobs, automated transport, urban stress, bad eating habits, and increased leisure time, designers will be looked upon to provide easy access to adult outdoor recreation facilities. In American "swinging single" complexes, where this is taken for granted, advertising emphasizes pools, courts, and saunas used as much (or more) for social contact as for exercise. At the other extreme, low-income projects may have play equipment for kids but nothing for adults.

Activities such as jogging, tennis, squash, and swimming are being demanded by all strata of society, not just by upper-income groups. In California, for example, tennis courts that were seemingly misplaced in low-income black areas a decade ago are now actively used by the local population.

Possible design responses

- Consider provisions for those sports currently in demand by the area's adult population.
- Provide a pleasing environment in which residents will feel tempted to walk or jog. (See "Footpaths and Pedestrian Circulation" in Chapter 12—Landscaping, Footpaths, and Site Furniture.)

- Where the site is too small to have its own adult recreation facilities, ensure that residents have access to nearby sports centers, parks, or clubs.

See also: Adjacent public facilities (71), Ball games (123), Off-site facilities (127), Leisure walking (186), User group territories (227).

146. Swimming pool

Where the budget permits, provide a swimming pool.

In moderate- to high-income U.S. and Canadian developments the most used and requested adult recreation facilities are swimming pools and tennis courts (Cooper, 1970b; Cooper and Corrie, 1970; Norcross, 1973; Norcross and Hysom, 1968). A pool may seem like a costly investment, but its considerable merits as a social focal point and as locale for children's and adolescents' recreation should be weighed. A pool engages children's attention far longer than most playgrounds, and parents can sunbathe while supervising. A pool provides a place where adolescent display and flirting are unofficially condoned; it engages the energies of boys who might otherwise turn to acts of vandalism. Thus it may soon pay for itself, not only in terms of residents' improved mental and physical health but in reduced maintenance costs for other portions of the site.

Pool maintenance and rules are sources of conflict; so residents should participate in resolving dilemmas such as adult versus family swimming, night use of pool by residents versus privacy of adjacent units, and use of pool area for drinking, barbecuing, and so forth versus pool area maintenance. A Canadian study concludes: "The pool is probably the most density-sensitive space in a project's community facilities. Perhaps it is because people are dressed more minimally and the medium is water. There is also a special sensitivity to water pollution and consequently to management maintenance services" (Beck, Rowan, and Teasdale, 1975b, 111).

Possible design responses

- Ensure that a pool is equally accessible to all households and is centrally located.
- Carefully fence pools so that small children will not fall in.
- Provide direct access within the housing development grounds—people do not like to walk along public roads in swimming attire.
- Provide a paddling or wading pool for children and places for supervising adults to sit.
- Locate the children's pool near adult swimming facilities.
- Provide adequate hard-surfaced and grassed areas (to walk on with bare feet in hot weather) around the pool, with seating for sunbathers and socializers.
- Provide fencing or planting screens for the entire complex to create a wind-free, semi-private setting and to screen adjacent units from noise.
- Provide dressing rooms and showers with toilets near the pool, especially where some dwelling units are far from the pool.
- Clearly display precise rules (determined by the users).
- Provide opportunities for tenant management.
- Do not plant vegetation that will drop leaves or berries in or near the pools.

See also: Adult sports (145).

147. Facility size

The quantity and size of community facilities should be commensurate with user demand.

This may seem an obvious statement, but clustered housing is replete with examples of underused or overused facilities, largely because planning standards are seldom based on user needs research. Designers or clients may have to do their own local research.

Possible design response

- Community facilities for a specific housing development should be designed for use by *non*residents only if that is specific local policy and if they can be scaled (and staffed) to meet the demands of both residents and nonresidents (Becker, 1974).

See also: Project size (2).

Parking

The car, many families' most valuable single possession, is essential for daily journeys to work, shopping, or school. People are naturally concerned about its physical safety—from theft, vandalism, or accidental damage. Observations in subsidized housing in the United States and Australia indicate that people will go so far as to drive over curbs, grassed areas, or playgrounds in order to park within sight of their dwelling. Ideally, residents of multifamily housing would have parking arrangements similar to those with typical detached or row house facilities—locked garages, private carports, or driveways. Because the design of much medium-density housing, and the wording of some government directives on subsidized housing, makes this impossible, the designer's minimal task is to provide a de-

cent alternative, that is, parking for each dwelling that is

1. Within reasonable proximity
2. Under casual surveillance from a number of units
3. Clearly separated from pedestrian and play areas
4. Arranged so that the number of parked cars visible from any one place does not create aesthetic blight

A housing development that is pleasing to its inhabitants in every other way can be marred by inadequate parking. One extensive American study of HUD-assisted housing found that satisfaction with parking is a relatively strong predictor of overall satisfaction (Francescato et al.,

Figure 153. Is this how we want our homes to look—all garage and no house?

204

Figure 154. Grouped garages *can* be provided in an attractive setting.

Figure 155. This scheme provides parking in grouped carports off a central cul-de-sac (to left), with houses, communal landscaped spaces, and play areas forming a looped sequence of spaces around it. (Hazelwood, Milton Keynes New Town)

1979). A quote from a study of a Chicago housing project is typical of many: "Residents felt that the parking space along the curb in front of their apartment should be theirs, and strongly resented finding the cars of visitors to other residents in 'their' spaces when they arrived home from work" (Weidemann and Anderson, 1979, 6).

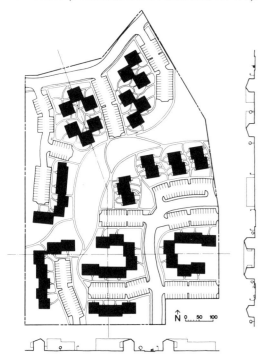

Figure 156. A low-rise townhouse and apartment development, ranked highly by residents in a study of thirty-seven HUD-assisted schemes. Each unit had access to parking on one side and to common landscaped space on the other. (Source: Francescato, 1980)

148. Vehicular segregation

Vehicle access and parking arrangements should respect the need for an uninterrupted network of safe landscaped spaces for children and adults.

Vehicle-free communal spaces should form an uninterrupted network throughout the site to enhance their use for playing, walking, or socializing. Ideally, they should form the core of a design around which buildings and parking are arranged. Too often the most powerful reason for clustering housing—to free land for pedestrian use—is violated in the site plan by filling up the created open spaces with cars. A creative site plan should bring cars reasonably close to dwellings without infringing on the quiet, pedestrian orientation of the site.

Possible design responses

- On medium to large sites, where parking must be clustered, locate parking on the periphery; leave the core of the site as vehicle-free communal space.
- On more limited sites provide parking in a central cul-de-sac with housing and communal landscaped spaces in looped sequence of spaces around it.
- To ensure children's safety, separate parking from play areas by the dwellings themselves. If this is impossible, locate the parking area such that only a small proportion of children has to cross it to get to play space.

- Locate parking in small groupings at one side of courtyards.
- Avoid situations where parking separates dwellings from communal landscaped space. If this is inevitable, ensure that roadways have bumps or other means of slowing down traffic.

See also: Children safe from cars (3), Pedestrian precinct (67), Woonerfs (70).

149. Vehicle speeds

Vehicular flow should be controlled by signs, changes in the roadway texture, and speed bumps.

This guideline is especially important where an access road is also used as a pedestrian walkway or frequently crossed by pedestrians.

Possible design responses

- At site entry points locate signs specifying a slow speed limit and warning that there may be children at play.
- Employ surface changes (asphalt to brick or cobblestones) to alert drivers to the need to slow down.
- Employ color or texture changes to warn drivers as they approach a pedestrian crosswalk. (It is generally not satisfactory for the crosswalk itself to be a rough-textured surface, however, because cautious pedestrians and people in wheelchairs will avoid it.)
- Where drainage gaps in speed bumps are necessary, make them as narrow as possible, and stagger their location to prevent motorcycles or mopeds from using them.
- Plant the shoulders adjacent to speed bumps with dense low trees or shrubs to prevent bypassing by vehicles.

See also: Children safe from cars (3), Traffic management (68), Woonerfs (70).

Figure 157. Barriers sometimes have to be placed on the grassed edges of roads to prevent drivers from avoiding the traffic bumps.

Figure 158. Locating parking between houses and a play area is *not* a good solution.

150. Locked garages

Where possible, provide each dwelling with its own locked garage.

Private garages not only shelter cars from the elements and potential theft or vandalism, but also provide a locale for storage, sheltered play, or a small work bench. But these latter activities are likely to occur only where the garage is adjacent to or incorporated within the dwelling; they are unlikely in private garage space located in an underground parking area or in a grouped area of garages located some distance from the dwelling.

Garages may be located at the end of the backyard (and accessed from the rear) to provide the yard with more screening for privacy (Untermann and Small, 1977). This is still close enough to the dwelling to encourage alternate uses and may be preferable for some activities (such as teenage band practice).

Possible design responses

- Locate private, lockable garages within or very close to dwellings.
- Ensure room in them for a small workbench.
- Where possible, provide a lockable storage closet within the garage.
- Provide at least one power point in the garage for lighting, power tools, and so forth.
- Locate support structures so that they do not interfere with opening car doors.

Figure 159. Make sure garages and car sizes are compatible.

Figure 160. Avoid locating garages so that they dominate the street scape and prevent passersby from enjoying personalized front yards.

- Design roofs to be high enough to accommodate vehicles with rear doors that swing up, roof racks, trailers, or converted vans.
- Design roofs in such a way that storage could be added above vehicle level.

See also: Secure garages (210).

151. Convenient parking

Where private garages are not feasible, a carport or driveway space is a preferable alternative.

Private garages were routinely provided, until recently, in council housing in Britain. This has not been the case in subsidized housing in the United States, Australia or, surprisingly, in Canada or Sweden, where the severity of the climate might suggest it should be. Personal observation in medium-density housing suggests that, in the absence of a garage, people prefer to park their cars in their own driveways, carports, or on the street outside their houses, rather than in a grouped parking area separated from the dwelling.

Possible design responses

- For security reasons ensure that, when a car is parked on the street or in a carport or driveway, it is visible from somewhere within the dwelling.
- Where two or three driveways or carports form a small cluster, provide landscaping or screening so that residents do not look out onto numbers of exposed cars, but permit a filtered view from the owner's dwelling for security purposes.
- Ensure that the positioning of parked cars does not block residents' views onto the street or passersby's views into the front yard—and thus inhibit the tending of a "display" garden.

- Provide lockable storage space in the carport or close to the driveway for car-related tools and materials. Where this might prove a security hazard, provide adequate equivalent space inside the dwelling.
- Where appropriate, ensure that the driveway or carport is wide and long enough to accommodate vehicles for physically disabled people. (See guideline 43 for details of barrier-free access.)
- Construct flat-roofed carports with two-story dwellings; the roofs can be used for roof gardens or even as the base for future room additions.

See also: Upper windows (208), Direct access (217).

Figure 161. Each household in this American row house scheme has one garage and one carport. Attractive detailing has created a sense of arrival and enclosure in each carport.

152. Small parking lots

Open parking lots should be relatively small and within view of some of the dwellings.

Open lots should be overlooked by at least some of the dwellings they serve. The fact that someone might be looking out of a window is a considerable crime deterrent.

In one Canadian development, where parking for more than two hundred cars was massed, residents feel that their homes look like "an army barracks" (MacLeod, 1977). The distribution of small parking areas around the site will ensure that parked cars do not dominate views and no car is too distant from the dwellings.

Possible design responses

- Provide parking in small lots, reasonably close to the dwellings they serve.
- Ensure that most of the parked vehicles are potentially visible from some of the dwellings. (This is less essential in low-crime areas.)
- Where a considerable amount of parking has to be provided in one sector of a site, break its mass down by positioning buildings and using dense planting.
- Lower the level of the parking area so that only the upper parts of cars are visible from dwellings. (This provides for surveillance while lessening visual impact.)

See also: Unobtrusive image (16), Assigned parking (157), Informal surveillance (217).

Figure 162. An attractive small parking lot in a British new town where adults can work on cars and children can safely kick a ball around.

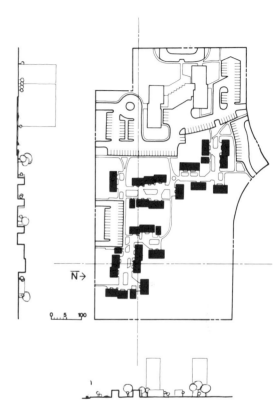

Figure 163. In a study of thirty-seven HUD-assisted housing schemes this was among the least satisfactory to the residents in terms of parking. They complained of vandalism to their vehicles parked on the edge of the site, out of sight of most dwellings. (Source: Francescato, 1980)

153. Grouped carports

Where parking in a moderate- or high-crime area is provided in grouped carports, these must be within view of some of the dwellings.

This guideline pertains to a common form of parking provision in American clustered housing: the communal, open-sided, but roofed carport, usually with assigned spaces. These carports are generally located on the edge of the site, a short walking distance to the apartments or townhouses. A roofed structure is necessary in many parts of the United States because of the need to protect cars from the extremes of heat or from snowfall.

Possible design responses

- Ensure that carport roofing material is capable of screening vehicles from extreme heat or heavy snowfalls and of withstanding the occasional exploratory escapades of children.
- In low-crime areas locate roofed, grouped carports on the site periphery.
- In high-crime areas ensure that the positioning and design of carports do not prevent casual surveillance of vehicles from inside the dwellings.

See also: Upper windows (208), Informal surveillance (219), Vulnerable materials (233).

Figure 164. This arrangement would work only in a low- or no-crime area because there is little casual surveillance of parked vehicles from the dwellings.

154. Parking access

Provide direct paved access from parking areas to dwelling entries.

Whether parking is in shared lots or in individual spaces, a direct route should be provided for ease of carrying babies or groceries, walking in wet weather, or maneuvering toddlers. In user surveys of clustered housing surprisingly few residents complain about having to walk from car to dwelling; apparently the walk, if it is not too long, is accepted as inevitable. A Canadian study suggests a distance of no more than 75 feet (23 m) (Beck, Rowan, and Teasdale, 1975b); an American study of an area with a milder climate recommends 100 to 200 feet (30 to 60 m) (Becker, 1974). This research, however, shows that in an ideal situation residents would prefer their cars closer to their dwellings, and would put up with fumes and noise, if a trade-off were possible.

Possible design responses

- Locate paths along the most direct route from parking to dwelling entries.
- Ensure that paths are
  - Well drained
  - Well lit
  - Level, with nonslip finishes
  - Away from dense shrubbery, which might conceal intruders
  - Wide enough to permit access by people in

wheelchairs (2 feet to 2 feet 2 inches [610 mm to 660 mm]).
—Wide enough to permit easy snow removal, where appropriate
—Sheltered from rain or snow
—Oriented so that winter sun will melt snow but paths will be protected from summer sun

• Locate dwelling entries no more than 200 feet (60 m) from parking.

See also: Snowmelt (177), Footpath design (183), Footpath lighting (191).

Figure 165. If direct access from parking to dwellings is not provided, residents will make shortcuts through planted areas.

155. Secure underground parking

Where parking facilities are underground or out of sight of the dwelling, ensure that they are secure, pleasant, well lit, and well ventilated.

Where a development is located in a moderate-crime or high-crime area and has unsupervised, shared parking facilities that anyone can enter, they may well attract criminal activity (vandalism, car theft, muggings, rape) and be avoided by residents (Cooper, 1972b; Cooper and Marcus, 1971; Department . . . , 1981b; Shankland . . . , 1977). Such parking areas should be accessible only by means of locked gates or should comprise private locked garages, although these too are prone to vandalism.

Many underground or multistory garages lacking locked entry points have met with so much vandalism and damage that they have had to be sealed off and car owners have been forced to fend for themselves on local streets (Shankland . . . , 1977). In one San Francisco co-operatively owned scheme residents successfully brought two vulnerable, semiunderground garages into use by raising funds to enclose them and ensuring that only legitimate users had keys (Cooper, 1970b). Consultants reviewing the potential use of an abandoned multistory garage in a problem development in South London recommended that the structure be demolished. Even conversion to lockable garages seemed a dubious investment because of lack of surveillance (Heffernan, 1977).

Possible design responses

- Where the provision of underground or multistory parking areas is inevitable, include limited entry points, each with a sturdy locked gate, or ensure that each resident has a lockable garage in this space with robust, vandal-proof metal doors ("garages within garages").
- Maximize casual surveillance by locating the structure near streets or walkways and by providing an "open" form of construction.
- In rehabilitating housing in high-crime areas consider converting underground or multistory garages to other uses—for example, gymnasium, youth club, community center, or workshop.

See also: Direct access (217), Lighting for safety (222).

156. Accurate parking provision

Ensure that parking is neither severely over- nor underprovided.

Underprovision forces people to jockey for spaces or engage in subterfuges to claim them and thus leads to strained neighbor relations; but the large, unused, hard-surfaced areas resulting from overprovision are unsightly and may anger people whose children are underprovided with play space or whose dwellings are too small.

Figure 166. In this low-income London housing project parking was very much overprovided; yet almost nothing was provided for children. An action study recommended this unused parking structure be demolished and the space used for needed landscaped play areas.

A case of overprovision is described in a study of a difficult-to-let estate in South London, where "patently absurd" parking requirements laid down by the local authority called for 110 percent provision, which resulted in "the loss of vast areas of ground level space which could have been given over to children's play etc. This waste of invaluable space plus the enormous capital outlay involved seems indefensible when it is considered that car ownership on estates averages 30%" (Heffernan, 1977, 34).

Parking standards are frequently based on the middle-income norm of one or two cars per family, even in public housing. In fact the majority of U.S. public housing tenants are living on unemployment or welfare benefits, and few can afford cars.

Possible design response

- Determine the appropriate level of parking provision per household on the basis of the following:
  - Current rates of car ownership
  - Stage in the family life cycle
  - Socioeconomic status of residents
  - Quality of local public transportation
  - Fuel costs (current and projected)
  - Availability of site area for parking
  - Other demands for open space (for example, children's play and adult sports).

See also: Assigned parking (157).

157. Assigned parking

Parking spaces in grouped parking areas should be assigned to specific dwellings and be clearly marked.

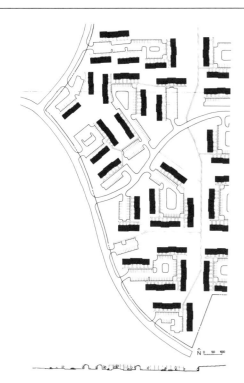

Figure 167 (a, b). The amount of parking is not always the problem. This scheme had the highest ratio of parking spaces per dwelling in thirty-seven subsidized projects studied—but one of the lowest ratings on parking satisfaction. The chief complaints were that spaces were unassigned and vehicles came too close to the windows. (Source: Francescato, 1980)

Because of conflicts between residents about use of unassigned parking spaces and because visitors may use a space someone has "acquired" through habitual usage, each space needs to be clearly marked. Addresses of units served are better than a separate parking numbering system, which will only add to the confusion that often already exists in clustered housing regarding orientation and way finding.

However, if parking spaces in high-crime areas are clearly linked to specific dwellings, an intruder could soon deduce who is not in and attempt a break-in. Residents in high-crime areas sometimes do not want their cars identified for fear of reprisals.

Possible design responses

- In low-crime areas, but *not* in high-crime areas, assign parking spaces in open lots or grouped carports to specific dwellings.
- Where some or all of the parking is on the street, arrange and enforce a system of resident parking permits so that outsiders do not use the spaces.

See also: Accurate parking provision (156).

158. Visitor parking

Visitor parking should be sensitively located and clearly identified.

On large sites, maps at the entrance help visitors park at the closest point to their destination and keep them from parking in residents' spaces.

One Canadian study suggests one visitor space for every ten units (Beck, Rowan, and Teasdale, 1975b), but rates will vary according to resident mix, availability, use of local public transit, and size of community, as well as from one country to another.

Possible design responses

- Identify all areas of visitor parking on maps at the entrances to developments.
- Locate visitor parking along the front side of dwellings or so that residents can see visitors as they approach dwellings.
- Stipulate in the resident's manual or lease agreements that residents are not permitted to park in visitor parking areas.

See also: Site map (23), Name sign (24), Visible dwelling numbers (28).

159. Car maintenance

Provide one or a number of hard-surfaced spaces with water and electrical connections.

In low-income housing, particularly in the United States, car and motorcycle maintenance provides a focus for adult male socializing. One Canadian study suggests a minimum of one 12 by 24 foot (3.6 by 7.2 m) space for each thirty to fifty cars (MacLeod, 1977). The function of the space should be made clear in a resident's handbook and/or with on-site notices.

Figure 168. When guest parking spaces are not identified, visitors park in residents' spaces, causing inconvenience and annoyance.

A study of middle-class New York condominiums found that cars being repaired in the common parking areas were considered basically unsightly, but repairs that took an hour or two were tolerated. A car taken apart and left there for days at a time was unacceptable (Tulin, 1978).

Possible design responses

- Provide protected open space for car maintenance, with water and electricity connections and lighting for nighttime use. In high-crime areas provide this space in a locked area (Larsson, 1980).
- Select a dark-colored flooring material, preferably of a variegated appearance, to hide oil stains.
- Provide drainage for car washing.
- Screen the space from the view of adjacent dwellings.
- Specify and enforce conditions of use so that major repair jobs do not monopolize spaces.
- Provide nearby seating for friends and observers.

See also: Workshops (139).

160. Cold-weather parking

In cold regions make special provisions in parking design.

One Canadian study recommends that all parking stalls be 9 feet (12.7 m) wide to provide adequate space for snow clearance (Barker, 1976). Parking design should acknowledge specific local conditions (wind direction, snow clearance patterns).

Possible design responses

- Provide plug-in block heating units (or power outlets) at each parking space.
- Provide large (above-average) parking spaces to allow for maneuvering, snow clearance, icy surfaces, snow falling from roofs, and so forth (Beck, Rowan, and Teasdale, 1975b).
- Provide places at the edges of parking areas where snow and leaves can be shoveled or blown.
- Design roofs and overhangs so that they shed snow easily but do not shed snow onto vehicular access areas.
- Select nonslip finishes for the floor of parking areas and adjacent footpaths to enable vehicles and pedestrians to maneuver safely.
- In wet climates provide sheltered parking spaces or at least a sheltered place for entering or exiting.

See also: Snow play (121), Snowmelt (177).

161. Hot-weather parking

In very hot climates residents should be provided with shaded parking to protect the paint finish of their vehicles.

Extreme temperatures and bright sun may fade paint, damage interior fittings (especially plastic), and make driving uncomfortable. In Adelaide, South Australia, a city with very hot, sunny summers, residents in a subsidized development frequently complain about the lack of weather protection for vehicles (Wirthensohn, 1976).

Possible design responses

- Provide as many dwellings as possible with garages or carports.
- Design flexible dwellings that will accommodate the addition of carports or garages.
- Plant trees that provide shade for cars and do not drop nectar, nuts, fruits, or cones on them. Where possible, select native trees that do not shed leaves.

See also: Grouped carports (153), Informal surveillance (219).

162. Recreational vehicle parking

Consider providing parking for boats, recreational vehicles, and other occasionally used vehicles.

In Canada, the United States, and Australia there is an increasing use of parking areas for boats, trailers (caravans), recreational vehicles, and the like. Unless special parking is provided, regular parking spaces or driveways may become cluttered with these vehicles, and residents' perceived sense of crowding may increase.

Possible design responses

- Provide a secondary, more remote parking area for recreational vehicles surrounded by high security fencing and locked at all times, especially in high-crime areas.
- Alternatively, provide tandem parking for each unit (that is, the outside vehicle must be moved before the inside one can be). The inside space is for infrequently used vehicles, such as R.V.s or second cars. This method uses space efficiently because the vehicles are parked close together (Untermann and Small, 1977).

12

Landscaping, Footpaths, and Site Furniture

The possibility of providing extensive areas of shared landscaping is clearly one of the primary advantages of clustered over detached housing in suburban locations and of clustered redevelopment over traditional, street-oriented housing in inner-city areas.

Several housing evaluation studies show that the exterior appearance of individual dwellings matters less to residents than the layout and landscaping of the scheme as a whole (Cooper, 1970b; Cooper and Corrie, 1970; Department . . . , 1972a; Lansing et al., 1970; Luedke and Associates, 1970; Norcross, 1973; Norcross and Hysom, 1968).

In several developments where either an attractive natural landscape was carefully preserved or considerable budget was allocated for new planting and maintenance, residents report tree growth to be one of the most important attributes of the site and say they go out walking for pleasure more frequently than in neighborhoods they had previously lived in (Cooper, 1972b; Marans and Rodgers, 1972).

In a major British study of the estate outside the dwelling the design and maintenance of the whole site correlates highly with overall housing satisfaction (Department . . . , 1972a). In British difficult-to-let estates it is generally the overall image, the dismal quality and lack of definition of semipublic outdoor spaces, as well as serious problems of management and maintenance, that arouse the greatest anger in tenants (Department . . . , 1981b,c). This is not to say, however, that additional landscaping is the prime means of improving tenants' morale and physically upgrad-

ing rundown and unpopular estates. In such situations the legacy of distrust between tenants and management needs to be broken down first. Better management, repair, and modernization of poor quality dwelling interiors, and measures to increase security, are likely to precede landscaping on tenants' lists of priorities. Simply adding landscaping may seem like a mere cosmetic treatment (Department . . . , 1981b,c).

For example, where a prewar "showpiece" estate in the Northwest London borough of Brent had deteriorated by the mid 1960s to the point that 75 percent of all households wanted to leave, a successful remedial program included the modernization of interiors, the addition of elevators, the reorganization of management, and the reduction of density, as well as extensive landscaping (Department . . . , 1981c). Bare asphalt courtyards were transformed to landscaped areas of grass, trees, shrubs, and parking bays; some streets were closed to through traffic; and an adventure playground, play hut, play field, and equipped areas for younger children were added. But in other settings—for example, Pruitt Igoe, St. Louis—even massive landscape improvements could do nothing to save projects so problem ridden that they eventually had to be demolished.

The guidelines in this chapter are divided into three broad sections: landscaping and planting, footpaths and pedestrian circulation, and site furniture.

Figure 169 (above). Apart from the reasonable cost, most residents chose to live here largely because of the green oasis effect of the landscaping. Asked if they would have preferred that money be spent on larger kitchens (minimally sized) or private garages and less on trees, the majority opted for trees. (St. Francis Square, San Francisco)

LANDSCAPING AND PLANTING

163. Landscaping importance

Landscaping should be treated as an intrinsic part of site design.

Designers need to make it clear to client, builder, lending authority, and management that landscaping, play equipment, fences, seating, and so forth are not "extras" that can be eliminated at the construction phase without altering the social and aesthetic effectiveness of the whole design. Where some or all of these features have been eliminated—usually by the builder to reduce costs—the social consequences are an unattractive environment, lack of play areas, reduced privacy, lack of gathering places, vandalism, or dissatisfaction (Cooper, 1972b; Department . . . , 1981b; Eikos Group, 1980; Zeisel and Griffin, 1975). For example, a clustered scheme in Cambridge, Massachusetts, was designed with the unit living rooms facing inward

onto a communal area where, it was hoped, adults would meet and children would play. But when the contractor eliminated garden fences, tree planting, play equipment, and site furniture in order to cut cost, the whole social intent of the scheme reversed. People hung out on the peripheral parking lots, where children could at least ride their bikes and where adults could pull out folding chairs. Although introverted site plans can be criticized for cutting people off from the neighborhood, in this case the neighborhood was industrial and had virtually no street life. The residents were left with an asphalt desert outside and a green desert inside.

Possible design responses

- Include landscape architects as part of the design team from the beginning of a project.
- In establishing budget priorities remember that site design and landscaping are critical to the overall success of a scheme.
- Maintain close liaison with building and landscaping contractors to ensure that they do not cut out intrinsic design elements that they perceive as extras.
- If budget cutbacks cannot be avoided, complete the "skeletal" design and develop a program with budget allocations to add remaining landscape features over time (Eikos Group, 1980).

See also: Pleasing milieu (10), Landscape quality (11).

Figure 170 (a, b). Residents could well resent the use of limited budgets on landscaping if it resulted in spaces like these. What is supposed to happen here? The real *use* of all outdoor spaces should be considered most carefully.

164. User-oriented landscaping

Landscaping should be planned with resident satisfaction as its chief concern.

In low-budget housing, areas of attractive trees and grass are sometimes put on the public side for show and dwellings face onto dreary asphalt courtyards or parking lots. This phenomenon can be observed all the way from prewar public housing in Britain to contemporary private apartment projects in suburban California. It is particularly unfortunate for families because children need a safe interior space to play in and stay-at-home parents or older folk appreciate a pleasant green view. An evaluation of a number of inner-London projects concludes, "the green and trees on the outside of the older estates (the *interiors* are asphalt) . . . offer a far less satisfying environment than the more recent estates where the grass and trees are *within* the blocks (Shankland . . . , 1977, 61).

Possible design responses

- In clustered schemes ensure that landscaping is never provided on the exterior (public) facade of a site at the expense of interior (semiprivate) spaces.
- Provide a pleasant view from living room and/or kitchen windows.
- Select species of trees that are tall enough so that residents above ground level will have a view out into (and not just down onto) pleasant greenery. (See guideline 12.)

See also: View from the window (12), Children as planners (99), Landscape installation and modification (179), Personalized landscape (180).

Figure 171. A strategically located back on this bench would have ensured that passersby would sit and look out into communal space, rather than infringe on the privacy of the dwelling.

165. Children in the landscape

Use of the site by children is a critical consideration in landscape design.

Figure 172. The saplings attached to these posts have died—small wonder. Unless sufficient interesting play objects are provided, children will be tempted to interact with *any* vertical elements in the landscape (trees, posts, bollards, bike stands, lampposts, and so on).

Several studies show that much visible outdoor damage in landscaped areas, although termed "vandalism" by some residents, is in fact the result of normal wear and tear by children at play. Because children between five and ten are the most frequent users of public open space in residential areas, the planting plan should allocate the maximum feasible amount of the site to their uses (Architecture . . . , 1966, 1969; Bowlby, 1969; Byrom, 1972; Committee . . . , 1972; Cooper, 1972a; Cooper Marcus, 1974; Department, 1972a, 1973a; Durard and Eckhart, 1973; Eikos Group, 1980; Gilmour et al., 1970; Hanke, 1964; Hole, 1966; Michelson, 1968; Medium . . . , 1977; Ministry . . . , 1967c; Shankland . . . , 1969). Otherwise parts of the site not intended for play will be taken over or trampled on (Cooper, 1972b; Cooper and Corrie, 1970; Cooper and Marcus, 1971; Shankland . . . , 1967; Zeisel and Griffin, 1975). Because there is a close correlation between good maintenance and overall residential satisfaction, it is especially important that landscaping be as "childproof" as possible.

Possible design responses

- Ensure that as much of the site as is feasible is accessible to children.
- Ensure that the routes of major desire lines (routes most frequently used by pedestrians) have hard-surfaced paths along them.
- Select sturdy, fast-growing, low-branching trees for children to climb.
- Plant semimature trees with stakes and mesh whenever possible; protect young trees with raised beds or with "keep off" planting such as roses or gorse.
- Avoid planting materials that may be tempting to play in, on, or under and that cannot withstand this treatment.
- Avoid grass *under* play equipment.
- Avoid the use of poisonous plant materials (for example, laburnum or oleander).
- Avoid the use of "hostile" plant material— that is, trees with thorns or prickly leaves or shrubs with sharp-edged or spiky growth— close to play areas or paths where children are likely to play.
- Specify robust site furniture.

See also: Children safe from cars (3), Playing everywhere (79), Unrestricted setting (84), Children's rights (85), Children as planners (99).

166. Ground shaping

Ground shaping and grading should be used to create interest on flat sites.

Building slopes, mounds, and berms is an excellent way to dispose of excavated soil from building and roadwork, and these are not costly design features. The slopes created can provide visual relief, help subdivide large spaces, and provide wind shields for people of all ages. They offer children rolling and sliding areas. Slides set into the side of a hill are safer than the freestanding variety and more accessible to disabled children.

Possible design responses

- Plan to use material excavated in building or road construction to create berms, slopes, or ground sculpture, especially in children's play areas.
- Be cautious that slopes likely to be used for snow sledding do not direct children toward vehicular areas.
- Ensure that ground shaping does not create drainage problems.
- Consider the use of berms to reduce traffic noise, subdivide spaces, or screen parking.

See also: Chapter 8—Common Open Space and the Needs of Children.

167. Paved areas

Avoid large, empty paved areas.

In subsidized housing when funds for site landscaping are tight, a quick and easy answer has often been to pave over large portions of the site with asphalt. This provides easy maintenance but results in a "hard" environment. If residents perceive the space outside their dwellings as hard—impersonal, ugly, and institutional—they are less likely to take responsibility for it than if it is domestic and attractive in scale and appearance (Newman, 1972; Sommer, 1974).

Possible design responses

- Pave only where necessary to enhance some specific function, such as pedestrian or vehicular circulation, parking, or unloading.
- Where a large paved area is intended for play, indicate its possible uses through line markings or equipment, but never provide this kind of surface as the *only* one on which to play.

See also: Pleasing milieu (10), Interesting landscaped spaces (73), Comfortable space dimensions (74), Incorporating the street (216).

168. Functional spaces

In selecting plant materials keep the actual use of every section of the site in mind.

Every planting decision on a housing site must be thought of in terms of function as well as visual appeal. Every portion of the site must be carefully planned for human, especially child, use. The whole site should be capable of sustaining fairly heavy use because many residents may be tied to it by virtue of low income, child-minding responsibilities, lack of transit, age, or disability (Cooper, 1972b, 1975). Unfortunately, books on planting design generally pay little or no attention to the social and psychological implications of planting plans, and few books on site design have concerned themselves with the important details of how the environment is actually used.

Possible design responses

- Divide the whole site into functional areas, each with a clearly specified purpose: a lawn area for ball games and sitting in the sun, buffer planting to maintain privacy in lower windows, shrubs as a windscreen for a seating cluster.
- When the site plan is nearing completion, double check its potential use and ask yourself what you expect to happen on every portion of the site. If there are sections with

no clear function, consult guidelines on children's and adults' needs to see if some potential site use has been overlooked.

See also: Tot lot location (90), Walk to play (102), Teenage hangouts (124), Community garden (141), Outdoor seating (192), On-site picnic (196), User group territories (227), Running the gauntlet (229), Conflicting uses (230).

Figure 173. The planting beds on this site make no functional sense and have been tramped by the children, leaving bare dirt to blow and spill onto the pathways. A design that may seem attractive on the drawing board or from ten floors up sometimes makes no sense on the ground.

169. Grassed areas

When considering the inclusion of a grassed area, the designer must decide whether its purpose is mainly for appearance or also for children's use.

Small grassed areas in developments with a high child density can be protected from excessive use by mounding, planting, or raising above footpath level. Such deliberate discouragement of child use, however, needs to be seriously debated before being decided upon. Perhaps children should be compensated with one large grassed area and a hard-surfaced ball-game or kickabout area. In a study of two problem estates in South London (both with high child densities) the landscaping in one scheme fared moderately well because areas of intensive circulation were paved, large lawn areas were provided, and some of these were mounded or raised above footpath level. In another scheme, which had many more small lawn areas, hard to maintain and easy to cut across, lawn areas soon became worn and muddy (Heffernan, 1977). The prediction of desire lines must be accurate if grassed areas are to be unscarred by muddy shortcuts.

Possible design responses

- Protect lawn areas not meant for play by mounding, raising them above path level, or planting.

- Design grassed play areas to:
  - Be large enough to equalize intensity of use
  - Have several points of access to avoid excessive wear and tear
  - Be separated from dwellings by some means (planting, grade difference, and so forth) to reduce noise and broken windows
  - Be well drained and located so that the sun will dry them out after rain.
- In grassy areas designed for heavy play where maintenance is a problem, consider allowing the grass to be unmaintained and unwatered.
- Avoid using low-level lights or irrigation sprinkler heads that protrude from the ground in grassed areas likely to be used for play.

See also: Playing everywhere (79), Children's rights (85), Ball games (123).

170. Trees

Employ trees as softening, space-enhancing, and shading elements at eye level.

The monotony of repeated facade designs can be broken by the appropriate use of trees. Trees can also screen potentially intrusive views across courtyards of limited dimensions and make such spaces seem larger, just as a room often seems larger after the placement of furniture. Apart from these aesthetic functions, trees are also essential elements in residential areas, to provide a link to nature, organic cycles, and seasonal rhythms and to enhance the microclimate.

Possible design responses

- Employ trees with open foliage where views across a relatively narrow space need to be filtered.
- Especially where it is likely that residents (the elderly or house-bound parents) will spend a considerable amount of time at home, provide views onto trees whose foliage exhibits seasonal changes and moves easily in a breeze.
- In areas with severe winters create views onto evergreen as well as deciduous species.
- Use trees of a height and texture so that their placement in a space of limited proportions enhances its size.

Figure 174. Strategically located planting can reduce the perceived density of a site by screening direct views of repeated facade designs.

- For safety, ensure adequate head room along pathways.
- Where the size of the space is appropriate, use mass plantings of the same species for visual strength and unity.

See also: View from the window (12), Comfortable space dimension (74), Varying spaces (75), Children's lookouts (109).

Figure 175. Too many trees planted in rows in a small space can make a site seem cluttered and render the space underneath unattractive.

171. Native species

Plant native species and retain existing trees.

Native species of plants and trees require less maintenance and are more likely to survive rough treatment or occasional unexpected weather conditions.

Possible design responses

- Retain existing mature trees on the site at all costs, especially those that are usable by children for climbing or Tarzan swings.
- Select species native to the region.
- When selecting exotic species, choose types native to comparable climatic zones.

See also: Open space maintenance (86), Tree maintenance (172), Landscape maintenance (181).

172. Tree maintenance

Choose trees so as to minimize maintenance.

The maintenance of landscaping has a strong influence on resident satisfaction. Especially in subsidized housing, where maintenance budgets may be low and there are large numbers of children, the selection of low-maintenance plant materials is important.

Possible design responses

- Children will inevitably climb trees; so select trees with a sturdy, low-branching system that enables them to do so.
- Do not place trees where their root systems may eventually disturb structural footings, curbs, or walks.
- Avoid species that need frequent trimming.
- Do not place species that frequently shed their leaves close to pools or ponds.
- Do not plant species that shed during wet seasons and whose leaves or secretions are particularly slippery (for example, linden in Britain) near pathways.
- Do not plant trees in or adjacent to parking areas if they would drop sticky nectar, nuts, or fruit onto the cars.

See also: Open space maintenance (86), Children's lookouts (109), Native species (171), Landscape maintenance (181), Maintenance policies (239).

173. Microclimate

Choose trees to enhance the microclimate and to act as a passive method of climate control for dwellings.

Plants reduce summer heat by blocking, absorbing, and scattering radiation and by the evapotranspiration process. If they are deciduous, they nevertheless allow the winter sunshine to penetrate. Deciduous trees used as windbreaks, however, are ineffective in winter.

Planting for climate control is a large subject in its own right. On this topic, readers are urged to consult books and manuals specifically for the region in which they are working.

Possible design response

- Select and locate trees so that they admit winter sun but shield people, buildings, metal play equipment, and so forth from summer sun.

See also: Trees (170), Privacy planting (176), Informal surveillance (219).

174. "Keep off" planting

Ground cover and shrub plantings should be used only where there is a logical reason to prevent use of a space.

Where plantings are used solely for ornamental purposes and there is a moderate to high density of children, they are likely to be trampled and become an eyesore (Architecture . . . , 1966; Cooper and Corrie, 1970; Cooper and Marcus, 1971).

Possible design responses

- Locate ground cover meant *not* to be walked on only where there is a specific need to keep people away (for example, for privacy or safety) or where mowing would be difficult.
- Locate ornamental shrubs only where there is a specific functional (such as screening) or aesthetic (such as foundation planting) need.
- Avoid ivy as a ground cover where it may prove attractive to vermin for their nests and runs.
- On windy sites avoid locating shrubs where litter lodging beneath them will become a maintenance problem.

See also: Playing everywhere (79), Unrestricted setting (84).

Figure 176. There were no fewer than seven species of plants and shrubs bordering this play area; its minimal size and children's need to run or tricycle around play equipment would suggest there should have been none.

Figure 177. Inappropriate use of planting: Thorny rose bushes are *not* the right choice for a play area of limited dimensions. Note the very small space to move around this jungle gym.

175. Shrubs for play

Where shrubs are to be planted for largely aesthetic purposes, consider using species that will also enhance children's needs for hiding spaces.

Most adults recall special places of their childhood, often unknown to their parents or other adults, where they could hide out. In modern housing developments the landscape is often scraped so bare that few such places remain (Cooper Marcus, 1978a).

Possible design responses

- Specify shrubs whose natural growth tendencies create "tunnels" or child-sized spaces beneath them.
- Specify shrubs that inhibit undergrowth and are high branching.
- Specify shrubs with dense foliage.
- Specify shrubs with harmless blossoms, berries, or "nuts." Avoid oleander and other poisonous flowers.
- Plant on fences creepers or vines that can create "tunnels" underneath.

See also: Playing everywhere (79), Play nests (116).

Figure 178. Inappropriate location of planting: A much better design here would have reversed planting and pathway, giving the houses on the left a buffer and children a place to bounce balls on the garage walls to the right.

176. Privacy planting

Use planting to enhance the privacy of ground-level dwellings.

In ground-level units with a double aspect one side will generally be screened by fenced private open space. But privacy on the other side is often minimal, especially if that side faces a street or public footpath.

Possible design responses

- Set buildings back at least 12 feet (3.6 m) from public footpath or street.
- If you cannot set buildings back, use thick planting or fencing to screen windows.
- Ensure that planting does not interfere with access to sun for microclimate control.

See also: Added privacy (30), Privacy screening (57), Orientation to sun (59), Microclimate (173), Yard surveillance (220).

Figure 179. Residents in this high-priced California development have to keep their drapes drawn all the time to maintain a sense of privacy because a public footpath passes close by and no buffer planting was provided.

177. Snowmelt

Ensure that planting in areas with cold climates does not impede the melting of snow and ice.

The shadow patterns of evergreen trees and shrubs can cause snow and ice to melt slowly from paths and steps, thus causing hazardous conditions for pedestrians.

Possible design response

- Calculate the winter shadow patterns of evergreen trees and shrubs, and ensure that these do not fall across frequently used pathways or steps.

See also: Hard-surface play (82), Parking access (154), Footpath systems (182).

178. Planting edges

All planted areas (other than lawns) next to hard surfaces should have wooden edges, raised borders, or retaining walls.

Edges prevent soil from washing over adjacent paths and minimize cutting across by cyclists or pedestrians. They can make all the difference between a tidy and an unkempt site (Architecture . . . , 1966; Cooper Marcus, 1971). Soil wash may seem like a minor problem, but it can suggest poor maintenance. Residents may respond by dropping litter, thus starting a cycle of disrespect for the environment.

Possible design responses

- Define all edges of planting areas with edging boards or retaining walls.
- Create retaining walls that can also be used for casual seating.

See also: Pleasing milieu (10), Outdoor seating (192), Seating environment (195).

Figure 180. Lack of edges between planted areas and hard surfaces will soon lead to unsightly soil washout.

Figure 181. Wooden or stone edges to planting beds can be designed to double as casual seating.

179. Landscape installation and modification

Although major items of landscaping need to be installed and established before occupancy, residents must have the opportunity to make later modifications.

Major routes, lighting, site furniture, play areas, grading, and planting should be established before the first residents move in. If they are not, there is a likelihood of vandalism, overuse of initially completed sections, or interference by children with planting work and equipment (Byrom, 1972; Committee . . . , 1972; Cooper and Corrie, 1970; Wilful . . . , 1971). "Fine tuning" of the landscaping by residents themselves might include determining the location of minor pathways (after desire lines are established), selecting plant materials to be planted adjacent to private yards, determining the size and location of community or children's gardens, or deciding the location of seating areas.

These measures will work only if sufficient budget has been allowed to implement residents' proposals once use patterns have been established. Residents should also have some collective means of altering or modifying the landscaping if it does not fit their needs as use patterns change (Byrom, 1972; Cooper, 1970b; Cooper and Corrie, 1970; Cooper and Marcus, 1971; Neighborhood . . . , 1973).

Possible design responses

- Establish major landscaping and circulation features before occupancy.
- Specify the kinds of features that residents may determine and implement themselves, and ensure that there is sufficient budget available.
- Recommend the establishment of a landscaping subcommittee of the home owners' or tenants' association, and ensure that this group has budget and decision-making powers.

See also: Subunit identity (21), Group territory (72), User-oriented landscaping (164); Personalized landscape (180), Maintenance policies (239), Resident's manual (241).

180. Personalized landscape

Provide planting spaces where individual households can add to the general landscaping of the development.

In a major study of residents' likes and dislikes in U.S. townhouses Norcross (1973) found considerable dissatisfaction with the monotony of facade designs. In many condominium developments, unfortunately, personalization of the facade by planting is against the rules; residents may do what they want only with their patios, which are generally out of public view.

Figure 182. The householder has added window boxes and picket fence, enhancing the basic wooden "wall" provided by the designer. (Suburban house near San Francisco)

Sometimes the rules are unstated. In certain British new town neighborhoods the landscaping in front yards is put in by the development corporation designers. Although no explicit rules

Figure 183. Pots and tubs full of flowers beautify this upper-level "street" in an inner-London scheme inhabited chiefly by elderly and retired people. When joints become stiff and strength is faltering, taking care of plants in pots can be a good substitute for tending a full-scale garden.

exist preventing people from replacing this planting, its very presence (and identical nature all the way down the street) is a disincentive to change.

Possible design responses

- Provide window boxes or shelves for flowerpots outside front windows.
- Provide an area for a flower or display garden.
- Leave small personal planting strips between patio/yard fences and communal or public open space.
- Ensure that lease or sales agreements do not preclude the personalization of landscaping in and around the entry within public view.

See also: Entry personalization (34), Display garden (62), User-oriented landscaping (164), Resident's manual (241), Tenant involvement (244), Resident responsibilities (245).

181. Landscape maintenance

Ownership and maintenance arrangements will affect what can be planned.

Maintenance of housing developments is considerably enhanced (and long-term costs reduced) when resident caretakers and gardeners are present, or at least when there is a full-time maintenance staff (Alexander, 1977; Cooper, 1970b; Department . . . , 1981b). With part-time service (or, worse still, once a week service) standards may deteriorate, and the vicious cycle of neglect-littering-vandalism-neglect is likely to commence.

Some evidence suggests that home owners (including residents of co-ops and condominiums) tend to treat their environment more carefully than do renters. Landscaping and hardware for the latter thus should be more vandal-proof (Cooper and Hackett, 1968; Norcross, 1973). (See Chapter 13—Security and Vandalism.)

Possible design responses

- Encourage the employment of a core of full-time maintenance personnel.
- Ensure an adequate operating budget to maintain the proposed landscaping.
- Where financially and socially appropriate, encourage cooperative ownership.

- Where residents pay a specific maintenance fee, ensure that all households have equal functional and visual accessibility to the amenities they are paying for (Byrom, 1972; Whyte, 1964).
- Specify maintenance responsibilities in a resident's manual or lease-sales agreement.
- Consider the employment of residents in maintenance work, especially those who may need to work part-time and close to home (teenagers, women, active elderly persons).

See also: Open space maintenance (86), Maintenance policies (239), Maintenance responsibilities (240), Resident's manual (241), Resident caretaker (243), Tenant involvement (244).

FOOTPATHS AND PEDESTRIAN CIRCULATION

The path system in any housing cluster must serve both for efficient direct movement from A to B and for informal, leisurely movement. Path users may be children on bicycles, parents with toddlers, people pulling laundry baskets or shopping carts, teenagers fooling around, adults out walking the dog, or people in wheelchairs with friends walking alongside. Different users will have varying needs for site furniture such as benches, drinking fountains, and litter containers.

The pathway system should be well designed, drained, and maintained. Because most use of the site takes place on or close to pathways, shortcuts around square corners, trampled planting along too-narrow routes, and litter dropped where no containers are provided are immediately noticed.

Too often, pedestrian movement is given considerably less thought than vehicle movement. For example, a recent British design guide on residential roads and footpaths devoted only six of its seventy pages to pedestrians (Department . . . Transport, 1977).

182. Footpath systems

Footpath systems should accommodate predictable patterns of pedestrian circulation.

Residents need pedestrian access to rubbish disposal, car parking, tot lots, older children's play areas, communal laundries, bus stops, shops, and elementary schools. They will use footpaths only if they form the shortest routes to these facilities. In a study of six traffic-segregated new town neighborhoods that apparently had well-thought-out footpath systems, nearly two-thirds of the residents report walking along main roads (with no pavements) and across landscaped areas to get to their destinations because these routes are shorter (Residential design . . . , 1975).

Footpath systems must recognize essential off-site facilities. The safety advantages of internal, segregated footpath systems in clustered housing sites are meaningless if residents must cross busy peripheral roads to reach essential services (Ministry . . . , 1967c).

Possible design responses

- Ensure that there is safe, direct, hard-surfaced access from every dwelling to needed on- and off-site facilities.
- Ensure that access to dwellings is direct and unambiguous.
- In a clustered housing site plan ensure that the shortest distance to amenities is via footpaths through the communal landscaped space, not via adjacent streets.
- Locate footpaths so that delivery personnel can take a direct route from vehicle to dwelling and from dwelling to dwelling without trampling the landscaping.

See also: Street linkage (78), Children on the move (80), Hard-surface play (82), Meeting neighbors (130), Parking access (154), Incorporating the street (216), Evening use (221), Running the gauntlet (229).

Figure 184. Pedestrians will usually follow the shortest route from A to B, whether or not an official path is provided.

183. Footpath design

Design footpaths to facilitate use and maintenance.

Possible design responses

- *Rounded corners and slopes* aid elderly and physically disabled persons and residents using shopping carts or baby carriages.
- *Pavements near entrances to buildings and communal facilities and at intersections between paths* should be wide enough so that a person and a cycle or skateboard can pass without one having to move off the path and so that people can stop to talk without blocking the route.
- *Handrails beside stairs and ramps*, along with benches and sitting areas, are especially important for elderly and physically disabled people and for children learning to walk.
- *Paths sloped to drain in wet weather or during irrigation* help prevent wet surfaces, which are a particular hazard to people whose mobility is impaired.
- *Paving textures should reflect their intended function.* Smooth surfaces are suitable for main pedestrian routes. Bricks or cobbles can be used to distinguish front entries from main footpaths or for adjacent "eddy" spaces, as long as they do not constitute barriers. These rougher textures are generally inappropriate for playgrounds, but attractive open textures such as brickwork may be suitable in seating areas adjacent to paths.
- *Clear definition of edges*, which prevents adjacent grass or planted areas from becoming worn, can be by means of a slight grade change, an edging strip, a retaining wall, or a sloped paved area. Ground cover edging does not prevent children from running or riding bikes across it.
- *Curb cuts* should be provided where paths connect with hard-surfaced areas to enable use by people in wheelchairs, wheeled vehicles, baby carriages, and so forth.

See also: Accessibility (43), Children on the move (80), Snowmelt (177), Planting edges (178), Footpath play (189).

Figure 185. A well-designed footpath taking account of the needs of children, cyclists, trees, and nearby residents.

184. Pedestrian demand

Footpaths should be designed with the type and volume of traffic in mind.

In Tapiola New Town (Finland) the path leading to the town center can quickly be recognized because it is considerably wider and of a different texture than any other path in the town. In Milton Keynes New Town (England) paths intended for cycling as well as walking are of red aggregate (unlike any other paths), and their intended use is well publicized throughout the town.

Figure 186. Children frequently play on footpaths close to home; paths should be designed to accommodate this activity. In this case the path is too narrow and adjacent planting is being trampled.

The design of paths that serve a specific purpose for relatively few people must be carefully considered. Where paths serve as back access to a row of terraced (row) houses, people may use wheelbarrows to move fertilizer, topsoil, or building materials into backyards. One such set of paths observed in a British new town was too narrow, had sloped planting areas on one side that encouraged mud to wash down across the path, and was made of paving stones set so far apart that heavy wheelbarrows or bicycles squelched in and out of the gaps, smearing more mud across the stones. Such microdetails make or break a pathway system.

Possible design responses

- Clearly identify path functions by using different surfaces, widths, signs, and so forth.
- Design paths for a single pedestrian 2 feet (600 mm) wide. Where two pedestrians are likely to be walking together or passing in opposite directions, make them 4 feet (1.2 m) wide (Department . . . , 1977).
- Where a person wheeling a stroller or a person in a wheelchair might need to pass, paths should be a minimum of 5½ feet (1.7 m) wide and path gradients should not exceed 1:12.
- Use smooth, even paving, and leave small gaps between paving stones.

See also: Accessibility (43), Footpath systems (182), Footpath design (183).

185. Paths and streets

Provide sidewalks along all streets in residential areas.

People should not be forced into pedestrian areas. Footpaths alongside streets are often equally safe and sometimes more interesting. It is a frequent oversight in British and Australian new towns to provide elaborate pedestrian networks through landscaped common spaces but no sidewalks along vehicular streets (Residential . . . , 1975). In U.S. clustered housing the opposite is sometimes true. Sidewalks along adjacent streets are provided, but designers ignore the need for path access from patios into common landscaped areas.

Possible design responses

- Provide pedestrian access along streets as well as separate pedestrian-only routes though landscaped spaces.
- Ensure that sidewalks are parallel to roads along their entire length; allow for a variety of spatial experience.
- Ensure that there are well-marked pedestrian crossings, especially on routes children are likely to take on errands.

See also: Footpath systems (182), Incorporating the street (216).

186. Leisure walking

Provide pathways for strolling or leisure walking.

Strolling routes should meander. All people, not just strollers, crave variety and are repelled by monotony. They move toward whatever excites curiosity—a space glimpsed from another space, a path that turns a corner and disappears. Such changing views involve them in the environment, evoke a pleasing sense of mystery or anticipation, and provide a sense of movement through space (Introduction . . . , 1978).

Where a development is adjacent to undeveloped land or forms part of a larger residential setting, pathway systems should allow resident pedestrians to range into these areas. Excellent examples of such integrated pathway systems can be observed in new towns in the United States (Reston, Columbia), Finland (Tapiola), Sweden (Vällingby, Fårsta), England (Stevenage, Milton Keynes, Runcorn), and Scotland (Cumbernauld, E. Killbride). In a planned unit development in New Jersey, residents used pedestrian paths through adjacent woods more than the community swimming pool featured in promotional literature. Two-fifths reported taking up walking for exercise since moving to the development.

Possible design responses

- Provide curvilinear paths without being arbitrary; a changing focal point provides interest on a walk.
- Provide the users of strolling pathways with a series of constantly changing views by means of building location, planting, or gradients.
- Create noticeable temperature changes by having some sectors fully exposed to the sun, some partially shaded, and some heavily shaded.
- Provide a variety of places to sit en route. (See guidelines 192 through 200 later in this chapter.)
- Provide a connection between on-site strolling paths and neighborhood walking or cycle paths without encouraging "outsiders" to pass through semiprivate or private on-site spaces.
- Ensure that meandering paths do not confuse those who wish to find a dwelling quickly; provide adequate signage and numbering.

See also: Space hierarchy (4), Visual complexity (18), Group territory (72), Interesting landscaped spaces (73), Footpath security (190), Site entry barriers (201).

Figure 187. Walking along paths that offer some variety and surprise is pleasant.

Figure 188. Traversing endless vistas is far less enjoyable.

Figure 189. Eaglestone. A study in Milton Keynes New Town asked residents what they remembered from a walk through their neighborhood. The residents in Eaglestone remembered 50 percent more places and landmarks than those living in Netherfield (see Figure 190).

Figure 190. Netherfield, where few landmarks were recalled.

187. Pedestrians passing by

When planning circulation routes, ensure that no population group will have to violate another's temporary territory while moving around the site.

Pedestrian routes should channel people *to* particular activity areas on the site, but should not force them to pass *through* the activity. A common mistake is to direct a pathway through a play area; it can be a hazard to passersby when children run from one piece of equipment to another; and it can be a hazard to the children at play if other children swoop through the play area on bicycles. Similarly, a pathway that forces adults to walk through a seating area taken over by teenagers may create a small crisis of "territorial infringement."

Possible design response

- Make sure that there is a clear distinction between entering an activity space and passing it by and that pathway design allows both to happen.

See also: Space hierarchy (4), Group territory (72), Tot lot location (90), Teenage hangouts (124), Running the gauntlet (229), Conflicting uses (230).

188. Footpath privacy

Locate footpaths so that pedestrians do not violate the privacy of nearby dwellings or yards.

Possible design responses

- Ensure that public paths do not pass next to the windows of dwellings.

Figure 191. When designing a site plan, consider both the nature of the barrier and the distance between public and private space. Passersby can easily look into the patio of this house. Some residents in this neighborhood have made their own modifications. (See Figure 182.)

- Where the distance between path and dwelling is problematic, screen with high, opaque fencing or buffer planting or create a grade difference, providing that does not constitute a barrier to physically disabled people.

See also: Added privacy (30), Private front path (37), Yard surveillance (220).

189. Footpath play.

Footpaths should be designed to accommodate children's play.

Studies of children's play show that moving around the neighborhood is their most common activity (Architecture . . . , 1969; Barker, 1976; Cooper Marcus, 1974; Department . . . , 1972a, 1973a; Hole, 1966; MacLeod, 1977; Neighborhood . . . , 1973). Footpaths should provide a safe and interesting play circuit for children—that is, circulation systems that link areas for sitting out or playing.

Possible design responses

- Make paths wide enough for both children on bicycles and adults (minimum of 4 feet [1.2 m]).
- Include a section of winding pathway so that children on bicycles can practice turning corners, "slaloming," and so forth.
- Avoid providing paths that will encourage fast cycling or noisy skateboarding on long downhill sections and sections close to dwellings.
- Discourage cycling in the vicinity of housing for elderly and disabled people.
- Select paving materials smooth enough for roller skating but not so smooth that they will be slippery in wet or icy weather.
- Connect dwelling entries and play areas by the shortest possible routes so that children do not create shortcuts.
- Design paths so that they circle all sides of play areas and widen at favorite points for children and teens to gather.

See also: Children on the move (80), Hard-surface play (82).

Figure 192. The design of this play area would have been much improved if, instead of paths "emptying into" the area, they had encircled it, providing space for hard-surface play around the sand and play structure.

Figure 193. Although footpaths should always be designed to accommodate reasonable play, some activities are hazardous or noisy.

190. Footpath security

Design paths to enhance security.

Pedestrian entrances to the site should be clear for the sake of residents and legitimate visitors but—at least in high- or moderate-crime areas—not so "welcoming" that all and sundry feel they have the right to enter and use the spaces inside. Paths should allow prescanning before use; however visibility should not necessarily mean an undifferentiated or uninteresting site.

Possible design responses

- Ensure that pedestrian site entrances clearly indicate the passage from public to semi-private space.
- Ensure that all footpaths are visible from adjacent dwellings.
- Channel pedestrian traffic so that people using footpaths, especially in the evening, may meet other residents.
- Align lighting and footpaths so that it is possible to see a considerable distance ahead at night.
- Avoid dense shrubbery close to paths or building entries.

See also: Neighborly surveillance (42), Site entry barriers (201), Informal surveillance (219), Lighting for safety (222).

Figure 194. Shrubs or trees that could allow criminals to hide should be avoided.

191. Footpath lighting

Design footpath lighting with care.

Lighting along paths should enable people to see their way and be seen by others in dwellings and using paths. Lighting should fall directly on paths and not cast dark shadows, especially on stairs.

Possible design responses

- Ensure that parking areas are adequately lit.
- Provide even lighting along paths.
- Ensure that lighting at entries is not blinding.
- Select fixtures that are sturdy and vandal-proof but do not appear "institutional."
- Provide shades to screen windows from direct rays or locate lights away from windows.
- Use light-sensitive switches or tuners for exterior lighting.
- Provide lighting for nighttime sports area use.
- Do not provide low, ground-level lights where higher-level lighting is not also provided or where children's play will damage the fixtures.

See also: Evening use (221), Lighting for safety (222).

SITE FURNITURE

192. Outdoor seating

A variety of pleasant outdoor seating locations will meet different needs.

People who must spend a lot of time sitting at home—because of child-minding responsibilities, infirmity, or age—may wish to sit outside for a change. A change of environment can lead to a change of mood or outlook. Yet benches are often "plonked" down on site with little concern for the experience of the sitter, looking straight into blank walls, patio fences, or walls of windows.

Possible design responses

• Provide outdoor sitting areas in all these locations:
—Adjacent to and slightly above preschool play areas
—Within viewing and calling distance of play grounds for five- to ten-year-olds
—Along frequently used pathways (if numbers of elderly or disabled people are housed on the site, every 200 to 300 feet [60 to 90 m] for frequent rests)
—Overlooking scenes of activity (for "watching the action")
—In quiet, secluded spots (for lovers and readers)
—In central, visible locations or close to a community building or basketball area
—For teenage socializing, arrange benches in L or U shapes for sizeable groups
—In locations overlooking attractive, green, quiet spaces in the development
—In elevated locations with a more distant view of the townscape

See also: Supervising adults (94), Teenage hangouts (124), Friendly encounters (131), Planting edges (178), Pedestrians passing by (187), Litter receptacles (200).

Figure 195. Why was the bench positioned here, presenting a boring view of repeated building forms?

Figure 196. The bench sitter's uninspiring view of concrete slabs and an oppressive high-rise building. This was the *only* bench provided in an inner-London scheme of 214 flats. (Robin Hood Gardens)

193. Sunny/shaded seating

In locating sitting areas be conscious of the local microclimate.

Possible design responses

- In regions warm enough to sit out on a sunny winter day locate benches in sheltered positions to catch the midday or early afternoon sun.

- In regions with variably cool to hot summers locate benches to give a choice between shade and sun.
- In predominantly hot regions locate most benches in positions shaded by trees or buildings.
- In windy locations provide seating sheltered by buildings, walls, or planting. If trees are used, evergreens are best (Cohen et al., 1979).

- In rainy regions place some benches in roofed shelters or gazebos facing an attractive view.

See also: Outdoor seating (192).

Figure 197. A pleasing seating design providing the choice of facing different directions and of sitting in the sun or dappled shade. (Apartments in a California suburb)

194. Seating variety

Provide a variety of sitting area designs.

Figure 198. Overprovision of benches: In this Thamesmead, London, courtyard there are no less than nine benches—but no play equipment. In the next courtyard there is play equipment—but no benches! Did the designer assume that children do not sit or that adults do not want to watch?

Children "plop" down on the grass, on a rock or wall, or on a bench, and then move on. Teenagers sprawl, fool around in a group, and arrange to "be seen" in semipublic locations. A harried adult may need a place to sit quietly alone. An elderly person may want a comfortable seat for a long time, to pass the time away. On-site seating should provide for a variety of sitting arrangements, locations, and outlooks.

Possible design responses

- Provide comfortable benches with backs for long-term sitting for elderly people.
- Provide wide, backless benches in semipublic locations for teenagers or children to sit or sprawl on or use as tables.
- Arrange some benches—with and without backs—in right-angled groupings so that two or more people can comfortably sit and talk.
- Provide some short benches (3 to 4 feet [0.9 to 1.2 m]) for people who want to be alone.
- Consider steps or retaining walls as casual seating.
- Provide resting places with space for a person in a wheelchair to fit into a conversational seating arrangement.

See also: Friendly encounters (131), Planting edges (178), Outdoor seating (192).

195. Seating environment

Pay close attention to the detailed design of seating areas.

Even if a distant outlook is initially considered in the siting of seating areas, the close-in visual/auditory/olfactory environment needs careful attention as well. Many people use a period of sitting outdoors for reflection or contemplation and are aided in their reflective moods by gently moving greenery, by the fine visual textures of nearby features, or by still or running water. Even unseen features, if they are nearby, can have a positive effect. People like to sit with something (plants, a wall) at their backs.

Possible design responses

- Consider the variety of colors, textures, and views visible from each seating location.
- Close to seating areas specify plant materials that will attract songbirds or butterflies.
- Provide a seating area near a small fountain, pool, or stream.
- Close to benches specify herbs or flowers with pleasant or evocative smells.
- Include plant materials that exhibit seasonal changes (leaves, blossoms, fruit).
- Provide small tubs of colorful annuals or perennials.
- Specify trees that make pleasing sounds in the breeze (for example, aspen, poplar) close to seating areas.
- Ensure that some seating is placed up against a wall, a berm, or an area of shrub planting.

See also: Trees (170), Microclimate (173), Planting edges (178), Outdoor seating (192).

Figure 199. Poor location of bench: Note that the bench partially blocks entry to the play area. Do we really want our children to play on model tanks?

Figure 200. Comfortable benches, but poorly located between two parking lots. How much better if they had been positioned in the adjacent shopping center, 200 feet (60 m) away. Providing a pleasing physical and social environment in which to sit is just as important as providing something to sit on.

196. On-site picnic

Provide picnic tables and barbecues.

Residents of low- or moderate-income developments, some of whom may not own cars or have easy access to a park, will appreciate a picnic table and barbecue in the communal outdoor space. People who can picnic in their own yard or at distant parks are unlikely to be interested.

Possible design responses

- Provide picnic tables and barbecues within easy access of dwellings, but in a semiprivate setting where users will not feel "on view."
- Locate the tables so that those sitting at them have a pleasant view.
- In regions with hot summers provide adequate shade.
- Locate the facility within view of a play equipment area.

See also: Tot lot location (90), Walk to play (102), Pedestrians passing by (187).

Figure 201. Picnic tables in a low-income, inner-city project. Residents using them feel very exposed, but because many do not have cars, they have nowhere else to go.

Figure 202. Picnic tables in a middle-income, suburban development. A pleasant, semiprivate location but, ironically, because most residents own cars, they prefer to picnic at a park or beach. This facility thus remains unused.

197. Child table

Provide a child-sized table and benches.

Figure 203. How much more useful here to have provided a child-sized table and benches rather than this overdesigned structure to "shade" two short benches.

Smaller children like to sit and draw, play games, talk, or read outdoors. Studies show that such play is much more common than active play on play equipment (Cooper Marcus, 1974; Department . . . , 1973a; Hole, 1966).

Possible design responses

- Locate a child-sized table and benches close to a play area or well-used pathway.
- Provide a hard surface under the table and a litter receptacle and drinking fountain nearby.
- Provide adequate shade in regions with hot summers and a roofed structure (gazebo or shelter) in regions with wet weather.
- Provide a normal-sized table and benches for adults and teenagers alongside the smaller furniture.

See also: Tot lot design (93), Undercover play (119), On-site picnic (196).

198. Drinking fountains

In regions with hot summers provide drinking fountains.

Because of differences in physiology and metabolism, children need to drink more frequently than do adults.

Possible design responses

- Provide a fountain with steps up or a low outlet for children as well as a high one for adults.
- Ensure adequate drainage.
- Locate a fountain on the edge of a sand play area so that overflow will dampen the sand.
- Provide fountains that can be used by people in wheelchairs and that have knobs that are easy for children or physically disabled people to turn on.

See also: Tot lot design (93), Sand play (95), Water play (96).

199. Public phones

Public phones are a high priority.

Provide several public telephones where many residents cannot afford private phones or in countries where it is not the norm to have a private telephone.

Possible design responses

- Locate public phones near the entries to dwellings in a well-lit, semipublic area.
- If there is only one public phone, avoid locating it within a room or communal space that may, at times, be locked up or where the noise level may be distracting.
- Ensure that at least one phone is low enough for use by children or a person in a wheelchair.
- Ensure that at least one phone is installed before the first residents move in.

200. Litter receptacles

On-site litter receptacles are a high priority.

It is astonishing how few housing schemes provide this essential amenity. This is partly because designers and clients of clustered housing are unaware of the extent to which common open spaces and access ways are actually used and partly because management fears that litter receptacles will be used for household garbage. If they recognized that such spaces are used as intensively for play and recreation as many parks, surely there would be a place to put litter.

Providing litter receptacles does not ensure that they will be used, but without them there is no point in blaming children for dropping candy wrappers on the ground.

Possible design responses

- Locate attractive litter receptacles along major pathways and close to all seating and play areas.
- Design litter receptacles so that they are easily emptied but not easily pushed over by a dog or child.

See also: Tot lot location (90), Teenage hangouts (124), Landscape maintenance (181), Outdoor seating (192), On-site picnic (196), Maintenance responsibilities (240).

13

Security and Vandalism

Crime is more of an issue in the United States than in other urban industrial nations, and many of the following guidelines are relevant specifically to North America. Crime rates in Britain, however, are rising steadily, and in these matters there is no room for complacency: Even where the requirements for reducing crime may conflict with client objectives, designers everywhere should be aware of the possibility of crime, if only because crime prevention techniques employed at the initial design stage are generally easier and cheaper than those employed in later redesign and rehabilitation work (Hough and Mayhew, 1982; Morris and Hawkins, 1970; Newman, 1976; Perlgut, 1982).

The failure of many U.S. public housing developments has been attributed to vandalism, crime, and the fear of crime. A vicious circle can be set up: Crime leads to the fear of crime, and this fear leads to the psychological withdrawal of residents and the disuse of outside buildings and grounds. This in turn sets up conditions that lead to further crime and abuse of the environment.

When plans are made to rehabilitate such projects, security improvements should receive high priority. Even in Britain surveys of rundown and stigmatized estates have found that most residents place security above aesthetics. In the rehabilitation of a vast, rundown, prewar London estate, for example, residents rejected plans to upgrade courtyards by landscaping in favor of courtyard floodlighting (Department

Donald Perlgut wrote the first draft of this chapter and contributed extensively to its revisions.

. . . , 1981c). In another such project new landscaping was given less priority than securing dwellings against break-ins.

In recent years many U.S. publications have examined crime prevention in housing projects (Brill . . . , 1979a,b; Perlgut, 1982b; Rouse and

Figure 204. An abandoned high-rise project in Liverpool, plagued by crime, vandalism, and social problems. Its inhabitants derisively named it "The Piggeries."

Rubenstein, 1978). These argue that both physical form and social environment play a major role in encouraging residents to improve the quality of life (and decrease the amount of crime) where they live. Despite his emphasis on design to solve crime problems, Oscar Newman readily admits that a housing development's social characteristics are stronger predictors of crime than its physical characteristics. In U.S. housing projects the three strongest indicators of crime are all functions of poverty, the standard variable of crime: the percentage of resident population receiving welfare, the percentage of families headed by a female receiving AFDC (Aid to Families with Dependent Children), and the per capita disposable income of the development's residents (Newman, 1976; Newman and Hersh, 1972).

An appreciation of the interaction between the physical design and the social characteristics of housing developments is critical to any security plan. A development may succeed with design mistakes, lack of needed services, or an imperfect tenant selection, but not with a volatile combination of the three.

An analysis of the location of crime in housing developments produces no major surprises (Rouse and Rubenstein, 1978; United States Department . . . , 1979). Potential criminals are attracted to the poorly lit and poorly surveyed parts of housing areas. Unsecured underground garages are obvious places for assault and vandalism. Ground-floor apartments are the most victimized, with top-floor apartments next be-

Figure 205. Signs of fear of crime: barbed wire in a high-crime San Francisco neighborhood.

cause of access from the roof and fewer opportunities for surveillance. Units that are visible from roads, well-traveled walkways, or nearby apartments suffer less from crime than others. In a major study of New York City public housing Newman (1972) identifies the areas of greatest crime in high-rise projects as enclosed spaces of buildings and grounds that are public in nature and that residents should be able to control or survey but cannot—stairwells, elevators, hidden lobbies, hallways, rooftops, and unclaimed grounds. These spaces are neither semiprivate (belonging to a particular group of dwellings) nor truly public and therefore under the surveillance of passersby. Ownership and responsi-

bilities are ambiguous, with residents unable to distinguish residents from outsiders. Many studies support Newman's claim that there is greater safety in developments with a clear hierarchical gradation of space from public territory to semiprivate to private spaces (Brill . . . , 1976b, c, d; Newman, 1972, 1976; Perlgut, 1981).

Newman (1971, 1976) uses the term *defensible space* for environments that exhibit physical characteristics—building layout and site plan—that function to allow inhabitants themselves to become the key agents in ensuring their own security. Newman's *Design Guidelines for Creating Defensible Space* (1976) identifies five separate design/management mechanisms that contribute, independently or collectively, to the creation of defensible space:

1. *Household allocation*: the assignment to different residential groups of the specific environments they are best able to utilize and control, as determined by their ages, lifestyles, socializing proclivities, backgrounds, incomes, and family structures
2. *Territoriality*: the territorial definition of space to reflect zones of influence of specific inhabitants. Residential environments should be subdivided into zones toward which adjacent residents can easily adopt proprietary attitudes.
3. *Surveillance*: the juxtaposition of dwelling interiors with exterior spaces and placement of windows to allow residents naturally to survey exterior and interior public areas of their living environments and the areas assigned for their use
4. *Environment*: the juxtaposition of dwellings— their entries and amenities—with city streets so as to incorporate streets within the sphere of influence of the residential environment
5. *Image*: the adoption of building forms and idioms that avoid the stigma of peculiarity that allows others to perceive the vulnerability and isolation of a particular group of inhabitants

A recent British critique of defensible space argues that, by legitimizing the presence of resi-

Figure 206. Defensible space measures such as territorial definition and casual surveillance make good sense for child rearing, even where there is no crime problem.

dents, defensible space can increase the possibility of crime by those who *are* residents (Mawby, 1977). This critique deserves attention, especially considering that many high-crime housing projects in the United States are known to be victimized primarily by those who live there (Newman, 1971; Newman and Hersh, 1972; United States Department . . . , 1979). A classic case is the redesign scheme for San Francisco's Yerba Buena East, which attempted to limit entry to several high-rise buildings via one scrutinized entry lobby. Because many of those committing crimes were residents, this strategy

failed to lower the crime rate significantly (Cooper, 1972b).

Reporting and combating crime in such situations is made more difficult by fear of reprisals. The pervasive fear of reporting crime (or suspicious behavior) in high-crime areas can undermine the success of redesign proposals to combat crime. If we add to this a disproportionate number of female crime victims in such settings (because female-headed households frequently make up from 60 percent to 90 percent of households in low-income housing) and a disproportionate number of male criminals, we have a very complex and sensitive social situation.

One must be wary of expecting "magic" social benefits from merely providing natural surveillance; the social makeup of residents and the quality of management may be equally relevant (McMurray, 1979; Perlgut, 1981, 1982). A Home Office Research Unit (U.K.) study of telephone kiosk vandalism found that kiosks that were overlooked were only marginally better protected than those that were not. The type of population living in the immediate vicinity was a much more important factor (Mayhew et al., 1979). There is little clear evidence to support the Newman thesis that, given the opportunity to "police" their immediate environment, people will do so. But given that much of Newman's thesis seems like good "common sense" and that surveillance is desirable for child rearing, regardless of its effects on crime, it would seem reasonable to maximize the incorporation of defensible space criteria where possible in the design of new housing developments.

Although design and hardware can certainly contribute to a sense of security, most security measures rely for their effectiveness on residents themselves. The best, and certainly the cheapest, technique of security planning is creating a viable and caring community of residents organized to protect themselves. People need the moral support of a community if they are to exercise their territorial rights; they must be able to rely on neighbors to help defend common territory. *Feelings* of security are a most significant factor. Unfortunately, in many U.S. low-income housing developments managers have discouraged resident organizations because they view them as a threat to their authority or because such organizations may voice demands that management is unable or unwilling to meet. In a crime-ridden housing development this unwillingness must be overcome: residents are ultimately the best agents for their own protection (Becker, 1977; Cooper, 1972b; Milne, 1976; Perlgut, 1978, 1982).

Other factors operating against the creation of viable communities in housing developments are poorly maintained common facilities for meeting casually—or a simple lack of them—and too great a heterogeneity of ages, ethnic origins, or life-styles within the population.

Management can help create community by limiting access by strangers, encouraging personal expression and territorial definition, providing a multipurpose room for meetings and recreation, developing a system for welcoming new residents and introducing them to their neighbors, and generally fostering casual meetings among residents (Cooper, 1972b).

Security education programs are another approach to prevention adopted in some U.S. developments and run by management, police crime prevention units, special city agencies such as San Francisco's Project-SAFE (which also helps tenants organize for security), or residents themselves. These programs generally emphasize a number of basic precautions (Barnes and Sarro, 1971; National . . . , 1976):

1. General precautions: keeping doors and windows locked; remembering newspapers, garbage, and mail; taking care of duplicate keys
2. Security procedures: use of entrance keys, storage areas, and mailboxes
3. Reporting procedures: how and when to report any trouble or suspicious occurrences to management or police
4. Protecting personal property: insurance, keeping sales slips and serial numbers, utilizing "Operation Identification" engraving of valuables with the owner's driver's license or similar number
5. Information about the neighborhood: streets, areas, and alleys to avoid; the availability of escort services
6. Self-protection: how to react during an assault, medical care

Such programs are generally adopted where high crime rates are established. They should be used cautiously where crime is not a problem because they may alarm residents and create unnecessary fears. Similarly, some of the "hardware" guidelines that follow may be inappropriate in secure or low-crime neighborhoods. They have been included for the "worst possible" situation.

One way of institutionalizing these guidelines would be to use them as a security review checklist for each site design in a problematic area. Police and other safety personnel can also evaluate the security implications of site designs. A few U.S. cities and towns have already hired and trained personnel for this undertaking (Blackman, 1966; Brill . . . , 1976b).

For further information on this chapter's guidelines the reader is referred to the following sources in the bibliography: Center for Residential Security Design (1973); National Center for Housing Management (1976); Newman (1972, 1976); William Brill Associates (1979a). Most of these references are to U.S. publications that may be difficult to locate in other countries. A recent bibliography by Donald Perlgut (1981a) gives a good selection of annotated references from the United States, Britain, and Australia.

The guidelines in this chapter are presented under subheadings: penetrability, territoriality, opportunities for surveillance, ambiguity, resident conflicts, vandalism, and management. These categories, and the analysis of security issues that stems from them, are based in part on Brill's (1979b) definitive treatment of factors of site analysis.

PENETRABILITY

One line of defense against crime is to make access more difficult to those spaces the criminal intruder wants to penetrate. This is hard in clustered or project designs where access to communal interior and exterior spaces is generally not controlled. This section considers three potentially penetrable areas: the site, building entrances, and individual dwellings.

201. Site entry barriers

Employ real or symbolic barriers to help discourage intrusion by strangers into communal landscaped spaces intended for use by residents only.

Some sites actually encourage intrusion. Typical incentives to undesired site penetration are footpaths or former street alignments that encourage cutting through the site, failure to distinguish between access intended for the public (delivery personnel, visitors, garbage trucks) and access intended for residents only, and unfocused pedestrian circulation through the site.

At the opposite extreme, a site strongly discouraging intrusion would be a courtyard arrangement of one- or two-story attached houses completely enclosing a common area accessible only via the houses (see Figure 209)

Between these two extremes falls the more normal situation, a site physically accessible to intrusion that has more or less effective *symbolic* barriers against it. Newman (1976) identifies three conditions for the success of symbolic barriers:

1. Intruders' ability to perceive and take heed of the meaning of symbols
2. The evident capacity of inhabitants of defined spaces or their agents to maintain control of their space
3. The capacity of the defined space to require intruders to make their intentions obvious

(That is, spaces must be defined so as to have a low tolerance for ambiguous use.)

The most successful crime-deterring situation exists where all these elements work together (Center . . . , 1973; Newman, 1971, 1972, 1976).

Figure 207. The narrow pathway and symbolic entrance suggests a transition into semiprivate space. Probably few nonresidents would intrude.

But the most crucial criterion is the second. The first and third criteria are often fulfilled in areas that remain crime-ridden because residents are fearful of challenging intruders or reporting crime. A recent study in the eastern United States shows that, although fences are powerful security features, only the presence of a person (occupant) provides a deferrent of comparable strength to a fence (Dockett, Brower, and Taylor, 1983).

Possible design responses

- Arrange buildings to minimize the number of entries into the site.
- Design vehicular and pedestrian circulation so that it is obvious how people and vehicles are to enter and leave the site.
- Locate site entries to enhance formal and informal entry surveillance.
- Create relatively narrow entries.

- Where a real barrier is called for, install wrought iron or tubular steel fences and gates. These are reasonably attractive in appearance, are difficult to vandalize, and require little maintenance. Avoid chain-link fences, despite their relatively low initial cost, because they are perceived as ugly and institutional.
- Avoid fencing the entire site and creating an exclusive or "fortress" image. However, when

Figure 208. A broader entrance and clear view into an attractive parklike setting might encourage nonresidents to enter or cut through the common open space of this scheme.

Example 1

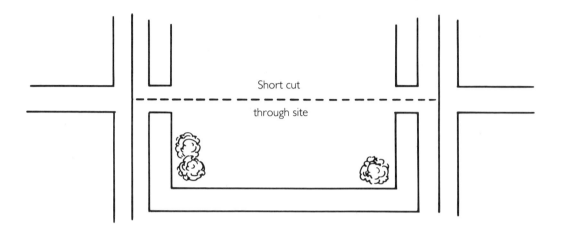

Short cut

through site

Figure 209. Where a former street has been closed to build a new housing scheme, neighborhood residents may still try to cut across the site unless buildings prevent it (example 1). In example 2 no strangers can enter the shared open space because it is almost completely enclosed by buildings.

Example 2

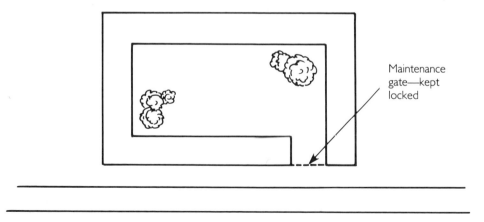

Maintenance gate—kept locked

a fortress is necessary, a fence is generally a better solution than a wall because it facilitates surveillance of adjacent areas, permits air circulation, and does not encourage graffiti.

- Eliminate opportunities for casual cutting through the site by strategically locating fences or low planting within the site and at site entry points. Low fences and walls can define the site perimeter, channel pedestrian movement to predetermined, controllable points, and, in the case of walls, serve as seating, thus contributing to surveillance at entry points. Low fences are suitable where seating needs to be discouraged (for example, where a cluster of teenagers might inhibit adults from using that entry point).
- Use bollards 3 to 5 feet (0.9 to 1.5 m) apart to separate and control pedestrian and vehicular traffic. Bollards may also double as casual seating, thus enhancing surveillance of the entry point. However seating will be used only by younger adults or children, and bollards do not prevent access by bicycles or motorcycles. A bollarded entry into a housing site for the elderly in Richmond, California, caused considerable anxiety to residents because it allowed entry by youthful motorcyclists seeking a shortcut through the site.

  Pressure-treated timber bollards, 8 by 8 inches (203 mm) square, are the best value in terms of comparable cost, useful life, maintenance requirements, and attractiveness. (This depends, of course, on timber availability.)

Although somewhat more expensive initially, bollards of precast concrete are probably the best choice if the budget allows. Pipe bollards are rather utilitarian and unattractive, but very durable and particularly suitable where occasional access by emergency vehicles is called for.

- Ensure that level changes used as symbolic barriers against vehicles do not preclude entry by persons in wheelchairs or by adults wheeling heavy shopping carts or strollers.
- Exercise caution in using a change in paving alone, for example, from public sidewalk to a brick or cobbled entry pathway. Although attractive, it is unlikely to deter intrusion by outsiders, especially at night. Paving changes can constitute serious problems for blind people and people using crutches, sticks, canes, or walkers and should therefore be discouraged except where the contrasted paving forms are of similar texture.

See also: Space hierarchy (4), Community identity (5), Edge treatment (22), Good management (238).

202. Visible lobbies

Design secure, visible lobbies and interior spaces.

Research on crime in multifamily housing shows that interior public spaces of buildings—lobbies, corridors, stairwells, and elevators—are most vulnerable, especially to such crimes of personal confrontation as assault, robbery, and rape. Such areas, although open to the public, are often without surveillance by passersby and police.

Possible design responses (Center . . . , 1973; Department . . . , 1974; Larsson, 1980; Newman, 1971, 1972, 1976)

- Equip shared entrances with locked doors, buzzers, intercoms, or entry phones. Ensure that buttons on buzzers and intercoms can be used by small children and that the operation is simple.
- Check that the unlocking mechanism and effort required to open doors are within the capacities of small children. Otherwise doors will be wedged open.
- Hidden areas and blind corners provide excellent hiding places for potential criminals. Where such features cannot be removed, provide mirrors, windows, and improved lighting.
- Encourage residents to linger in the lobby for social reasons.
- In particularly vulnerable areas consider hiring adult residents as part-time "door monitors."

- Make the area around the main entrance clearly distinguishable from public walkways leading to it so that persons entering will feel distinctly that they are entering an area controlled by residents.
- Use transparent materials between 2 and 7 feet (0.6 and 2.1 m) off the floor in parts of walls and doors at major entry points. If vandalism is a problem, choose unbreakable glass or similar material.
- Provide lobby doors with secure key-operated locks. (The key should not open apartment doors.) Lobby doors should open out; in-swinging doors are easier to kick in.
- Where large numbers enter a building via one entry (for example, a high-rise elevator structure), consider providing an unlocked outer lobby housing the intercom system and an office from which a guard can informally survey the space. Legitimate visitors could pass through a locked door to an inner lobby containing elevators, mail boxes, notice boards, waiting area, and so forth.
- Ensure that lobby/vestibule areas are visible from the exterior by providing large, unbreakable, glazed areas and high interior lighting levels.

See also: Neighborly surveillance (42), Shared entry (44), Corridor access (49).

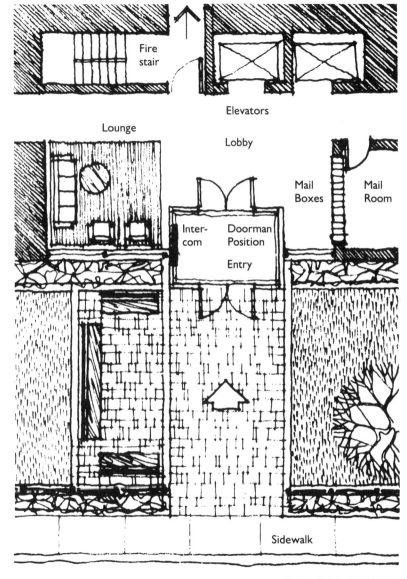

Figure 210. In this design there are places to sit inside and outside the entrance, encouraging casual surveillance. Visitors cannot gain entrance through the second set of double doors until they have been "buzzed" in by a resident. (Source: Newman, 1976)

203. Sturdy doors

Provide high-quality, sturdy construction for all exterior doors.

The major security tests of door material are its ability to withstand efforts to force entry and its ability to retain securely its attached locking devices.

Possible design responses

- Provide doors a minimum of 1¾ inches (44.5 mm) thick. The toughest door material is metal, but solid-core wood doors are relatively secure and preferred for appearance, unless they are too expensive.
- In high-crime areas avoid hollow-core wood doors, thin wood panel (less than ½ inch [12.7 mm]) doors, and glass-paneled doors, even though they may be braced for added strength.
- Avoid fitting entry hall glass panels where breakage could permit easy access to the lock or latch.
- Ensure that entry hall glass panels are too narrow to permit physical access by an intruder.

See also: Visible entry (36), Vulnerable materials (233).

204. Sturdy locks

Provide sturdy locks on all exterior doors.

Locks must withstand or seriously delay not only simple forced entry, but also sophisticated criminal intrusion. Simple latch hooks can be opened in two minutes by unskilled burglars, in fifteen seconds by skilled ones.

Possible design responses (Barnes and Sarro, 1971; Center . . . , 1973; National . . . , 1976; Newman, 1976; United States Department . . . , 1974)

- Provide key-in-door, dead bolt, or dead latch locks at least 1 inch (25.4 mm) long. (Two or more locks are often recommended by security experts, with the secondary one being a vertical bolt or 1½ inch [38 mm] horizontal bolt lock.)
- If the lock extends beyond the door, provide a beveled ring or escutcheon plate covering to prevent forcible removal by a gripping tool.
- In general avoid spring latches. They provide insufficient security.
- On doors with glass panels have key-operated locks on both the exterior and interior so that intruders cannot break the glass, reach in, and undo the lock.
- Design locks and doors to make it simple for a new tenant to change locks.

See also: Secure garages (210), Secure storage (211).

205. Peeping out

Make it possible for residents to see who is at the door before opening it.

Possible design responses

- Provide an entryway visible from the dwelling (for example, from a side window).
- Provide a glassed-in entry porch with *two* locked doors so that the visitor standing at the exterior door can be viewed by the resident standing at the interior door.
- Install a fish-eye lens or peephole on solid exterior doors. It should contain a double glass and a wide-angle lens and be no larger than ¼ inch (6.35 mm).
- Provide a case-hardened steel chain that allows the door to be opened 2 inches (50.8 mm) for talking to strangers. (Some slide chains have a locking mechanism that prevents use of a thumbtack [or piece of tape] and rubber band to pull back the slide mechanism and remove the chain from the track.)

See also: Added privacy (30), Entry path location (38), Front porch (40).

206. Sliding doors

Provide sturdy hardware for sliding glass doors.

Sliding glass doors, which are easily jimmied, bent, and lifted out of their frames, are especially vulnerable on the ground floor.

Possible design responses

- In medium- or high-crime areas avoid sliding patio or balcony doors. Use standard-sized swinging doors with a keyhole only on the inside.
- Provide sliding patio doors with dead bolt, key-operated locks, unbreakable laminated glass, and sturdy frames. For extra security provide an extra safety bar and lock bolted to the floor.
- Have sliding doors slide to the *inside* of the stationary glass panel. (Although doors sliding to the outside may provide a better weather fit, they are a security risk.)

See also: Access to private open space (54), Balcony off living room (65).

207. Mail slot

Avoid illegal entry by means of the mail slot.

In areas where mail is delivered directly through a mail slot in the door, take care to ensure it does not permit illegal entry. A British security study warns: "A juvenile arm can reach through a BS 2911 letter plate to the shoulder, and operate a lock up to about 16 inches (400 mm) away—over 50 percent of people arrested for housing-breaking are juveniles" (Security . . . , 1970, 4).

Possible design response

- Ensure that the front door letter slot is as small as possible and located as far as possible from the lock.

208. Upper windows

Avoid detailing designs that will assist entry into upper-floor windows.

Some architectural solutions can innocently provide the burglar with easy access to upper-floor windows. Once a burglar has gained access to one, he or she has easy access to other apartments on the same floor.

Possible design responses

- Avoid porches or low-level balconies with horizontal side slots that can be used as ladders.
- Avoid continuous private balconies.
- Avoid skylights in high-crime areas. Never place skylights next to trees or other easily accessible places.
- Avoid external pipework that could serve as a ladder.
- Avoid flat-roofed appendages and extensions.

209. Fire escapes

Design fire escapes to minimize illicit access.

Possible design responses

- Use ladders with a weight balance (or similar) mechanism. Ensure that the lowest rung is no nearer than 12 feet (3.6 m) from the ground.
- Ensure that the ground underneath the fire escape is clear of large plantings and is easily visible.
- Ensure that all fire exits can be locked from the outside and are outfitted with panic hardware utilizing a dead bolt lock (preferably vertical) and perhaps an alarm that sounds when the door opens. The effectiveness of such alarms depends on the speed and consistency of response. They may constitute a nuisance because teenagers sometimes set them off to harass local officials (Center . . . , 1973; National . . . , 1976).

Figure 211. A fire escape covered with lumber to prevent illegal access to flat roofs. Such measures should be weighed against the possible barrier they would present to residents in a fire.

210. Secure garages

Provide all garages with security and high visibility.

The car is an expensive family possession; every precaution should be taken to ensure that it can be parked overnight in a place that is secure from theft or vandalism.

Possible design responses

- Where possible, provide each unit with a locked garage visible from the dwelling.
- If density and site requirements demand underground or "decked" parking, provide only a limited number of entry points and a secure lock for each.
- If the parking area is neither fully visible nor capable of having all entries locked, provide individual garages. (These should be constructed of robust metal or concrete, *not* of wood, which can easily be vandalized.)
- If building access is limited, limit entry through the garage as well (Center . . . , 1973; National . . . , 1976; Newman, 1976). A door leading from an underground parking area to a building's interior must be treated with the same security precautions as a main entryway; doors should be self-closing and key or card operated.

See also: Locked garages (150), Grouped carports (153), Secure underground parking (155), Vulnerable materials (233).

Figure 212. Because these open garages could not be seen from the dwellings, they became locales for vandalism and theft, and the residents essentially abandoned them in favor of street parking.

Figure 213. In later phases of the same housing scheme individual locked garages were provided and proved successful. (Geneva Terrace, San Francisco)

211. Secure storage

Provide strong and securable storage rooms for use by personnel.

A housing development uses many pieces of valuable equipment. Storage rooms should be of adequate size, windowless, and preferably in a basement area (National . . . , 1976).

See also: Entry storage (51), Sturdy locks (204).

212. Utility meters

Protect utility facilities and meters in high-crime areas.

Such expensive facilities as hot water heaters, heating furnaces, water pipes, and fire hoses should be protected from vandalism and accidental damage. Utility meters (water, gas, electric) should be enclosed with wire mesh or similar protection, although they still should be convenient and accessible to service people (Perlgut, 1982).

TERRITORIALITY

Site planning should help residents lay claim to the space adjacent to their units and, as a group, assume control and responsibility for semiprivate areas—such as courtyards—shared by a number of households. Successful site design clearly provides a hierarchy of spaces: from public spaces open to everyone (streets), to semiprivate spaces intended for specific geographic or demographic groups (courtyards, play areas, seating for the elderly), to private spaces intended for individual households (dwellings and adjacent private open space). Inadequate site design occurs where only two categories of space are present: public space, which anyone can enter, and private dwelling space. With a hierarchy of spaces several "lines of defense" are created.

In considering an existing site, be alert to both the probable lack of a space hierarchy and the lack of positive feelings of territoriality. The following conditions (Brill . . . , 1979b) indicate such deficiencies:

- Areas adjacent to dwellings have not been demarcated or personalized, and there are few cues indicating that these spaces are used (for example, chairs on porch, plants in pots, toys on path).
- Communal landscaped spaces appear poorly maintained or unused, and there is no demarcation between these and semiprivate areas.

- Buildings and landscaping have been badly vandalized.
- Buildings and site present a negative image to residents or outsiders.

213. Territorial zones

Subdivide residential environments into specific territorial zones.

All spaces within a housing development should be treated as "zones of influence" of specific groups of inhabitants to encourage their proprietary attitudes. Residents are likely to protect semiprivate space that they feel "belongs" to them. Conversely, they may not relate to semipublic or public areas such as open stairwells, hallways, courtyards, parking lots, or adjacent streets. Territorial definition can be largely symbolic, not necessarily preventing access with physical barriers but psychologically discouraging it. It thus has the added advantage of being inexpensive (Becker, 1977; Center . . . , 1973; Newman, 1971, 1972, 1976).

Possible design responses

- Divide large sites into visually identifiable clusters, using fencing, planting, and building placement to reinforce the division.

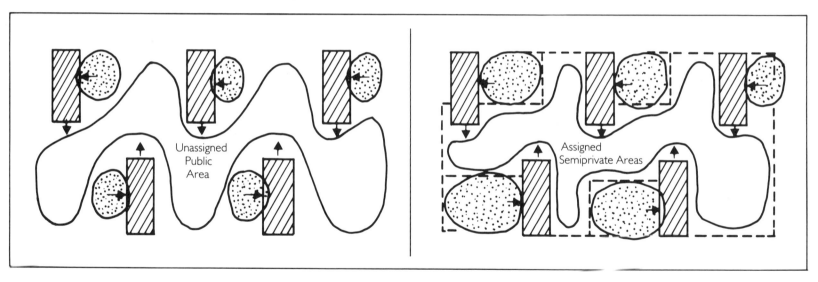

 Building Entry

Secondary Exit

 Semipublic Area Adjacent to Building Entry

Fencing

 Building

Figure 214. The unassigned public area in the left-hand sketch is a prime locale for crime. In the right-hand sketch, clearly defined entrance courts plus fencing around the whole site help discourage criminal intrusion. (Source: Newman, 1976)

- Design the communal space of each cluster so that it is visible to all the dwellings it serves, cannot be used as a shortcut by non-residents, and encourages cluster residents to come out, use the space, and become visually and socially acquainted.
- Develop a management policy that permits and encourages residents to maintain or modify these communal spaces jointly.
- Create semiprivate back and front yards for each ground-level unit, with fencing or planting to delimit these spaces from communal areas. Ensure that management permits and encourages their personalization by residents.
- Use distinctive paving to "assign" site areas, such as entry courts, to particular groups of buildings or dwellings. A paved entry court, for example, will contribute to the extension of the territory of that building into the site and may subtly reinforce residents' territorial claims.

A variety of paving materials and patterns, identifying use areas and entry zones, may contribute to residents' sense of security and add visual interest. The following are reasonably attractive surfaces that require minimal maintenance: concrete paving scored on a 3-foot (0.9 m) grid, exposed aggregate, precast concrete pavers, hexagonal asphalt pavers, brick paving, or brick grids in concrete paving. Surfaces to be avoided are gravel (maintenance and use problems) and asphalt (maintenance problems and aesthetic unattractiveness) (Brill . . . , 1979a).

Take great care when using paving to avoid irregular surfaces, which might make the site inaccessible to people in wheelchairs or those using prosthetic devices. Nonslip surfaces should be provided to ensure ease of access by physically disabled people.

See also: Space hierarchy (4), Community identity (5), Subunit identity (21), Territorial expression (29), Display garden (62), Group territory (72), Interesting landscaped spaces (73), Friendly encounters (131), Landscape installation and modification (179), Personalized landscape (180), Tenant involvement (244), Resident responsibilities (245).

214. Entrance group

Limit the number of households sharing an entrance.

In most multistory buildings interior circulation areas—entries, lobbies, corridors, stairs, and landings—are for the common use of residents. If the number of users of these areas is small, they are more likely to be perceived as semiprivate, and the residents can more easily enforce social norms (Larsson, 1980; Newman, 1971, 1972, 1976). For this reason blocks subdivided by separate sets of stairs serving limited numbers of units are preferable to deck- or corridor-access blocks. In a study of vandalism in fifty-two inner-London estates, Wilson (1978) found that deck-access and elevator-access blocks suffer more damage than stair-access or gallery-access buildings, where fewer people share an entryway. Any building with an open entry, particularly where this is used as a through route to other locations, tends to suffer high rates of vandalism. In a design and management evaluation of eighteen inner-London public housing projects, the authors conclude that deck and continuous gallery access ways can become 'anonymous' and end up belonging to no one in particular (Shankland . . . , 1977a).

Possible design response

- Limit the number of households sharing each building entrance to between three and eight. In circumstances where there is considerable

Figure 215. A small entry court, such as this one, with many windows looking into it, is less likely to be the scene of a crime than a large, anonymous, semipublic space. (Setchell Road, Southwark, London)

demographic and life-style homogeneity, it may be possible for up to a dozen households to share satisfactorily (Newman 1971, 1972, 1976).

See also: Shared entry (44), Dwelling cluster (132).

OPPORTUNITIES FOR SURVEILLANCE

Formal surveillance is undertaken by police, caretakers, and security guards. Equally important is informal surveillance, which involves the casual observation of neighbors, children, and visitors by residents as they go about their daily lives. It can be facilitated by the positioning of windows and gardens, the location and design of pathways and play areas, the quality of lighting and landscaping, and the avoidance both of large, ambiguous spaces and of small, secluded ones. The feeling that others will see if help is necessary reassures residents that they are not alone, and this encourages use of communal areas. This, in turn, improves security because intruders will rarely trespass if they think they are being observed.

Opportunities for formal and informal surveillance may be lacking under the following circumstances (Brill . . . , 1979b):

- The arrangement of buildings and access does not permit residents, police, or security personnel to observe activities on the site.
- Site and building entrances are not located or designed to encourage observation of people entering or leaving.
- Recreational, sitting, and walking spaces are screened from the view of residents inside their units.

- Planting, walls, fences, or buildings block the view along pathways, out of entrances, or into adjacent open spaces.
- The site is not adequately and evenly lit at night.

Figure 216. Gallery-access buildings suffer from the highest rates of vandalism in Britain. But at least some are now on regular police beats.

215. Superblocks

Consider the security risks of traffic-free superblocks.

Large superblocks with interior pedestrian circulation suffer higher crime rates than projects of comparable size and density in which existing city streets continue through the site (Newman, 1972, 1976). In high-crime areas housing sites larger than a U.S. city block (300 by 500 feet [90 by 150 m] in San Francisco, for example) are best subdivided by through streets, and the scale of neighboring city blocks is best maintained (Jacobs, 1961; Newman, 1972, 1976). Through streets mean direct access to buildings by car and bus and more patrolling by police. In Britain some large, vulnerable projects are now patrolled by police on foot, but this is a rarity in the United States.

See also: Density and form (1), Project size (2), Traffic management (68), Sidewalk activities (69), Woonerfs (70).

216. Incorporating the street

Incorporate local streets into the site plans of new developments.

Early planning manuals concerned with inner-city renewal encourage housing developments to turn their backs on city streets, but this strategy produced an unfortunate "fortress" appearance and rendered adjacent streets in medium- and high-crime areas even more vulnerable. If a development's buildings include the city streets in their zone of influence, residents are more likely to concern themselves with these areas and help create safer neighborhoods. (Angel, 1968; Hollingshead and Rogler, 1963; Holme and Massie, 1970; Hough and Mayhew, 1982; Jacobs, 1961). Passing cars, traveling at moderate speed, may provide additional surveillance.

Possible design responses

- Orient buildings to adjacent city streets.
- Design building entries for as few families as possible so that each household will identify more strongly with the street outside its unit.

See also: Shared entry (44), Pedestrian precinct (67), Traffic management (68), Woonerfs (70).

217. Direct access

Provide direct access to buildings from parking lots, public transit, and city streets.

If building entrances are not close to parking lots, public transit stops, and city streets, residents may face long, dangerous nighttime walks home.

Possible design responses

- Plan street-oriented building entrances for nighttime accessibility.
- Design a short, direct walk from parking lot or bus stop to building entry.
- Ensure that pedestrian routes to building entries are well lit and unobscured by planting.

See also: Convenient parking (151), Parking access (154), Footpath Security (190), Footpath lighting (191).

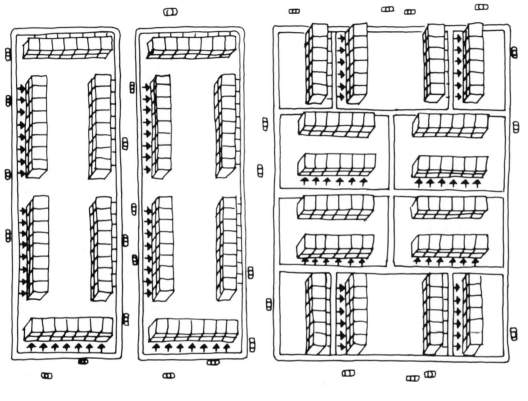

A.

Outward facing project.

Arrows designate entries.

B.

Inward facing project.

Arrows designate entries.

Figure 217. In a high-crime area the scheme on the left is preferable to that on the right because every house has direct access from the street. (Source: Newman, 1976)

218. Resident allocation

Allocation policies can promote or discourage informal surveillance.

In high-crime areas households likely to be home most of the day—for example, elderly people or parents of very small children—should be located close to particularly vulnerable site entry points to facilitate natural surveillance. Elderly people and female heads of households—the two groups most likely to be victims of crime—should be housed in locations where natural and police surveillance are effective. Out-of-the-way units, where neighbor surveillance is unlikely, should not be allocated to households of working adults where dwellings are likely to be empty all day.

Possible design response

- Locate households likely to have an adult at home most of the day close to vulnerable site entry points to facilitate informal surveillance.

See also: Life cycle clusters (7), Managing security (237).

219. Informal surveillance

Place windows and orient entries to maximize natural surveillance of the site.

Even in low- or no-crime areas, designing for surveillance facilitates supervision of children in family housing. In high-crime areas good general visibility and constant use not only deter crime but also help make residents feel secure. The feeling of security is especially important because the judgment that an area is unsafe is self-fulfilling: People will avoid using it and so actually make it less safe (Angel, 1968; Center . . . , 1973; Hollingshead and Rogler, 1963; Holme and Massie, 1970; Hough and Mayhew, 1982). Of course, measures to encourage surveillance must not violate privacy needs.

Surveillance alone, however, has no magic effect. Residents are unlikely to challenge strangers or call the police when they see something suspicious unless they know they can rely on neighbors to back up their territorial claims. Particularly in public housing there is often resistance to challenging strangers or calling the police for fear of retaliation.

Possible design responses

- Ensure that each dwelling entry is visible from at least two other dwellings.
- Place windows of frequently used rooms (kitchen, living room) so that natural sur-

veillance of nearby entries and communal open spaces can take place casually.
- Ensure some degree of homogeneity within the community (especially by age or life-style) so that residents feel a sense of cohesion.

See also: Visible entry (36), Neighborly surveillance (42), Overlooking (58), Balcony off living room (65), Tot lot location (90), Home turf (128), Grouped carports (153).

Figure 218. A delicate balance must be struck between designing for ease of surveillance and designing for privacy. Residents of this London scheme were very concerned about the lack of privacy from passersby, yet wanted to leave their drapes open to let in the sun. (Acorn Place, Camberwell, London)

220. Yard surveillance

The enclosure of private open space should not prevent surveillance.

Although fences can provide privacy, they may also provide cover for a potential criminal. For this reason in the redesign of one crime-ridden California development (Acorn, Oakland), the high patio fences between adjacent units were left intact for privacy, but end fences separating the patios from communal areas were reduced from 6 to 4½ feet (1.8 to 1.4 m) to facilitate surveillance in and out.

Possible design response

- Fence private open space sensitively so that surveillance into and out of the space is enhanced without infringing too greatly on dwelling privacy.

See also: Added privacy (30), Neighborly surveillance (42), Yard linked to common space (55), Privacy screening (57), Privacy planting (176).

221. Evening use

Encourage casual use of the environment during evening hours.

Active use of an environment automatically brings it under surveillance. Because crime rates are much higher during the evening (although burglary rates are higher in the daytime), entry design and orientation should encourage evening activities such as sitting on front porches or taking evening walks. This presupposes an attractive environment and adequate night lighting (Angel, 1968; Holme and Massie, 1970; Hough and Mayhew, 1982; Jacobs, 1961).

Possible design responses

- Focus pedestrian movement after dark along a few well-used entry and exit routes.
- Provide comfortable places to sit and socialize near building entrances.
- Provide separate areas for teenagers so that territorial conflicts do not occur.

See also: Teenage hangouts (124), Footpath security (190), Footpath lighting (191), Outdoor seating (192), Public phones (199), Running the gauntlet (229).

222. Lighting for safety

Well-used public access ways require bright, even, and vandal-proof lighting.

Possible design responses (Center . . . , 1973; National . . . , 1976; Newman, 1976; United States Department . . . , 1974; Ward, 1973)

- Select lights that do not have excessive glare and generate no dark shadows.
- Select vandal-resistant and easy-to-maintain light fittings.
- Light all heavily used spaces with the power of 5 to 10 footcandles (Newman, 1971, 1972). (The useful ground coverage of an elevated light fixture is roughly twice its height. A 150-watt incandescent lamp mounted 8 feet [2.4 m] from the ground can provide adequate light for 16 feet [4.9 m] along a walk. Higher fixtures are safer from vandalism, although, if fixtures are mounted higher than the second floor, people may feel as though they are in a compound.)
- Design lighting for elderly people with special care: About twice as much actual brightness is required to create the same degree of perceived brightness for a sixty-year-old as for a twenty-year-old, and the ratio increases even more for people in their seventies.

See also: Footpath security (190), Footpath lighting (191).

223. Management office

Locate the management office at a central visible point.

A well-located management office can maximize the "policing" and surveillance potential of personnel and make visitors and strangers aware of an "official" presence. But an office designed and located so as to be an overpowering presence defeats its own purpose. (See also Chapter 14—Management, Maintenance, and Refuse Disposal.)

Possible design responses (Berkeley . . . , 1980; National . . . , 1976; United States Department . . . , 1974, 1976)

- Ensure access to the office by both residents and outsiders.
- Take security precautions to protect money, keys, and other valuables stored in the office.

See also: Small meeting room (134), Supervised facilities (140), Maintenance responsibilities (240), On-site office (242).

224. Safe meeting places

Locate social rooms close to other heavily used areas.

Facilities where residents meet casually or formally should be close to other heavily used areas to permit casual surveillance by passersby. Separate areas, however, should be provided for teenagers to minimize conflict with other residents. In one crime-ridden public project in Los Angeles, which has six hundred units on a 43-acre site, the only community facility is a gymnasium next to a parking lot. Because the lot is the site of regular gatherings of violent teenage gangs, residents express fears about attending activities in the gymnasium even in daylight (Perlgut, 1978).

Possible design responses (National Center . . . , 1976; National Housing . . . , 1978; Perlgut, 1978; Teitz, 1975)

- Locate social rooms near building lobbies or near a central trafficked route.
- Avoid locating social space in basement areas.
- Locate teen social space so that noise or hanging out will not annoy or threaten other residents.

See also: Small meeting room (134), Supervised facilities (140).

225. Safe laundry rooms

Minimize opportunities for vandalism of laundry rooms.

Because they are used intermittently and contain expensive equipment, laundry rooms are especially vulnerable to vandalism.

Possible design responses

- Locate laundry rooms near building lobbies, management offices, or central, well-trafficked pedestrian routes, not in out-of-the-way locations such as basements.
- Provide laundry rooms with attractive seating areas, community notice boards, drink machines, and tables for folding laundry to encourage their use and surveillance by residents.
- Keep laundry rooms locked and allow access only to residents.
- Provide individual locked and metered power points for washers and dryers that can be operated only by individual residents' keys. (In this system, working successfully in New South Wales Housing Commission flats in The Rocks, Sydney, Australia, the electricity used is automatically charged to each unit's electricity bill.)
- Install equipment that requires tokens ("tickets").

- Have management or other personnel patrol laundry rooms.

See also: Laundry facilities (137), Management office (223), Maintenance policies (239).

226. Alarm systems

In vulnerable locations or in existing developments where the original layout provides little natural surveillance, electronic alarm systems may be appropriate.

The effectiveness of alarm hardware is directly tied to security "software," to the people responsible for responding to the alarm.

Selection of a proper alarm system should be based on the system characteristics desired: Is deterrence of crime or apprehension of criminals the primary goal? Should the system be visible to deter attempted burglary? Or should it be hidden to increase the likelihood of apprehending a burglar?

AMBIGUITY

A space is ambiguous when it lacks symbolic, functional, or verbal cues as to how it is to be used, whom it is for, who should control its use, and who should maintain it. Ambiguity may have serious consequences in crime-prone neighborhoods.

Brill (1979b) suggests that a dangerous ambiguity may exist under the following conditions:

- The overall site design does not present a "readable" hierarchy of well-defined public, communal (semiprivate), and private spaces. (See guideline 4.)
- The site contains spaces that, because their intended use is unclear, are unused or taken over for antisocial activities. (See guideline 168.)
- The site contains areas whose purpose may be clear (for example, tot lot) but that are unacceptably located and therefore unused. (See guideline 90.)
- The site contains "unclaimed" areas, apparently not within the domain of any dwelling or dwellings. (See guidline 213.)
- The site contains large, unused, hard-surfaced or grassy areas neither subdivided into comfortable spaces nor furnished to suggest specific activities. (See guidelines 74 and 167.)
- The site contains spaces taken over by outsiders for loitering or cutting across and avoided by residents. (See guideline 5.)

Figure 219. When residents themselves have to paint directions on a wall, there is something wrong with the site design, the graphics system, or both.

Figure 220. A poorly sited and unused play area can become a problematic, ambiguous space in a high-crime area.

Figure 221. The ambiguity of this balcony—is it shared or private?—creates easy access for a burglar.

227. User group territories

Ensure that each identified user group has a place on the site for its preferred outdoor activities.

It is not enough to provide open space and assume that residents will use it "appropriately." People require cues as to what a space is for (Becker, 1977). Although children and adolescents require fewer cues than adults (and therefore will make do with whatever is provided), adults may not appreciate what children do (and where they do it). To avoid both the misuse of outdoor spaces and conflicts between adults and youths, make the use of semipublic areas unambiguous.

Possible design response

• Ensure that each age group within the housing development has one or more outdoor spaces that are its indisputable territory and that each of these spaces is located and "furnished" appropriately.

See also: Group territory (72), Tot lot location (90), Walk to play (102), Teenage hangouts (124), Functional spaces (168).

228. Buffer zone

Create a buffer between dwellings and communal open space.

In older housing projects (for example, interwar projects in Britain or U.S. schemes of the 1940s and 1950s) it was common practice *not* to provide yards for ground-level units. Communal areas frequently abutted directly against the outer walls of ground-level dwellings, bringing children at play close to windows and giving burglars ready access to windows and doors. In a study of vandalism on London estates, Wilson (1978) found that such dwellings are particularly susceptible to damage. Another British report on building security (Mawby, 1977) found that they are particularly susceptible to burglaries.

Possible design response

• Where possible, provide clearly delimited yards as buffers; otherwise provide raised planting beds as buffers between private interior and communal outdoor use.

See also: Territorial expression (29), Added privacy (30), Transitional filters (39), Common space boundary (77), Personalized landscape (180), Footpath privacy (188).

Figure 222. Attractive and adequate fencing is provided in this Australian housing project to screen private patios from shared open space.

RESIDENT CONFLICTS

Conflicts among residents can occur when two incompatible activities are located next to each other or when two resident groups are forced to compete for the same space (Brill . . . , 1979b). Conflicts can lead to quarrels, which may give rise to criminal activity or to the resentful withdrawal of one group from the disputed space. In either case the potential for community social cohesion and the likelihood that anticrime measures will be effective are diminished.

229. Running the gauntlet

Ensure that no resident group, while going about its daily business on the site, will have to "run the gauntlet" through an area dominated by others.

A preschool play space at the back of a Berkeley, California, minipark remained unused because parents and small children were fearful of passing by rowdy young men playing on a basketball court that dominated the narrow entry to the park. A similar situation in a Los Angeles public housing development resulted in nonuse of part of the site by elderly people harassed by teenagers (Perlgut, 1978).

Possible design responses

- Locate the dwellings of particularly vulnerable groups (elderly people, families with small children) close to the services and facilities they frequently use (shops, seating areas, play spaces).
- Minimize the likelihood of a potentially intimidating group (that is, young men or teenagers) taking over spaces that others frequently pass by or through: locate a space for teenagers on a cul-de-sac or provide routes allowing others to bypass the space.

See also: Group territory (72), Ball games (123), Teenage hangouts (124), Pedestrians passing by (187).

230. Conflicting uses

Ensure that potentially conflicting activities are not placed next to each other.

In numerous housing developments children's play areas have been closed or relocated because their location close to dwellings caused noise problems (Department . . . , 1981b, c). This guideline is especially important in high-crime neighborhoods, where any social irritant may be "the last straw."

Possible design responses

- Separate potentially noise-producing activities from dwellings.
- Locate them in partly sunken or screened places, as long as the screening does not create a place where crime might occur.
- Relocate a conflicting activity (for example, an "offending" basketball court might be located on a partially used parking lot).
- Screen activities that are potentially dangerous to bystanders (such as baseball) when they cannot be located away from other uses.
- If proximity cannot be avoided, buffer conflicting activities with dense planting or mounding.

See also: Tot lot location (90), Sibling play (104), Ball games (123), Teenage hangouts (124).

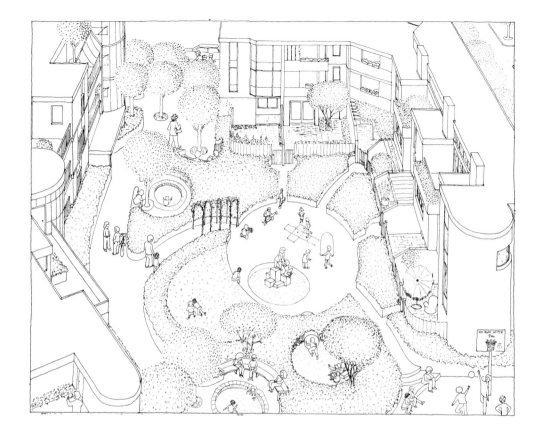

Figure 223. There are several situations in this scene where residents might feel they are violating the territory of a particular user group by passing along certain pathways.

VANDALISM

In many tight, high-density urban schemes (whether high-crime or not) problems may occur because intensive use of the site results in normal wear and tear or in vandalism. Although the latter is more likely to be an antisocial activity rather than a crime, it may cause bad feeling and considerable tension among residents—particularly between adults and youth.

The following guidelines fall into three categories: those cautioning against too high a density of children and youth (that is, limiting the perpetration of vandalism), those urging the provision of adequate facilities for youth (that is, distracting the perpetrators of vandalism), and those dealing with vandal-proof materials (that is, making vandalism more difficult).

Figure 224. Is graffitti vandalism or a legitimate expression of frustrated and powerless youth?

231. Child density

Design with particular care where child densities are high.

The Lambeth Inner Area Study, which examines in detail eighteen problem estates in that inner-London borough, concludes that problems of noise, vandalism, and neighbor disputes are likely to be more marked once a child density figure exceeds thirty per acre (Shankland . . . , 1977b). A parallel study, looking specifically at vandalism in fifty-two inner-London estates, found that all building forms are likely to experience vandalism once the number of children (aged five to sixteen) exceeds five per ten dwellings (Wilson, 1978). A Canadian study of nine government-owned, medium-density family housing developments found an apparent relationship between vandalism and lack of facilities and programs for children (Larsson, 1980). However, in some areas with high child densities there has been little vandalism, probably because of good site planning, design, and management.

Possible design response

- Use ratios of adults to children of less than three to one and densities of more than thirty children to the acre as "warning devices." They signal the need for careful site planning, special provision for child recreation, and more-than-adequate maintenance.

See also: Density and form (1), Life cycle clusters (7), Interesting landscaped spaces (73), Playing everywhere (79).

232. Taking risks

If adequate facilities for adventurous play are not provided, children and teenagers are likely to take risks in and on buildings.

If legitimate outlets for adventurous behavior are not provided, children are likely to climb on garage roofs, use elevators as play objects, and generally use the environment in a "delinquent" manner. However, because one motivating element in vandalism is "forbidden fruit," even with the most challenging play area or imaginative site planning some children will prefer to climb on garage roofs.

Possible design responses

- Ensure that structures likely to attract climbing or exploring children are either made sturdy or designed so that scaling them is impossible.
- Provide alternative, challenging play areas.
- Establish an adventure playground or an area of unmaintained, child-proof, natural vegetation.

See also: Playing everywhere (79), Leftover spaces (83), Unrestricted setting (84), Play on site (101), Children's preferences (107), Tarzan swings (108), Adventure playground (113).

233. Vulnerable materials

Avoid the use of highly vulnerable materials.

Vandalism may be approached as a more general problem of maintenance, of overuse, misuse, or neglect, rather than of outright malicious destruction (Wilson, 1978). Much of what we term *vandalism* is actually hard but legitimate use or modification of facilities to meet user needs. Vandalism and poor maintenance set up their own vicious circle: If parts of a site are easily worn or damaged and not immediately repaired, further wear or malicious vandalism may not be readily visible, and the physical fabric may soon deteriorate (Becker, 1977; Wilson, 1977).

Possible design responses

- Specify materials that withstand normal hard use and can easily be replaced.
- Use standard-sized panels, panes, and fittings to facilitate replacement.
- The original designer should prepare maintenance manuals for management to facilitate speedy repairs.

See also: Play equipment upkeep (147), Children in the landscape (165), Functional spaces (168), "Keep off" planting (174), Good management (238), Maintenance policies (239).

234. Attractive materials

Although robust materials are a wise precaution, do not use them at the expense of appearance.

The "maintenance" school of management specifies vandal-proof materials and fixtures and "keep-off" landscaping. This can result in a drop in amenity standards and an overall image that is bleak, institutional, and cold. Ironically, this may offer a challenge to vandals. The "appearance" school of management steers a middle course between the unsightliness of wilful damage and the bleakness of "hard architecture" (Sommer, 1974) and vandal-proof materials. We recommend the latter approach.

Possible design responses

- Avoid obvious "problem" materials such as the following, listed in "Wilful Damage on Housing Estates" (1971):
  —Soft-textured wall finishes that can be easily scratched or damaged (especially in entry or access ways)
  —Light-colored wall finishes next to planting beds where rainfall or irrigation is likely to cause unsightly staining
  —Glass in vulnerable positions, particularly along much-used public access routes
  —Tiles or glass below the height of ground-level windowsills, especially where adjacent ground is used for play

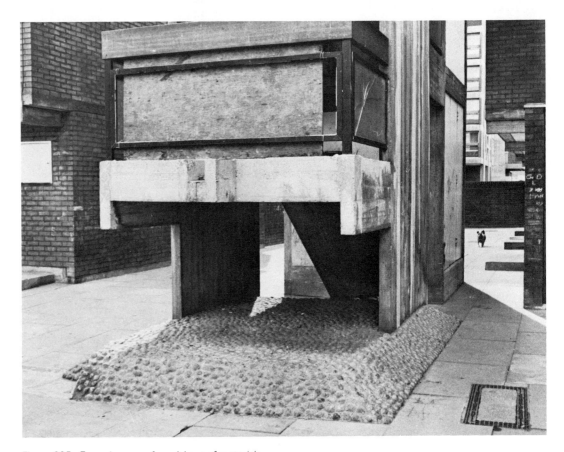

Figure 225. Excessive use of vandal-proof materials can create a depressing, institutional environment.

Figure 226. This path was made by a newspaper boy who continued to cut across the planted area despite management attempts to dissuade him by planting a tree. Is this vandalism or normal wear and tear of an environment inadequately provided with footpaths?

—"Up-and-over" garage doors of inadequate strength
—Plastic-covered light fittings that can be burned
—External copper and lead piping, which are vulnerable to theft
—Painted metal or wood posts or fences in playgrounds or public spaces
—Flimsy paneling or lightly constructed wood fencing in public areas
—Loose pebbles or rocks in landscaping

See also: Locally acceptable materials (17), Attractive play materials (111).

235. Prompt repairs

Maintenance staffing and budgeting must allow for the prompt repair of damage.

Whether deliberate or not, damage left unrepaired is a cue to further misuse of the environment. This is particularly the case in low-income developments at higher densities (Dillingham, 1971). A study by the British Building Research Station (Wilful . . . , 1971, 3) states:

Buildings and site works in a dilapidated state breed vandalism. . . . Persistence in the repair of damage and removal of defacement is essential if headway is to be made against the problem. Deterioration in appearance can arise from causes other than vandalism, such as accidental damage, misuse or ordinary wear and tear, or weathering, decay, corrosion and other forms of failure; if these are allowed to develop, conditions favoring vandalism can become established in an estate previously free from it or re-established in one from which it has been eliminated.

A Canadian study found that a "quick fix" policy reduces vandalism in family housing, especially if it is accompanied by a strengthening of the authority of on-site management to insist on responsible behavior by adults and children (Larsson, 1980).

Possible design response

- Allocate funds to permit speedy repair of damaged or worn parts of the housing environment.

See also: Open space maintenance (86), Landscape maintenance (181), Maintenance responsibilities (240), Resident caretaker (243), Play equipment upkeep (247).

Figure 227. A child leaving this house and entering the play area is likely to trample shrubs planted in the wrong place. Will the behavior be labeled "vandalism"?

236. Mailboxes

Locate mailboxes so as to minimize the possibility of vandalism and theft.

Where mail is delivered directly through a mail slot in the door, care needs to be taken to ensure that it does not permit illegal entry. (In Australia and the United States mail is usually delivered only to the property line.)

In high-crime areas letter boxes are frequently subject to vandalism. They are also pried open, especially on days when welfare or pension checks are known to be delivered. Therefore, the design of individual and grouped letter boxes requires careful attention.

Possible design responses

- If mail slots are provided, ensure that the front door letter slot is as small as possible and located away from the lock (at least 400 mm).
- Locate individual mail slots in property fences, if delivery to the door is not possible.
- Ensure that individual or grouped letter boxes are visible from dwellings.
- Specify letter boxes that are deep enough so they cannot be pried open.
- Specify letter boxes of sturdy, fireproof construction and fit them with a strong key-operated lock.
- Provide contrasting street numbers on letter boxes and dwelling entries.

MANAGEMENT

The emphasis in this chapter has been on environmental manipulation, that is, "defensible space." A complementary approach, termed "manageable space" by one writer (Perlgut, 1982), recognizes that changes in the physical environment alone are not enough: Management must facilitate the education of residents in precautionary anticrime measures and in organization for their own security.

The list of techniques in the following guideline touches on the major points of manageable space. For further details see the following works in the bibliography: Brill, 1979a, b; Gardiner, 1978; Perlgut, 1981a, 1982b; Rouse and Rubenstein, 1978; U.S. Department of Housing and Urban Development and U.S. Department of Labor, 1979.

237. Managing security

Employ effective management techniques to minimize crime. (Becker, 1977; Cooper, 1972b; Hough and Mayhew, 1982; National Center . . . , 1976; National Housing . . . , 1977, 1978; Newman, 1976; Perlgut, 1978, 1981b, 1982b; Teitz, 1975; United States Department . . . , 1979).

Management can take the following steps:

- Encourage resident organizations to be concerned with security issues.
- Utilize existing local crime prevention programs.
- Institute resident security education programs if they are not otherwise available.
- Develop a system of orientation (including handbooks and introduction to neighbors) for new residents.
- Encourage resident neighborliness and dwelling personalization.
- Make judicious use of resident patrols.
- Develop special "escort" programs as needed.
- Take great care in allocating residents to dwelling units, using a system that follows recommended methods.
- Enforce high standards of resident screening and utilize eviction only when really necessary.
- Generally coordinate all security efforts with residents.

- Contact police directly and negotiate to alter or increase patrol and other services.
- Use police and other outside security experts to inspect the development for unsafe areas.
- Utilize any available outside sources to supply funds for security personnel and other strategies.
- Develop a comprehensive crime reporting system; encourage reporting of all crimes; and keep accurate statistics.
- Provide informal surveillance, and maintain high visibility of management and maintenance workers around the housing development.
- Actively coordinate security planning with neighboring developments, city agencies, and other relevant parties.
- Maintain buildings and grounds at a high level of repair.

See also: Open space maintenance (86), Landscape maintenance (181), Resident's manual (241), Tenant involvement (244), Resident responsibilities (245).

14

Management, Maintenance, and Refuse Disposal

MANAGEMENT AND MAINTENANCE

Good management is essential to the success of any multifamily housing development. In subsidized rental housing, for example, different rates of crime, vandalism, rent arrears, and vacancies are often more attributable to management policies than to the composition of the residential population, the design of the dwellings, or the geographical location of the developments (Perlgut, 1982). Large, impersonal, centralized bureaucracies have, on balance, poor success rates. Local, decentralized, responsive, and flexible management styles seem to work better.

Good management thus leads to happier tenant-landlord or tenant-landlady relationships. In a New York State study the four major factors contributing to residents' evaluations of *appearance* were found to be maintenance, landscaping, outside materials, and building shape and layout (Becker, 1974). Maintenance is an important management responsibility: "For many residents appearance is almost synonymous with good upkeep. Well-maintained grounds, no litter, and no junk lying around were a prerequisite to satisfaction with any more specific design feature" (Becker, 1974, 65).

A major study of eighteen public housing estates in the inner-London borough of Lambeth concludes:

> A "good" estate, that is, one where people feel happy and settled, is not just one in which a few particularly important features are well handled, but one in which the balance between a multiplicity of factors comes out on the credit side. Thus on an average estate, excellent management may be counter-balanced by poor design features. On the other hand, a bad estate may contain several excellent design features which are overwhelmed by poor management or by the way in which the residents use the place. (Shankland, 1977a, 45)

Significantly, the quality of the environment on the estates surveyed (ranging from large to small, prewar to contemporary) depends more on the way it is maintained and cared for than on the design standards.

238. Good management

Design can facilitate or inhibit good management.

A key element in the design of multifamily housing (for whatever income group) is its capacity to be easily managed and maintained. Because several studies show maintenance levels to be a crucial factor in resident satisfaction, carefully scrutinize the initial design for its maintenance potential.

Possible design responses

- Use high-quality, acceptable building materials.
- Avoid vulnerable materials (glass) or surfaces (white stucco) in semipublic entrances or access ways.
- Provide unambiguous distinctions between private, communal, and public spaces.
- Avoid pedestrian access ways that cut through sites.
- Provide adequate play space for children.
- Clients should propose a contract with designers that extends several years into the occupancy of a scheme so that design problems can be rectified as they appear.

See also: Space hierarchy (4), Locally acceptable materials (17), Established play areas (97), Teen entertainment (126), Site entry barriers (201), Vulnerable materials (233).

239. Maintenance policies

Physical design should take account of projected management, maintenance, and repair policies.

Before a design is finalized, the design team, client, management, and, if possible, prospective residents should discuss proposed maintenance and repair policies so that projected maintenance costs are kept within the bounds of proposed budgets. For example, if the budget for gardeners is limited, landscaping must be robust, use native species, and have low maintenance needs or the whole site will soon have an unkempt appearance. If the equipment replacement budget is low, care should be taken to install hard-wearing play equipment, street furniture, and so forth.

The documentation of difficulties in problem housing developments shows over and over that many would have been avoided if management policy on dwelling allocation, maintenance, and replacements had been integrated into the design process from the start. Prior management experience on how certain kinds of hardware are used or how maintenance costs compare between different access arrangements should be an essential and high-priority feature of programming and design discussions. All too often design discussions on new or rehabilitated housing include higher echelons of the client bureaucracy but exclude members of the maintenance staff who might best judge the long-term effectiveness of key design decisions. The conclusion

of a report on a disastrous London housing project laments:

> The hasty design and construction of Lakeside [pseudonym] has been repented at leisure by the local authority departments concerned, and regretted even more by tenants. The lack of any effective housing management participation in the design, one of the major reasons for the problem, has now been remedied for future schemes, but this has come too late for the estate. The sheer scale and the design of the estate are fundamental problems which cannot be modified. The physical improvements which have already been made . . . may marginally improve the quality of life . . . but eventually . . . the possibility of demolition is one that will have to be considered. (Department . . . Environment, 1978, 56–57)

Another, more hopeful, section of this report on difficult-to-let estates discusses the complete reorganization of the Housing Department of Newcastle (which manages 45 percent of the housing stock of that city). This has resulted in some significant management improvements, including:

1. Reclaiming certain responsibilities from a powerful planning department
2. A system of five-yearly planned maintenance that increases efficiency and opens opportunities for "preventative" maintenance
3. Decentralization of housing management to area offices where three estate officers are

responsible for all management functions of seven hundred dwellings (One area office had more inquiries in a day than the same office previously had in a week when located in a more remote civic center.)

In other examples cited in this study the marked improvement of problem housing developments was always brought about by a *combination* of environmental, management, maintenance, and tenant allocation procedures. The following management/maintenance improvements proved most effective:

1. Increasing the number of maintenance staff and particularly the proportion who are *resident*, each with a specific portion of a project to take care of (This proved particularly popular with staff and residents alike.)
2. Assigning management staff to a particular group (about seven hundred seemed to be the norm) instead of sharing responsibilities with others
3. Decentralizing office locations for area and project officers to locate them in or near the development they served, thereby ensuring their availability to tenants who called in to talk about maintenance or social problems
4. Having the architects prepare a manual detailing the make and size of each item of hardware to facilitate reordering of replacement parts and a planned system of preventative maintenance

Most of these improvements revolve around increasing the level of *responsibility*—of caretakers toward a piece of the environment, of

estate officers to a particular group of families, of maintenance staff toward long-term upkeep. This parallels a comparable concern for upgrading tenants' responsibilities toward each other and the physical environment by means of "defensible space" improvements. These heartening changes in policy recognize the root cause of many housing problems: alienation—of people from each other, of people from their jobs, of people from significant areas of the physical environment.

Possible design responses

- Locate management offices in or near the housing developments they serve.
- Install hard-wearing equipment if the replacement budget is low.
- Specify robust, mature plant materials if the landscape maintenance budget is low or problematic.
- Involve maintenance staff in the design process to advise on the long-term effectiveness of alternate proposals.
- Specify dwelling units for maintenance staff or management assistants.
- Have architects prepare a manual of hardware for maintenance staff to facilitate reordering.

See also: Open space maintenance (86), Tree maintenance (172), Landscape maintenance (181), Management office (223), Vulnerable materials (233), Resident's manual (241), Play equipment upkeep (247).

240. Maintenance responsibilities

Management and resident responsibilities on site should be clearly spelled out.

Because the level of site maintenance is highly correlated with resident satisfaction, it is particularly important that residents have a clear and unambiguous demonstration of management's concern for this issue. Maintenance problems have often been exacerbated by oversights in original designs: no litter containers near play areas, inadequate edging around planting beds or sandboxes, inadequate provisions for garbage disposal.

If maintenance responsibilities are not made clear, bad feelings may develop between management and residents. Generally, the most successful arrangement is one where management is responsible for *all* shared spaces, inside and out (for example, keeping the site free of litter, dog excrement, standing water, and snow; repairing evidence of vandalism; replacing worn-out equipment; and keeping community facilities and shared entryways clean, safe, and in good repair). Resident responsibilities can embrace their own dwelling, private open space, and any parking space within the confines of the dwelling. In general, delegation of shared stairway or hallway cleaning to residents is not successful and can create bad feelings among neighbors. However, a resident- or management-organized special task, such as the annual painting of a shared stairway or periodic project "clean-up" days, can contribute to a sense of community and collective responsibility.

See also: Open space maintenance (86), Planting edges (178), Landscape maintenance (181), Litter receptacles (200), Prompt repairs (235).

241. Resident's manual

Designers and management should prepare a resident's manual.

A booklet describing how the designers and management expect and hope the development will be used should be prepared and distributed to all residents. It should be written in nontechnical and nonbureaucratic language and should be translated into the languages of the major resident groups. It should also be attractive and well illustrated, or it will tend not to be used. And it should be more than a book of "house rules." It might include the potential advantages and disadvantages of certain dwelling locations (that is, very neighborly to very private); the possible uses of public outdoor spaces; suggestions on interior maintenance, repainting, tree and shrub selection, simple home repairs (for example, blown fuses, blocked sinks), and possible furniture arrangements; phone numbers to call for repairs or emergencies; the location of nearest schools, hospitals, public agencies, and so forth. One successful manual especially pleased residents of a housing project for the elderly with a section that named and described the various species of trees and plants used in the communal areas. Such a manual is especially important when development design or layout is unconventional in any way (Cook, 1972).

Many studies of communities with shared outdoor space report confusion over whether the space is purely aesthetic or intended also for play, who is responsible for maintenance, who has the right to use it, and so on (Becker, 1974; Byrom, 1972; Cooper, 1975; Cooper Marcus, 1974; Department . . . , 1973a; Department . . . , 1981a). The policy concerning use of shared open space must be clear to both management and residents and should be made explicit in the design and/or resident's manual. Although children will use almost any space with a minimum of cues, adults need more specific indicators of permitted or desirable activities (Madge, 1964).

The benefits of a good manual are many. It may reduce the number of unnecessary maintenance requests for minor repairs and thereby reduce management costs. It can provide a set of rules that residents can use as the basis of their own negotiations to resolve conflicts; if the basis for regulations is understood, residents are more likely to accept them, or to propose their own reasonable alternatives.

See also: Children's rights (85), Landscape maintenance (181), Maintenance responsibilities (240).

242. On-site office

Where possible, provide a management office on site.

A manager who is readily available for payment of rents and receipt of complaints and requests for repairs will make residents' day-to-day lives much easier. This is especially true of lower-income developments, where residents may not have bank accounts (for ease of rent payment by mail) or telephones (for ease of reporting needed repairs). "Absentee" relationships should be avoided.

Although selection of managers and their methods of management may be beyond the architect's influence, he or she should be aware that the success of the development will rest very strongly on management and on resident relations with the manager.

Possible design response

- Locate an on-site management office near public telephones and mailbox.

See also: Management office (223).

243. Resident caretaker

Resident or full-time caretakers are essential to successful management.

A study of inner-London housing projects, ranging from very successful to problem ridden, concludes that a resident caretaker (termed in some U.S. housing authorities a *resident assistant*) is a key element in housing management. "The best caretakers manage to fill other roles as well as their routine responsibilities. Some of them may act as social workers, keeping an eye on elderly and infirm tenants and sorting out minor disputes. They are vital mediators between tenants and the providers of services such as refuse disposal, landscaping, and building maintenance" (Shankland . . . , 1977a, 45). Those housing schemes with resident caretakers were better maintained and less vandalized than those without resident caretakers.

In estates administered by the Greater London Council the resident staff system was changed in 1971 to using a mobile team that made routine maintenance visits or could be called in an emergency via special "assista-phones" located at key spots on the estates. This change was later recognized as a mistake: Levels of maintenance and resident satisfaction are lower than on estates with resident caretakers. The previously cited inner-London study concludes that new measures are necessary: In order to facilitate the difficult task of recruiting resident staff, they will need to be accorded a status that befits their tasks, have adequate

backup services (cleaning, gardening, and so forth), and be offered the attraction of better housing.

Where resident caretaking is impossible, there should at least be a full-time team of maintenance workers with spatial responsibilities clearly laid out and with adequate office and equipment storage space. A comparison of two medium-density San Francisco projects (with comparable middle-income families), one with a mix of resident and nonresident full-time caretakers and gardeners and one maintained by a "flying squad" service that visited in a van once a week, reveals a distinct difference in levels of maintenance and care. In the former project, standards were extremely high, with beautifully maintained landscaping and a complete absence of litter, vandalism, or graffiti (despite a location adjacent to a high-crime, low-income neighborhood). The project with the mobile service was plagued by problems of vandalism, litter, and poor maintenance, despite an apparently more salubrious, semisuburban situation. Maintenance staff in the first project were always on site, enabling people to get to know them. They took pride in their work and were not hesitant to chide local children who might be about to damage the landscaping. A mobile team obviously cannot have the same pride in its work or perform the often crucial task of "social control" (Cooper Marcus' observations, living at the first scheme—St. Francis Square—and consulting at the second—Geneva Terrace).

Possible design response

- Provide an office and housing for a resident caretaker that is centrally located yet affords some privacy.

See also: Children in the landscape (165), Landscape maintenance (181), Prompt repairs (235).

244. Tenant involvement

Consider increasing the amount of tenant participation in management.

Experiments ranging from more representation of tenants on housing management committees to the complete transfer of ownership and control to tenants' cooperatives are now ongoing in the United States and Britain. Research on various methods of increased participation is as yet inconclusive, but generally, in Britain and the United States, the strength of a tenants' association or co-op depends largely on the hard work and initiative of a relatively few residents. When these individuals move away or the burden becomes too heavy, the association may collapse. Despite the egalitarian ideal of more participation, the day-to-day lives of most low-income tenants (and especially those with particular burdens, such as single parents with full-time jobs) do not afford much energy for evening meetings or door-to-door canvassing. Thus when far-seeing housing authorities in London—such as Lambeth and Camden—formally requested tenants' ideas about ways they could be involved in management, there was little response (Shankland . . . , 1977a). Some tenants suspect "tenant participation" as a means of off-loading work onto them by management. An evaluation of design and management on eighteen inner-London estates concludes: "What most tenants desire is not a greater stake in management, but a more efficient and humane version of the present system" (Shankland . . . , 1977a).

Reporting a large number of studies, a British review of the literature on problem housing estates concludes, "freedom of choice, identified in the literature as an extremely important element of individual satisfaction, is not available to most council tenants, who see themselves as 'pawns in the housing game'" (Attenburrow, 1978, 4). The findings reveal many housing departments to be "authoritarian," "over-restrictive," "paternalistic," "bureaucratic." Many problem estates appear to have been created by "ghetto" housing policies, where families with similar "deviant value sets" have been concentrated on older, less-attractive estates "where their morale is sapped further by physical neglect and the deteriorating structural and visual environment" (Attenburrow, 1978, 4). Not surprisingly, some residents are reported as responding with "creeping demoralisation," "despondency and apathy," and the development of "anti-authoritarian attitudes."

The social mixing or balancing of populations has, in a few cases, had beneficial results, but only where the estate had certain positive attributes to start with (reasonably small size, good location, domestic-scale buildings) (Cooper, 1970b; Sarkissian, 1976). The U.K. Department of the Environment has urged local authorities dealing with "problem" estates always to combine resident involvement (on more than a token level) with management and physical improvements. In most U.S. rehabilitation schemes resident involvement in major redesign decisions has been found to be not only politically advisable, but of enormous benefit in the long-term success of modernized projects. This involvement is generally more successful when there is some degree of tenant homogeneity.

See also: Pleasing milieu (10), Children as planners (99).

245. Resident responsibilities

The greater the level of responsibility accorded to each resident, the easier will be the task of management.

Although there is little conclusive proof, plenty of circumstantial evidence suggests that the more individuals (in a housing, working, or educational setting) are permitted some control over the maintenance and personalization of their territory, the more satisfied they will be, and the fewer the problems for management and maintenance staff. Studies of students allowed to paint and alter their dormitory rooms at the University of California at Davis indicate a parallel rise in satisfaction levels and a lowering of vandalism and maintenance costs. Studies of open-plan office environments indicate greater satisfaction when employees are allowed to personalize their environments. When asked if they would rather have the housing authority maintain their front yards or do it themselves, the majority of residents in a U.S. housing project voted to do it themselves because it allowed a greater sense of pride and territory (Cooper, 1975). The San Francisco Housing Authority has recently changed its policy on gas stoves and refrigerators for its tenants. These were formerly provided and maintained by the authority; now they are purchased and maintained by the tenants, resulting in higher levels of maintenance and resident satisfaction. Similar changes in policies regarding tenant choices have been established in other English-speaking countries,

notably in Australia, where public housing management is undergoing critical reviews in all states.

With the freedom to make reasonable changes and improvements, housing residents (whether tenants or owners) are likely to invest energy and money in personalizing and modifying their dwellings and may be less likely to move than if they did not have this opportunity. Socially, this activity may encourage interaction among neighbors (borrowing tools, asking advice, trading skills); aesthetically, it will add diversity to the environment. For many people each improvement they make to their home environment enriches their commitment to it. In a community where many have been able to act out this commitment, there will probably be a stronger sense of community surveillance and looking out for each other's welfare (see Chapters 5 and 13).

See also: Territorial expression (29), Articulated facade (31), Personal additions (32), Neighborly surveillance (42), Display garden (62), Personalized landscape (180), Resident's manual (241).

246. Domestic Animals

> Housing developments should be designed to allow residents to keep domestic animals, within certain limits.

Provision should be made, if at all possible, for residents to keep pets. Taking care of a pet can be an important learning experience and can fulfill significant nurturing needs in childhood. Pets can provide companionship for those living alone and sometimes form a useful bridging device in opening conversations with fellow residents. Recent research indicates a connection between human-animal interaction and reduced stress levels evidenced in lowered blood pressure. Dogs can be an important source of security, especially for the elderly and disabled and those who live alone and when walking on local streets after dark is potentially hazardous.

Although the keeping of cats or rabbits or caged birds in housing schemes seems to provoke few problems, a number of studies report conflicts between dog owners and those without pets, over fouling the green areas and small children getting harassed (Cooper, 1975). A study of inner-London housing projects reports that open spaces were overrun by dogs, grassed areas and access ways were fouled, and children and old people were frightened. In that study residents spoke nostalgically of the days when there was stronger management control and dogs were not allowed (Shankland . . . , 1977a). In a San Francisco high-rise project the major problems were the barking of dogs tethered on balconies and the fouling of flat roofs used as exercise areas.

In many U.S. and British projects there has clearly been a rise in dog ownership (particularly of large, "fierce" breeds) as local crime rates have increased. Many housing authorities have had to relinquish their "no dogs" rules in the face of tenant pressures. The problems remain, however.

In a Berkeley, California, park a large dog running field (fenced from other park users) is highly successful. Most housing developments, however, would not have sufficient open space to devote to this.

In Utrecht, Holland, an alternative to pets is a small zoo of domestic animals near a high-density housing area where children can observe and pet the animals without maintaining them. In Britain and Denmark adventure playgrounds near housing projects encourage children to keep and care for small pets, such as rabbits and goats. In Germany "youth farms" outside some cities permit children to visit and help maintain working farms. In Britain the development of "city farms" on vacant sites in inner-urban areas has permitted children to assist in the care of rabbits, goats, and horses and to learn to ride.

These are all very laudable developments, but they should be viewed as additions rather than alternatives to the very basic right of keeping a pet in one's own home.

Possible design responses

- Designate one part of the development as pet-free so that those who strongly object to neighbors with pets can choose this option.
- Restrict the size of dogs that can be owned.
- Strictly enforce leash laws.
- Enforce heavy penalties on residents whose animals make a development dirty or dangerous.
- Require a damage deposit.

See also: Resident's manual (241).

247. Play equipment upkeep

Play equipment should be inspected and repaired regularly.

Because play equipment comes in for a great deal of hard wear (and sometimes abuse), it should be regularly inspected and damaged items should be replaced. All too frequently in public housing projects the swings are chained up by management (preventing use) or damaged parts are removed and never replaced. This is *not* a good solution in human relations or long-term maintenance terms. Children read the message—correctly—that they do not matter and are likely to abuse other elements of the environment in retaliation. Maintenance budgeting must include a sufficient amount for play equipment renewal.

See also: Safe play (105), Prompt repairs (235), Maintenance responsibilities (240).

REFUSE DISPOSAL

A few studies cite inadequate refuse disposal as a focal point of resident-management disputes. Although designers are unlikely to be able to influence the quality and frequency of collection service, they should take such service into account in their designs and pay special attention to the design and location decisions affecting refuse disposal that *are* within their bailiwick.

In a major American study of thirty-seven HUD-assisted projects, most developments observed had disposal areas that were poorly designed, located, and maintained (Francescato et al., 1979). Two basic recommendations are: provide more than adequate space to handle refuse disposal needs; ensure that collections are frequent enough.

Figure 228. One of the differences between a high- and low-income housing development can be seen in the way garbage disposal is handled. In this expensive development near San Francisco individual garbage cans are hidden in locked storage spaces, close to entries.

248. Garbage disposal

If possible, provide private garbage areas close to kitchen entrances.

Most families prefer to have their own garbage cans. For each dwelling the number of cans or plastic bags should be tailored to the collection service. Variations in family size should also be allowed for; larger families will produce more garbage and need more room for its disposal. In several studies the larger the family, the more frequent are complaints about garbage disposal. Cans should be easily accessible for pickup, yet screened from view of the dwelling interior and garden.

See also: Back and front entries (41), "Front" and "back" customs (56).

249. Bulky refuse

Provide for the disposal of bulky items that cannot be handled in the normal way.

Even the best thought-out garbage schemes break down when no provision has been made for the occasional disposal of large domestic items, such as storage boxes, worn-out furniture, and broken-down appliances. If there is no official place to leave these, they will inevitably be "dumped" somewhere in the development or on adjacent land, creating a rundown impression that may lead to further desecration in the form of littering or vandalism. Provide one or a number of special fenced enclosures and indicate clearly (via notices and the resident's handbook) what they are for and what arrangements management has made for regular pickup by the garbage department.

Possible design response

- Provide a special fenced enclosure for bulky items that are to be collected periodically, and make clear to residents how it is to be used.

See also: Resident's manual (241).

250. Garbage chutes

Where garbage chutes are provided, particular care should be taken in their design and location.

Many studies report complaints regarding refuse disposal via chutes. If refuse chutes are provided, precautions are necessary.

Possible design responses

- Provide hoppers and chutes large enough so as not to become blocked with normal-sized refuse.
- Ensure that hoppers are designed so that children can use them because they are often sent out with the garbage.
- Make other provisions for the disposal of bulky items of refuse.
- Ensure that hopper surrounds are easily maintained and cleaned.
- Ensure that hoppers are undercover but also easily accessible to the families they serve.
- Locate chutes so that they do not pass by bedrooms of dwellings, thus causing disturbance when used late at night.

See also: Shared entry (44), Maintenance policies (239).

251. Dumpster location

Where garbage is handled by communal dumpsters, each disposal point should serve a specific number of units and be clearly accessible to them.

A successful method frequently employed in low-rise, multifamily U.S. housing is the communal dumpster. Several households dispose of their refuse in a large steel container instead of in individual garbage cans. Pickup costs are less than for individual cans. Dumpsters should be located on convenient pedestrian circulation routes so that refuse can easily be disposed of while on the way to the car, school, or shops. Refuse areas more than 100 feet (30 m) from a building entrance will generally be considered inconvenient; they should be much closer. If dumpsters are located too far from units, children who have been allocated the chore of taking out the garbage may end up leaving a trail of rubbish behind them.

If the distribution of dwellings and of garbage disposal facilities has not been clearly thought through, a slightly less convenient point may be underutilized and a more convenient point over-utilized, causing overflow and hygiene problems. If the choice has to be made between locating a facility for convenience of collection and locating it for convenience of disposal, the latter should take precedence, although it should never be so close to dwellings as to create problems with odors or banging dumpster lids. A blank end wall of a building, with no door or windows

immediately adjacent, is a possible location. If various locations are being considered, the choice should reflect the needs of large households, which produce more refuse.

Possible design responses

- Locate dumpsters adjacent to well-used pedestrian circulation routes.
- Locate dumpsters no more than 100 feet (30 m) from building entrances.
- Locate dumpsters for convenience of disposal of garbage.
- Locate dumpsters near blank, windowless end walls.
- Locate dumpsters to meet needs of the largest households.

See also: Pleasing milieu (10).

Figure 229. A communal dumpster must be located close to the households that use it and be easy to open, convenient to empty, and screened from view. This example fits all those criteria.

252. Dumpster collection

Locate dumpsters with consideration for collection (and lack of obstruction of other functions).

Vehicles that collect refuse from shared containers are both large and heavy. Therefore a parking area or roadway should be within reasonable distance of them. Dumpsters on wheels are designed to be rolled, which means that the collection point does not have to be immediately adjacent to collection vehicle parking. If it is more convenient for residents, dumpsters should be located "inside" the site, with adequate wide and straight pathways between the dumpster location and the collection vehicle.

One study reports inadequate consideration of the weight of such vehicles, with the result that summer-heated asphalt became depressed where the vehicle parked, causing a hazardous condition for play and car parking (MacLeod, 1977). The dumpster area—if in a parking lot—should not cause visibility problems for approaching cars; in cold regions it should not cause a problem for snow clearance vehicles. Whatever the location, a water source nearby will allow the area to be easily hosed down.

See also: Vehicular segregation (148).

253. Dumpster screening

Screen garbage dumpsters from view.

Because of the size of dumpsters and their potential for spills, it is even more important to screen dumpsters than individual bins. Yet all too often in low-income projects dumpsters are just distributed around the parking lots or, worse still, lined up in full view of dwellings. This is just another unsubtle message that low-income residents do not matter; it would be unthinkable to handle refuse this way in higher-income developments. Therefore care should be taken in screening dumpsters from view, including views from upper floors. Materials should preferably

Figure 230. A tastefully screened garbage area. Ironically, this may also become a favorite place to play because it is of child-sized dimensions.

be unpainted wood or concrete block to avoid unsightly chipping of painted or stuccoed surfaces. Design of the dumpster area should include a gate wide enough to allow disposal personnel to pull the dumpster out conveniently. This may seem obvious; yet we have observed many cases where moving dumpsters in and out is so difficult that garbage personnel end up leaving them permanently *outside* the screened areas.

Because children are naturally attracted to all kinds of on-site "furniture," whether intended for play or not, design dumpster screens so that these can be used for casual play without too many hazards. In windy locations the screening design should ensure that there will not be a problem with garbage being blown around from unlidded or unclosed dumpsters.

In developments where pets are permitted and/or in regions where scavenging animals such as raccoons are present, a roofed screening structure should be designed to keep out these marauders.

Possible design responses

- Use unpainted wood, brick, or concrete block fencing to screen dumpsters.
- Provide a gate wide enough to allow the dumpster to be moved.
- Ensure that screens are sturdy enough to withstand casual play.
- Provide a roof on the dumpster enclosure.
- Create an enclosure that is not accessible by dogs or other animals that are attracted to garbage.

254. Dumpster selection

Select refuse dumpsters for ease of use.

Some dumpsters are remarkably inefficient. Some are so high that a small person or child could never reach the lid; some lids are so heavy that few can open them, or, once open, they are left that way, causing problems with smells and flies.

As is the case with most communal facilities, the fewer the number of families sharing each facility (refuse hopper, garbage shed, and so forth), the greater the sense of individual responsibility and the better the upkeep of that facility.

Possible design responses

- Provide lids that can easily be opened and closed.
- Provide dumpsters with well-fitting lids that do not make a loud noise when dropped or pushed shut.
- Avoid rolling doors that could freeze shut in regions with cold winters.
- To ensure accessibility by children, provide a set of wooden steps.

Glossary of Environmental and Related Terms

Definition of Some American Environmental Terms

Apartment. A living unit in a building that contains three or more units and has some common services or facilities.

Block. An urban area enclosed on all sides by public streets.

Condominium. A way of subowning an apartment house or other multiple dwelling so that each space is owned or mortgaged at whatever point it rests in space, on or off the ground.

Cooperative. Joint ownership of a building; the total building is owned proportionately by shares in stock.

Den. A small, informally furnished room often used by the "man of the family" for hobbies, an office, collections, and so forth.

Duplex. A two-family dwelling in which the living units are one above the other or side by side.

Flat. Any one floor of a building two or more stories high, each floor of which constitutes a single dwelling unit and has a private street entrance. It usually is in a single family (detached) house that has been converted.

Ground cover. Low, dense plants that carpet the ground and require no cutting or other maintenance. Most common in the United States are ivy and myrtle (Vinca minor).

High rise. Multiple-story building served by elevators.

Planned unit development. A housing scheme with the following characteristics: dwellings in clusters, some of the site reserved for shared open space, much or all of the housing in the form of townhouses or apartments, higher density per acre than conventional, single-family housing.

Radburn-type layout. Experimental American garden suburb, only one portion of which was built in New Jersey in the 1920s. Designed by Henry Wright and Clarence Stein. First attempt to segregate pedestrians (particularly children) from automobiles by way of a central, shared green space with footpaths that pass under streets by tunnels.

Retaining wall. Wall built to contain and hold back earth on one side.

Row housing. Three or more dwellings with party or common walls in which all dwellings have an entry at grade (ground level).

Stoop. A porch, platform, or entrance stairway at a building entrance. From Dutch *stoep*, which in Amsterdam allowed refuge above flood water at a building entry.

Subdivision. An area originally under a single ownership that has been subdivided into plots intended or used for building purposes.

Terms with No Widely Accepted American Equivalent

Block (Canadian, British). A large building or set of buildings (for example, Corbu's Marseille Block).

Gallery- or deck-access building (Canadian, British). Multistory apartment structure with open gallery (single-loaded) corridors extending the length of the structure at each level, onto which the individual apartments open. Where the gallery is wider than the usual 4 or 5 feet (1.2 or 1.5 m), this access way is often termed a *deck* (not to be confused with the American term *deck*—a wood-floored platform jutting out from a private house or apartment and used for recreation, like a patio).

Leisure center (British). Building or group of buildings serving the general public of a community or neighborhood for recreational activities.

Linked housing (Canadian). Two-story houses linked by means of adjacent garages.

Maisonette (British). An apartment unit with two stories, linked by an internal private stair.

Maisonettes (Canadian). Two-story units with entrances off a common interior corridor on the lower floor, upper floors back to back.

Point block (British). High-rise block in which flats are closely grouped around elevators, that is, only about four flats per floor. This is in contrast to a slab block or gallery-access building.

Stacked housing (Canadian). One- or two-story dwellings stacked one on top of the other, usually two or three units high, each with a private exterior entrance from grade or gallery.

ENVIRONMENTAL TERMS USED IN VARIOUS ENGLISH-SPEAKING LOCATIONS COMPARED

American Term	British English	Canadian English	Australian English	New Zealand English
Apartment	Flat	Apartment	Flat; home unit	Flat
Atrium house	Courtyard house	Court house/atrium house	Courtyard house	N.E.T.*
Back porch	Verandah, porch	Verandah, porch	Back verandah	Back porch
Berm	Mound	Berm	Earth berm	Berm
Blacktop, asphalt	Tarmac	Asphalt paving	Asphalt	Asphalt
Block (that is, city block)	N.E.T.*	Block	Block	Block
Cinder block	Breeze block	Concrete block	"Besser" block	Concrete block
Closet	Cupboard, wardrobe	Closet	Cupboard, wardrobe, built-in robes	Cupboard, wardrobe
Condominium	Flying freehold	Condominium	Strata title	Strata title
Co-op housing	Housing cooperative, housing association	Co-op housing	Co-op	Co-op
Day-care center	Nursery, creche	Day-care center	Day-care center, creche	Day-care center
Dead storage	Store	Dead storage	N.E.T.*	N.E.T.*
Den	Study	Den	Den, study	Study
Dumpster	Skip	Container	N.E.T.*	Bin, Skip
Duplex	Semidetached, two units, side by side	Duplex = one unit above another; double, semi-detached = two units, side by side	Duplex	Semidetatched
Elevator	Lift	Elevator	Lift	Lift
Family room	Parlour, family room	Family room	Family room	Family room, rumpus room
Faucet	Tap	Tap	Tap/faucet	Tap
First floor	Ground floor	Ground/first floor	Ground floor	Ground floor
Flat	Flat	Apartment	Flat	Flat

American Term	British English	Canadian English	Australian English	New Zealand English
Garbage	Rubbish	Garbage	Garbage, rubbish	Rubbish
Garbage chute	Refuse hopper	Garbage chute	Garbage chute	Garbage chute
Garden	Flower or vegetable bed	Vegetable garden, flower garden	Flower bed, vegetable garden	Flower or vegetable bed
Grade	Ground level	Grade	Ground level	Ground level
High rise	High rise, point block, tower block	High rise	High rise	High rise
Jump rope	Skipping	Skipping	Skipping	Skipping
Jungle gym	Climbing frame	Play structure	Climbing frame, jungle gym	Jungle gym, climbing frame
Lavatory, toilet	Cloakroom, loo	Washroom, powder room	Toilet	Toilet
Living room	Living room, sitting room, front room, parlor, lounge**	Living room	Lounge room, living room	Lounge, living room
Lot	Curtilage, lot	Lot	Block	Section
Median strip	Central reservation	Median	Median strip	Median strip
Mobile home	Mobile home, caravan	Mobile home, trailer	Mobile home, transportable home	Caravan
Moving van	Removal van	Moving van	Removal van	Removal van
Multifamily housing	Block of flats	Multifamily housing	Block of flats, medium-density housing	Multiunit housing
Orientation	Aspect	Orientation	Orientation	Orientation
Parking lot	Car park	Parking lot	Car park	Car park
Parking strip	Verge	Shoulder	Nature strip	Verge
Planned unit development (P.U.D.)	Grouping of buildings on site, often traffic-segregated layout	Planned group building project	Cluster housing, villa units, group housing	N.E.T.*
Project	Housing estate	Project, development	Project, development	Housing estate

American Term	British English	Canadian English	Australian English	New Zealand English
Public housing	Council housing, local authority housing	Social housing, public housing	Public housing	State housing, council housing
Recreational vehicle (RV), trailer	Dormobile, camper	RV	Large camper, van caravan	Caravan, camper van
Rent	Let, rent	Rent	Rent, let	Rent
Row house, town house	Terrace house	Row house, town house	Row house, terrace house, town house	Town house
Sidewalk	Pavement	Sidewalk	Footpath	Pavement, footpath
Single-family dwelling	Detatched house	Single-family detached house	Detached house, single dwelling	Detached house
Single-loaded corridor, access balcony	Gallery access, deck access	Single-loaded corridor (interior), access gallery (exterior)	Gallery access	Gallery access
Speed bump	Sleeping policeman	Speed bump	Speed bump	Judder bar
Stoop, porch	Porch	Porch	Front verandah, porch	Porch, front porch
Store, market	Shop	Store	Shop	Shop
Stroller	Push-chair	Stroller	Pusher, stroller	Push-chair
Subdivision	Estate development	Subdivision	Subdivision, estate	Subdivision
Victory garden, community garden	Allotment	Allotment garden	Community garden	Allotment
Walk-up apartment	Block of flats without a lift, staircase access	Walk-up apartments	Block of flats, home units	Block of flats
Woonerf	Mixer-court	N.E.T.*	N.E.T.*	N.E.T.*
Yard	Garden	Yard, garden	Yard, garden (if planted)	Garden, backyard

*N.E.T. = No Equivalent Term
**The range of terms is due to subtle class distinctions in the name of this room.

Bibliography

Ackermans, E. 1970. "The vicinity of the home used as a play area." *Netherlands Institute for Preventative Medicine.*

Adams, Anthony. 1975. *Your energy-efficient house: Building and remodeling ideas.* Charlotte, Vt.: Garden Way.

Ahlbrandt, Roger S., Jr., and Paul C. Brophy. 1976. "Management: An important element of the housing environment." *Environment and Behaviour* 8, 4 (December).

Aiello, James, Barry Gordon, and Thomas Farrell. 1974. "Description of children's outdoor activities in a suburban residential area: Preliminary findings." *Man-environment interactions: Evaluations and applications,* edited by Daniel Carson. Washington, D.C.: Environmental Design Research Association.

Alexander, Christopher, Sara Ishikawa, Murray Silverstein, et al. 1977. *A pattern language.* New York: Oxford University Press.

———. 1979. *A timeless way of building.* New York: Oxford University Press.

"Alexandra Gardens environmental improvements: A report for Alexandra Gardens tenants." 1980. London: Support (February). Mimeo.

Altman, Irwin. 1975. *The environment and social behavior: Privacy, personal space, territory, crowding.* Monterey, Calif.: Brooks/Cole.

American National Standards Institute, ANSI A177.1 R.80. 1980. *Making buildings and facilities accessible to and usable by the physically handicapped.* New York: American National Standards Institute.

American Society of Landscape Architects Foundation. 1975. *Barrier free site design.* Washington, D.C.: U.S. Department of Housing and Urban Development.

Angel, S. 1968. *Discouraging crime through city planning.* Working Paper no. 75. Berkeley: Institute of Urban and Regional Development, University of California.

Appleyard, Donald. 1979. "Home." *Architectural Association Quarterly* 11, 3.

———. 1981. *Livable streets.* Berkeley: University of California Press.

Appleyard, Donald, and Mark Lintell. 1972. "The environmental quality of city streets: The residents' viewpoint." *Journal of the American Institute of Planners* 38, 2 (March).

Architecture Research Unit. 1966. *Courtyard houses, Inchview, Prestonpans.* Edinburgh: Architecture Research Unit, University of Edinburgh.

———. 1969. *Traffic separated layouts in Stevenage New Town.* Edinburgh: Architecture Research Unit, University of Edinburgh.

Attenburrow, J. J., A. R. Murphy, and A. G. Simms. 1978. *The problems of some large local authority estates—an exploratory study.* Building Research Establishment Current Paper, C.P. 18/78. Garston, England: Building Research Establishment, Department of the Environment.

Auckland Regional Authority Planning Division. 1974a. *Multi-unit housing: Part 1, Patterns and problems.* Auckland. Auckland Regional Authority Planning Division.

———. 1974b. *Multi-unit housing: Part 2, Planning controls.* Auckland: Auckland Regional Authority Planning Division.

————. 1974c. *Multi-unit housing: Part 3, Peripheral development*. Auckland: Auckland Regional Authority Planning Division.

Babbie, Earl R. 1973. *Survey research methods*. Belmont, Calif.: Wadsworth.

Back, Kurt W. 1962. *Slums, projects and people: Some psychological problems of relocation in Puerto Rico*. Durham, N.C.: Duke University Press.

Bagot, Patricia. 1971. *A comparative study of three forms of housing tenure*. Edinburgh: Architecture Research Unit, University of Edinburgh.

Balmforth, Nick, and Wendy Nelson. 1978. *Jubilee Street: Pebble Mill's guide to adventure play*. London: British Broadcasting Corporation.

Barker, Eric J. 1976. "Tenant participation in housing design: A report on experimental public housing projects in Winnipeg and Brandon, Manitoba." Written in association with Stecheson, Frederickson, Katz, Architects, Winnipeg, and sponsored by CMHC. Winnipeg. Mimeo.

Barnes, Robert E., and Ronald Sarro. 1971. *Are you safe from burglars?* Garden City, N.Y.: Doubleday.

Beamish, Anne. 1980. *Child-pedestrian safety in residential environments*. Monograph 1. Ottawa: Central Mortgage and Housing Corporation.

Bechtel, Robert, and Rajendra Srivastrava. 1978. *Post occupancy evaluation of housing, A final report on contract #H2405*. Department of Housing and Urban Development. Washington, D.C.: U.S. Government Printing Office.

Beck, Robert J., Robert Rowan, and Pierre Teasdale. 1974. "The evaluation of family satisfaction with the design of the stacked maisonette." *Man-environment interactions: Evaluations and applications*, Vol. 5, *Methods and measures*, edited by Daniel Carson. Washington, D.C.: Environmental Design Research Association.

————. 1975a. *Site design requirements: Vol. 1, User-generated program for low-rise multiple dwellings*. Montreal: Centre de Recherches et d'Innovation Urbaines, Université de Montréal. (Report produced for the Central Mortgage and Housing Corporation, Ottawa, Canada.)

————. 1975b. *House design requirements: Vol. 2, User-generated program for low-rise multiple dwelling housing*. Montreal: Centre de Recherches et d'Innovation Urbaines, Université de Montréal. (Report produced for the Central Mortgage and Housing Corporation, Ottawa, Canada.)

Becker, Franklin D. 1974. *Design for living: The resident's view of multifamily housing*. Ithaca, N.Y.: Center for Urban Development and Research, Cornell University.

————. 1976. "Children's play in multifamily housing." *Environment and Behaviour* 8, 4 (December).

————. 1977. *Housing Messages*. Stroudsberg, Pa.: Dowden, Hutchinson and Ross.

Becker, Franklin D., with Stephanie Ashworth, Douglas Beaver, and Donald Poe. 1977. *User participation, personalization, and environmental meaning: Three field studies*. Ithaca, N.Y.: Cornell Program in Urban and Regional Studies, Cornell University.

Beer, Anne R. 1975. "Children's play—A study of the problems in housing areas in Sheffield." Sheffield: Department of Landscape Architecture, University of Sheffield. Mimeo.

————. 1982. "The development control process and the quality of the external environment in residential areas." *Landscape Research* 7, 3.

Bengtsson, Arvid. 1970. *Environmental planning for children's play*. New York: Praeger.

————. 1972. *Adventure playgrounds*. New York: Praeger.

Berg, M., and E. A. Medrich. 1980. "Children in four neighbourhoods: The physical environment and its effect on play and play patterns." *Environment and Behaviour* 12, 3.

Berk, Sarah Fenstermaker. 1980. "The household as workplace: Wives, husbands and children." In *New Space for Women*, edited by Gerda R. Wekerle, Rebecca Peterson, and David Morley. Boulder, Colo.: Westview Press.

Berkeley Planning Associates. 1980. "Urban initiatives anti-crime program: Evaluation of the proposals by the housing authorities of the cities of Los Angeles, Richmond and San Francisco." Berkeley, Calif.: Berkeley Planning Associates.

Bjorklid, Pia. 1982. *Children's outdoor environment*. Stockholm: Stockholm Institute of Education.

Blackman, A. 1966. "The role of city planning in child pedestrian safety." *American Behavioral Scientist* 10.

Block, Herbert, and Gilbert Geis. 1962. *Man, crime and society: The forms of criminal behavior*. New York: Random House.

Boehm, Edgar. 1980. "Youth farms." In *Innovation in play environments*, edited by Paul F. Wilkinson. London: Croom Helm.

Booth, A., and D. Johnson. 1975. "The effects of crowding on child health and development." *American Behavioral Scientist* 18.

Boudon, Philippe. 1972. *Lived-in architecture: Le Corbusier's Pessac revisited*. Cambridge, Mass.: MIT Press.

Bowlby, John. 1969. *Attachment and loss*. New York: Basic Books.

Bridges, John E. 1973. "Security system 'by' the residents 'for' the residents." *Journal of Housing* 6 (June).

Brill, William, Associates. 1976a. *Controlling access in highrise buildings: Approaches and guidelines*. U.S. Department of Housing and Urban Development. Washington, D.C.: U.S. Government Printing Office.

———. 1976b. *Victimization, fear of crime, and altered behavior: A profile of the crime problem in Capper Dwellings, Washington, D.C.* U.S. Department of Housing and Urban Development. Washington, D.C.: U.S. Government Printing Office.

———. 1976c. *Victimization, fear of crime, and altered behavior: A profile of the crime problem in Murphy Homes, Baltimore, Maryland*. U.S. Department of Housing and Urban Development. Washington, D.C.: U.S. Government Printing Office.

———. 1976d. *Victimization, fear of crime, and altered behavior: A profile of the crime problem in William Nickersen, Jr. Gardens, Los Angeles, California*. U.S. Department of Housing and Urban Development. Washington, D.C.: U.S. Government Printing Office.

———. 1979a. *Planning for housing security: Site elements manual*. Prepared for U.S. Department of Housing and Urban Development, Office of Policy Development and Research. Washington, D.C.: U.S. Government Printing Office.

———. 1979b. *Planning for housing security: Site security analysis manual*. Prepared for U.S. Department of Housing and Urban Development, Office of Policy Development and Research. Washington, D.C.: U.S. Government Printing Office.

Brolin, B. C., and John Zeisel. 1968. "Mass housing: Social research and design." *Architectural Forum* 129, 1 : 66–71.

Brower, S. 1974. "Recreational uses of space: An inner city case study." In Vol. 7, Social Ecology, *Man-environment interactions: Evaluations and applications*, edited by Daniel Carson. Washington, D.C.: Environmental Design Research Association.

Building and dwelling on women's terms: A short report on a conference. 1979. Kungalv, Sweden (May).

Budgaard, Aase, Jan Gehl, and Erik Skoven. 1982. "Soft Edges" (an English summary of Bløde Kanter). *Arkitekten* 21.

Bussard, Ellen. 1974. "Children's spatial behavior in and around a moderate-density housing development: An exploratory study of patterns and influences." Master's thesis, Department of Design Analysis, Cornell University.

Byrom, Connie. 1979. "Privacy and courtyard housing." *The Architects' Journal* 151, 2 (January): 101–104.

Byrom, J. B. 1972. *Shared open space in Scottish private enterprise housing*. Edinburgh: Architecture Research Unit, University of Edinburgh.

Canada Mortgage and Housing Corporation and Canada Design Council. 1979. *National housing design competition 1979*. Ottawa: Canada Mortgage and Housing Corporation.

Caplow, T., and R. Forman. 1950. "Neighborhood interaction in a homogeneous community." *American Sociological Review* 15.

Cappon, Daniel. 1971. "Mental health in the high rise." *Canadian Journal of Public Health* 62.

Cardew, R. V. 1980. "Flats in Sydney: The thirty per cent solution?" In *Twentieth century Sydney: Studies in urban and social history*, edited by J. Roe. Sydney: Hall and Hemonger.

Carman, John. 1971. "Safety and security in multi-family housing complexes." *Journal of Housing* 28, 6 (June): 277–81.

Carrasco, Frank F., W. Gary Wilkins-Vigil, and Nathan Auslander. 1977. "Chicano children and their outdoor environment: Barrio, housing project and rural settings." Denver, Colo.: Juarez-Lincoln Center. Mimeo.

Cavanna, Roger. 1974. "Backyard options in residential neighborhoods." Master's thesis, Department of Landscape Architecture, University of California, Berkeley.

Center for Environmental Structure. 1969. *Houses generated by patterns*. Berkeley, Calif.: Center for Environmental Structure.

Center for Residential Security Design. 1973. *A design guide for improving residential security*. U.S. Department of Housing and Urban Development. Washington, D.C.: U.S. Government Printing Office.

Central Mortgage and Housing Corporation (Canada). 1978. *Post-occupancy project evaluation report phase one*. Ottawa: Central Mortgage and Housing Corporation (June).

Chase, Elizabeth, and George Ishmael. 1980. "Outdoor play in housing areas." In *Innovation in Play Environments*, edited by Paul F. Wilkinson. London: Croom Helm.

Cheek, Becky. 1973. *Planning playgrounds for day care*. Atlanta, Ga.: Southeastern Day Care Project,

Southern Regional Education Board (130 Sixth Street, NW, Atlanta, Ga. 30315).

Cheshire County Council. 1976. *Design and housing-roads*. Chesire County Council.

Childhood City Newsletter. 1979a. "Children and urban open space." Edited by Don S. Cook, Christine Hoffman, and Lisa Cashdan. No. 17. New York: Graduate School and University Center, City University of New York.

———. 1979b. "Teen environment." Edited by Mark Francis and Vanessa Nobile. No. 16. New York: Graduate School and University Center, City University of New York.

———. 1980a. "Participation." Edited by Carol Baldassari, Roger Hart, and Mike Lockett. No. 22. New York: Graduate School and University Center, City University of New York.

———. 1980b. "Scandinavian report." Edited by Mark Francis, Roger Hart, Lynn Paxson, Cecilia Perez, and Leanne Rivlin. No. 19. New York: Graduate School and University Center, City University of New York.

Clarke, R. V. G. 1978. *Tackling vandalism*. Home Office Research Study no. 40. London: Her Majesty's Stationery Office.

Coates, Gary, and Henry Sanoff. 1973. "Behavioral mapping: The ecology of child behavior in a planned residential setting." In *Proceedings of the Third Annual Conference of the Environmental Design Research Association*. Los Angeles: University of California at Los Angeles.

Cohen, Uriel, Anne Hill, Carol Lane, Tim McGinty, and Gary Moore. 1979. *Recommendations for child play areas*. Task III of contract no. DACA 73-78-C-0005 for U.S. Department of the Army, Office of the Chief of Engineers, Special Projects Branch, Washington, D.C. Milwaukee: Community Design Center, Inc., with Center for Architecture and Urban Planning Research, University of Wisconsin.

Committee on Housing Research and Development. 1972. *Families in public housing: An evaluation of three residential environments in Rockford, Illinois*. Research report. Urbana-Champaign, Ill.: University of Illinois.

Connell, Bettye Rose. 1975. "Behavioral science research for design decision-making: The processes of programming and evaluation and an evaluative case study of multi-family housing." Master's thesis, College of Human Ecology, Design and Environmental Analysis, Cornell University.

Cook, Barbara E. 1972. "Survey evaluation for low-cost low-rent public housing for the elderly, Pleasanton, California." Berkeley, Calif.: Sanford Hirshen and Partners, Architects. Mimeo.

Cook, J. A. 1969. *Gardens on housing estates: A survey of user attitudes and behaviour on 7 layouts*. Building Research Station current papers 42/69. Garston, England: Building Research Station.

Cooney, E. W. 1974. "High flats in local authority housing in England and Wales since 1945." In *Multi-storey living: The British working class experience*, edited by Anthony Sutcliffe. London: Croom Helm, and New York: Harper & Row.

Cooper, Carla, and Bill Sims. 1978. "A post-occupancy evaluation of the fourplex condominium." *Housing and Society* 1.

Cooper, Clare. 1970a. "Adventure playgrounds." *Landscape Architecture* 61, 1 (October): 18–29, 88.

Cooper, Clare. 1970b. *Resident attitudes towards the environment at St. Francis Square, San Francisco: A summary of the initial findings*. Berkeley: Institute of Urban and Regional Development, University of California. Working paper no. 126.

Cooper, Clare. 1971. "St. Francis Square: Attitudes of its residents." *American Institute of Architects Journal* 56, 6 (December): 22–25.

Cooper, Clare. 1972a. "The house as symbol." *Design and Environment* (September).

Cooper, Clare. 1972b. "Resident dissatisfaction in multi-family housing." In *Behavior, design and policy aspects of human habitats*, edited by William H. Smith. Green Bay: University of Wisconsin.

Cooper, Clare. 1974a. "Children in residential areas: Guidelines for designers." *Landscape Architecture* 65 (October): 372–77.

Cooper, Clare. 1974b. "The house as symbol of self." In *Designing for human behavior*, edited by Jon Lang, Charles Burnette, Walter Moleski, and David Vachon. Stroudsberg, Pa.: Dowden, Hutchinson and Ross.

Cooper, Clare. 1975. *Easter Hill Village: Some social implications of design*. New York: Free Press.

Cooper, Clare, and John Corrie. 1970. "Geneva Terrace: A strategy for the future." San Francisco. Mimeo.

Cooper, Clare, and Phyllis Hackett. 1968. *Analysis of the design process at two moderate-density housing developments*. Berkeley: Center for Planning and Development Research, University of California.

Cooper, Clare, and Stephen Marcus. 1971. "Observations at three San Francisco redevelopment agency housing developments." San Francisco: San Francisco Redevelopment Agency. Mimeo.

Cooper Marcus, Clare. 1974. "Children's play behavior in a low-rise, inner city housing development." In *Man-environment interactions: evaluations and applications*, edited by Daniel Carson. Washington, D.C.: Environmental Design Research Association.

Cooper Marcus, Clare. 1977. "User-needs research in housing." In *The form of housing*, edited by Sam Davis. New York: Van Nostrand Reinhold.

Cooper Marcus, Clare. 1978a. "Remembrance of landscapes past." *Landscape* 22, 3 (Summer).

Cooper Marcus, Clare. 1978b. "Salvaging a troubled public housing project." *American Institute of Architects Journal* 67, 11 (September).

Cooper Marcus, Clare, and Lindsay Hogue. 1977. "Design guidelines for high-rise family housing." In *Human response to tall buildings*, edited by Don Conway. Stroudsberg, Pa.: Dowden, Hutchinson and Ross.

Cooper Marcus, Clare, and Robin C. Moore. 1976. "Children and their environments: A review of research, 1955–75." *Journal of Architectural Education* 29, 4 (April): 24–25.

Cost effective site planning. 1976. Washington, D.C.: National Association of Home Builders.

Coulson, N. J. 1980. "Space around the home: Do residents like what the planners provide?" *The Architects' Journal* 24 (December).

County Council of Essex. 1973. *A design guide for residential areas*. Tiptree, Essex (U.K.): Anchor Press.

Cowburn, W. 1967. "Housing in a consumer society." *Architectural Review* 142, 849:398–400.

Coyle, Tom. 1973. *Design guidelines for condominium housing*. Ottawa, Canada: Architectural and Planning Division, Central Mortgage and Housing Corporation.

Danger on the playground. 1978. London: Fair Play for Children.

Danish National Institute of Building Research. 1969. *Children's use of recreational areas.* Copenhagen: Danish National Institute of Building Research.

Dao Tang Duc and Jan McMurray. 1977. "Housing preference in New Zealand: Interim report no. 2—An Overview." Research paper 77/3. Wellington, New Zealand: National Housing Commission.

Darke, Jane. 1978. "The primary generator and the design process." In *New directions in environmental design research* (proceedings, E.D.R.A. 9 Conference), edited by W. Rogers and W. Ittelson. Stroudsberg, Pa: Dowden, Hutchinson and Ross. Also in *Design Studies* 1 (July, 1979).

Darke, Jane, and Roy Darke. 1969a. *Physical and social factors in neighbour relations.* London: Centre for Environmental Studies. Working paper no. 41.

———. 1969b. *Suburban housing estates: Physical and social characteristics.* London: Centre for Environmental Studies. Working paper no. 40.

———. 1970. *Health and environment: High flats.* London: Centre for Environmental Studies. Working paper no. 10.

———. 1972. "Sheffield revisited: Evaluation of Park Hill flats." *Built Environment* 1, 10.

———. 1979. *Who needs housing?* London: Macmillan.

Darke, Jane, Bryan Lawson, and Christopher Spencer. 1979. "Surveying the users: Some people are never satisfied." Paper given at International Conference on Environmental Psychology, Guildford, Surrey.

Davey, Judith. 1976. "Social aspects of housing: A bibliography." The influence of social factors in New Zealand, a review of the literature and annotated bibliography. Research paper. Wellington, New Zealand: National Housing Commission.

———. 1977. "Social factors and housing need in New Zealand: An overview." Research paper 77/1. Wellington, New Zealand: National Housing Commission.

Davidoff, Paul. 1980. "Respect the child: Urban planning with the child in mind." In *Innovation in play environments*, edited by Paul F. Wilkinson. London: Croom Helm.

Davis, Sam. 1977. *The form of housing.* New York: Van Nostrand Reinhold.

Dean, John. 1966. "Housing design and family values." In *Urban housing*, edited by William L. C. Weaton et al. New York: Free Press.

Dee, N., and J. C. Liebman. 1970. "A statistical study of attendance at urban playgrounds." *Journal of Leisure Research* 2.

Department of the Environment (U.K.). 1971a. *New housing in cleared areas: A study of St. Mary's Oldham.* Design Bulletin 22. London: Her Majesty's Stationery Office.

———. 1971b. "Survey of four medium-rise high density estates." Sociological Research Section. Mimeo.

———. 1972a. *The estate outside the dwelling: reactions of residents to aspects of housing layout.* Design bulletin 25. London: Her Majesty's Stationery Office.

———. 1972b. *Spaces in the home: Bathrooms and WC's.* Design Bulletin 24, part 1. London: Her Majesty's Stationery Office.

———. 1972c. *Spaces in the home: Kitchens and laundering spaces.* Design Bulletin 24, part 2. London: Her Majesty's Stationery Office.

———. 1973a. *Children at play.* London: Her Majesty's Stationery Office.

———. 1973b. "High density housing: A current DOE development." Housing Development Directorate paper 1/73. London: Department of Environment. Reprinted from *The Architect's Journal* (3 January 1973).

———. 1974. "The Quality of local authority housing schemes." Housing Development Directorate paper 1/74. London: Department of Environment. Reprinted from *The Architect's Journal* (27 February 1974).

———. 1976. "Children's playground." Housing Development Directorate occasional paper 2/76. London: Department of the Environment.

———. 1977. *Recreation and deprivation in inner urban areas.* London: Her Majesty's Stationery Office.

———. 1978. "Difficult to let council housing: Case studies 2, Post war estates." Housing Development Directorate occasional paper x/78. London: Department of the Environment. Mimeo, draft.

———. 1981a. *An investigation of difficult to let housing, Vol. 1: General findings.* Housing Development Directorate occasional paper 3/80. London: Her Majesty's Stationery Office.

———. 1981b. *An investigation of difficult to let housing, Vol. 2: Case studies of post war estates.* Housing Development Directorate occasional paper 4/80. London: Her Majesty's Stationery Office.

———. 1981c. *An investigation of difficult to let housing: Vol. 3, Case studies of pre war estates.* Housing Development Directorate occasional paper 5/80. London: Her Majesty's Stationery Office.

Department of the Environment (U.K.), Housing Development Directorate, and Greater London Council. 1978. *Housing appraisal kit—A complete social survey package.* London: Department of the Environment.

Department of the Environment and Department of Transport (U.K.). 1977. *Residential roads and footpaths: Layout considerations.* Design bulletin 32. London: Her Majesty's Stationery Office.

Derman, Asher. 1974. "Children's play: Design approaches and theoretical issues." *Man-Environment Systems* 4, 2 (March).

"Design criteria." 1967. *Official Architecture and Planning* 30, 3 (March).

Design criteria for the development of sheltered play spaces in medium to high density housing projects. 1980. Research project 11. Ottawa: Canada Mortgage and Housing Corporation.

Dillingham Corporation (SUA Division). 1971. *A study of crime prevention through physical planning.* Los Angeles: Southern California Association of Governments.

Dingemans, Denis. 1975. "The urbanization of suburbia: The renaissance of the row house." *Landscape* 20, 2.

Dockett, Kathleen, Sidney Brower, and Ralph B. Taylor. 1983. "Residents' perceptions of site-level features: People, problems, planting and fences." *Environment and Behaviour* 15, 4 (July): 419–37.

Duhl, Leonard J. 1963. *The urban condition: People and policy in the metropolis.* New York: Basic Books.

Durard, R., and D. R. Eckhart. 1973. "Social rank, residential effects, and community satisfaction." *Social Forces* 52, 4.

Durlak, Jerome, Barbara Duncan, and Gwennyth Emby. 1976. *Suburban children and public transportation in metropolitan Toronto.* Toronto: Ministry of State for Urban Affairs.

Edmonton Social Services, Social Planning Section. 1978. "Design guidelines for multiple family housing." First draft. Mimeo.

Egar, Ruth, and Wendy Sarkissian. 1982. "Reviewing the Australian suburban dream: A unique approach to neighbourhood change with the family support scheme." Paper presented to the 52nd congress of the Australian and New Zealand Association for the Advancement of Science, Macquarie University, N.S.W.

The Eikos Group (Planning and Environmental Design Group Ltd., Vancouver). 1980. *Children's perceptions of a play environment: A study of three low cost housing developments in Vancouver.* Research project 4 for International Year of the Child. Ottawa: Canada Mortgage and Housing Corporation.

Ellis, Peter. 1977. "Chalvedon housing area, Basildon: A social psychological evaluation." *The Architects' Journal* 166, 37:485–94.

———. "A social psychological study of the outside spaces in the Chalvedon housing area." London: Ahrends, Burton and Kuralek, Architects. Mimeo.

Erley, Duncan, and Martin Jaffe. 1979. *Site planning for solar access*. Washington, D.C.: U.S. Department of Housing and Urban Development.

Esbensen, Steen B. 1979. "An international inventory and comparative study of legislation and guidelines for children's play spaces in the residential environment." For the United National Committee of Nongovernmental Organisations for the International Year of the Child. Ottawa: Canada Mortgage and Housing Corporation. Mimeo.

Evans, E. B., B. Shub, and M. Weinstein. 1971. *Day care: How to plan, develop and operate a day care center*. Boston: Beacon Press.

Fairley, William, and Michael Liechenstein. 1971. *Improving public safety in urban apartment dwellings: Security concepts and experimental design for New York City Housing Authority buildings*. New York: New York City Rand Institute.

Fanning, I. M. 1967. "Families in flats." *British Medical Journal* 4.

Festinger, Leon, Stanley Schacter, and Kurt Back. 1950. *Social pressures in informal groups: A study of human factors in housing*. New York: Harper and Row.

Fjeldsted, Brenda. 1980. "'Standard' versus 'adventure' playgrounds." In *Innovation in play environments*, edited by Paul F. Wilkinson. London: Croom Helm.

Francescato, Guido, Sue Weidemann, James R. Anderson, and Richard Chenoweth 1980. *Residents' satisfaction in HUD-assisted housing: Design and management factors*. Washington, D.C.: U.S. Government Printing Office.

Freeston, R. 1980. "Garden City clippings: Cliches obscure facts." *Royal Australian Planning Institute Journal* 18.

Fried, Marc. "Grieving for a lost home." In *The urban condition*, edited by L. Duhl. New York: Basic Books.

Friedberg, Lawrence. 1974. "Comparative perceptions of residential environment and 'home' image, verbal responses and physical reference." Master's thesis, Cornell University. As quoted in Becker, 1977.

Friedmann, Arnold, Craig Zimring, and Ervin Zube, 1978. *Environmental design evaluation*. New York: Plenum Press.

"Front and back: Problems of the threshold." 1967. *The Architects' Journal* 146, 21:1307–12.

Fyson, Anthony. 1976. *Change the street*. London: Oxford University Press, in association with Chameleon/Ikon.

Gans, Herber J. 1961a. "The balanced community: Homogeneity or heterogeneity in residential areas." *Journal of the American Institute of Planners* 27, 3 (August).

———. 1961b. "Planning and social life: Friendship and neighbor relations in suburban communities." *Journal of the American Institute of Planners* 27, 2 (May).

———. 1962. *The urban villagers*. Glencoe, Ill.: Free Press.

———. 1967. *The Levittowners*. New York: Pantheon.

———. 1973. "The possibilities of class and racial integration in American new towns: A policy-oriented analysis." In *New towns: Why and for whom?*, edited by H. S. Perloff and N. C. Sandberg. New York: Praeger.

Gardiner, Richard A. 1978. *Design for safe neighborhoods: The environmental security planning and design process*. National Institute of Law Enforcement and Criminal Justice, Law Enforcement Assistance Administration. Washington, D.C.: U.S. Government Printing Office.

Gatt, Carmel. 1978. "Privacy in private outdoor spaces in multi-family housing projects." Master's thesis, Department of Architecture, University of British Columbia.

Gehl, Ingrid. 1971. *Bo-miljo*. SBI Rapport, 71. Copenhagen.

Gehl, Jan. 1977. *The interface between public and private territories in residential areas*. Parkville, Victoria: Department of Architecture and Building, Melbourne University.

———. n.d. "Housing, site planning, urban design." Mimeo.

"Getting down to play maintenance." 1979. In *Care in the home*. London: Royal Society for Prevention of Accidents, U.K.

Gilmour, Andrew, et al. 1970. *Low-rise high density housing study*. Edinburgh: Architecture Research Unit, University of Edinburgh.

Gittus, Elizabeth. 1976. *Flats, families and the under-fives*. London: Routledge and Kegan Paul.

Goldberg, Juliana V. 1974. *Managing a successful community association*. Washington, D.C.: Urban Land Institute.

Goldsmith, Selwyn. 1967. *Designing for the disabled*. New York: McGraw-Hill.

Goodman, M. 1974. "The enclosed environment." *Royal Society of Health Journal* 94, 4 (August).

A good place to bring up kids. 1978. Children's Environments Advisory Service (Polly Hill, Advisor). Ottawa: Central Mortgage and Housing Corporation.

Grady, Ethel F. 1967. *Values and attitudes of selected homemakers in economically deprived families toward housing.* Bulletin 391, University of Rhode Island, Agricultural Experiment Station.

Gray, John. 1979. "Housing on a human scale." Report read at the Housing Centre National Conference, U.K., April 4 and 5. Reprinted in *Housing Review* 28, 4 (July–August): 103–106.

Greenie, B. B. 1976. *Design for diversity: Planning for rational man in the neo-technic environment, an ethological approach.* New York: Elsevier.

Griffin, Mary E. 1973. "Mount Hope Courts: A social physical evaluation." American Civilization senior honors thesis, Brown University.

Gutman, Robert. 1965–66. "The questions architects ask." *Transactions of the Bartlett Society* 4.

———. 1966. "Site planning and social behavior." *Journal of Social Issues* 22, 4 (October).

Guttinger, V. A. 1977. "Small children and traffic." *Ekistics* 43.

Habraken, N. J. 1972. *Supports: An alternative to mass housing.* New York: Praeger.

Habraken, N. J., J. T. Boekhold, P. J. M. Dinjens, and A. P. Thijssen. 1976. *Variations: The systematic design of supports.* Cambridge, Mass.: Laboratory of Architecture and Planning, MIT.

Halkett, Ian. 1976. *The quarter-acre block: The use of suburban gardens.* Canberra: Australian Institute of Urban Studies.

Hall, Edward T. 1966. *The hidden dimension.* Garden City, N.Y.: Doubleday.

Hanke, Byron R. 1964. *The homeowners association handbook.* Washington, D.C.: Urban Land Institute.

Hanson, Dennis, Min Kantrowitz, Richard Nordhaus, and Robert E. Strell. 1978. "Subsidized housing in Albuquerque: Design evaluation, analysis and recommendations." (Design and Planning Assistance Center, University of New Mexico.) Albuquerque, N.M.: Albuquerque/Bernalillo County Planning Department.

Harries, Keith D. 1974. *The geography of crime and justice.* New York: McGraw-Hill.

Hart, Roger. 1973. "Review of theory and research on children's relationship to the physical environment." In *Children in the residential setting*, by A. M. Pollowy. Montreal: Université de Montréal, Centre de Recherches et d'Innovation Urbaines.

Hart, Roger. 1978. *Children's experience of place.* New York: Irvington (Halstead).

Hart, Roger, and Louise Chawla. 1982. "The development of children's concern for the environment," *Zeitschrift für Uniweltpolitik*, special issue on environmental psychology. (J. Wohlwill and N. Watts, eds.) Berlin: International Institute for Environment and Society, 271–94.

Hartman, Chester. 1963. "Social values and housing orientations." *Journal of Social Issues* 19 (April).

Hayden, Dolores. 1980. "What would a non-sexist city be like? Speculations on housing, urban design, and human work." *Signs: A Journal of Women in Culture and Society*, special issue on women and the city, 5, 3 (spring supplement 1980): 170–87.

———. 1981. *The grand domestic revolution: A history of feminist designs for American homes.* Cambridge: MIT Press.

Heffernan, David. 1977. *Difficult-to-let: What are the difficulties?* (A study of two high density sixties estates for the London borough of Lewisham). Report A78:R3. Edinburgh: Architecture Research Unit, University of Edinburgh.

Heideman, Lawrence M., Jr. 1976. "Tapiola: An unique experimental design separating socio-economic class from housing and community environmental factors in health and well-being." *Urban Ecology* 2.

Heraud, B. J. 1968. "Social class and the new towns." *Urban Studies* 5.

Hester, Randolph. 1975. *Neighborhood space.* Stroudsburg, Pa.: Dowden, Hutchinson and Ross.

Hill, Polly. 1980. "Toward the perfect play experience." In *Innovation in play environments*, edited by Paul F. Wilkinson. London: Croom Helm.

Hinshaw, Mark, and Kathryn Allot. 1972. "Environmental preferences of future housing consumers." *Journal of the American Institute of Planners* 38, 2 (March).

Hoinville, Gerard, Roger Jowell, et al. 1978. *Survey research practice.* London: Heinemann.

Hole, Vere. 1966. *Children's play on housing estates.* National Building Studies research paper no. 39. London: Her Majesty's Stationery Office.

Hollingshead, A. B., and L. H. Rogler. 1963. "Attitudes towards slums and public housing in Puerto Rico." In *The urban condition*, edited by L. H. Duhl. New York: Basic Books.

Holme, Anthea, and P. Massie. 1970. *Children's play: A study of needs and opportunities*. London: Michael Joseph.

Hough, Mike, and Pat Mayhew, eds. 1982. *Crime and public housing*. Proceedings of a workshop held in September 1980. Research and Planning Unit paper 6. London: Home Office.

"Housing and the environment." 1967. Special issue of *Architectural Review* 142, 849:332–42, 359–62.

Housing families at high densities. 1978. Vancouver: Vancouver City Planning Department.

Housing Research and Development Program, University of Illinois at Urbana-Champaign. 1974. *Site improvement handbook for multi-family housing*. State of Illinois, Department of Local Government Affairs, Office of Housing and Buildings.

"Housing: The home and its setting." 1968. *The Architects' Journal* 148, 37:493–554.

Huntoon, Maxwell. 1971. *Planned unit development: A better way for the suburbs*. Washington, D.C.: Urban Land Institute.

Hurtwood, Lady Allen of. 1968. *Planning for play*. London: Thames and Hudson.

Ineichen, Bernard J. 1972. "What kind of neighbours do you want?" *New Society* 22.

An introduction to housing layout: A GLC study. 1978. London: The Architectural Press.

Jackson, R. H., ed. 1977. *Children, the environment and accidents*. Turnbridge, Kent: Pitman Medical Publishing.

Jacobs, Ellen, and Peter Jacobs. 1980. "Street play: recreating networks for the urban child." In *Innovation in play environments*, edited by Paul F. Wilkinson. London: Croom Helm.

Jacobs, Jane. 1961. *The death and life of great American cities*. New York: Random House.

Jacobs, Peter, and M. Charney. 1975. *Street works: Generating public open space*. Ottawa: Canada Ministry of State for Urban Affairs.

Jeffery, Clarence Ray. 1970. *Crime prevention through environmental design*. Beverly Hills, Calif.: Sage.

Jephcott, Pearl, with Hilary Robinson. 1971. *Homes in high flats: Some of the human problems involved in multi-storey housing*. Edinburgh: Oliver and Boyd.

Johnson, Laura Climenko, Joel Shack, and Karen Oster. 1980. *Out of the cellar and into the parlour: Guidelines for the adaptation of residential spaces for young children*. Research project 9. Ottawa: Canada Mortgage and Housing Corporation.

Johnston, Judith. 1978. "Demographic change and housing needs." Research paper 78/2. Wellington, New Zealand: National Housing Commission.

Johnston, R. J. 1971. *Urban residential patterns: An introductory review*. London: G. Bell.

Jowell, Roger, Richard Berthoud, and Ellen Johnson. 1971. "Runcorn community study. Report on exploratory phase." London: Social and Community Planning Research. Mimeo.

Kakalik, James S., and Sorrel Wildhorn. 1971. *Private police in the United States: Findings and recommendations*. Vol. 1. Santa Monica, Calif.: Rand Corporation.

Katz, Robert. 1966. *Design of the housing site: A critique of American practice*. Urbana, Ill.: Small Homes Council, Building Research Council.

Kautz, Barbara Ehrlich. 1974. "Social integration of tenants in scattered site public housing." Master's thesis, Department of City Planning, University of California, Berkeley.

Keller, Suzanne. 1968. *The urban neighborhood: A sociological perspective*. New York: Random House.

———. 1981. *Building for women*. Lexington, Mass.: D. C. Heath.

Kendon, Olive. 1979. *Because they asked*. London: Children's House Society.

Kent Planning Officers. 1976. *Housing design guide*. Maidstone, England: Kent County Council.

King, Ross. 1974. "Progress report on study: 'Medium density housing for Australia.'" Australian Housing Standards Task Force, information paper 11 (October). Mimeo.

Klein, J. 1965. *Samples from English cultures, vol. 1: Three preliminary studies, aspects of adult life in England*. London: Routledge and Kegan Paul.

Klein and Sears. 1980. *Lost and found: Recycling space for children*. Research/Planning/Architecture. Research project 8. Ottawa: Canada Mortgage and Housing Corporation.

Knights, Kay. 1977. "City farms." *The Association of Agriculture Journal*. (Autumn).

Kriesberg, Louis. 1968. "Neighborhood setting and the isolation of public housing tenants." *Journal of the American Institute of Planners* 34, 1 (January).

Kritchevsky, Sybil, and Elizabeth Prescott. 1969. *Planning environments for young children—Physical space*. Washington, D.C.: National Association for the Education of Young Children (1834 Connecticut Avenue, NW, Washington, D.C. 20000).

Kuper, Leo. 1953. "Blueprints for living together." In *Living in towns*, edited by Leo Kuper. London: Cresset Press.

Ladd, Florence C. 1972. "Black youths view their environments: Some views on housing." *Journal of the American Institute of Planners* 38, 2 (March).

Lamanna, R. A. 1964. "Value consensus among urban residents." *Journal of the American Institute of Planners* 30, 4 (November).

Landscape Architecture Program (Project director: Mark Francis). 1981. *Children in Village Homes, a participatory study of child ecology with implications for design of the Village Homes playground.* Davis: Environmental Planning and Management, University of California.

Lansing, J., and E. Mueller, with N. Barth. 1964. *Residential location and urban mobility.* Ann Arbor: Institute for Social Research, University of Michigan.

Lansing, John, et al. 1970. *Planned residential environments.* Ann Arbor: Institute for Social Research, University of Michigan.

Larsson, Nils K. 1980. *The nature of child-related maintenance and vandalism problems in C.M.H.C. family housing projects.* Research project 3 for International Year of the Child. Ottawa: Canada Mortgage and Housing Corporation.

Laurie, Ian, ed. 1979. *Nature in cities: The natural environment in the design and development of urban green space.* Chichester, England: Wiley.

Leoffler, Margaret. 1967. *The prepared environment.* New York: Educational Facilities Laboratories.

Lerup, Lars. 1977. *Building the unfinished: Architecture and human action.* Beverly Hills, Calif.: Sage.

Lifchez, Raymond, and Barbara Winslow. 1979. *Design for independent living: The environment and physically disabled people.* New York: Whitney Library of Design.

Lindheim, Roslyn, Helen Glaser, and Christie Coffin. 1972. *Changing hospital environments for children.* Cambridge, Mass.: Harvard University Press.

Littlewood, Judith, and Anthea Tinker. 1981. *Families in flats.* London: Her Majesty's Stationery Office.

Locke, Hubert G. 1969. *Urban crime and urban planning.* Detroit: Wayne County Planning Commission.

Lofland, John. 1971. *Analyzing social settings: A guide to qualitative observation and analysis.* Belmont, Calif.: Wadsworth.

Luedke, Gerald, et al. 1970. *Crime and the physical city.* Washington, D.C.: National Institute of Law Enforcement and Criminal Justice.

Lym, Glen Robert. 1980. *A psychology of building: How we shape and experience our structured spaces.* Englewood Cliffs, N.J.: Prentice-Hall.

Lynch, Kevin. 1977. *Growing up in cities. Studies of the spatial environment of adolescence in Cracow, Melbourne, Mexico City, Salta Toluca and Warszawa.* Cambridge, Mass., and Paris: MIT Press and UNESCO.

MacLeod, John B. 1977. "Open space and walk-up apartments: A case study of user needs and landscape design." Practicum for master's degree, Department of Landscape Architecture, University of Manitoba, Winnipeg. Mimeo.

Madge, J. 1964. "Privacy and social interaction." Paper delivered to the Bartlett Society, December 8. Mimeo.

Maizels, Joan. 1961. *Two to five in high flats.* London: Housing Centre.

Manthe, Donald. 1979. "Post evaluation of Farum Midpunkt." Student research paper, California Polytechnic State University, San Luis Obispo, California. Mimeo.

Marans, Robert W., and W. Rodgers. 1972. *Toward an understanding of community satisfaction.* Ann Arbor: Institute for Social Research, University of Michigan.

Margaret, Sister (Catholic Social Service). 1971. "Resident satisfaction survey at Banneker Homes, San Francisco." Unpublished.

Marks, Harold. 1957. "Subdividing for traffic safety." *Traffic Quarterly* 2 (July): 308–25.

Massachusetts Housing Finance Agency. 1974. *A social audit of mixed-income housing.* Boston, Mass.: Massachusetts Housing Finance Agency.

Matsushita, Dan, Associates Ltd. 1979. *The potential of roof deck play spaces.* Research project 15. Ottawa: Canada Mortgage and Housing Corporation.

Mawby, R. 1977. "Defensible space: A theoretical and empirical appraisal." *Urban Studies* 14, 2:169–79.

Mayhew, P., R. V. G. Clarke, J. M. Burrows, N. M. Hough, and S. W. C. Winchester. 1979. *Crime in public view.* Home office research study no. 49. London: Her Majesty's Stationery Office.

McMurray, Jane. 1979. "Housing preferences in New Zealand: Interim report no. 3—Sections." Research paper 79/3. Wellington, New Zealand: National Housing Commission.

A medium-density housing study. 1977. Report NHA 5155. Ottawa: Central Mortgage and Housing Corporation.

Michelson, William. 1968. "Most people don't want what architects want." *Transaction* 5, 8 (July–August): 37–43.

———. 1976. *Man and his urban environment: A sociological approach*, 2nd ed. Reading, Mass. Addison-Wesley.

———. 1977. *Environmental choice, human behavior, and residential satisfaction*. New York: Oxford University Press.

Miller, A., M. C. Courtis, and J. Cook. 1965. *Radburn layouts: A case study*. Garston, England: Building Research Station (U.K.).

Miller, A., and J. Cook. 1967. "Radburn estates revisited: Report of a user study." *Architect's Journal* 1 (November).

Milne, Phillipa. 1976. "Open space design in Radburn and medium density planning: Some social considerations." Adelaide: South Australian Housing Trust. Mimeo.

Milton Keynes Development Corporation, Planning Department. 1978. "Major play facility monitoring study." Milton Keynes, England. Mimeo.

Ministry of Housing and Local Government (U.K.) 1961. *Homes for today and tomorrow*. (The Parker Morris Report). London: Her Majesty's Stationery Office.

———. 1967a. *Landscaping for flats*. Design Bulletin 5. London: Her Majesty's Stationery Office.

———. 1967b. *The needs of new communities*. London: Her Majesty's Stationery Office.

———. 1967c. "Housing at Coventry: A user reaction study." Sociological Research Section. *Official Architecture and Planning* 30, 12:1746–65.

———. 1968a. *House planning: A guide to user needs with a check list*. Design bulletin 14. London: Her Majesty's Stationery Office.

———. 1968b. "Woodway Lane, Coventry: Interim report." London. Mimeo.

———. 1969a. *The family at home: A study of households in Sheffield*. London: Her Majesty's Stationery Office.

———. 1969b. *Family houses at West Ham: An account of the project with an appraisal*. London: Her Majesty's Stationery Office.

———. 1970. *Families living at high density: A study of estates in Leeds, Liverpool and London*. Research and Development Group. London: Her Majesty's Stationery Office.

Mitchell, G. D., T. Lupton, M. W. Hodges, and C. S. Smith. 1954. *Neighbourhood and community: An enquiry into social relationships on housing estates in Liverpool and Sheffield*. Liverpool: Liverpool University Press.

Montgomery, Roger. 1966. "Comments on 'fear and the house-as-haven.'" *Journal of the American Institute of Planners* 32.

———. 1977. "High-density, low-rise housing and the changes in the American housing economy." In *The form of housing*, edited by Sam Davis. New York: Van Nostrand Reinhold.

Moore, Gary T. 1981. *Child care facilities and equipment*. Washington, D.C.: U.S. Government Printing Office and Department of Labor, Women's Bureau.

Moore, G. T., U. Cohen, and T. McGinty. 1980. "Design patterns for children's environments: Synopsis of a two-year research and development project." In *People and the man-made environment*, edited by R. Thorne. Sydney, Australia: I.B. Fell Housing Research Unit, University of Sydney.

Moore, Robin C. 1980. "Generating relevant urban childhood places: Learning from the 'yard.'" In *Innovation in play environments*, edited by Paul F. Wilkinson. London: Croom Helm.

———. 1985. *Childhood's domain: Play and place in childhood development*. London: Croom Helm.

Moore, Robin C., and Donald Young. 1978. "Childhood outdoors: Toward a social ecology of the landscape." In *Human behavior and the environment*, edited by I. Altman and J. Wohlwill, vol. 3. New York: Plenum Press.

Morris, Norval, and Gordon Hawkins. 1970. *The honest politician's guide to crime control*. Chicago: University of Chicago Press.

Mulvihall, R., and S. McHugh. 1977. "A preliminary investigation of housing imagery and the acceptability of innovation in housing estates." Planning Division working paper 2. Dublin: An Foras Forbartha.

Muscovitch, Arthur. 1980. *Child's perception of the neighbourhood*. Research project 5. Ottawa: Canada Mortgage and Housing Corporation.

Nahkies, G. E. 1974. "Multi-unit residential development in Christchurch." *New Zealand Geographer* 30:151–65.

National Capital Development Commission, Australia. 1978. "Traffic noise and its effect on site selection and design of dwellings." Technical paper 25. Canberra: National Capital Development Commission.

National Center for Housing Management. 1976. *The housing manager's resource book*, Ch. 5: "Security." Washington, D.C.: National Center for Housing Management.

National Commission on Urban Problems (Douglas Commission). 1969. "The development, objectives and adequacy of current housing code standards." In *Building the American city*, report to the Congress and the President of the United States. Washington, D.C.: U.S. Government Printing Office.

National Housing Law Project—Multifamily Demonstration Program. 1977. "Acorn Housing Development: Comprehensive audit and recommendations." Berkeley, Calif. Mimeo.

————. 1978. "Jackie Robinson Garden Apartments: A comprehensive review with recommendations." Berkeley, Calif. Mimeo.

National Institute of Law Enforcement and Criminal Justice. 1974. *Residential security*. Washington, D.C.: U.S. Government Printing Office.

National Recreation and Park Association. 1976. "Proposed safety standards for public playground equipment." Working draft no. 5, developed for the Consumer Product Safety Commission. Arlington, Va.

"Neighborhood design study: Progress report 3." 1973. Baltimore: Department of Planning.

Newman, Oscar. 1969. *Physical parameters of defensible space, past experiences and hypotheses*. New York: Columbia University Press.

————. 1971. *Architectural design for crime prevention*. National Institute of Law Enforcement and Criminal Justice. Washington, D.C.: U.S. Government Printing Office.

————. 1972. *Defensible space: Crime prevention through urban design*. New York: Macmillan.

————. 1976. *Design guidelines for creating defensible space*. National Institute of Law Enforcement and Criminal Justice. Washington, D.C.: U.S. Government Printing Office.

————. 1976. *No place to rest his head* (90-minute film). Washington, D.C.: U.S. Department of Housing and Urban Development.

————. 1980. *Community of interest*. New York: Anchor/Doubleday.

Newman, Oscar, and Barry Hersh. 1972. *Immediate measures for improving security in existing residential areas*. New York: Center for Residential Security Design.

Newman, Oscar, and Stephen Johnston. 1974. *Model security code for residential areas*. New York: Institute for Community Design Analysis.

Newson, John, and Elizabeth Newson. 1968. *Four years old in an urban community*. London: George Allen and Unwin.

————. 1976. *Seven years old in the home environment*. London: George Allen and Unwin.

Nicholson, C., and H. Marsh. 1968. *Children's outdoor activities on three medium density estates*. Sociological Research Section, Ministry of Housing and Local Government. London: Her Majesty's Stationery Office.

Norcross, Carl. 1973. *Townhouses and condominiums: Residents' likes and dislikes*. Institute Special Report. Washington, D.C.: Urban Land Institute.

Norcross, Carl, and John Hysom. 1968. "Apartment communities: The next big market." Technical bulletin 61. Washington, D.C.: Urban Land Institute.

Noren-Bjorn, Eva. 1982. *The impossible playground*. West Point, N.Y.: Leisure Press.

O'Brien, N.J. 1972. "A comparative behavioral study of row housing developments." Institute of Urban Studies, University of Winnipeg. Mimeo.

Open space in housing areas: Documentation of a colloquium. 1972. Stockholm: National Swedish Institute for Building Research.

Opie, Iona, and Peter Opie. 1969. *Children's games in streets and playgrounds*. Oxford, England: Clarendon Press.

Oppenheim, A. N. 1966. *Questionnaire design and attitude measurement*. London: Heinemann.

Osmon, Fred Lin. 1971. *Patterns for designing children's centers*. New York: Educational Facilities Laboratories.

Parish, Shirley, and David Parish. 1972. "A study of four Bridgeport housing developments." Bridgeport, Conn.: Zane Yost and Associates. Mimeo.

Parks, Thomas William. 1979. "Post occupancy evaluation: An overview and a case study of married student housing at the University of New Mexico." Master's thesis, Department of Architecture, University of New Mexico, Albuquerque.

Paterson, John, David Yencken, and Graeme Gunn. 1975. *A mansion or no house: A report for UDIA [Urban Development Institute of Australia] on consequences of planning standards and their impact on land and housing*. Melbourne: Hawthorne Press.

Pederson, Britt. 1980. *Small communal laundries in blocks of flats*. Article 6702014. Stockholm: Swedish Council for Building Research.

Perez, Cecilia, and Roger A. Hart. 1980. "Beyond playgrounds: Planning for children's access to the environment." In *Innovation in play environments*, edited by Paul F. Wilkinson. London: Croom Helm.

Perin, Constance. 1972. *With man in mind: An interdisciplinary prospectus for environmental design.* Cambridge, Mass.: MIT Press.

———. 1977. *Everything in its place: Social order and land use in America.* Princeton, N.J.: Princeton University Press.

Perlgut, Donald. 1978. "Security in H.U.D. subsidized and insured family housing projects. An analysis of the problems and some proposals for the future." Prepared for the National Housing Law Project, Berkeley, Calif. Mimeo.

———. 1981a. *Crime prevention and the design and management of public developments: Selected and annotated references from Australia, the United States and the United Kingdom.* CPL bibliography no. 53. Chicago: Council of Planning Librarians.

———. 1981b. "Crime prevention for Australian public housing." *Forum: Australian Crime Prevention Council Quarterly Journal* 4, 3.

———. 1982a. *Crime prevention and the design of public developments in Australia: Selected case studies.* Social Planning and Research Unit. Adelaide: South Australian Institute of Technology.

———. 1982b. "Manageable space: Proposals for crime prevention in subsidized housing." Paper presented at the Third International Symposium on Victimology, Muenster, Westphalia, West Germany, September 1979. In *The victim in international perspective,* edited by Haus J. Schneider, Berlin and New York: Walter de Gruyter.

Perlman, Janice. 1976. *The myth of marginality: Urban poverty and politics in Rio de Janeiro.* Berkeley: University of California Press.

Phelps, L., and John Fabbri. 1971. *Crime prevention: Before the fact and after the fact.* Richmond, Calif.: Richmond Police Department.

Pickett, K., and D. Boulton. 1974. *Migration and social adjustment.* Liverpool: Liverpool University Press.

Play areas for low-income housing. 1972. Champaign: Housing Research and Development Program, University of Illinois.

Pollowy, Anne-Marie. 1977. *The urban nest.* Community Development Series, vol. 26. Stroudsberg, Pa.: Dowden, Hutchinson and Ross.

Popenoe, David. 1977. *The suburban environment: Sweden and the United States.* Chicago: University of Chicago Press.

Poyner, Barry, and Nigel Hughes. 1979. "The effects of selling council houses on the care and maintenance of estates." (Outline of research project). London: Tavistock Institute of Human Relations. Mimeo.

Prescott, E., E. Jones, and S. Kritchevsky. 1972. *Day care as a child-rearing environment.* Washington, D.C.: National Association for the Education of Young Children.

Proshansky, Harold M., and Robert D. Kaminoff. No date. "Environmental quality and developmental outcomes." In "Prevention of retarded development in psychosocially disadvantaged children," edited by M. J. Begab, H. Garbes, and H. C. Haywood. Mimeo.

Pyron, B. 1972. "Form and space in human habitat: Judgmental and attitude responses." *Environment and Behaviour* 4, 1:87–120.

Rabeneck, Andrew, David Sheppard, and Peter Town. 1973. "Housing flexibility?" *Architectural Design* 43 (November).

———. 1974a. "Housing flexibility/adaptability?" *Architectural Design* 49 (February).

———. 1974b. "The structuring of space in family housing: An alternative to present design practice." *Progressive Architecture* 55, 11 (November): 100–106.

Raimy, Eric. 1979. *Shared houses, Shared lives.* New York: J. P. Tarcher.

Rainwater, Lee. 1966. "Fear and the house-as-haven in the lower class." *Journal of the American Institute of Planners* 32 (January).

———. 1973. *Behind ghetto walls: Black families in a federal slum.* Chicago: Aldine. (Republished, London: Penguin Books, 1973).

Rapoport, Amos. 1968. "The personal element in housing: An argument for open-ended design." *Royal Institute of British Architects' Journal* 75, 7:300–307.

———. 1969. *House form and culture.* Englewood Cliffs, N.J.: Prentice-Hall.

———. 1978. "The environment as an enculturating medium." In *Priorities for environmental design research,* edited by Sue Wiedemann and James R. Anderson. Washington, D.C.: Environmental Design Research Association.

———. 1980. "Environmental preference, habitat, selection, and urban housing." *Journal of Social Issues* 36, 3.

Redevelopment Agency of the City of Oakland (California). 1972. "New housing development guidelines." Mimeo.

Reizenstein, Janet E. 1975. "Linking social research and design." *Journal of Architectural Research* 4, 3 (December): 26–38.

Relph, E. 1976. *Place and placelessness.* London: Pion.

Reppetto, Thomas A. 1974. *Residential crime.* Cambridge, Mass.: Ballinger.

Residential design feedback: Report of studies. 1975. Milton Keynes, England: Planning Directorate, Milton Keynes Development Corporation.

Residential development handbook. 1978. Washington, D.C.: Urban Land Institute.

Rich, Peter. 1966. "Notes on low rise high density housing." *Arena, the Architectural Association Journal* 81, 900 (March): 242–44.

Robinson, Julia Williams. 1975. "Housing and upward mobility: A comparison study of Liberty Plaza rowhouses and Hanover apartments." Student term paper, University of Minnesota. Mimeo.

———. 1980. "Images of housing in Minneapolis: A limited study of urban residents' attitudes and values." Master's thesis, Department of Architecture, University of Minnesota.

Rothblatt, Donald, Daniel Garr, and Jo Sprague. 1979. *The suburban environment and women.* New York: Praeger.

Rothenberg, M., D. G. Hayward, and R. R. Beasley. 1974. "Playgrounds for whom?" In Vol. 11–12, *Man-environment interactions: Evaluations and applications.* Edited by Daniel Carson. Washington, D.C.: Environmental Design Research Association.

Rouse, Victor W., and Herb Rubenstein. 1978. *Crime in public housing: A review of major issues and selected crime reduction strategies, vol. 1: A report; vol. 2: A review of two conferences and an annotated bibliography.* Prepared by American Institute for Research for the U.S. Department of Housing and Urban Development, Office of Policy Development and Research. Washington, D.C.: U.S. Government Printing Office.

Ruddick, J. G. 1969. "Personalisation and mass housing." Fifth-year study. Birmingham, England: School of Architecture.

Saile, David G., et al. 1971. *Activities and attitudes of public housing residents.* Champaign: Housing Research and Development Program, University of Illinois.

———. 1972. *Families in public housing: An evaluation of three residential environments in Rockford, Illinois.* Champaign: Housing Research and Development Program, University of Illinois.

Sandels, Stina. 1975. *Children in traffic,* rev. ed. London: Paul Elek.

———. 1979. *Unprotected road users: A behavioural study.* Skandia report no. 3. Stockholm: Skandia Insurance Company.

Sandvik, Gloria, Barbara Bate Shellenbarger, and Margaret Mahoney Stevenson. 1973. *Resident evaluation of four planned unit developments: Eugene, Oregon.* Eugene, Ore.: Eugene Planning Department.

Sarkissian, Wendy. 1976. "The idea of social mix in town planning." *Urban Studies* 13 (October).

Sarkissian, Wendy, and Warwick Heine. 1978. *Social mix: The Bournville experience.* Bournville, England, and Adelaide, Australia: Bournville Village Trust and South Australian Housing Trust.

Scarr, Harry A., Joan L. Pinsky, and Deborah S. Wyatt. 1973. *Patterns of burglary,* 2nd ed. U.S. Department of Justice. Washington, D.C.: U.S. Government Printing Office.

Schorr, A. 1963. *Slums and social insecurity.* Washington, D.C.: U.S. Department of Health, Education and Welfare, Social Security Administration.

Scottish Local Authorities Special Housing Group. 1977. *Tenant response: Results of the initial series of housing appraisal kit surveys.* Edinburgh: Scottish Local Authorities Special Housing Group.

———. 1978. *Children at play—preliminary discussion paper.* Edinburgh: Scottish Local Authorities Special Housing Group.

"Security." 1970. *Building Research Station Digest* 122:18.

Seidel, Andrew D. 1980. "Factors influencing conceptions of information quality in the production and utilization of environment and behavior research." School of Architecture and Environmental Design, State University of New York at Buffalo. Mimeo.

Shankland, Cox and Associates. 1967. "Social survey, Childwall Valley Estate, Liverpool." London and Liverpool: Shankland, Cox and Associates. Mimeo.

———. 1969. *Private housing in London: People and environment in three Wates housing schemes.* London: Shankland, Cox and Associates.

Shankland, Cox Partnership, in association with the Institute of Community Studies. 1977a. "Housing management and design: Inner area study, Lambeth." IAS/LA/18. London: Department of the Environment. Mimeo.

———. 1977b. "People, housing and district: Inner area study, Lambeth." IAS/LA/5. London: Department of the Environment. Mimeo.

Simmie, J. 1974. "Inequality and social mix." Seminar paper. London: Centre for Environmental Studies.

Site planning bibliography. 1974. Ottawa: Canada Mortgage and Housing Corporation.

Smith, Barry, and David Thorns. 1978. "Housing need and demand characteristics: First stage report." Research paper 78/1. Wellington, New Zealand: National Housing Commission.

————. 1979. "Constraints, choices and housing environments." Research paper 79/1. Wellington, New Zealand: National Housing Commission.

Sommer, Robert. 1969. *Personal space: The behavioral basis of design*. Englewood Cliffs, N.J.: Prentice-Hall.

————. 1974. *Tight spaces: Hard architecture and how to humanize it*. Englewood Cliffs, N.J.: Prentice-Hall.

South Australian Housing Trust. 1977. "Choice in trust housing: Notes on estates seminar." Unpublished paper. Adelaide, Australia. Mimeo.

Spivack, Mayer. 1978. "The design log: A new informational tool." *AIA Journal*, 67, 12 (October): 76–78.

Stevenson, Anne, Elaine Martin, and Judith O'Neill. 1967. *High living: A study of family life in flats*. Melbourne: Melbourne University Press.

Stewart, W. F. R. 1970. *Children in flats: A family study*. London: National Society for the Prevention of Cruelty to Children.

Stimpson, Catharine R., Elsa Dixler, Marta J. Nelson, and Katheryn B. Yatrakis, eds. 1981. *Women and the American city*. Chicago: University of Chicago Press.

Stop de kindermoord. 1975. Amsterdam: Stop de Kindermoord.

Streets ahead. 1979. London: Design Council, in association with the Royal Town Planning Institute.

Suttles, Gerald. 1970. "Deviant behavior as an unanticipated consequence of public housing." In *Crime in the city*, edited by David Glaser. New York: Harper & Row.

————. 1972. *The social construction of communities*. Chicago: University of Chicago Press.

Sutton, A. J., and D. T. Richmond. 1975. "Walk-up or high rise: Residents' views on public housing." Sydney: Housing Commission of New South Wales.

Taylor, Nicholas. 1973. *The village in the city*. London: Maurice Temple Smith (in association with *New Society*).

Taylor, Lord Stephen, and Sidney Chave. 1964. *Mental health and environment*. London: Longmans.

Teasdale, Pierre. 1980. *Project parapluie: A user generated shelter design for the recreation of school-age children in a Montreal housing project*. Ottawa: Canada Mortgage and Housing Corporation.

Teitz, Michael B. 1975. *Multifamily failures, Vol. 1B: Statistical analysis* (with Richard Dodson); *vol. 2: Case studies; vol. 3: Conclusions and recommendations*. Prepared by Berkeley Planning Associates. San Francisco: U.S. Department of Housing and Urban Development, Region IX.

Thayer, Robert L., Jr. "Designing an experimental solar community." *Landscape Architecture* 67, 3 (May): 223–28.

————. 1980. "Conspicuous non-consumption: The symbolic aesthetics of solar architecture." In *Proceedings of the eleventh annual conference of the Environmental Design Research Association*, edited by R. Stough and A. Wandersman. Washington, D.C.: Environmental Design Research Association.

Thomsen, Charles H., and Alexandra Borowiecka. 1980. *Winter and play: Design guidelines for winter play environments on the Canadian prairie*. Ottawa: Canada Mortgage and Housing Corporation.

Thorne, R., ed. 1982. *Medium density housing in Sydney: Survey of users and general attitudes in two housing forms*. Sydney: I. B. Fell Research Centre, University of Sydney.

Tonigan, Richard, et al. 1970. *Child care and development centers, model neighborhoods, Albuquerque, New Mexico; or Mr. Architect: This is how we want our centers to perform*. Albuquerque, N.M.: Institute for Social Research and Development, University of New Mexico.

Tudor Walters Report. 1918. "Committee appointed to consider questions of building construction in connection with the provision of dwellings for the working classes in England and Wales and Scotland." London: Her Majesty's Stationery Office.

Tulin, Steven Jay. 1978. "Residents' use of common areas in condominium developments." Master's thesis, Department of Environmental Analysis, Cornell University.

Turner, John. 1976. *Housing by people: Towards autonomy in building environments*. London: Marion Boyars.

United States Consumer Product Safety Commission. *Hazard analysis—Playground equipment*. Washington, D.C.: U.S. Consumer Product Safety Commission, Bureau of Epidemiology.

————. 1981. *Handbook for public playground safety. Vol. 1—General guidelines for new and existing playgrounds; vol. 2—Technical guidelines for equipment and surfacing*. Washington, D.C.: U.S. Government Printing Office.

United States Department of Housing and Urban Development (HUD). 1963. *Minimum property standards for multi-family housing*. Washington, D.C.: U.S. Government Printing Office.

———. 1974. *Housing management handbook 7460.4: Security planning for HUD-assisted multi-family housing*. Washington, D.C.: U.S. Government Printing Office.

———. 1976. *Defensible space and security: A partially annotated bibliography*. Library Division. Washington, D.C.: U.S. Government Printing Office.

———. 1977. *Preliminary findings from the field study: Report of the task force on multi-family property utilization. PR* Washington, D.C.: U.S. Government Printing Office.

———. 1980. *Energy conservation for housing: A workbook*. HUD no. 002651. (Available from HUD user, P.O. Box 280, Germantown, Md. 20874.)

United States Department of Housing and Urban Development and Department of Labor. 1979. *Urban initiatives anti-crime program guidebook*. Washington, D.C.: U.S. Department of Housing and Urban Development.

Untermann, Richard, and Robert Small. 1977. *Site planning for cluster housing*. New York: Van Nostrand Reinhold.

Urban Land Institute. 1969. *The pros and cons of cluster housing*. Washington, D.C.: Urban Land Institute.

Vancouver City Planning Department. 1978. *Housing families at high densities*. Vancouver, B.C.: Vancouver Planning Department.

Verwer, Domien. 1980. "Planning and designing residential environments with children in mind: A Dutch approach." In *Innovation in play environments*, edited by Paul F. Wilkinson. London: Croom Helm.

Veterans Administration, Department of Veterans Benefits. 1978. *Handbook for design: Specially adapted housing*. Washington, D.C.: U.S. Government Printing Office.

Victoria University of Manchester, School of Architecture. 1975. *Access in dwellings: A report on a housing research project*. Manchester: Revell and George.

Vischer, Jacqueline, and Clare Cooper Marcus. 1982. "Design awards: Who cares?" In *Knowledge for design: Proceedings of 13th annual conference of Environmental Design Research Association*. College Park, Md.: Environmental Design Research Association.

Vischer Skaburskis Planners. 1980. *False Creek area 6 phase 1: Post-occupancy evaluation final report*. Prepared for Canada Mortgage and Housing Corporation.

Ward, Colin, ed. 1973. *Vandalism*. New York: Van Nostrand Reinhold.

Ward, Colin. 1978. *The child in the city*. London: The Architecture Press.

Watkins, William B. 1980. "Play environments in arid lands." In *Innovation in play environments*, edited by Paul F. Wilkinson. London: Croom Helm.

Webb, Eugene J., et al. 1966. *Unobtrusive measures: Nonreactive research in the social sciences*. Chicago: Rand McNally.

Weeks, J. K. 1966. "A new concept in law enforcement: Vertical policing." *Police* 11, 1 (September/October).

Weidemann, Sue, and James Anderson. 1979. *Resident heterogeneity in multi-family housing: A source of conflict in space*. Urbana-Champaign: Housing Research and Development Program, University of Illinois.

Weinberger, B. 1973. "Liverpool estates survey." Centre for Urban and Regional Studies, Liverpool. Research memo, October 25.

Weininger, Otto. 1980. "How high shall we rise? The great unanswered question." In *Innovation in play environments*, edited by Paul F. Wilkinson. London: Croom Helm.

Weiser, Galia. 1980. "City streets: The child's image as a basis for design." In *Innovation in play environments*, edited by Paul F. Wilkinson. London: Croom Helm.

Wekerle, Gerda, Rebecca Peterson, and David Morley. 1980. *New space for women*. Boulder, Colo.: Westview.

White, L. E. 1946. *Tenement town*. London: Jason Press.

———. 1970. "The outdoor play of children living in flats: An inquiry into the use of courtyards as playgrounds." In *Environmental psychology*, edited by H. M. Proshansky, W. Ittleson, and L. Rivlin. New York: Holt, Rinehart and Winston.

White, Thomas, et al. 1975. *Police burglary prevention programs*. Washington, D.C.: National Institute of Law Enforcement and Criminal Justice.

Whyte, William H., Jr. 1956. *The organization man*. New York: Simon and Schuster.

———. 1964. *Cluster development*. New York: American Conservation Association.

———. 1980. *Social life of small urban spaces*. Washington, D.C.: Conservation Foundation.

"Wilful damage on housing estates." 1971. *Building Research Station Digest* 132 (August): 1–4.

Wilkinson, Paul F., ed. 1980. *Innovation in play environments*. London: Croom Helm.

Wilkinson, Paul F., and Robert S. Lockhart. 1980. "Safety in children's formal play environments." In *Innovation in play environments*, edited by Paul F. Wilkinson. London: Croom Helm.

Wilkinson, Paul F., Robert S. Lockhart, and Ethel M. Luhtanen. "The winter use of playgrounds." In *Innovation in play environments*, edited by Paul F. Wilkinson. London: Croom Helm.

Willis, Margaret. 1957. "Private balconies in flats and maisonettes." *The Architects' Journal* 125, 3236 (March): 372–76.

———. 1963a. "Designing for privacy: (1) What is privacy?" *The Architects' Journal* 137, 22 (May): 1137–41.

———. 1963b. "Designing for privacy: (2) Overlooking." *The Architects' Journal* 137, 23 (June): 1181–87.

———. 1963c. "Designing for privacy: (3) Personal relationships." *The Architects' Journal* 12 (June).

Willmott, Peter. 1962. "Housing density and town design: A pilot study of Stevenage." *Town Planning Review* 33 (July).

———. 1963. *The evolution of a community: A study of Dagenham after forty years*. London: Routledge and Kegan Paul.

———. 1964. "Housing in Cumbernauld—Some residents' opinions." *Journal of the Town Planning Institute* 50 (May).

Willmott, Peter, and Michael Young. 1960. *Family and class in a London suburb*. London: Routledge and Kegan Paul.

Wilson, Hugh, and Lewis Womersley. 1977. "Inner area play." Inner Area Study, Liverpool, IAS/LI/14. London: Department of the Environment. Mimeo.

Wilson, Sheena. 1977. "Vandalism and design." *Architect's Journal* 26 (October).

———. 1978. "Vandalism and 'defensible space' on London housing estates." In *Tackling vandalism*, edited by R. V. G. Clarke. Home Office research study no. 40. London: Her Majesty's Stationery Office.

Wilson, Sheena, and Michael Burbidge. 1978. "An investigation of difficult to let housing." *Housing Review* 27, 4.

Wirthensohn, Horst. 1976. *User-need analysis: A guide in designing inner-city medium-density housing in Adelaide, South Australia*. Bachelor of Architecture thesis, School of Architecture and Building, South Australian Institute of Technology, Adelaide, South Australia.

Wood, Elizabeth. 1961. *Housing design: A social theory*. New York: Citizens Housing and Planning Council.

Woonerf (residential precinct): A different approach to environmental management in residential areas. 1977. The Hague: Royal Dutch Touring Club.

Woonerf: Revised translation of the minimum standards and new traffic regulations and signs. 1978. Amsterdam: Royal Dutch Touring Club.

Worthen, Helena. 1975. "How does a garden grow?" *Landscape* 19, 3 (May).

Yancey, W. 1971. "Architecture, interaction and social control: The case of a large-scale public housing project." *Environment and Behaviour* 3, 1.

Young, Michael, and Peter Willmott. 1957. *Family and kinship in East London*. London: Routledge and Kegan Paul.

Young, T. 1934. *Becontee and Dagenham: The growth of a housing estate*. Becontee (UK): Becontee Social Survey Committee.

Zeisel, John. 1973. "Symbolic meaning of space and the physical dimension of social relations: A case study of sociological research as the basis of architectural planning." In *Cities in change*, edited by J. Walton and D. Carns. Boston: Allyn and Bacon.

———. 1975. *Sociology and architectural design*. Russell Sage Social Science Frontiers Services, no. 6. New York: Free Press.

———. 1981. *Inquiry by design: Tools for environment-behavior research*. Monterey, Calif.: Brooks/Cole.

Zeisel, John, and Mary E. Griffin. 1975. *Charlesview Housing: A diagnostic evaluation*. Cambridge, Mass.: Architecture Research Office, Harvard University.

Zeisel, John, Gayle Epp, and Stephen Demos. *Low rise housing for older people: Behavioral criteria for de-*

sign. U.S. Department of Housing and Urban Development. Washington, D.C.: U.S. Government Printing Office.

Zeisel, John, and Polly Welch. 1981. *Housing designed for families: A summary of research*. Cambridge, Mass.: Joint Center for Urban Studies of MIT and Harvard.

Zerner, Charles. 1977. "The street hearth of play: Children in the city." *Landscape* 22, 1 (Autumn).

Illustration Credits

Copyright belongs to (name of photographer in parentheses, if known):

Architectural Review—Fig. 7 (William Toomey), 13 (de Burgh Galway), 40 (Sydney Newberry), 67 (de Burgh Galway), 70 (Michael Reid), 102 (de Burgh Galway), 173 (de Burgh Galway), 218 (de Burgh Galway).

The Architects' Journal—Fig. 39 (William Toomey), 42 (H. Herzberg), 43 (Martin Charles), 68 (William Toomey), 76 (R. Inglis), 79 (Sam Lambert), 86 (H. E. Meyer), 95 (Sam Lambert), 98 (Martin Charles), 106 (John Mills), 152 (John Mills), 154 (Sam Lambert), 206 (William Toomey).

Architectural Press—Fig. 2 (Sam Lambert), 27 (Richard Bryant), 29, 31 (Richard Bryant), 155 (Richard Bryant), 180 (Martin Charles), 185 (Martin Charles), 215 (Richard Bryant).

Milton Keynes Development Corporation—Figs. 25, 99, 190 (all by John Donat).

Runcorn Development Corporation—Fig. 24 (Brian Williams).

Crown Copyright (reproduced with permission of Controller of Her Britannic Majesty's Stationery Office)—Fig. 71.

Greater London Council—Fig. 23.

Project PLAE (Play and Learning in Adaptive Environments)—Figs. 135, 138.

- Photos reproduced with permission of The Architectural Press, London—Figs. 18, 23, 24, 28, 39, 99, 142.

- Illustrations from G. Francescato, S. Weidemann, J. Anderson, and R. Chenoweth. 1980. *Residents' Satisfaction in HUD-assisted Housing: Design and Management Factors.* Washington, D.C.: U.S. Government Printing Office. Reproduced with permission from the authors—Figs. 15, 21, 90, 91, 156, 163, 167a & b.

- Illustrations from Oscar Newman. 1976. *Design Guidelines for Creating Defensible Space.* National Institute of Law Enforcement and Criminal Justice. Washington, D.C.: U.S. Government Printing Office. Reproduced with permission of the author—Figs. 210, 214, 256.

- Illustrations from Architecture Research Unit. 1969. *Traffic Separated Housing Layouts in Steverage New Town.* Edinburgh: Architecture Research Unit, University of Edinburgh. Reproduced with the permission of John Byrom—Figs. 16, 17, 62.

- *Illustration from Residential Design Feedback: Report of Studies.* 1975. Milton Keynes, England: Planning Directorate, Milton Keynes Development Corporation. Reproduced with permission from Milton Keynes Development Corporation—Fig. 73.

Compositor:	G&S Typesetters, Inc.
Text:	10/12 Gill Sans Light
Display:	Gill Sans Bold and Extra Bold
Printer:	Malloy Lithographing, Inc.
Binder:	John H. Dekker & Sons